Miles
0 100 200 300 400 500

TROPIC OF CANCER

Atlantic Ocean

BAHAMA

DOMINICAN
REPUBLIC San Juan

VIRGIN
ISLANDS

ANGUILLA
ST. MARTIN
ST. EUSTATIUS
ST. KITTS
GUADELOUPE
DOMINICA
MARTINIQUE

LESSER ANTILLES

CUBA

HAITI

Santo Domingo

PUERTO
RICO

GREATER   ANTILLES

ST. LUCIA

ST. VINCENT
GRENADINES
GRENADA
TOBAGO
TRINIDAD

JAMAICA   Caribbean   Sea

CURACAO   BONAIRE
ARUBA

SOUTH
AMERICA

Caracas

Savannah River

Charleston

osa

Montgomery

Altamaha R.

Savannah

Atlantic
Ocean

FORT
FREDERICA

onecah R.

Choctawhatchee R.

Chattahoochee River

Flint R.

Apalachicola

Ochlockonee R.

River

St. Marys R.
Ft.

Atlantic
Ocean

Pensacola

Tallahassee

Suwannee R.

St. Augustine

CASTILLO DE
SAN MARCOS
FORT
MATANZAS

Apalachicola

FLORIDA

Gulf of Mexico

Miles
0 50 100 150

THE EARLY JEWS OF NEW ORLEANS

By Bertram Wallace Korn

American Jewry and the Civil War (1951)

Eventful Years and Experiences: Studies in Nineteenth Century American Jewish History (1954)

The Centenary Edition of Solomon Nunes Carvalho's Incidents of Travel and Adventure in the Far West (1954)

The American Reaction to the Mortara Case: 1858–1859 (1957)

Letters of Baron Corvo to Leonard Moore (1960)
    (with Cecil Woolf)

Benjamin Levy: New Orleans Printer and Publisher (1961)

Jews and Negro Slavery in the Old South, 1789–1865 (1961)

Retrospect and Prospect (1965)
    (on behalf of the Central Conference of American Rabbis)

The Early Jews of New Orleans (1969)

THE EARLY JEWS
OF NEW ORLEANS

BERTRAM WALLACE KORN

AMERICAN JEWISH HISTORICAL SOCIETY

Waltham, Massachusetts • 1969

Library of Congress Catalog Card Number: 70–86334

COPYRIGHT © 1969 BY

THE AMERICAN JEWISH HISTORICAL SOCIETY

PRINTED IN THE UNITED STATES OF AMERICA

PRESS OF *Maurice Jacobs,* INC.

1010 ARCH STREET, PHILADELPHIA, PA. 19107

For Judy
in honor of your Confirmation
and for Buddy
in honor of your Bar Mitzvah

The publication of this volume has been supported by

THE ENDOWMENT FUND OF
THE JEWISH WELFARE FEDERATION OF NEW ORLEANS,
        A. B. KUPPERMAN, *President*
        MORTON GABA, *Executive Director*

THE LUCIUS N. LITTAUER FOUNDATION,
        HARRY STARR, *President*

THE RABBI'S PUBLICATION FUND OF
REFORM CONGREGATION KENESETH ISRAEL, PHILADELPHIA,
        LOUIS SCHWERIN, *President*

Table of Contents

CONTENTS

Preface

I have felt a fond attachment for New Orleans ever since my friend and teacher Rabbi Julian B. Feibelman of Temple Sinai first introduced me to its charm almost thirty years ago. Three years later, at the behest of beloved Myra and Bernard H. Eichhold, I assumed rabbinical leadership of my first congregation—Shaaray Shomayim of Mobile, Alabama. At least once a month my friend Joseph Bear would take me with him to New Orleans on some excuse or other. On none of those visits in 1940 or 1943 did it ever occur to me that I would become involved in this study of the beginnings of Jewish life in New Orleans.

Over the years of my research into various aspects of American Jewish history, I had touched on themes of importance to New Orleans: the nature of Judah P. Benjamin's feelings about Judaism; Judah Touro's strange indifference to his religion until the last years of his life; Benjamin Levy's pioneering career as a bookseller, printer and publisher. But as a matter of simple fact, I never intended to write this book.

Some years ago I began to assemble material for a study of Jewish life in the ante-Bellum South; a monograph on *Jews and Slavery in the Old South* was one product of that effort. As I surveyed the available resources, I discovered that very little thorough research had been done into the earliest periods of New Orleans Jewish history, and I decided that I would have to do some basic digging myself. I presumed that little would be found, but I had to make certain. Much to my astonishment, the more deeply I delved, the more I uncovered—a host of early Jewish settlers who were totally unknown to those who had previously written brief essays on Jewish life in the city; a number of colorful personages who fascinated me so profoundly that I had no alternative but to try to learn more about their experiences; and some distinctive, perhaps unique, aspects of Jewish life in the community—or better, accounting for the lack of a sense of community before 1827–28—which struck me as being worth more than brief reference in a larger framework.

I was, then, ambushed into writing this book. This research has taken an inordinate amount of time, and yet it has given me more pleasure than any other work I have essayed. This is partly because I have made so many friends in the process—hundreds of librarians, scholars, students, researchers and just plain people, who have generously contributed material to these pages, or have helped me to find it. Had I lived in New Orleans this work would have been finished in one-quarter of the time. Much of the hunt had to be carried on through correspondence, microfilms, photocopies and notes made by research assistants. But on a number of occasions it was my privilege to be able to work in New Orleans libraries, museums and depositories of historic materials. These trips brought me the great pleasure of spending time with my colleagues Rabbis Julian B. Feibelman and Leo A. Bergman, and with my friends Dorothy and Shepard Shushan, in whose lovely home I was so warmly welcomed and permitted to make my New Orleans headquarters. To them and to all the others who have helped with hospitality, encouragement and information—whose names I have tried to list in the Acknowledgements—I offer my sincere appreciation.

The first and second drafts of this book were written during the summers of 1966 and 1967 in the hospitable surroundings of the American Jewish Archives at the Hebrew Union College in Cincinnati, while I was given time off by my long-suffering but sympathetic congregation. The rich collections which my beloved teacher, Professor Jacob Rader Marcus, has assembled at the Archives during the twenty years which have passed since its foundation, made it possible for me to do much checking and doublechecking while engaged in the writing process. The staff of the Archives exemplifies the highest standards of helpfulness which a research institute can offer. My thanks go as always to Professor Marcus for his unfailing encouragement and assistance as I struggled with knotty problems of synthesis and narrative.

I know that some members of my congregation have thought at times that I dwelt in the past as much as in the present. All the more am I gratified that they have indulged my research and detective work so uncomplainingly. They have afforded me the widest latitude in pursuing my second career as a student of history. They even provided me with a former president, Mr. Charles C. Pollack, who helped to translate some of the myriad of French documents with which I have had to deal.

Two other men rate a special word of gratitude: Professor Jack D. L. Holmes of the University of Alabama at Birmingham, and Mr. Winston De Ville of Alexandria and Chapel Hill. Dr. Holmes has constantly placed at my disposal his rich knowledge of the Spanish colonial period of Louisiana, and Mr. De Ville, the most ubiquitous student of French archival resources in all of Louisiana, has hunted far and wide to help me locate elusive pieces of isolated information. Both of these friends and co-workers have helped me to achieve an intimate comprehension of the colonial period. For the later, American period, I have been ably helped by Mr. and Mrs. H. L. Forsyth, dedicated students of Louisiana genealogy and joyous friends to all who are interested in New Orleans history, who always seemed to be able to come up with a new lead whenever I ran into a deadend. An entire section of Acknowledgements lists the names of the innumerable folk who have assisted in the research for this volume. Mention must be made here, however, of these: Mrs. Michell Jacques, who typed the original manuscript and has proof-read the book into print; Mrs. Herbert Greenspan, Miss Imelda McGonigle, Mrs. Leonard Sarner and Mrs. Hyman Penn, my secretaries, who participated in its preparation in many ways; my colleague, Rabbi Abraham I. Shinedling, who helped me get the manuscript ready for the press and has prepared the index; Bernard Wax, the Director of the American Jewish Historical Society, who has shown devoted interest in the success of this project; and Dr. Maurice Jacobs, my friend, the printer, who cares about the book as much as I do.

My choice of a biographical rather than a thematic approach was made somewhat reluctantly. It would have been far easier to have described the activities of these New Orleans people in terms of the various categories of life—economic, political, social, cultural, etc.—pursuing a comparative method. But the clarity achieved by this sort of treatment would have blurred the view of them as whole persons and as members of families, which I have attempted to achieve. Because they were, in such large measure, isolated persons rather than members of a Jewish community, it seemed to me essential to present them as distinct individuals. I have reverted to the thematic approach only in regard to their religious views and practices because here, as a group, they offer a sort of case study in the tension between accommodation and continuity which underlies all of American Jewish history.

My terminus ad quem requires some explanation to those who will be scandalized that I have not attempted to delineate in any great detail the experiences of the New Orleans Jewish community beyond the 1840's. Although I do devote some attention to the life stories of some early Jews who lived even into the 1890's, and much effort to the attempt to achieve an understanding of Judah Touro's later years, my primary concern has been with the origins of the community, the tracing of the story up to the point somewhere in the late 1830's or early 1840's when New Orleans began more closely to resemble other Jewish communities throughout America. Some aspects of distinctiveness did continue—a higher rate of intermarriage; a greater number of transients; a more urgent need for institutions like the Touro Infirmary and the Jewish Widows' and Orphans' Home; a lengthy delay in the creation of a genuine Reform congregation—but most developments in New Orleans can best be understood in relation to those in other major communities in the South and throughout the nation. If God spares me, I still hope to move on to an evaluation of the nature of Jewish life in the South prior to the outbreak of the Civil War. In such a study, more can be said about the further growth of New Orleans Jewry than would have meaning here.

One further explanation is in order: I was altogether astonished at the mountain of material about the Monsanto family which turned up in the later years of my research. I had presumed, without justification, that others had worked exhaustively in colonial Louisiana materials and had found nothing about early Jews.

The Monsanto story is another reason for the distinctiveness of the New Orleans Jewish community's origins; it is altogether different from Jewish experiences in the British colonial areas on the Atlantic coast. And I am equally grateful that the pursuit of the Monsanto family into British West Florida records revealed so much additional material about the first Jewish settlers in my old Southern home, Mobile.

Ordinarily a work like this would be accompanied by a formal and formidable bibliography, but I believe that this would be unnecessary. A collation of all of the manuscript and published sources to which reference is made in the notes would simply add to the length of the book, but would serve no useful purpose; nor could a bibliography legitimately include all of the thousands of books and pamphlets whose pages I have turned in the vain hope of discovering some reference to my people. Suffice it to say that I have hunted for material in every logical or illogical source noted in the standard Louisiana bibliographies; turned cards in the catalogue of every major library in the New Orleans area; and read through every available issue of New Orleans newspapers, in the original form or on microfilm, from the earliest issue to the end of 1842. I have preferred to concentrate my attention on the notes, some of which are, perhaps, too tightly packed with detailed information; but I should not want any fellow researcher to miss any hint of a detail which I have succeeded in discovering. The course over which I have plodded has been too arduous for me to refrain from sharing anything that I have found.

Although I have attempted to exploit relevant source materials with as much thoroughness as possible, New Orleans possesses an embarrassment of manuscript riches. The Notarial Archives, in particular, are incredibly informative. It would take most of the rest of my life to search through every notarial volume in the basement of the Civil District Court Building in New Orleans for additional data about the life of these people whom I call "my people" because I feel as though I have brought them back to life. But I do not think that additional years of such research would change very much in this volume, although a great deal of specific data, particularly about the business careers of some of my dramatis personae, would indeed be of interest. I hope that some candidates for master's and doctor's degrees in Louisiana universities will undertake further research along these lines. It will undoubtedly be illuminating.

Even more to the point are the similar records in parish (the Louisiana equivalent of county) court houses throughout the state, which I have not even seen, let alone searched. Rural Louisiana presents yet another challenge to students of local Jewish history. I am certain that much new material about Jews during the period from 1810 to 1840 will be uncovered in such caches of manuscripts.

Basically I conceive of this book as the story of people, not just any people, but people who are—were—part of the People Israel, the People of mystery, of pain, of hope. Always an enigma to others as well as to themselves, these who belonged to the People Israel fled through the night, over continents, and across the ocean, in search of freedom, opportunity and self-realization. In the process of flight and settlement, many of them lost their sense of relatedness to the People Israel, and abandoned their personal identity as Jews, but even this was part of the search. Many had endured too much to be content any longer to be regarded as inferiors—in an age when the Jewish religion had not yet found a way of surviving in the modern world. If they wanted to forget that they were Jews, we can understand even that. But though individuals may end their search on bypaths, the People itself persists, rediscovers itself, renews itself. Despite every obstacle, challenge, danger and difficulty, somehow Israel manages to survive to face another day, and even finds it possible to live creatively and to wring a blessing from the Most High.

B.W.K.

Wyncote, Pa.
April 1, 1969.

Chronology

1718   Founding of New Orleans by the French.

1754–63 French and Indian War, between France (joined in 1761 by Spain) and England, the American colonial equivalent of the European Seven Years' War (1756–63).

1762   Treaty of Fontainebleau (November 3), by which France ceded New Orleans and the Louisiana colonial area west of the Mississippi River to Spain, as compensation for Spain's impending loss of Florida to Great Britain.

1763   Treaty of Paris (February 10), ending the Seven Years' War and France's colonial empire on the American continent. French Louisiana east of the Mississippi was surrendered to the British; this area included the lower third of the present states of Mississippi and Alabama. The British divided their new possessions, French eastern Louisiana and Spanish Florida, into British West and East Florida.

1766   Arrival in New Orleans of the first Spanish governor, Antonio de Ulloa.

1769   Arrival in New Orleans of the second Spanish governor, General Alejandro O'Reilly.

1779   Capture of Baton Rouge, Manchac and Natchez from the British by the Spanish under Governor Bernardo de Gálvez.

1780   Capture of Mobile by Gálvez.

1781   Capture of Pensacola by Gálvez.

1800   Treaty of San Ildefonso (October 1), by which Spain ceded New Orleans and Louisiana west of the Mississippi to France. Formal transfer November 30, 1803.

1803   Louisiana Purchase Treaty between the United States and France (April 30). Formal transfer December 20, 1803.

1810   Revolt of West Florida settlers in the Baton Rouge area against Spain (September 23) and annexation of the area by the United States (October 27).

New Orleans was French from 1717 to 1766; Spanish from 1766 to November 30, 1803; French from November 30, 1803, to December 20, 1803; American from December 20, 1803.

Baton Rouge was French from 1717 to 1763; British from 1763 to 1779; Spanish from 1779 to 1810; American from 1810.

Mobile was French from its founding in 1702 to 1763; British from 1763 to 1780; Spanish from 1780 to 1813, when it was seized by the United States, which had claimed it since 1803.

Pensacola was Spanish from about 1699 to 1763; British from 1763 to 1781; Spanish from 1781 to 1814, when it was taken over briefly by the British before Andrew Jackson seized it for the United States.

List of Illustrations

THE EARLY JEWS OF NEW ORLEANS

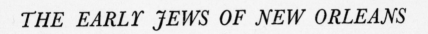

I

The Colonial Experience

1. Jews in the French Caribbean

Just as the 1492 expulsion of the great Jewish community of Ferdinand and Isabella's Spain drove shock-waves of refugees to every conceivable area of open or clandestine settlement in Europe, North Africa and Asia Minor, so the minor diaspora which resulted from the capture of Dutch Brazil by the Portuguese in 1654 scattered another significant Jewish community into the nooks and crannies of a newer world. Wherever they could find a haven, hospitable or begrudging, temporary or permanent, these Spanish and Portuguese Jews, called Sephardim, sought to settle. Some went back to the Old World, to the security of Amsterdam, even to London, but many, apparently, having taken the adventurous voyage to the Western Hemisphere, attempted to establish themselves in the islands and ports of the Caribbean and Atlantic. A few found their way, by accident, to the bleak, bustling town of New Amsterdam that Peter Stuyvesant ruled on the North American mainland. Stuyvesant's heavy-handed effort to prevent them from remaining in the colony evoked the strong protest of the Jews of Amsterdam to the directors of the Dutch West India Company. They complained that

> ". . . The French consent that the Portuguese Jews may traffic and live in Martinique, Christopher and others of their territories, whither also some have gone from here, as your Honors know. The English also consent at the present time that the Portuguese and Jewish nation may go from London and settle at Barbados, whither also some have gone. . . ."[1]

The Jewish burghers of Amsterdam might well have mentioned that Jews had perhaps settled in Martinique even before the

1

French added the island colony to their New World possessions in 1635, and that refugees from Brazil had fled not only to Martinique and St. Christophe, but also to Guadeloupe.[2]

This is not to suggest, however, that the status of the Jews in the French islands during the seventeenth century was idyllic. Some of the leading statesmen in the homeland and in the colonies realized full well that every brain and pair of hands, even Jewish, brought added strength to the island frontiers, but conservative religious and economic forces continually agitated against this permissive view. Controller-General Jean Baptiste Colbert supported the liberal attitude so vigorously that Louis XIV issued a formal decree on May 23, 1671, which authorized Jews to remain in "la Martinique et les autres Isles habitués par mes sujets."[3] But in 1685 this tolerant policy was reversed in the first published compilation of laws for the regulation of slavery in the colonies, the *Code Noir*; one section of that code ordered the banishment of Jewish settlers from the French island colonies:

> "It is our wish, and we decree, that the edict of the late King of glorious memory, our greatly honored lord and father, dated April 23, 1615, be carried into effect in our Islands and, by these Presents, We command all our officers to chase out of our Islands all Jews who have established their residence there whom, as declared enemies of the Christian faith, We command to get out in three months, counting from the day of the publication of these Presents, upon penalty of the confiscation of their persons and property."[4]

The edict of 1615 had not been applied to the Marrano merchants of Bordeaux and other commercial centers of southern France—they continued to enjoy a special status. Similarly, although some Jews may have been expelled from the French West Indies, or denied admission to them, as a result of the decree of 1685, certain privileged Jewish entrepreneurs continued to maintain residence and conduct their businesses in the islands. Members of the noted Gradis family, for instance, developed extensive commercial and agricultural holdings in Martinique and Saint-Domingue (the present-day Haiti) early in the eighteenth century.[5]

2

2. JEWS IN EARLY LOUISIANA?

The Caribbean islands were far more attractive to ambitious, resourceful Jews like the Gradis family than the Louisiana colony which was abuilding so painfully and so slowly on the Gulf Coast mainland. Despite the efforts of the brothers Pierre Le Moyne d'Iberville and Jean Baptiste Le Moyne de Bienville, who exhibited great confidence in the potential promise of Louisiana, the colony languished "in a state of confusion, with quarreling factions, abandoned concessions, habitations, and farms, and an immoral and generally worthless French citizenry."[6] There is no positive documentary evidence known to the writer that any Jew came to Louisiana during the early years of the colony.[7] Such immigrants to Louisiana as Jacob David, shoemaker, Romain David, tailor, Robert and Genevieve Jacob, and a soldier named Louis Salomon, all of whom arrived in 1719, have been regarded as Jews simply on the basis of their names, but no contemporary document identifies them as Jews or Jewish converts to Christianity.[8] Nor is there evidence that any of the early German colonists who settled in the area called "the German coast" were known to their fellows as Jews. The religion of almost every one of these early Germans is recorded; none is identified in available lists or documents as a Jew or as a convert from Judaism. It is natural for the historian seeking Jewish relevance to be attracted to such names as Marx, until he discovers that the first Marx in Louisiana was named Balthazar, and that he gave his religion as Roman Catholic.[9] The search for early Jews in Louisiana should continue, but researchers ought to agree that names alone can hardly be offered as conclusive evidence.[10]

In a similar vein, the ban on the residence of Jews in the Louisiana *Code Noir* of 1724 should not be regarded as presumptive evidence of the actual presence of Jews in the colony. A much more likely explanation is that the text of the 1724 *Code* (which was drawn up in Paris, not in Louisiana) was based in large measure upon the prior document of 1685, which had been issued before the establishment of the settlements on the

3

Gulf Coast. The section on the Jews varied only slightly in the new version:

> "The edict of the late King Louis XIII, of glorious memory, dated April 23, 1615, shall be executed in our province and colony of Louisiana: this being done, We enjoin the Directors General of the said Company, and all our Officers, to drive out of the said country all Jews who may have established their residence there. These, as declared enemies of the Christian name, We command to leave in three months, counting from the day of the publication of these Presents, upon penalty of the confiscation of their persons and property."[11]

One of the variations, it will be noted, is a greater uncertainty in this document about the actual presence of Jews than in the 1685 version, as if to say that no report of the settlement of Jews in Louisiana had reached Paris.

The inclusion of a ban on Jewish settlement as Article I, and on the practice of any religion other than the Catholic as Article III, in a code which regulated Negro slavery in the colonies, has seemed to baffle certain historians. Charles Gayarré, for instance, voices his mystification: "By what concatenation of causes or ideas, these provisions concerning the supremacy of the Roman Catholic religion and the expulsion of the Jews came to be inserted in the Black Code, it is difficult to imagine."[12] But it is not so difficult once we recognize that the basic motivation was a missionary concern for the souls of the Negro slaves: if Jewish landowners could practice Judaism, they might feel free to convert their slaves to their own religion. Only a double-edged denial of the right of Jews to settle, and of the freedom to practice any faith other than the Catholic, would guarantee the proper Catholicization of the slaves. Since the time of the Emperor Constantius (339), legislation of the Roman Empire, of Church Councils, and of individual states, had sought to support the spread of Christianity by prohibiting the holding of Christian slaves, and even of potential slave converts to Christianity, by Jews, as well as the conversion of slaves to Judaism by their Jewish owners.[13] But whatever the background of the *Code Noir*, it should not be regarded as positive evidence that Jews who would be subjected to its provisions had already come

4

to Louisiana. This is not to suggest, however, that they would have been welcomed into the colony. A bureau document of the Company of the Indies, dating from 1716 or 1717, urged the exclusion of Jews because they would be politically unreliable and economically too aggressive. "Those of Portugal [who are in France now] give us a good example of what to avoid."[14] It is idle to wonder what would have happened if a Jew had tried to settle in the colony. It should be recognized, however, that if Jews did not attempt to settle in Louisiana, their avoidance of the area was not motivated by their fear of rejection or banishment, but rather by their awareness of the fact that the colony's languishing economic condition offered them little opportunity of making a living in their accustomed commercial pursuits.

The extensive economic potential of Louisiana was seen clearly by one Jew who never settled there, but whose vision, if acted upon, might have stimulated the kind of growth the colony sorely required. This Jew was Abraham Gradis of Bordeaux, whose family, as we have noted, had already established commercial branches in the Caribbean and who, in 1748, organized the highly successful Society of Canada venture for the promotion of commerce in the northern colony. In the same year, Gradis proposed the establishment of a similar company which would exploit the commercial and agricultural opportunities he perceived in the Louisiana settlement. The key to the problem, as Gradis saw it, was the massive importation of Negro slaves into the colony under the auspices of the King—he suggested ten thousand slaves over a period of five years. These slaves would be utilized primarily for the clearing and cultivation of land. Some of the lumber would be used for construction, and the excess would be exported. The major objective of all this activity would be "a lucrative trade in all our manufactures with New Spain [Mexico], a commerce now inaccessible to the French because of the sea. Through overland caravans into this colony, the Spaniards could secure our merchandise and wares in exchange for gold and silver. . . ." Gradis' memorandum which embodied these recommendations to the French government was submitted from Bordeaux on May 21, 1748. It was filed without comment or action.[15]

Very possibly, however, even though Gradis' plan was not carried out, the first contacts of Jews with Louisiana were through trade rather than permanent settlement. The earliest located transaction on record concerns a cargo of goods worth 14,162 piastres and 2 reales, which Josue Henriques, Jr., a Jewish businessman in Curaçao, shipped to one Bertrand in New Orleans some time before July, 1748. Bertrand accepted the consignment, sold it and absconded with the proceeds. On July 19, 1748, the Layssard brothers, Jean Baptiste and Etienne, who were apparently Henriques' correspondents in New Orleans, petitioned Vincent d'Auberville, Commissaire Ordonnateur of the Province and First Judge of its Superior Court, for the seizure of Bertrand's property in New Orleans, so that Henriques might be reimbursed for his losses. D'Auberville approved the petition on July 19, and the required notice was served at Bertrand's residence on August 3. In September, a Bertrand associate admitted possession of merchandise worth 4,132 piastres which belonged to the fugitive, but insisted that he would not voluntarily surrender it. The incomplete record of the case ends here.[16] There may, of course, have been many other commercial contracts during the 1740's and 1750's between Jews in the Caribbean area and merchants and customers in New Orleans of which no record remains because they did not become the subjects of such legal wrangling as this.

3. The *TEXEL* Affair

Within a decade of Henriques' trouble, however, a few Jewish merchants and their families had finally established themselves in New Orleans. Attention was called to their presence in the colony, which violated the first article of the *Code Noir*, in the barrage of correspondence which documents the complex "*Texel* affair." As a result of the arrival in New Orleans in January, 1759, of the ship *Texel* which gave its name to this cause célèbre, the hostility which had long been simmering between the Governor of the colony, Chevalier Louis Billouart de Kerlérec, and the Commissaire Ordonnateur, Vincent Pierre Gaspard de Rochemore, burst into the open. The *Texel* had come to New Orleans from Jamaica on a *parlementaire* voyage. *Parlementaire* shipping ventures were a well-known feature of the Seven Years' War (1756–1763) in the colonial areas. Originally designed to encourage the exchange of prisoners of war, they developed into speculative trips to enemy territory for the sale of cargoes of scarce merchandise. A few prisoners would serve as the excuse for the shipment of sorely needed goods to an enemy port. Kerlérec welcomed these opportunities to obtain foodstuffs and other commodities for his colony, even at high prices. Rochemore opposed the Governor's policy. The *Texel* arrived in the Governor's absence. The Ordonnateur, in an effort to establish his authority and demonstrate his virtue, accused Kerlérec of violating the intent of the law and of sharing in the profits of such cargoes. He therefore seized the *Texel* and imprisoned its captain. Kerlérec, on his return to town, released the ship and the captain, and reprimanded Rochemore for taking the law into his own hands. Both men, of course, wrote reports to Paris to justify their conduct. The captain of the ship was a Jew named David Dias Arias, who died in New Orleans before he was able to leave the colony. In Curaçao, years before, Dias Arias had married Gracia Yesurun, daughter of Haham Rephael Yesurun (1678–1747). The rabbi was so unlucky as to countersign a heavy note of indebtedness for him; when Dias Arias found himself unable to pay his debts, he fled Curaçao and took refuge in Jamaica. The rabbi had to sell all his possessions in order to raise just one-quarter of the huge sum for which he was now responsible. An unsavory character, at best, was Dias Arias, to become the subject of so intense a colonial furore. The conflict between the two highest officials of the colony and their supporters dragged on for years, culminating in the dismissal of Rochemore and the resignation of Kerlérec. Long after Louisiana had been ceded to the Spanish, their families brought suits and countersuits in the courts of France and wrote memoirs on the case.[17]

It was clearly an accident that the owner of this *parlementaire* ship happened to be a Jew. Dias Arias was probably no different

7

from the other commercial adventurers who participated in this legalized smuggling business. But Rochemore had little liking for Jews anyway, and used their presence in New Orleans as another argument to justify his seizure of the *Texel* and his defiance of the Governor:

> ". . . The sale of the cargo [after it was released by Kerlérec] has been accomplished by the Captain [Dias Arias] of this ship in the stores of the Jews established in this colony. The Captain has received the money for it, and has left the river after having had time during a two months sojourn, at complete liberty in this city, to gather knowledge of the weakness of this colony, and to carry away such commodities as he wished. One of these Jews left in another ship a short time after without declaring his destination and without a passport; and, furthermore, this is the custom in this colony on the part of those who leave for foreign and enemy colonies, to receive the approval of the Governor, who alone knows their designs. . . .
>
> "These Jews, who according to the edicts and ordinances must not remain in a colony more than three months, under penalty of imprisonment and confiscation of their property, are forming establishments here the progress and the danger of which have been observed by the whole country. There are, at present, six of them here, and I do not include those of the ship of Dias Arias, engaging in commerce both wholesale and retail, with the same freedom as French businessmen. The merchants and other inhabitants of this colony are persuaded that the Jews are only tolerated here as a means of raising money, through a tax that I know nothing of. . . ."[18]

Thus Rochemore marshalled his accusations against the Jews: they were spies for the enemy; they were weakening the colony through the exportation of commodities; they were bribing the Governor to obtain permission to remain; and they were an economic danger to the inhabitants of the colony. Had Rochemore gained the upper hand in his struggle with the Governor, or had Kerlérec agreed with his position, there is no doubt that the Jews would have been summarily expelled. But, fortunately for them, Rochemore's defiance did not prevail, and they were permitted to remain.

4. THE FIRST DOCUMENTED JEWS IN NEW ORLEANS

Unfortunately we do not know the names or activities of all of the six Jews to whom Rochemore and his clique referred, nor do we know precisely which one was the first to settle permanently in Louisiana. That distinction may quite possibly belong to a person whose name and affairs are unrecorded in any document, but more likely than not it should be accorded to Isaac Rodrigues Monsanto. In early 1757, Monsanto and his associate, Manuel de Britto, then in Curaçao, chartered the sloop *St. Joseph* from its owner Charles Guillaume, for a voyage to New Orleans. Manuel Monsanto, Isaac's brother, was a passenger on the ship, probably for the purpose of supervising the sale of the cargo in New Orleans. Isaac Monsanto and de Britto may have gone ahead to New Orleans, while the ship stopped at Saint-Domingue. Either on its way to New Orleans, or on its return, the ship was captured in the Bay of Monte Christi by a New England privateer, the *Black Snake*, under the command of Captain Ebenezer Tyler, and taken to Providence, Rhode Island. After its arrival there, Manuel Monsanto and his associates gave their power of attorney for the recovery of the sloop to Jacob Rodriguez Rivera, a prosperous Jewish merchant of Newport, R. I., on June 8, 1757. De Britto meanwhile hastened to Rhode Island to help to secure the release of the ship, which was finally accomplished through the payment of a ransom, but the cargo was apparently confiscated because it was destined for, or had come from, a French port. The *St. Joseph* was loaded with rum and once more set out for the Caribbean area, only to be captured by another privateer, this time, apparently, for good. A series of suits and countersuits ensued in the courts of Saint-Domingue and New Orleans, beginning in late 1757 and continuing until 1763. Guillaume sued for the rent of the ship while it was in British custody; Monsanto and de Britto sued for the expenses involved in fitting and refitting the ship and for the profits anticipated from the sale of the rum, which they said Guillaume's agent, one Perpignot or Perpina, had hijacked for sale in Saint-Domingue—

the reason that the sloop was captured by the British the second time. The final judgment of the New Orleans court in 1763 cannot be found, but the case was so confused and complicated that neither party had all the right on its side—the real problem was that the British privateers were too efficient.[19]

It is not clear whether Isaac Monsanto had already decided to transfer his business operations from Curaçao to New Orleans before the *St. Joseph*'s voyage, in view of that port's great need for consumer goods due to the war, or whether his enforced stay in New Orleans to pursue the case through the courts persuaded him that this would be a good location for his activities. It is also possible that Isaac Monsanto had already become discouraged by the highly competitive commercial atmosphere in Curaçao, which was perhaps the most active entrepreneurial port in the Western Hemisphere at the time. But whether through accident or design, by October 24, 1758, at the latest, Isaac had established himself in New Orleans. On that date he made some purchases at the auction of the property of Claude Joseph Villars Dubreuil, the deceased Contractor of Public Works. One of these purchases was "a little Negro girl named Quetelle," for whom he paid 1,400 livres. He was obviously setting up a household; hence his need for a slave.[20]

5. THE MONSANTO FAMILY IN THE HAGUE AND CURAÇAO

Isaac Monsanto was born at The Hague, Holland, in October, 1729, the eldest son and second child of David Rodrigues Monsanto, a native of Amsterdam, and his wife Ester Levy. Monsanto was a Sephardic Jew; Ester was an Ashkenazi (Central European) from Münster in Germany.[21] The father is first mentioned as the clerk of Sir Solomon de Medina in 1715, but he may have served in that capacity prior to that time; Medina had already established his residence at The Hague in 1705 after moving to the continent from England in 1702 in order to remain in close contact with the Duke of Marlborough, for whose armies he was a major supplier of transportation and foodstuffs. William III had knighted Medina on June 23, 1700,

in recognition of his financial services to the Crown and to Marlborough. He was the first professing Jew so to be honored by a British monarch. By the time of David Monsanto's employment, however, Medina had lost much of his immense wealth, and after Marlborough's disgrace in 1711, his connection with momentous affairs of state had ended. Nonetheless, Medina was still a man of substance and influence, and we may be certain that David Monsanto's responsibilities as his secretary-bookkeeper were arduous and weighty. Sir Solomon was still supervising his business operations and investments in England and the Netherlands from The Hague, and was continuing to attempt to retrieve money he had loaned to Marlborough. David Monsanto was both loyal and efficient: he remained in Medina's employ until the latter's death at the age of eighty in 1730, and continued to serve Lady Ester de Medina and the executors while the estate was being settled, at least until 1739. Sir Solomon reposed such confidence in his clerk that he left him a bequest of 400 guilders, plus an additional 1,500 guilders following Lady Ester's death—a larger legacy than Sir Solomon's bequests to his own grandchildren, and the third largest beyond the family circle. Unfortunately, Medina's affairs were so tangled, and his debts so enormous, that David Monsanto probably never collected even a fraction of this inheritance.[22]

During his employment by Medina, who must have been fairly generous to him, David Monsanto had saved enough money to make an investment in the Compagnie van Beleninge, a municipal bank of The Hague; to contribute modest amounts of money to the building fund of the Honen Dal Congregation, which dedicated its new synagogue in 1726; and to establish a family. He married Ester Levy in the synagogue in 1726 or 1727 and sired his first child, Sara, in 1728. At least eight other children, in addition to Isaac, came of this union. Probably because the anticipated legacy from the Medina estate would make him a fairly substantial citizen, David decided, in 1732, to register his marriage to Ester in the civil records of The Hague, and to have a civil wedding ceremony performed. This was not an unusual procedure; Protestants, too, had the privilege of choosing between a civil or religious wedding ceremony, and sometimes decided on both. During the 1730's, David was

11

apparently a fairly prosperous man. He probably pursued some of the business interests in which he had been involved with Medina, and also represented clients in business transactions by exercising their power of attorney, much as he had done for Medina. In 1736 he was elected to an expensive honor by his congregation, and to equally expensive office the following year. In 1741 he served as trustee of an estate. But by late 1742, apparently, he had fallen on hard times. Perhaps he had been borrowing against the anticipated Medina legacy, which by then had become a forlorn hope. He left The Hague for Germany, probably in an effort to recoup his fortunes, but to no avail. When he returned in 1745, he notified the authorities that he did not have the money to pay the special tax which had been levied to meet the cost of Dutch participation in the War of the Austrian Succession. Beginning in 1746, David Monsanto and his family were maintained by the Jewish community, now united by the merger of the two congregations, Honen Dal and Beth Jacob, which had taken place during his absence, in 1743. This man who, as secretary of the wealthy Medina, had kept the records of investments in the hundreds of thousands of pounds sterling, was now reduced to accepting a monthly stipend from the community of which he had once been a fairly substantial member. On Passover he received gifts of *matzos*, and on Hanukah both clothing and money. He who had gratefully accepted and paid for the high honor of serving in 1736 as the "Bridegroom of Genesis" on *Simchas Torah* (the Festival of Rejoicing in the Torah, celebrated on the last morning of the Feast of Tabernacles in the autumn), now served as a *minhanista*—that is, one of the group of unemployed, idle and retired men who, in exchange for a small allowance, were required to attend services in the synagogue every weekday, in order to assure the presence of the mandatory quorum (*minyan*) of ten men necessary for the conduct of public Jewish worship.[23]

The available evidence for the birth years of the children of David and Ester Monsanto is confused and contradictory. We know definitely that Sara, the eldest, died in January, 1736, and that a third child, Jaël, was eight months old in January, 1732. But the registration of birth of some of the other children does not give their names; and later testimony of the children themselves offers various ages which contradicts their statements on other occasions. The best guesses that we can offer are only approximations: Jaël may be the daughter named Judith who was one of the oldest children and who later lived in Saint-Domingue; Joseph may be the child born in 1733, and Manuel was born probably in 1734. There is a big jump in time to the other children, although still other children may have been born and died during the intervening years in that age of severe infant mortality—Gracia (1743?); Angélica (1744?); Eleanora (1745?); Jacob (1746?); Benjamin (1747?). We know definitely that Jacob and Benjamin were still young enough to be pupils in the synagogue school in The Hague in 1753–54. We also know that Ester, probably exhausted by child bearing and rearing, by poverty and want, died in July of 1747. If all the children were hers, as we believe, that is the terminal date for their birth. David Monsanto was too poor to pay the fee for the registration of Ester's death and burial.[24]

After years of dependence on communal funds for their support, in late 1754 the Monsanto family decided to take the bold step of beginning life anew. They made application to the officers and board of The Hague Jewish community for a grant which would enable them to emigrate to Curaçao. A total of 600 florins was offered to them; this included the 120 florins which they ordinarily received each year, aside from special gifts on holidays.[25] Many European Jewish communities during this period, and later, got rid of their paupers by dispatching them to other cities in the Old and New Worlds, but one wonders if in this case, at least, the decision to strike out for new opportunities was not made by the paupers themselves. Although the subsidy was given to David, the titular head of the family, it would seem unlikely that it was he who made this momentous decision: from what hidden reserve of psychic energy could he have summoned the imagination and courage to start a new life after eight years of poverty and failure? In view of Isaac's subsequent leadership of the family, it seems far more probable that it was he who was unwilling any longer to submit to dependence and want, and that it was his ambition and aggressiveness which precipitated the move to the New World. Isaac may well have promised his father that he would take care of his brothers and sisters if David would agree to this drastic action—but promise or not, his future conduct indeed demonstrated his willingness to assume responsibility for the rest of the family.

No record has been discovered which marks the Monsanto family's arrival in Curaçao, but it seems reasonable to suppose that it was in 1755. Actually, the first reference to any member of the family in the Curaçao archives relates to the ill-fated *St. Joseph* voyage of 1757, but the family would have had to be in Curaçao[26] for at least a while in order to accumulate the funds necessary for that venture. It is, of course, possible that Isaac and Manuel had made the trip alone at first, with the rest of the family following later, but this seems unlikely in view of the family's tightly-knit unity in later years in Louisiana. At any rate, by 1758 Isaac and Jacob both possessed certificates as brokers in Curaçao, while the father was pursuing his old occupation of representing the legal interests of clients by utilizing their power of attorney. Far from being a solicitor or barrister, let alone attorney-general of the colony, a legend which persists among some of his descendants—all that David Monsanto or any other Jew could do was to participate in a legal transaction by exercising the power of attorney of a client who was out-of-town or was too busy to be present.[27]

We have no certain knowledge of which brothers and sisters Isaac took with him to New Orleans in 1757–58. There is definite evidence that Manuel did remain in Curaçao, carrying on an import and export business there, but he may have been engaged in these ventures on Isaac's behalf. The last records in Curaçao relating to David and Manuel date from the summer of 1763. It may have been then that the family closed down its Curaçao headquarters, Manuel moving to New Orleans to join Isaac, and probably taking along with him Manuel de Britto, who apparently up until then had spent more time in Curaçao than in New Orleans. The date and place of David Monsanto's death are not known. Although his name is not listed in the incomplete burial records of Curaçao, he may possibly have died there in the summer of 1763, when members of the family seem still to have lived there. It was surely not in New Orleans, for, as we shall see, a bequest by David to his daughters in New Orleans was later described as having come to them in the form of a shipment of cargo. Perhaps the most probable location of David's death was Saint-Domingue, where his son Joseph settled, and where his daughter Judith (Jaël?) lived with her husband Moïse Julien. Whatever David's fate, it is clear that he had succeeded in reestablishing himself at least to the extent that he was able to leave some money to his three daughters. The move to Curaçao had indeed given him a new opportunity in life.[28]

Manuel Monsanto and Manuel de Britto probably took along with them to New Orleans another Jew, Isaac Henriques Fastio, who was to outlive most of the Monsanto brothers and sisters in Louisiana. Fastio, a native of Bordeaux, had probably established himself in Curaçao by April, 1757, when his wife Ester left Bordeaux for Curaçao by way of Amsterdam, with their four daughters in tow, accompanied by her brother Abraham Rodrigues and a forty-six-year-old servant, Abraham García. Fastio and Manuel Monsanto were partners in some complex export operations in 1763 which brought them into conflict with the son of the late governor of Curaçao. Perhaps Manuel Monsanto, de Britto and Fastio were compelled to leave Curaçao after this disastrous venture which, apparently, plunged them into debt. At any rate, Fastio was in Louisiana by 1766 at the latest, participating in some business ventures with Isaac Monsanto. Although he may have opened a store in New Orleans, it is more likely that he moved almost immediately to Pointe Coupee where he spent most of his active business life in Louisiana. His death record in 1804 states that he had been a Louisiana resident for "about 50 years," but so far as we can trace his movements, he could not have moved to New Orleans until 1763 at the earliest. Possibly Isaac Monsanto had prospered so well that he could now also support Manuel and de Britto; he may also have promised to give Fastio a share in some of his ventures. The transfer to New Orleans may also have been stimulated by the end of the Seven Years' War, and the expectation that business opportunities in New Orleans would be more attractive than in Curaçao.[29]

15

6. ISAAC MONSANTO AND COMPANY IN NEW ORLEANS, 1758–1769

New Orleans had indeed offered ample opportunity for Isaac to demonstrate his capacity for aggressive and imaginative commercial activity. Assisted by the continuing scarcity of consumer goods created by the interminable warfare between England and France, the absence of competition from the largely indolent French settlers, the useful contacts which he already had established in Curaçao and possibly in Saint-Domingue and elsewhere, and the ready help of his younger brothers, he succeeded in becoming a prosperous merchant during the period 1758–69. Isaac Monsanto seems to have had a vigorous, out-going personality, and to have made friends easily. Not only did Governor Kerlérec refuse to eject him and the other Jews, but he seems to have taken a friendly interest in Isaac, which the latter reciprocated. Monsanto was one of twenty-nine merchants who signed a statement on April 29, 1763, which praised Kerlérec's efforts to encourage the commerce of the city during the war.[30] Kerlérec continued to maintain business relations with Monsanto even after his return to France. In 1766 he wrote to Monsanto from Paris about the sale of some cypress, and reported that "Mr. Gradis, who is here now, spoke to me about 600 quarts of flour you have in your store. I promised him I would do what I can to help you."[31]

The Gradis firm of Bordeaux was one of a large number of correspondents with whom Isaac Monsanto had business dealings during the period 1758–69. On occasion, Monsanto acted as their agent and collected funds due them from customers in New Orleans, and, similarly, Monsanto was sometimes asked by Louisiana clients to arrange for the transfer of credit from the Gradis firm to New Orleans.[32] Monsanto also transacted business with other firms, whose headquarters were in Bayonne, La Rochelle, Bordeaux, Paris, Cadiz and London. In the Caribbean area, he sent cargoes to, and received them from, Saint-Domingue, Cuba, Vera Cruz, Campeche, Jamaica,

Martinique, Curaçao and St. Eustatius.[33] Nearer home, the Monsanto company had customers and clients in the Louisiana settlements and posts at Rapides, Pellas Creek, Bayou Manchac, the German Coast, Houma, Opelousas, Natchitoches and Pointe Coupee.[34] Ranging farther afield on the mainland, he shipped goods to New York City, Pensacola and Mobile in the British colonies, and up the Mississippi to Natchez and to more distant posts in the Arkansas and Illinois country.[35] Consignments from these areas were also shipped to Monsanto in New Orleans. Like other merchant shippers, Monsanto established limited partnerships for specific ventures: in 1765, for instance, he chartered a ship for a voyage to Vera Cruz, carrying a cargo of liquor and other merchandise, with Kerlérec's successor as Governor, Jean Jacques Blaise D'Abbadie, as a partner.[36] It was not unusual for Royal Governors and other officials to participate in business ventures like these, but it is reflective of their attitude towards the Jews that neither Kerlérec nor D'Abbadie hesitated before dealing in this way with Isaac Monsanto.

The broad geographical range covered by Monsanto's interests was equalled only by the variety of commodities which he handled in both wholesale and retail quantities. The merchandise which he traded ranged from handkerchiefs to guns, from canvas to lumber, from cordage to indigo, from sugar to lime, and from bullocks to slaves.[37] The latter were not only bought and sold singly, but en masse. In 1768 the firm had an interest in a contracted shipment of eighty slaves who were, however, never delivered to New Orleans.[38] Monsanto made frequent purchases at auction, the most important on record being the Trianon plantation of the late Chevalier Bernard de Vergès, the engineer who had been in charge of public works. This plantation, which Monsanto bought in 1767 for 5,500 livres, was located a few miles above New Orleans, across the Mississippi, with a frontage of seventeen and a half arpents on the river. The plantation house was fifty feet long, with eleven rooms and front and rear galleries. It was a palatial residence for the time, with outbuildings and slave quarters. De Vergès had been in debt to Monsanto for 2,000 livres, but the estate was bereft of cash. Since this was a time of severe commercial

17

depression, it is entirely possible that Monsanto purchased the plantation only to protect his interest in the estate.[39] There is no indication that he ever occupied the plantation house or intended to become a planter. He was a businessman, and he was compelled to give daily attention to his affairs.

According to a court record of 1766, living with Isaac in his combination home, store and warehouse on Chartres street[40] were his sisters Angélica and Gracia, his brother Manuel, a man named Abraham Robles (apparently not related), a mulatto slave from Martinique named Valentin, a number of other slaves including a little girl and a male whose name was Baptiste Manuel Monsanto, and Jean Baptiste Marcellin Lomère, a thirty-five-year-old French weaver who had boarded with Monsanto for about seven years. Whether de Britto lived with Monsanto when he was in town—he was probably the traveling partner in the firm—we do not know. Lomère, who had always seemed a little peculiar, created a stir in September, 1766: Robles found him chasing the little Negro slave girl and brandishing a stick at her; Robles seized the stick, and Lomère promptly attacked him with a knife and stabbed him four times. In the subsequent trial, the Attorney-General demanded a fine for the state, 800 livres in damages for Robles, imprisonment and banishment of Lomère: "to be returned to his family [in France], to be confined for the rest of his days as a mad man, known by several of his acts." But before Lomère was shipped out of the colony, Monsanto and de Britto were required to return to him the 5,000 piastres gourdes which the weaver had deposited with the firm.[41]

Lomère was not the only Louisiana settler who used Monsanto as a banker; many others deposited money with him—including his sisters Gracia, Angélica and Eleanora, who left with him the money they inherited after their father's death[42]—and he, in turn, was indebted to many of his fellow residents.[43] Hard money was always scarce in a frontier area like Louisiana, and especially during the period of Monsanto's business activity in New Orleans.[44] Many of his customers required credit over a long period of time, and he sometimes had to enter suit to secure payment after the passage of many years. Louis Marie Populus de St. Prother, for instance, bought some merchandise from him on credit in 1764; the debt was still unpaid in 1773 when, with interest and charges, it had almost doubled. On occasion, even when a customer was finally ready to remit payment, the bill of exchange might not be honored. On May 15, 1765, John Stuart, the Superintendent of Indian Affairs for the Southern Colonies of Great Britain, then making his head-quarters in Pensacola, bought merchandise from Monsanto worth two hundred pounds. Two years later he paid him with a bill of exchange on Charles Ogilvie of London which was eventually protested.[45]

Skins were frequently used in lieu of cash in large-scale dealings throughout the area. Monsanto owed a large sum of money to the Pensacola firm of McGillivray and Struthers long enough for John Fitzpatrick, their agent in New Orleans, to put angry pressure on Isaac in April, 1769. Fitzpatrick reported to his Pensacola superiors that

"... I delivered your Letter to Mr Monsantto and intimated him that he must Not think of baffling me any longer about the payment & that if Continu[s] Pleading his Accostmed Excuses I would present a petition to the Councl to Request they would see me Redressed by giving me up the Neoxus [a ship which belonged to Monsanto?] Untill an Entire Satisfaction was made for what he ows...."

Isaac promised to do what he could as soon as possible. Shortly afterward he left for the Illinois country to buy skins; Fitzpatrick sent word to Pensacola as soon as he received reports of Monsanto's imminent return. Finally, on July 17, Isaac was back in New Orleans, assuring Fitzpatrick that boatloads of skins were on their way to New Orleans, and that some would be taken directly to Pensacola where McGillivray and Struthers could take in trade the entire amount of the debt at the rate of 37 sols per dried skin and 42 sols for a skin without the hair removed. The unsettled conditions of the time prevented the fulfillment of the agreement, however, and in September Fitzpatrick was still trying to obtain the money, although he admitted that cash was dreadfully difficult to find anywhere in New Orleans.[46]

7. MONSANTO'S SERVICE TO THE BRITISH IN WEST FLORIDA

Some years earlier, Isaac Monsanto had a desperate need for cash in connection with an important service which he rendered to the British authorities in Mobile and Pensacola in 1764–65, when they were preparing to send an expedition up the Mississippi in order to take possession of the Illinois country, in keeping with the provisions of the Treaty of Paris which ended the Seven Years' War. According to a report which the Louisiana Governor, D'Abbadie, sent to the Minister of Marine in Paris, the British Commandant at Mobile had "struck a bargain with M. Monsanto, a merchant, for furnishing bateaux, utensils, etc., which would be necessary for this convoy, by the terms of which he promised to send him also ten thousand livres upon his arrival at Mobile, and to send advances in proportion to the successive expenses which he will be obliged to make; but, since the first sum has not yet been sent, the preparations for the expedition have been stopped and the only activities that M. Monsanto has performed while waiting consist in repairing five or six bateaux...."[47] This report was written on January 29, 1765, but Isaac Monsanto had already been waiting impatiently for several months for the initial payment which had been promised to him by John Lind, captain of a British schooner. Lieut. Alexander Maclellan of the British forces had tried to reassure Monsanto, in a letter dated November 10, 1764, which said in part:

"... Since you ask my advice I counsel you quite frankly not to stop the proceedings. I do not know at all the powers or the orders that Mr. Lind had in these matters. His Excellency Mr. D'Abbadie showed me a copy of the agreement between you and the said gentleman, according to which he was to pay you the amount of 2000 piastres instantly upon his arrival in Mobile. Since this was not done because of the different money used, you have been inconvenienced a bit at the present time, but you will no doubt be reimbursed and I hope that will be soon. ... If the papers for the rent of the boats have been drawn up, please send them to me as there is a chance that I will leave [New Orleans] for Pensacola tonight. . . ."[48]

Monsanto had still not received any payment from the British by January 23, 1765, when he wrote an importunate letter to Major Robert Farmar, the British Commandant at Mobile:

"This moment I received the honor of your two letters by Mr. Campbell, bearing date the 21st decr. & 4th Jany. by which I see you order me to continue the work, in order that every thing may be ready, and that you will send me the dollars and bills of Exchange by the first opportunity. As you have not done it as yet, the want of money I find has been the occasion, that some want unfortunately is found here, and is the occasion of my finding my self very much put to it; I Imagined I deserved the preferance [sic] to Mr. Dupart who has recd. 1400 dollars, when at the same time his work is done by his own Negro's, for whom he advances nothing; and I am obliged to do every thing with ready money, for which I have paid a great Interest, (and I can't find what I have occasion for to continue the work). I was in hopes from this motive that money would have been sent, and It is now more than a month since you mentioned it. I should have been very glad [if] you had at least sent me a part.—I have been afraid for some time past on account of the bills of Exchange, but now I have more reason than ever from the news spread abroad by an English vessel just arrived from pensacola, that all your Bills were returned protested. I flatter myself that this News is false, but it is made public all over the Town, which you may be assured will prevent me negotiating the bills; there is a means of making easy this payment, by sending me good skins at 50 sols a pound french weight, delivered to me here, which makes half a dollar gourde—

"If You have not sent the money on the receipt of this, I beg Sir you would not defer It, You know I am obliged only to deliver the Boats two months after the first payment. They may be ready sooner, and I don't doubt but you will likewise, if not, You'l be so good as to send somebody to receive them, once finished I cannot take charge of them, besides I shall have occasion for the last payment. I hope likewise to be indemnified on account of the augmentation of my expenses, and for the Interest of the money I have been obliged to pay, from my not receiving It according to agreement—Be persuaded that every thing shall be done with all possible zeal, concerning what may be usefull to you, which is my reason for now offering you my services in praying you would believe that Nobody is more respectfully

Sir

Your most humble

and most Obedt. Servant

Monsanto—

"[Post-Script:] Mr. Pittman & Stuart are arrived, as they came away eight days after Mr. Campbell, I was in hopes of touching what you did me the honor to mention in your letter, which was to be sent me the first opportunity; I hope It will soon come."[49]

Pressing as his needs were, and eager as he was for this contract to be completed, poor Isaac had to wait even longer for British colonial bureaucratic legalism to inch its way forward. Major Farmar submitted a petition to Governor George Johnstone, on February 20, 1765, urging that Monsanto be paid in skins, despite the prohibition of such exports for the purpose of trade:

"... your Petitioner is necessitated to represent to your Excellency, that the important service of taking possession of the country of Illinois is entirely retarded and put a stop to, for the great inconvenience of the general want of money, which at present prevails in this Province, that it will be impossible to proceed according to the express orders of the Commander in Chief, unless some expedient is fallen upon to discharge the different expences [sic] of the contracts works &c occasioned by this intended expedition.

"Your petitioner therefore prays that your Excellency would take the above into your Serious Consideration, and that the law prohibiting the exportation of Deerskins to any foreign parts may be suspended till twelve hundred weight of deerskins is shipped and transported to New Orleans, in order to pay part of the contract concluded with Mr. Monsanto on the part of the Government for providing and repairing a sufficient number of Batteaux to transport His Majesty's troops to the said country of Illinois, as this appears the only salutary measure to put

22

immediately into execution the orders received from Headquarters and fully to answer the expectation of Government
thereupon."

The petition was bounced back and forth from Farmar to
Johnstone to the Provincial Council. The Council criticized its
legal form, so Farmar had to resubmit it. Then he was asked
to come in person to answer questions, but he protested that he
was so ill that he could not appear and could only answer questions sent to him in written form. Eventually the Council
decided to proceed with the project by requesting the revenue
officer not to "obstruct the exportation of that quantity of
Skins," but suggested that the packages "should be inspected
and sealed" so that no more than the required number would
be shipped to New Orleans. The same duty would be paid by
the colonial government as though the skins were being sent
to commercial buyers in Great Britain. Most of the payment,
however, was made in drafts—£1,405.18.8 in March and £397
on April 1, 1765. The expedition finally departed for the North,
and Monsanto must have heaved a sigh of relief—but his troubles
with the British had not quite ended, for in December he was
sued for their wages by boatmen who returned from the Illinois
country in a bateau belonging to "his Britanique Majesty."[50]

8. THE FIRST JEWS IN MOBILE AND PENSACOLA

Major Farmar's problems, on the other hand, had just begun.
Trapped in a power struggle between the British civil and
military authorities, he was court-martialed in 1766 for em-
bezzlement and misappropriation of funds. It was a complex
and lengthy case, but Farmar was finally acquitted. One of the
charges made against him was "For sending flour belonging
to the King to New Orleans, and selling it or attempting to
sell it there, by means of one Pallachio, a Jew."[51]

Joseph de Palacios and his two Jewish partners, Samuel Israel
and Alexander Solomons, who did business in New Orleans
under the French as well as in Pensacola and Mobile under

23

the British during this period, had arrived in the West Florida Province in late 1763 or the beginning of 1764. On February 2, 1764, just six months after the British took possession of the area from the French in accordance with the provisions of the Treaty of Paris, these "three English merchants residing in this city [Mobile]," purchased a lot "in the street of the burying place ... fronting the [King's] Indian House." This property, for which they paid 200 Spanish dollars, included a house and other buildings. One should note that while Mobile had been a French possession, no Jewish merchant had been sufficiently attracted by its commercial possibilities to undertake to settle there, but no sooner were the British in command, than these merchants arrived in this now new frontier. On May 8, 1764, de Palacios and Solomons (Israel is not mentioned in this deed) bought another property, three lots of ground, including a house planked above and below, raised on a brick foundation, covered with shingles, and consisting of "a Hall, a Chamber and alcove, another Chamber and a Cabinet," with a brick chimney, a kitchen, oven, stove and garden court. For this property they were to deliver to the seller, Claude Mortal, nicknamed Chalan, two hundred barrels of flour, two hundred weight each, "good, sound and merchantable," within five months. The firm of de Palacios, Solomons and Israel was engaged in transactions with Major Farmar very early, for on July 20, 23 and 24, 1764, Alexander Solomons was in New York City receiving cash from Judah Hays for part of a Bill of Exchange which Farmar wrote on the Lords of Treasury for £700.[52] The partners were also moving back and forth between Mobile and Pensacola; since the Spanish had previously controlled Pensacola, these may well have been the first Jews in the town. On February 9, 1765, their applications for building lots and garden lots in Pensacola were approved. Palacios was assigned lot number 29 and Solomons number 35, lots that backed on to each other, while Israel was granted number 44. In the West Florida Provincial Council minutes, the three names were listed under "first class choices," in sequence, as though the partners had stood in line together.[53] On November 2, 1765, the Governor ratified the grants to Israel and de Palacios; Solomons' must also have received approval because he later mortgaged his lots.[54]

24

The following year, 1766, another Jew received assignments of land in Pensacola, including town and garden lots number 119, and additional grants of 50 and 500 acres. He was Isaac Mendes, formerly of Jamaica, who had come to West Florida even earlier than the three partners. As early as the fall of 1763, Mendes sold £25 worth of goods for use as "Indian presents" to Governor Johnstone. It is possible that this man is identical with the Isaac Mendes who was in Albany with the British troops in 1756. If so, he may have been a trader who traveled with a particular regiment.[55] At any rate, Mendes did not remain in the colony very long. By May, 1766, he was in debt to Charles Strachan and Company to the amount of £293.7½. It was probably in order to collect funds for the payment of the bill that, in July, he mortgaged his town lot number 119 and his dwelling place to one Manuel Josephson (possibly the New York and Philadelphia Jewish leader of the same name who became well-known in post-Revolutionary times) for $560, and a month later he and John Crozer sold lot number 23 for $375. In October, 1766, Mendes transferred title to his town and garden lots numbered 119, and to his home, to Benjamin Ward, in settlement of a debt of 1,200 Spanish milled dollars which Mendes owed to Ward. Mendes probably left Pensacola soon after these transactions, for he does not again appear in the records.[56]

The grants of land which were received by Mendes, de Palacios, Israel and Solomons draw our attention to their political status in the British province. Alexander Solomons and Samuel Israel had been born probably in London; Mendes appears to have been a Jamaican. We do not know enough of the background of de Palacios to tell where he was born, but if he had not possessed proof of naturalization, he would not have qualified for grants of lots in Pensacola. The "Act to encourage Foreigners to come into and settle in this Province," passed by the House of Assembly of West Florida on December 22, 1766, and subsequently approved by Governor Johnstone, provided for the naturalization of foreigners in residence for a minimum of three months who were willing to take the oath of allegiance and to pay a small fee. Naturalized persons were to have the same "Immunities and Rights" as natural born citizens. This act was specifically designed to attract French Roman Catholics, and therefore noted that Catholics were to be treated the same as Protestants, and "upon being Naturalized . . . shall be Intitled to have and possess Town Lotts and Tracts of Land on the same conditions prescribed to his Majesty's Protestant Subjects." The act also guaranteed the free exercise of the Roman Catholic faith "because no People can be truly happy though under the greatest enjoyment of Civil Liberties if abridged of the freedom of their Consciences as to their Religious Professions." Lots were to be set aside in Pensacola and Mobile for the construction of Catholic "Churches or Chappels." The act further stipulated that Catholics were to be given the right to sit on juries and to cast ballots in elections. The only privilege not included was that of election or appointment to office. No list of naturalized foreigners has been located in the West Florida Papers, so it is impossible to tell whether de Palacios and Israel were naturalized there, or brought proof of their status with them from some area of previous residence. The Jewish religion was not mentioned in the act, but the freedom of conscience provision undoubtedly applied to these Jews, although there is no reason to believe that there were ever enough of them to form a quorum for religious worship.[57]

Meanwhile, Solomons, de Palacios and Israel continued to fulfill Major Farmar's assignments. In April, 1765, they billed him for £215.11.9; this included the purchase of boards and nails for a brig, hire of the brig, pilotage to Mobile, a lost anchor, and the transportation of some troops and their gear to the brig. Perhaps it was because they were so close to Farmar that Solomons joined twenty-one other inhabitants of West Florida in sending a complaint about Governor Johnstone's administration to the Lord Commissioners for Trade and Plantations, in April, 1766.[58]

The partners do not seem to have been particularly successful. In 1765 they purchased the well-known plantation outside of Mobile known as "Lis Loy," but had to mortgage it to a merchant in Pensacola who foreclosed on them the next year. In November, 1765, they borrowed £610 from John McGillivray, William Struthers and William Trewin, using their headquarters in Mobile and three Negro slaves as collateral. In

1767, Solomons mortgaged his town and garden lots in Pensacola to Patrick Morgan, who foreclosed in 1774. In 1767–69, the partners owned one less slave, for they paid taxes on only two. The tax was a dollar a head. The account of the Provincial Treasurer reads, in an amusing but informative shorthand, "Jews on 2." Things went from bad to worse: in 1769 de Palacios petitioned the West Florida Assembly for relief from imprisonment as a debtor to the Frenchman who had sold "Lis Loy" to the partners: "That the Petitioner was become Insolvent and had been Confined upwards of Two Years, and was reduced to the lowest Ebb for the want of necessary support . . . That he was confined at the Suit of a Monsieur Montberault of New Orleans who lately removed with his Family for Old France, and had left no Orders with his Attorney for the Releasement of the Petitioner." Within a month, de Palacios was free, but he apparently never succeeded in gaining a secure economic foothold.[59]

In 1773, de Palacios was in trouble again. A New Orleans citizen to whom he had been in debt for almost 3,000 livres since 1766 sued the court for permission to seize one of his slaves in New Orleans. At the trial a witness testified that the still insolvent Jew was "absent in Pensacola and . . . was accustomed to come to [New Orleans] without presenting himself to the public and . . . it was not easy to be able to see him on these occasions." In other words, de Palacios was still dodging his creditors, although he was obviously attempting to do some business.[60]

Samuel Israel is a vague, indistinct person. He never appears alone, but always as a member of the team. Perhaps he did not spend much time in the province.[61] Alexander Solomons was more successful than de Palacios; at least, there is no record of his having been imprisoned for debt. In 1770, Joseph Badon of Mobile mortgaged one hundred head of large horned cattle to Solomons as security for the payment of a bill of exchange for £150 on a Bordeaux merchant. Alexander's brother Haym, who was not a member of the firm, signed as a witness to this transaction and, again, a year and a half later, when the same mortgage was transferred to another merchant. Haym was a clerk for McGillivray and Struthers in Pensacola. He remained in West Florida longer than the others. On May 10, 1779, he was one of the "Gentlemen Freeholders and Principal Inhabitants of West Florida" who signed a petition to the Lord Secretaries of State. They pledged their loyalty to the Crown and affirmed their abhorrence of the Revolutionary ideas of the Atlantic coastal colonies, but protested against the favoritism and corruption of Governor Peter Chester's administration. When the Governor wrote to London in 1780 and denounced the signers of the petition, he belittled Haym Solomons as "a Hireling about Mr. McGillivary's home."[62]

In March, 1772, Alexander Solomons, "Late of Mobille in the Province . . . but now of the Town of Pensacola . . . Merchant," took a mortgage of five hundred and fifty Spanish milled dollars from Peter Rochon of Dog River, near Mobile, on fifty head of the "Largest and best Cattle" on his plantation. If the debt, plus accrued interest, were not paid by the clearance of a bill of exchange in Solomons' hands, Rochon was bound to supply "a sufficient number of Persons and Horses to Drive the aforesaid fifty Cattle to Pensacola," and defray the cost of slaughtering enough cattle to pay off the debt. The same month Solomons signed as a witness when a German couple sold some land near Natchez; he witnessed a second deed for the same people in 1774.[63]

De Palacios did not remain in British West Florida long enough to be there when the Spanish captured the colony in 1780–81. He was gone by 1778, when he took the oath of allegiance to the new state of South Carolina as a "transient person." But he was not a visitor for very long. He remained in Charleston, married there in 1785, and became an active member of the Jewish community.[64] Alexander Solomons disappears from view after 1774, but his brother Haym was still in West Florida when the Spanish under Gálvez took it from the British in 1780–81. He fled with William Struthers to Georgia, went up to Charleston to sell some skins, and decided to stay there. He had to be approved by a patriot committee whose duty it was to ferret out Loyalists. Haym presumably did not tell the committee about the petition of 1779 in which he pledged his loyalty to Great Britain. Gershom Cohen, who vouched for Haym as "a man of good character," probably knew nothing of that prior declaration either. Haym, who said he was born in England but left there when very young, may not have had very strong political opinions in any direction. He probably went along with the trend of the time, whatever it was wherever he happened to be. At any rate, he liked Charleston well enough to make his home there, carrying on an auction business until his death in 1801.[65]

9. THE ARRIVAL OF A NEW SPANISH GOVERNOR IN NEW ORLEANS AND THE EXPULSION OF THE JEWS

Dreary as was the financial plight of de Palacios in British territory, Isaac Monsanto's fate was ultimately far worse. Though the continued residence in New Orleans of the Monsanto family, de Britto, Fastio and possibly other Jews of whom we have no knowledge,[66] was clearly in contravention of the *Code Noir*, Rochemore had been the only official who questioned their presence during the French regime. No one else seems to have attempted to dislodge them from their very comfortable and profitable position. Isaac Monsanto, above all, was as secure as he could desire to be. He conducted his business affairs, purchased property both real and movable, traveled freely throughout the colony and back and forth into such foreign areas as British West Florida, engaged in transactions which involved the Governor and other lesser officials, and sued in the courts and was sued. He also assumed an official legal role: in 1762, he acted as a translator for the Superior Court of Louisiana.[67]

But that same year, 1762, France and Spain signed the secret Treaty of Fontainebleau, in which the French ceded the Louisiana colony west of the Mississippi, and the city of New Orleans, to the Spanish. This was to compensate Spain for her loss of Florida to the British, in the general settlement which marked the end of the Seven Years' War. The news of this change of regime may have troubled Monsanto when it was formally made public, for he well knew that Spain had never tolerated the presence of Jews in her American colonies, and

29

that Spanish economic policy was highly restrictive. But his fears, and those of other Louisianians, were lulled to sleep by Spain's long delay in taking formal possession of the new territory. It was not until March, 1766—more than three years after the treaty had been signed—that the new Spanish governor, Antonio de Ulloa, arrived in New Orleans. Ulloa was given so little support by Spain's colonial administrators that he was compelled to rely on his French predecessor, Captain Charles Philippe Aubry, to run the colony . . . further reason for Monsanto to relax. Very little had really changed. But in October, 1768, Ulloa published a list of new commercial regulations, quite in keeping with Spain's traditional colonial practice, which would have driven Monsanto and other merchants in New Orleans out of business. Resentment against these restrictive ordinances, and against other Spanish actions, aroused a number of French Creole leaders to such a pitch of indignation that they chased Ulloa out of the colony. While Monsanto took no part in the uprising, he probably agreed with the general sentiment that the Spanish would let the colony go without a fight. But he and other merchants and the leaders of the rebellion were very wrong in their decision to stay. Monsanto's delay in making plans to leave New Orleans proved to be very costly.

The second Spanish governor, Lieutenant General Don Alejandro O'Reilly, who reached New Orleans on August 17, 1769, was a different kind of man from Ulloa, and he had far stronger forces at his command than were ever given to Ulloa. O'Reilly was a soldier who had the fixed intention of remaking the unsuccessful French province into a genuine Spanish colony. He meant to enforce the law. His first attention was directed to the foolhardy revolutionaries who had refused to acknowledge the reality of the French cession of Louisiana to Spain, and who had succeeded in driving his predecessor out of Louisiana. Even while the rebel leaders were on trial, leading to their imprisonment or execution,[68] O'Reilly set about guaranteeing stricter enforcement of the Spanish colonial trade regulations.

On September 1, 1769, John Fitzpatrick, the British commercial agent in New Orleans, reported to his employers in Pensacola that ". . . Things are in a very Critical State here at present as the General Will not Allow any foreigners to Vend their Merchant Dise here in Future; they are allowed to Dispose of what they had in Store before his Arrival of which they ware all Obliged to give in an Inventory to him. . . ." Seven days later, he wrote, "I intend Leaving this place shortly as all English subjects who are not Married or have no fixed settlements [farms] here are Ordered away by His Excellency General O Relly . . . No English Subject is allowed to land any thing here. . . ." On September 11, Fitzpatrick told another British firm that "it is Immagined that all the English Subjects here will Shortly be obliged to leave it which is Reasonable to Expect being Universally known the Spanish Government will not allow any Foreigners in their American settlems. therefore we Must submit to their Accustomed Rules of Government. Altho such as has any outstanding Debts rely on his Excellency's Clemency for Time to recover them the result of wch God only knows." Unable to secure an extension for the collection of debts, he placed his papers in the hands of a local merchant, and, on September 21, reported that he intended leaving for Mobile the following day.[69]

O'Reilly approached his problem systematically: first the British, then other businessmen. Since it was impossible for any merchant to have observed to the letter every Spanish commercial regulation which had been promulgated during Governor Ulloa's ineffectual administration, O'Reilly had no difficulty in nailing all of them with charges of illegal trade. On October 17, 1769, he wrote to Fray Julian de Arriaga, Minister of the Indies, that he had obtained a confession of guilt from two Genevan brothers named Duraldes "who were dealing in diamonds, watches, gold caskets and other jewelry, galloons, laces and other costly goods . . . [in] illegal trade [with] Campeche and Vera Cruz. . . ." He ordered these brothers and twelve other merchants to leave the province before the end of October, "together with three Jews named Monsanto, Mets,[70] and Brito,[71] who had also made some illegal shipments and had correspondents in Vera Cruz, Campeche, the nearby presidios, and other places."[72] O'Reilly believed that he had broken the back of illegal trade by requiring the departure of all of these merchants: "By pursuing this same course with equal care, I can assure you that the value of the

31

illegal shipments which can be made from this colony to the other dominions of the King in America will be very small. This is the important objective."[73]

There is no extant document in which O'Reilly proclaimed the expulsion of all foreign Protestant and Jewish merchants, but this was the understanding of O'Reilly's intention among the British officials in the West Florida Province, who were following developments in New Orleans very closely. Lieutenant-Governor Montfort Browne reported to London on October 8, 1769, that, after the rebel leaders had been sentenced, ". . . a General Pardon to the Rest of the Inhabitants has since been published most of whom have taken the oath of Allegiance to the King of Spain; such as would not were allowed a Month's time to Settle their affairs and Depart, the English to a man and all protestants and Jews are driven from there; Count O'Rilly is detested for his Inhumanity and falsehood. . . ."[74]

In a communication to his superiors, dated October 17, 1769, O'Reilly seemed to refer to the religion of the Jews as a major factor in the decision to expel them: "There are to leave this province during the current month two Jews, named Brito and Mets, and before the end of the next month the Jew Monsanto, for the reason that all three are undesirable on account of the nature of their business and of the religion they profess."[75] Isaac Monsanto, who had gotten along so well with the easygoing French officials, especially with Governors Kerlérec and D'Abbadie, was apparently unable to believe that O'Reilly was serious about the order of expulsion. He misunderstood the reason, and assured the new Governor that he had not taken any part in the ill-fated rebellion, and was loyal to the new administration. Unfortunately this Monsanto letter cannot be located; he may even have offered to take the oath of allegiance to the Spanish King. But, on December 26, 1769, O'Reilly rejected Monsanto's appeal, although the deadline for his departure had obviously been delayed:

"In regard to the demand which you have made to me, Monsieur, concerning the conduct which you have maintained in this colony during the uprising which took place here, I render you the full justice which is due you, and [state] that you were not opposed to the Government of his Most Catholic Majesty.

32

"The departure which I require of you and your entire family is specifically a consequence of an order of the King which expressly forbids all Jews from residing in this state.

"I am, Monsieur, etc."[76]

But O'Reilly was not telling the entire truth to Isaac Monsanto. Fitzpatrick knew and accepted the facts of life; he was willing to recognize that the Spanish Governor's motive was primarily economic. Religion and nationality were really secondary. O'Reilly was finding one way or another of ridding his colony of almost all of its successful merchants, including some of the wealthiest Frenchmen who had every right to remain.[77] O'Reilly wanted Spanish authority to dominate the colony's economic life. That the Jewishness of Monsanto and his partners was not a major factor in their expulsion is confirmed by the Spaniards' failure to disturb a petty country storekeeper like Isaac Fastio who, in all probability, had long since left New Orleans to set up business in Pointe Coupee. As we have already noted, de Palacios was in and out of New Orleans during early Spanish rule; he had to dodge his creditors, but the civil authorities did not try to exclude him because he was a Jew. Moreover, as we shall shortly see, it was only a brief time before one or another member of the Monsanto family visited Louisiana or returned there to live. Ultimately all of them resumed residence in Louisiana under Spanish rule, and seem not to have been challenged by any official. Perhaps, then, the truth went even deeper than Fitzpatrick imagined. Too much economic power may have been concentrated in the hands and strongboxes of the seventeen or so merchants who were expelled, and of the rebels whose wealth was confiscated. If so great a proportion of the commerce of New Orleans were monopolized by a small number of merchants, what gain would Spain derive from the colony? Certain it is that the edict of expulsion was tantamount to the confiscation of the assets of the merchants who were affected by O'Reilly's edict.

The partners had probably been trying desperately to arrange the Monsanto firm's affairs, to collect debts and sell off their holdings, but due to the scarcity of cash and the disoriented state of commercial affairs, they had as little success as Fitzpatrick, and they were far more deeply involved than he. The lack of specie among their local customers was only one part of the problem. Their transactions covered such a wide geographic area and transportation was so slow that it was actually impossible for them to settle their accounts in three months. Hundreds of firms and individuals in the Mississippi valley and in the Caribbean area were in their debt, and they in turn owed money to suppliers as far away as Europe. Even a year would not have given them enough time to round out their affairs and close their books. They were, therefore, compelled to place their fate and fortune in the hands of men who probably had no interest in seeing that they would receive any proceeds from the settlement of their affairs. By December 18 Monsanto and his partners had drawn up memoranda listing their debits and credits; these, together with all of their papers and files, were turned over to two court-appointed syndics or receivers, Nicholas Forstall and Jean Joseph Duforest.[78]

Although it is clear that Monsanto's firm was one of the largest in New Orleans, it is impossible to assess his net worth at the time of his expulsion. The documents relating to his affairs are known only in manuscript and printed summaries, and in papers scattered through the Spanish and French manuscripts in the safe of the Cabildo in New Orleans. It cannot even be discerned if Monsanto's debts outweighed his credits, but this is unlikely. The settlement of his New Orleans business interests continued for many years; in 1785, fifteen years after his expulsion, two hundred and sixty-nine separate files of bills, accounts, receipts, memoranda, deeds, contracts and notes were still in the hands of syndics, but the notarized list does not give their dates or any hint of their contents. For at least two more years, suits were still being entered in the New Orleans courts by creditors seeking their share of the remaining property. The two sets of syndics had undoubtedly eaten up a great deal of the assets while distribution was taking place. It is important to note, however, that beyond Isaac Monsanto's constant need for cash, a perennial problem in the colonial areas, there was no sign that he was in financial difficulty before the expulsion. Monsanto's was a large and prosperous business until O'Reilly's order.[79]

10. THE MONSANTO FAMILY IN EXILE

What alternatives were open to the Monsanto clan as they prepared to leave New Orleans? They could have attempted to convert to the Roman Catholic faith in the hope of being permitted to remain in Louisiana, but Isaac was apparently too loyal to his ancestral faith to follow this course of action; had he desired to abandon Judaism he would have done so long before danger arose—for he and his family had already been subjected to the constant pressure of the dominant faith for many years. It is, however, not even certain that apostasy would have secured the remission of O'Reilly's order. The Governor's successor, Colonel Don Luis de Unzaga y Amézaga, who took command of Louisiana in March, 1770, indicated this quite firmly in a letter which he wrote during his first month in office: "In all our realms of America it is forbidden by law to admit any foreigners, not even the French, who are Christians [i.e. Roman Catholics] being exempt from this law, much less persons recently converted for their own private ends."[80] If they could not remain in New Orleans, then, where should they go? They could seek refuge in the nearest mainland colony beyond the Spanish frontier, that is, in the British West Florida capital of Pensacola, where Isaac had done business over the years, where there were already a number of Jews in business (although, as we have seen, they were none too successful), and where other refugees were fleeing.[81] But was trade in Pensacola brisk enough for Isaac to support his large household? Jamaica or one of the British seaboard colonies, such as South Carolina, Palacios' eventual destination, would offer another opportunity for a fresh start, but Monsanto had apparently not established very fruitful contacts in these areas. Saint-Domingue was even more promising because Isaac had relatives and correspondents in that French island, and its life and trading conditions were not dissimilar to those of Louisiana. The actual decision was to move to the closest possible point, Pensacola.

Precisely when Isaac Monsanto and the members of his household left New Orleans is not recorded in any document.

35

It may be that they arrived in Pensacola as early as January 11, 1770, for Isaac signed a promissory note on that day to John Waugh of London, "Mariner," for 457 milled dollars, equal to £106.12.8, mortgaging his slaves Prince and Princess as security. It is entirely possible that Waugh was the captain of the ship on which the family left New Orleans, and that, being unable to pay for their passage and the transportation of whatever luggage and possessions they brought with them, Isaac had to execute a note for the expenses of the trip.[82] On June 1, 1770, Isaac borrowed 435 Spanish milled dollars, 5 and ¾ reales, at eight per cent interest from his old correspondents John McGillivray and William Struthers. His Negro slaves Caesar and Dolly were the collateral. The deed begins, "I, Isaac Monsanto late of New Orleans, now of the Town of Pensacola in the province. . . ."[83] How many of the members of his household came with him is in doubt. It is possible that Isaac's brothers scattered in various directions in an effort to find safety and security. Certain it is that Manuel was expected to turn up at the Natchitoches Post in the spring of 1770. On June 16, 1770, Athanase de Mézières y Cluny, Lieutenant-Governor of Natchitoches, reported to Governor Unzaga:

> "Of the two Englishmen whom I have sent to your Lordship's presence and [notice of whose] return to this villa you deigned to give me under date of May 15, last, only Guillermo Ovarden [William Warden] has arrived; concerning him and Señor Manuel Monsantto I am punctually fulfilling my orders from your Lordship. . . ."[84]

Whether Manuel attempted to reach Natchitoches is not recorded. If he did, the likelihood is that he was turned away.[85]

For the time being, at least, there was no place in Spanish Louisiana in which the Monsanto family could reside. But they could be closer to the colony than Pensacola. John Fitzpatrick traveled from New Orleans to Mobile, and then journeyed to the settlement of Manchac on the Mississippi River at the junction of the Iberville River, within a very few months. Fitzpatrick chose Manchac because he knew that there would be ample opportunity for trade with the inhabitants of Spanish Louisiana since "in all Likelyhood Goods henceforward will be very Scarce in Orleans," and the French and Spaniards "will always find Means to pay for What they want; in Deer skins Indigo Cotton Tobaco Rice & Cash." The Monsanto brothers had either maintained a storehouse in Manchac all along, or got there first and established themselves in one of the few serviceable structures. When Fitzpatrick arrived he complained about "the heavy Expencess my precipitated Departure from Orleans has Caused, Occasioned by Genel. Oreyleys ill natured proceedings; also in Building my self a house as none here was Habitable Except them Occupied before my Arrival by Monsantos Brothers & Mr. Bradley. . . ."[86] Fitzpatrick reported on August 30, 1770, that one of the Monsanto brothers was expected back in Manchac from New Orleans in the near future. From that time on, one of the brothers was usually in the Manchac settlement, which was their headquarters, participating in the brisk, illegal trade that sprang up over the border of the Mississippi River despite the Spanish prohibition of traffic with the British merchants.[87]

Whether Isaac actually established residence in Pensacola is not known. He appears in the court records from time to time, usually in reference to loans and debts. On November 9, 1771, John Scott secured a judgement for £212.8, with interest, against Monsanto in the General Court of Pleas. Monsanto mortgaged his slaves Caesar, Dolly, Prince and Princess, to Scott. The debt was paid on March 28, 1772. Two days later Isaac was writing to Brigadier General Frederick Haldimand asking for a loan of two hundred piastres to be repaid in a few months, with the slave Jen as surety. He also reported that one of the Duralde brothers, his fellow exiles from New Orleans, had absconded to Saint-Domingue, and that their cargo of plank boards and other merchandise, just arrived, was no help at all to the Duraldes' creditors (including both Haldimand and Monsanto). Obviously, Monsanto was not the only former New Orleans merchant who was in desperate straits as a result of O'Reilly's order of expulsion. On January 25, 1772, Isaac mortgaged his slave Fanchonet to John Ritson of Pensacola for 270 Spanish milled dollars. The slaves were apparently the only property he had been permitted to carry with him from New Orleans. He mortgaged them again and again, to raise money for investment in trade goods which he or his brothers sold wherever they could. In March, 1772, he mortgaged the perennial Caesar, Dolly, Prince and Princess to John Stuart, Superintendent of Indian Affairs of the Southern British colonies, with whom he had been doing business since 1765. The deed was registered in December, and Stuart had to foreclose on Prince and Princess in February, 1773.[88]

While the brothers were attempting to reestablish themselves in business in Manchac, Angélica remained in Pensacola long enough to be courted by and married to George Urquhart, a young Protestant Scotsman who had been in Pensacola since 1766. Urquhart had done business with Isaac previous to the expulsion, and witnessed a deed for him in June, 1770. Urquhart family tradition reports that the marriage took place early in 1772 in Pensacola. By July 30, 1772, George was at his plantation on the British side of the Mississippi, writing a letter to Angélica in New Orleans addressed to "Madame Urquhart." She was probably on her way from Pensacola to her husband's plantation, "Semhas Vale." The letter, interestingly enough, is addressed to her in care of "Monsr. Forestall;" she was staying with one of the syndics of Isaac's property! Her older son, Thomas, was born in Baton Rouge on June 25, 1773.[89] However long some members of the family remained in Pensacola, at least one of them, Eleanora, went on to Saint-Domingue to join the brother and sister who lived there. She was married to Pierre André Tessier de Villauchamps at Cap Français on that island on February 7, 1773. Her first child, Charles André Tessier, was born there on October 3, 1775. The next year the Tessier family moved to Louisiana, bringing Eleanora back home.[90]

Isaac seems to have been unable to reestablish himself in business to any degree. Previously a strong, bold man of affairs who was willing to undertake any venture, he strikes a pathetic figure from 1770 until his death in 1778. Constantly borrowing money, he apparently was unable to fight his way back to financial security. Perhaps the Spanish confiscation had not only driven him from home and familiar surroundings, but also had broken his will. Some indication of Isaac's financial condition may be gathered from the petition which Gracia, Angélica and Eleanora submitted to the New Orleans court and Governor Unzaga some time between 1770 and 1773, in which they asked that the amount of 1,095 pesos and 6 reales, which they had left on deposit with Isaac from their inheritance from their father, be granted them from the assets of his firm in the hands of the syndics. They said that Isaac "having been obliged to leave this city because of the laws of the Kingdom, and leave his business unfinished . . . is in complete poverty because of his great losses . . . the said brother not having that sum of money. . . ." They may have been exaggerating to some degree, but Isaac's situation was certainly well known; Governor Unzaga would not have acceded to their request if he had believed that Isaac could well afford to repay his sisters.[91]

John Fitzpatrick had no liking for Isaac when they were both in New Orleans. In exile, Fitzpatrick mocked him when he appeared at Manchac in December, 1773:

> ". . . Mr. Isaac Monsanto came here the Other day & had some Cotton Checks for sale & as I was in Much want of [them] And as he . . . sold them very Cheap I bought to the Amount off $102, and drew on your house [Miller and Swanson of Mobile] for the payment, as I imagined you would have no Cash to disburse in the affair; I hope you will not think hard of my Drawing on you; for if I thought you should have the money to pay, I should not have drawn on you. . . ."[92]

In other words, Isaac Monsanto could go hang for the money, even though the goods were cheap, and Fitzpatrick needed them!

In November, 1774, Isaac was staying with Angélica and George Urquhart near Baton Rouge. The next month, he spent at least nine days in New Orleans, recording his power of attorney to Francisco Liotau, and swearing to the settlement of all accounts (from the French days) between himself and the estate of one Grimaul. The latter notarial record describes Isaac as "passing through the city."[93] In June, 1775, he was in Pointe Coupee, where Manuel, and Eleanora and her family had settled. He was in some kind of business deal with George Urquhart at the time, and had correspondence with Oliver Pollock of New Orleans about it.[94] By the time of his death in April or May of 1778, he had apparently settled in a house on the land of François Allain in Pointe Coupee. The inventory of his affairs was in no way as complicated as the lists of business transactions he left behind in New Orleans in 1769–70. His personal property was valued at 4,550 piastres; it consisted of trunks, furniture, clothing, a cypress strong box containing 400 livres, some books, a perpetual almanac, a pistol and a clock; he also had some merchandise which included two cases of sugar and a container of coffee. One side of the house had been used as Isaac's store, and a small cabin had served as his storehouse. He owed 5,765 piastres, while his customers were indebted to him for 24,955 piastres. He had sold five slaves to Manuel and Jacob the previous November. Such was the end of Isaac's business career: from a large warehouse in New Orleans, with ventures on three continents, to an insignificant little store in Pointe Coupee.[95]

11. MATTERS OF RELIGIOUS IDENTIFICATION AND PRACTICE

There is no question but that Louisiana became an exception to the traditional Spanish colonial policy of rigid exclusion of Jews. Once the Monsanto family had been driven out of New Orleans and had been deprived of their position of prominence in its commerce, they were allowed to return without interference; and Isaac Fastio seems not to have been disturbed at all, probably because his commercial activity was too minor to interest O'Reilly. But the members of the Monsanto family revealed an equally indifferent attitude to Judaism. They had, in the first place, moved away from Curaçao with its synagogue, its large Jewish community and its flourishing Jewish life, and deliberately chose to live in New Orleans, where there was only a small handful of Jews. It is possible that they tried for a time to observe Jewish religious customs in their home, but there is no evidence of this; certainly objection would have been voiced if they had attempted to conduct Jewish religious services during the French regime. They had remained in New Orleans for eleven or twelve years without contact with organized Jewish life. Now that they were compelled to leave

Louisiana, at least partly because of their religion, they did not choose to establish residence in a place like Charleston or Curaçao where they would be able to participate in a full Jewish life. They either could not or would not stay away from Louisiana. Whether it was Isaac's fear of his inability to re-establish himself elsewhere, or an unrealistic expectation that he would be able to regain control of his affairs in Louisiana, or a strong sense of belonging which all of the brothers and sisters had developed for the colony, the specific motivation really makes no difference. The important fact is that the family refused to take advantage of this opportunity to move to some community where they could practice Judaism. While there is no evidence that the brothers and sisters ever held a family meeting to determine what role Jewish identification would play in their future, it is hardly a coincidence that none of the three sisters married during their time of residence in New Orleans, with its large male population, while they did marry so soon after their enforced departure from the city— Angélica and Gracia in British West Florida and Eleanora in Saint-Domingue, all three to non-Jews. It is almost as though they had attempted to preserve their identity, if only in a negative way, while they were in New Orleans, but subsequently decided to bow to circumstances, to take on the protective coloration of the environment, to act for all practical purposes as though they had been born Christians, and to ignore the religion in which they had been reared but which was now only a memory. In a certain sense, the Monsanto brothers and sisters became Marranos, Jews living like Christians in the eyes of the outside world, without, however, making any effort to preserve their ancestral heritage in secret—in fact, they became secularists, because Judaism no longer meant anything to them, and Christianity did not arouse their interest. This is the only interpretation which can be given to their behavior.

Before sketching the further events of the lives of the Monsanto brothers and sisters, it may be useful to assess the available evidence relating to their personal, individual religious convictions and identification throughout the years after the expulsion.

Benjamin, the youngest member of the clan, was the only brother who took a bride, and the only Louisiana sibling who married within the faith. In 1787 he married Clara la Mota, the twenty-two-year-old daughter of Solomon la Mota and Rica Coen of Curaçao, who had been in New Orleans at least since the previous September, when she purchased a female slave.[96] We do not know why Clara came to New Orleans, whether to marry Benjamin or for another reason. The possibility exists, at any rate, that Benjamin had visited Curaçao on a business trip and fallen in love with her there, bringing her to New Orleans later. In Curaçao they might have been married in the synagogue. In New Orleans, they underwent strict Spanish Catholic legal procedures: Benjamin had to provide witnesses to testify that he was a bachelor, that he had not promised to marry anyone else, and that he had his brother Manuel's permission to marry. He and Clara affirmed that they had been baptized in the Catholic faith at birth. This was obviously untrue, because Benjamin's attendance at the Jewish school at The Hague in 1753–54 is documented in that community's records. But this affirmation proves that Benjamin was not a convert, for in that case he would have offered evidence of his adult baptism.[97]

Nevertheless, the wedding had to take place in the St. Louis Parish Church of New Orleans because there was no other place in town where a wedding could be held, and no person other than a Catholic priest could officiate. Father Antonio de Sedella, later known affectionately as Père Antoine, stated in his ecclesiastical record of the ceremony that Benjamin, "together with his contracting party, made public abjuration of their errors in the mode and form which is prescribed in her ritual, Our Mother the Holy Church. . . ."[98] Roman Catholic authorities have been unable to explain the meaning of this phrase; according to present practice, the formula refers to the Profession of Faith which is made by converts before baptism. But neither Benjamin nor Clara appears in the St. Louis Cathedral Baptismal Registers! It is possible that the officiating priest used both the convert's formula and the affirmation of baptism at birth in order to protect himself from possible ecclesiastical censure for officiating at the wedding of non-Catholics, for it was not until 1792 that special regulations were issued for the registration of the weddings of non-Catholic (Protestant) persons by Catholic priests in Louisiana. The entire matter becomes even more confused and ironic when we realize that only a few months later—on July 21, 1787—Governor Miró was officially notified that Father de Sedella had been designated Commissioner of the Holy Inquisition in Louisiana, and, because he feared the effect this news would have on the many Protestant British and American settlers whom he wished to encourage to remain in the colony, Miró forbade the priest to exercise this function and hustled him out of New Orleans.[99] We have no way of knowing whether Père Antoine knew that the bridal couple was Jewish, but Benjamin and Clara do not seem to have attempted to hide their origin in Natchez, where they lived most of the time. Even a stranger who visited the town in 1790–91 heard that they were Jews. Major Samuel S. Forman, who traveled down the Mississippi from Ohio to Natchez, wrote in the account of his trip that "in the village of Natchez resided Monsieur and Madam Mansanteo—Spanish Jews, I think—who were the most kind and hospitable of people."[100] But in 1785, when Benjamin testified as a witness at the trial of Jorge Rapalie for treason, the record states that "having taken due oath on the Holy Gospels according to the usage of his religion, he was asked whether he swore by God and promised the King to speak the truth upon the points on which he will be questioned."[101] This was the customary oath taken by the Protestants in the Spanish colony, especially in the Natchez area, where there were large numbers of them. The record of Benjamin's death on September 30, 1794, is couched in the standard, formal phrases which were used for all Catholics; he was buried in St. Louis Cemetery No. 1.[102] Benjamin's will, dictated the day before his death, but not signed by him because he was already so weak, began with pious Catholic formulas of faith which the notary may have inscribed automatically. Benjamin did, however, request "three masses for the repose of my soul." We have no way of telling what these Catholic rites meant to him.[103] Clara married a second time; she followed the example of her sisters-in-law when she became the wife of a non-Jew, Captain William Scott, some time before

1800.[104] Clara and William Scott had one child which was baptized as a Catholic at its death at the age of two in April, 1802.[105] Clara herself was buried in the St. Louis Cemetery No. 1, after her death on July 19, 1822, at the age of fifty-seven. Her funeral mass was conducted by the same Père Antoine who had married her to Benjamin thirty-five years before.[106]

Of Eleanora's religious experience we know nothing other than a few ritual records. Her grandchild, Marie-Eulalie Roques, was baptized at St. Louis Church on September 5, 1798, with Clara acting as godmother. But Eleanora had already died and been buried from the Church on April 8, 1796. Her funeral record, unlike the others, fails to use the customary formula relating to last rites.[107] Gracia's husband, Thomas Topham, was British, and was therefore probably a Protestant. Her will, dated December 8, 1790, does not mention religious matters, but her Catholic funeral record, January 3, 1791, uses the customary ritual formulas.[108] Both Jacob and Manuel took oaths "by God and the Cross, according to law," when they testified in the New Orleans court on June 28, 1785, in one of the final hearings relating to the disposition of Isaac's property.[109] Manuel had several slaves baptized in St. Gabriel Church, at the Iberville Post, south of Baton Rouge, on April 22 and 23, 1781, but this would not necessarily be proof of anything— even Jews who were synagogue members in later periods did not express any interest in converting their slaves to Judaism.[110] Jacob left no will, but he, too, was buried from St. Louis Church, on June 5, 1789.[111] Manuel wrote two wills. In the first, dated March 8, 1792, he contributed "two reales for each of the Churches of the city," and bequeathed a pearl rosary to his sister Angélica. Both bequests were omitted from his second will, February 23, 1795, which was necessitated by the sudden death of Benjamin. Had he already given the rosary to Angélica?[112] Manuel's death on July 10, 1796, is recorded without the usual description of last rites. It is impossible, of course, to tell whether various priests entered their records differently, one in a more cautious, another in a more mechanical fashion, or if, indeed, this sort of omission has any significance at all.[113]

Actually, we are attempting to do the impossible when we try to assess any person's religious feelings solely on the basis of formal records. Who can tell what any religious ceremony, of any faith, means to another person? Human emotions are so variable that a religious service may have a more profound effect one day than it does the next. All we possibly can do is surmise that since the Monsanto siblings were born into Judaism, and we have been unable to discover a record of conversion to Christianity of any one of them, they must therefore have been no more devoted to Christianity than to Judaism.

There is one exception to this generalization: Angélica, who eventually seems to have become a devoted member of the Episcopal Church. If so, this was due to the influence of her second husband, Dr. Robert Dow, whose father had been a Presbyterian minister in Scotland, and who was an early leader of Christ Church of New Orleans, founded in 1805. Dow was senior warden of the Church from 1807 to 1815 and was a close friend of Bishop Philander Chase while he was serving in New Orleans. Members of the family recall hearing about a copy of the Episcopal Book of Common Prayer which Dr. Dow had presented to Angélica.[114] Her will, dated June 16, 1821, in contradistinction to the formalized statements utilized in the wills of some of her brothers and sisters, seems to express sincere, personal piety:

"... I commend my soul to the Lord of life, steadfastly believing that through the merit and satisfaction of His Son, Jesus Christ, I shall obtain pardon for my transgressions, and that having finished these days of misery and mortality, I shall inherit everlasting quiet, and I give my body to the earth, whereof it was made, to be decently interred without any pomp or superfluous expense, in humble hope, that it shall rise a glorious body at the general resurrection...."[115]

Doctor Dow was not guided by Angélica's wish for modesty. The tomb he erected over her grave was one of the most striking in the Girod Street Cemetery and, after the relocation of the remains of those buried therein, the obelisk was removed to the Louisiana State Museum on Jackson Square: "The singular monument consisted of a freestone obelisk surmounting a brick tomb. On it, in high relief, was carved a skull and crossbones, a grim memorial that could well have been conceived by a man of medicine. The words 'Memento Mori' are chiseled beneath it and the date '1821' above it."[116] On the front of the monument were carved the words: "SACRED/ to the memory of/ ANGÉLICA/ consort of/ Doctor Dow/ died Oct. 21, 1821,/ aged 72 years./ Whose deportment as a Wife,/ a Mother and a member of Society,/ was too conspicuous,/ to require Eulogium,/ being rarely equaled/ and never excelled." Among the Urquhart family papers is a manuscript eulogy of Angélica written by General James Wilkinson of military and conspiratorial fame; in it, Wilkinson referred to Angélica's religious fervor:

> ". . . This lady was a member of the Episcopal Church, a regular communicant at the Lord's table, she was pious without profession, and religious without affectation . . . in conversation with an old friend who had visited her not more than twelve hours before her decease she observed: 'I now feel so well that I think I may live five or six years longer, to-morrow being Sunday I will go to Church and give thanks to God for his goodness to me.' The intention was known to Him from whom no secret is hidden and we trust the immortal spirit has received the reward of those who die in the Lord. . . ."[117]

It is ironic that of all the members of the family who had participated in religious functions of one kind or another in the St. Louis Catholic Church—where she and Robert Dow were married on September 9, 1781[118]—Angélica alone should have become not only a sincere Christian, but a Protestant Christian! Angélica's adoption of Christianity may be explained by either of two factors: perhaps she possessed a natural bent towards piety—if Judaism could not be her religion in any genuine sense, then she would become a Christian; or, more likely, her gratitude and attachment to Dr. Dow were so strong that she said to him, like Ruth of old, "thy God shall be my God."

At least one of the Fastio girls, on the other hand, was formally converted to Roman Catholicism. Elizabeth, who gave her age as thirty-two, was baptized on April 4, 1782, at St. Francis Church in Pointe Coupee. If her age is correct, she is probably the daughter who was listed as Judica, age six, in the Bordeaux embarkation records of 1756. Elizabeth's conversion had nothing, apparently, to do with marriage, since it was three years before she was married, in the New Orleans St. Louis Church, to John George Noeherberg or Noerberg, a native of Philadelphia, who was a Protestant. Elizabeth died in New Orleans in 1796, and was buried in St. Louis Cemetery No. 1. Nothing else is known of the life of the other Fastio girls or of their mother. If Elizabeth's sisters married at all, it must have been out of the faith, just as the Monsanto girls did; and Ester Fastio, like her husband, probably died under Catholic auspices, just as, to all intents and purposes, they had lived as nominal Catholics.[119]

12. Gracia Monsanto and Thomas Topham

The West Florida Protestant marriage records cannot be located anywhere, but it may have been in Manchac rather than in Pensacola that Gracia was married to Thomas Topham. During the period 1772–77 he was applying for grants of acreage and town lots in the Manchac area.[120] John Fitzpatrick referred to Topham as a partner of one Proffit in the Natchez area in 1776.[121] Topham had written Isaac's will on January 1 and April 12, 1778, but he pleaded the pressure of business after Isaac's death, and was not present as an executor at the inventory which was taken beginning on May 7.[122] He did, however, make an appearance at the inventory of Angélica's husband's estate in February, 1779.[123] On April 12 of that year he and Gracia sold a lot and two houses, located in Ascension Parish, to Jacques Cantrelle.[124] In June, 1780, he sold two slaves to Angélica.[125] He was still in business with Proffit in 1780, but this is the final reference to him which has come to light, prior to September 22, 1784, when Gracia received 5,669 pesos from Manuel and Jacob and Robert Dow which they had set aside for her from her deceased husband's estate. There was a dispute over Topham's affairs with merchants in London, which had to be settled by arbitration; this London reference suggests that Topham had originally come from England.[126] Since we know so little of Topham's business life, it is difficult to venture any statements about him. His will cannot be found, but Gracia's, executed in 1790, indicates that she led a fairly comfortable life: in addition to unspecified amounts of cash, she bequeathed nine slaves to her brothers and sisters and her Urquhart and Tessier nephews and niece. Among the prized possessions which she named in her will and specified as gifts to various relatives were: a large mirror, a large chair with arms, a silver setting for twenty-four, a porcelain coffee pot with matching cups, shoe buckles, two damask table cloths, two dozen napkins, and a picture painted on glass. These provisions reflect a meticulous, sentimental woman who cherished the things she touched, a loyal and affectionate sister and aunt who distributed her possessions in such a manner that each member of her family received something from her.[127]

13. ELEANORA MONSANTO AND PIERRE TESSIER

We know somewhat more about Eleanora's life after her marriage to Pierre Tessier in Saint-Domingue in 1773 and her return to Louisiana in 1776. She seems to have been the only one of the Monsanto sisters to make a really bad match. In November, 1779, she was desperate enough to go to court to petition for a property separation from her husband. He was then in prison as a debtor; his liabilities amounted to 1,579 pesos, while his land, house, outbuildings and four slaves in Pointe Coupee were worth only about 1,570 pesos. Her dowry at the time of the marriage had been 6,000 livres with an additional 2,000 livres in linen, jewelry, silverware, and the like. (Where did all this come from, in 1773, when Isaac had so little? From Eleanora's brother Joseph and sister Judith in Saint-Domingue, where the marriage took place?) Tessier had made a gift of 4,000 livres to her at that time. Now, she complained, he had been so cavalier with her funds that the only remaining assets which could possibly replenish her dowry account were the land, house and slaves, which the creditors were attempting to take away from her. She petitioned the court, therefore, to assign to her all of the assets of the family, to declare her free of responsibility for Pierre's debts, and to grant her complete control over the remaining property without the need of consulting her husband. This is the earliest recorded case of such a suit in Spanish Louisiana judicial history. Eleanora's attorney contended that Tessier's "bad conduct" accounted for the shrinkage of his own and Eleanora's property, and assured the court that she could be trusted with control "because of her good conduct and executive ability." The witnesses on her behalf, George Castles, Marcos Olivares and Angélica's husband-to-be, Dr. Robert Dow, testified that "they have known Pedro Andres Tessier, at Pointe Coupee, for a long time, he is an abandoned man, possessed of many vices and bad, dissipated habits. He is unable to work and it is also well known how he has wasted the greater part of his wife's dowry." Strong words—strong enough to persuade Governor Gálvez to approve the petition, and to instruct the Commandant at Pointe Coupee, Don Carlos de Grandpré, to conduct an inventory of the Tessier property, with the creditors as witnesses.[128] One of the first things Eleanora did was to get rid of three of the slaves by selling them to her brother-in-law-to-be, Dr. Dow.[129] What ultimately happened to Pierre Tessier cannot be discovered. He apparently outlived Eleanora, for she is not described as a widow in her death record. But she was a good manager; when her daughter Marie-Eulalie married Pierre Roques in May, 1795, Eleanora was able to give her a dowry of 3,000 pesos, although part of this money may have come by inheritance from Eleanora's siblings.[130] Her son, Charles André Tessier, redeemed the family name from the dishonor which Pierre's dissolute conduct had cast upon it. Beginning in 1796 he served as Secretary of the Spanish colonial government. After the Louisiana Purchase, he became an aide-de-camp to Governor William C. C. Claiborne, achieving the rank of Major in the Territorial Militia, and held the office of Parish Judge in East Baton Rouge from 1815 to 1846. On August 13, 1813, Governor Claiborne wrote of him to Secretary of War John Armstrong:

"... This Gentleman is a native of Louisiana, and a member of an extensive and influential family [;] his education has been respectable, & he has acquired by Traveling a considerable knowledge of the man [sic] and of things.—To a very commanding

graceful person he unites the most polished manners, and altho'
his partiality for the ladies may have betrayed him into some
imprudencies, his deportment has been so conciliatory, & his
integrity, bravery & honor so well established that his ac-
quaintances hold him in very high estimation.—Tessier during
the Territorial Government was one of my aids and is now a
Major in the Militia of the State.—I think him worthy of a
like Commission in the Regular service;—But if this cannot be
obtained I recommend him for a Captaincy. . . ."

So far had the son gained acceptance among his fellow-citizens
that they identified him with his prosperous and civic-minded
cousins, Angélica's sons, Thomas and David Urquhart, rather
than with his worthless father. We may be certain that Angélica,
with her strong sense of family unity, had a good deal to do
with encouraging her nephew.[131]

14. ANGÉLICA MONSANTO AND GEORGE URQUHART

Angélica's life was the longest, happiest and most fruitful of
all. Her first husband, George Urquhart, who had come to
Pensacola in February or March of 1766, was born in Aberdeen-
shire, Scotland, in the mid-1730's; his mother was a Forbes of
Blackton. He may have been in Middlesex County, England,
before his journey to America. He secured generous grants of
land shortly after his arrival, and achieved swift recognition
as a leader in the colony. In 1766, he was appointed Deputy
Collector of His Majesty's Customs at Pensacola; in 1771 he
signed as a witness at the treaty between the administration and
the Congress of Chiefs of the Upper Creek Tribes. His first
expectation was to become a planter in the Pensacola area, but
his original land grant was not fertile enough; he secured another near the Tunica village, but in 1772 decided to settle
on the Mississippi opposite Louisiana. Meanwhile he had been
engaged in various business transactions, and had borrowed
money in fairly large amounts. Once in the Manchac area, he
served as a Justice of the Peace, and succeeded in apprehending
the murderers of some nearby French people; he also was a

member of the Assembly of the Province. Urquhart was a dynamic, aggressive man in the best sense of the word, a builder, a good pioneer for such an area as British West Florida. He died in February, 1779, of "a Sore Breast and cough which turned into consumption." Angélica for a time considered the possibility of leaving Louisiana and moving to Scotland with her children, but George's mother thought she would be wise not to do so, in view of the distance and her own age.[132] It was probably to be near her brothers that Angélica moved to New Orleans with six-year-old Thomas and one-year-old David. So she petitioned the court, in September of 1779, for permission to sell the plantation, explaining that she had found a purchaser willing to pay 400 pesos more than its assessed worth, and that the property was "daily deteriorating" because of neglect. The sale took place in December, 1779; the price was 1,400 pesos.[133] So ended George Urquhart's dream of a planter's life in the New World.

15. ANGÉLICA MONSANTO AND DR. ROBERT DOW

It was only a brief time before Dr. Robert Dow, physician to the Royal Hospital of New Orleans, was courting Angélica. Another Scotsman, the son of Robert Dow, a Presbyterian minister, and Juana (Janet) Adie, Dr. Dow had left Scotland for the West Indies, and then had gone on to Louisiana in 1776. He began his practice of medicine in New Orleans in 1778. Prior to their wedding, he and Angélica appeared before a notary on May 10, 1781, to register their financial affairs. Angélica brought to the marriage a total worth of 13,390 pesos, of which sum almost 5,500 pesos was in trust for her two sons. Her dowry was in the form of notes and credits, in addition to furniture, household possessions and eight slaves. Dow himself gave 2,000 pesos to Angélica as his dowry. The wedding was performed on September 9, 1781.[134] Dow was an outstanding personage in New Orleans for more than four decades, a highly regarded participant in cultural, religious and medical affairs, and a deeply valued friend to many. Years later Charles Gayarré described him as "full of genial, exhuberant kindness for all his fellow human beings, of a florid complexion, of convivial habits . . . Dr. Dow was a great authority, and no member of his profession ever acquired more popularity. . . ." Governor Claiborne paid tribute to him as being "at the head of his profession and universally beloved, because of his amiable disposition, his humanity and his urbanity." Claiborne offered him a seat in the Louisiana Legislature in 1804, but Dow felt that his obligations to his family and patients precluded his acceptance of that responsibility.[135]

Angélica and Robert Dow were a good match. Angélica possessed a warm, cheerful personality that shone from her face. She was loving, kind and gracious. Her home was always open to guests. In 1787, when James Wilkinson, an utter stranger, came to New Orleans on the first of his controversial visits, it was in the Dow home that he stayed; Angélica and David became his "respectable, dear and honoured friends." In his eulogy of Angélica thirty-four years later, Wilkinson made special mention of the soirees in the Dow home, No. 7 Condé street between Dumaine and St. Ann (into which they moved in 1784): "A prominent and universally acknowledged trait of character which distinguished Madame Dow was her generous hospitality. She always spread a sumptuous table and health permitt[ing] every respectable stranger and a long list of the most distinguished inhabitants partook of the urbanity and good cheer of her home." The Dow couple loved the theater and took a box when the first professional company opened its stage in New Orleans.[136]

Equally as important to Angélica as Dr. Dow's affection for her was his strong and generous behavior towards her sons, one of whom did not remember his father at all, and the other only a little. Letters from Dow to Angélica's sons, in 1802 and 1821, which have fortunately been preserved by the Urquhart family, are written in warm, affectionate and genial terms. One begins with the words, "My dear Friends Thomas & David, for I dislike the formal Name of calling You my Step Sons. . . ." In her will, Angélica paid tribute to her husband "as a small testimony of my gratitude and love which he has during the whole period of our happy union, manifested towards me," and charged her sons to give him their unstinting respect "from a grateful remembrance of that attention and care which my dear husband bestowed on their education from their early life up to manhood." To him she bequeathed, so long as he lived in Louisiana, the income from her property—worth about $8,000—and to his nephew in Scotland, a pair of silver candlesticks together with a silver tray and snuffer, all initialed T.G.T. (Thomas, Gracia Topham) "which were presented to my dear husband by my deceased sister. . . . And I particularly charge my dear husband with the accomplishment of this bequest, in order that the said plate may remain in his family as a memento of mine."

In 1821 Dr. Dow estimated that their joint property was worth about $32,000, including their home, some land in Baton Rouge, their shares of stock in the Louisiana Bank, and some notes for loans. He was a good manager, and she had business sense too; they invested in real estate and bought and sold a number of slaves throughout the years. She was proud that their financial situation was so good, and he attributed this to "our joint endeavors." This substance permitted them to lead a comfortable, satisfying life all their days.[137]

Dow made several trips to Europe, one in 1785–86 in connection with "urgent family business." Before he left, John Fitzpatrick wished him "Great Success in your undertaking, and a safe retourn to your familly," when he asked him to take a letter to London.[138] The second trip lasted, perhaps, as long as two years. He had left New Orleans by July 7, 1800, when Angélica entered into the first of two slave transactions in his absence; on August 23, 1800, he was in Philadelphia, visiting with the famous Dr. Benjamin Rush, who made this entry in his commonplace book: "Dr. Dow from Orleans breakfasted with me. He was on his way to Scotland after an absence of 23 years. He said at Orleans the natives and old settlers who went out of town and came in again took the yellow fever last year, but no other natives or old settlers. He said diseases of the skin were very common in Orleans. He told me Don Gálvez, the Governor of Florida, made it a practice to retire when he was angry, and drink a bottle of Claret to compose his body and mind." After this professional talk and gossip, on to Europe. Perhaps it was in connection with the settlement of his mother's estate, for the previous year he had sent a power of attorney to his nephew in Scotland. Dr. Dow was still in Europe in July, 1802, when he wrote to Thomas about the cession of Louisiana by Spain to France: ". . . it is very much to be feared, the Inhabitants there, will gain nothing by the change of Government or new Masters. It is a fixed Maxim & Principle of this Government [he was writing from France] that every Colony Should pay its own Expences, and Impositions will infallibly be laid on the People. . . ." He paid a call on Madame Miró and Baron Pontalba, distinguished friends from New Orleans now living in a château outside of Paris, and found Pontalba "apprehensive that his Property at New Orleans will decrease in its value. . . ."

Most important is the suggestion in Dow's letter that he had been expecting Angélica to join him in Europe for a permanent change of residence. The letter is addressed to Thomas at Bordeaux and Dr. Dow begins by saying that he was "a little Surprised and disappointed, as you may well conceive at finding your good Mother not along with you. She has been playing Cross Purposes with me . . . however I have no Reflexion to make on her Conduct being convinced that She has acted for the best, and now that I am sure we are to have her in Britain, we shall endeavour to make her happy there and I shall hurry home to her as soon as posible, and then there will be an end to my Rambling Disposition. . . ." But the good Doctor was deceiving himself if he thought he could drag Angélica away from New Orleans. Despite his dislike for the climate of New Orleans—he considered it to be "malarial and debilitating," the source of so much of the disease in the area—he returned to the city and stayed there. It was not until after her death that he would move back to Europe; perhaps she knew that this would happen, and that was why she restricted the income from her estate to such time as he remained in Louisiana. But he would not stay; about two years after her death he moved to Europe. In 1840–41 he was still living in England, but family papers contain no further information about him.[139]

16. MONSANTO FAMILY UNITY

Angélica's affectionate reference to Gracia's gift of the silver candlesticks and other pieces, thirty-one years after Gracia's passing, is a telling example of Monsanto family closeness. Shining through the tedious and repetitious verbiage of legal documents are constant reminders that the Monsanto brothers and sisters maintained a fiercely close and typically Jewish family relationship throughout the years. Benjamin paid the expenses of Eleanora's suit for property separation from her husband; Jacob acted in her behalf in selling off three slaves to Angélica's husband-to-be. Jacob was a witness at the signing of Angélica's marriage agreement with Doctor Dow. Manuel and Jacob and Angélica's husband acted as guardians of Gracia's property after her husband's death. Isaac and Gracia's husband were present at inventory of George Urquhart's estate. They did not even feel distant from their Saint-Domingue brother and sister: Gracia, Benjamin and Manuel made bequests in their wills to Joseph; Gracia and Manuel to Judith. They were, quite naturally, worried about the fate of their family during the revolution on the island. Manuel, the last of the Monsanto brothers to die, said very sadly in his will, because he had not heard from Judith for a long time, that "if on account of the revolution [she] has moved to another country and because of this circumstance she has died, I name in her place her daughter Da. Raquel, my niece, who will inherit her share instead."[140] And so it continued through the years, this Monsanto protectiveness, probably instilled in them through the example of Isaac's generous assumption of responsibility for his brothers and sisters in the early years, and strengthened by the experience of adversity in 1769–70 when they were flung out into the world. Although French and Spanish law required the participation of family members in many legal matters, the Monsanto children never followed the example of their neighbors by engaging in the typical suits and countersuits over financial questions that frequently marred the unity of other colonial families. As a matter of fact, the only recorded family disagreement was fomented by Clara, Benjamin's widow, when she refused to

55

accede to her late husband's wish that his and Manuel's settlement with their creditors should take precedence over her own claims on his estate.

17. MANUEL, JACOB AND BENJAMIN MONSANTO
IN BUSINESS

For more than twenty years prior to Benjamin's death in 1794, the three younger brothers operated a business consortium in undisturbed harmony, first under Isaac's leadership, then with him as a somewhat minor partner, and finally without him after his death. There is, however, no precise mention of Benjamin in any documentation during the 1770's other than as an executor of Isaac's estate. This may be because he was the youngest brother and therefore not empowered to sign for Manuel and Jacob. In his correspondence, John Fitzpatrick refers to the Monsanto store in Manchac frequently from 1770 through July of 1781. Jacob and Manuel were dealing in dry goods, cattle, slaves and other merchandise. They were traveling back and forth to New Orleans. They had as much trouble finding hard money as Isaac always did, and paid their debts in notes and bills of exchange. On October 6, 1773, Fitzpatrick refers to Manuel as though he is established in Pointe Coupee, and not just visiting.[141]

In July, 1772, Jacob petitioned the Council of West Florida for the customary grant of three hundred acres "opposite the Spanish Settlement of Point Coupee," as though he intended establishing himself as a farmer. But the petition was denied on the ground that he had not become a naturalized resident: "It was the opinion of the [Council] that the Petitioner cannot hold lands—untill naturalized, being a Foreign Jew." This was an interesting answer; it demonstrated that there was no objection to his being a Jew, but that he, like every other alien, needed to go through the simple steps required for naturalization. Jacob did not protest that he was not a Jew, nor did he undergo naturalization so far as we know.[142]

As has already been noted, the Spanish gave no further trouble to the Monsanto brothers and sisters because of their religion, after the family was driven out of New Orleans in 1769–70. Beyond Governor Unzaga's reference to Manuel in June, 1770, there is no further mention in official Spanish documents of objection to the presence of these Jewish people. O'Reilly's successors were less successful than he was in the enforcement of commercial regulations—trade between Manchac and Louisianians continued at a merry pace until West Florida was captured by the Spanish under Gálvez in 1779. Restrictions against Protestant settlers were formally eased over the years; by the 1790's there was an affirmative policy of encouraging such immigrants, and some of these, like Dr. Dow, became prominent residents.[143] The Monsanto brothers did not actually settle in New Orleans as full-fledged residents until the early 1780's, but there seems to have been no objection to their traveling in and out of New Orleans as early as August, 1770, and doing business there. This may be the real reason that Jacob did not want to be naturalized as a British subject in 1772—because he still considered himself a Louisianian and was only waiting for a propitious and advantageous time to return permanently to the colony. It is surely significant that even Isaac, with all the bitterness he must have felt towards the Spanish, came back to settle, and die, in Louisiana.

But there was one occasion when Jacob got into trouble with the Spanish colonial government. In January, 1773, he arrived in Natchitoches in a canoe with a Canadian and two Negroes and a cargo of contraband merchandise. When Lieutenant-Governor de Mézières discovered that the contents of the canoe did not match the certified bill of lading, he threw Monsanto and the crew into prison, seized the cargo, and requested instructions from Governor Unzaga. In March, the Governor ordered Mézières to send Monsanto, his companions and the cargo to New Orleans. There the very desirable merchandise was sold at public auction, and the proceeds of 2,112 reales deposited in the public treasury. Monsanto was apparently released on parole, and promptly fled the city. He was tried in absentia in October, and sentenced to "five years of presidio duty at Oran." Meanwhile another Monsanto shipment, carried

by one La Derrive, an employee of the firm, to the Rapides
Post in September, 1773, had been seized by the commandant
of that settlement; this cargo consisted of illegal trade goods
worth 298½ reales. The Council of the Indies in Madrid did
not get around to considering the case of Jacob Monsanto until
1776; they then criticized the Governor for some imperfections
in his report of the case, and questioned the ability of a sheriff
who would be so lax as to permit his prisoner to escape. But
apparently the Spanish colonial authorities were not really
interested in imprisoning smugglers; Monsanto was not the
only merchant who was apprehended and then permitted to
escape after his property was confiscated—three other smugglers
had the same experience. So far as we know, no official attempted
to arrest Jacob during subsequent trips into the colony; his trial
appears to have been a mere formality. But what is most instructive about the entire record of these proceedings is that
Jacob is not identified either as an unwanted Jew, or as a member
of the family of merchants which had been expelled from
Louisiana just a few years before. Matters had indeed changed
since O'Reilly's departure.[144]

In October, 1773, the West Florida Province declared a
moratorium on land grants, and it was not possible for the
Monsanto brothers to obtain land for the time being. Manuel
and Jacob did, however, request a special favor in March, 1775:

> "Read the Petition of Manuel and Jacob Monsanto setting forth
> as follows—viz.—That your Petitioners have for several years
> past kept a Store on the Lands reserved for His Majesty's use at
> Manchack. That having frequently petitioned your Excellency
> and your Predecessors for a Grant of Lands on this River which
> however it has not been their good fortune to obtain and being
> now desirous to Erect a small Dwelling House or Store on the
> abovementioned reserved Land for carrying on their business of
> Merchandize they therefore humbly pray your Excellency and
> Honors will Grant them permission to Erect Buildings for that
> purpose on the Ground which they have occupied since their
> residence at Manchack being at the upper end of the old Cleared
> Ground, and that they may peaceably possess the same untill it
> shall be wanted for His Majesty's use at which time they beg to

have the Liberty to remove their said Buildings or to dispose of them in such other way as they shall be able. And your Petitioners as in duty bound will ever pray &c.—"

No mention here of the reason for the negative response to the prior request; this was simply an effort to make life and business more comfortable while they were still trading out of Manchac. This petition was viewed with favor:

"It was the unanimous advice of the Board that the prayer of the Petition should be Granted—Upon which His Excellency ordered that Manual [sic] and Jacob Monsanto the Petitioners should have Liberty to reside and occupy their several Buildings at Manchack until the Lands whereon they stand is required for the King's use—and that they may have Liberty to remove all their property when they are ordered off said Land this being the same indulgence that was given to Mr. Fitzpatrick in Council on the 17th of February in the year 1772."[145]

Manuel and Jacob, in other words, were to be treated as though they were British subjects. And so indeed they continued to be regarded: in September, 1776, when grants were again available, Jacob applied for a grant of 450 acres on the claim of family right ("His family consists of himself and Seven Negroes") and 1,000 acres through purchase. No mention was made in this petition of the reason for previous denial, and no one brought it up at the Council meeting: he was given 700 acres. Surely he had not become naturalized. Was it because he had become more prosperous, or because George Urquhart, his brother-in-law, was so prominent in the area in which he wished to settle, or because the disturbed conditions in the Atlantic seaboard colonies had aroused justifiable apprehensions about the safety of the West Florida Province—and happy settlers were valued, particularly those whose trading activities at Manchac were so important? Probably all of these factors were involved. The land granted to the Monsanto brothers was just north of George Urquhart's plantation on the Mississippi.[146]

So the brothers were up and down the Mississippi River, from New Orleans to Manchac and Baton Rouge and on to

Pointe Coupee and Natchez. They did business with a New Orleans merchant like Oliver Pollock, sold Captain Pierre Joseph Favrot some equipment for repairs at Fort Baton Rouge, took a mortgage on some land and on a schooner on the river, and borrowed cash from George Urquhart when things became tight.[147] By 1780 Benjamin had established himself in Pointe Coupee in business with his brother Isaac's old associate, Isaac Fastio. Fastio and Isaac Monsanto had engaged in commercial transactions at least as early as 1766; in fact, Fastio was still trying to recover the large sum of 3,330 pesos, 5½ reales, from Isaac's syndics. It is obvious that Fastio did not blame Isaac or the brothers for the financial confusion of Isaac's affairs: he had taken part in the inventory of Isaac's possessions on May 7, 1778, and now he was quite happy to join together with Benjamin in various business dealings over a period of at least eight years—until 1788, when they dissolved the partnership which had been created "only by faith through a private agreement"— not by a notarized, public document. But the termination of the partnership was announced publicly, and entered into the records of the Commandant of Pointe Coupee Post: it stipulated that Fastio had no claim on Benjamin's possessions, "consisting of a plantation at this post, slaves, furniture, utensils, animals, etc., and all other goods he possessed elsewhere."[148]

Benjamin appears to have been the "country" representative of the firm after Manuel and Jacob closed the Manchac store and moved their headquarters to New Orleans, where they lived on Toulouse street. Together as a team, sometimes each on his own account—for it was another loose partnership, without formal papers—they bought and sold land, acted as agents for the collection of debts, bought or attempted to buy goods at auction, even a ship, bought and sold slaves, and engaged in a general wholesale and retail business as well, much along the lines of Isaac's prior commercial activities. Among the many items which they are recorded as selling are the following: sugar, butter, salt meat, West India rum, soap, tobacco, indigo, cloth, English shoes, linen trousers, thread stockings, hats, beaver skins, ship cable and horses. Only one detailed account has survived the ravages of time; it is a list of the items which the

Monsanto brothers supplied to Santiago Lemelle, a planter in Attakapas, during 1783–84:

8	dishes	4	ells of ribbon
2	pitchers	1	pair of woolen stockings
1	dish and 1 ladle	1½	ells of flannel
2	water jars	2½	ells of coarse carpet
18	flasks of brandy	1	pair of silk bandages
7	colored linen handkerchiefs	1½	ells of blue cloth
1½	ells of brown cloth	1½	ells of white flannel
4	ells of Rouen linen	3	ells of linen
3½	ells of calico	3	ells of linen for the Negroes
2	ells of cottonade	1	box of tea
6	ells of dull linen		

The total cost of these products was 118 pesos, 6 reales. But Lemelle did not pay in cash. He manufactured candles on his plantation, and the Monsanto brothers took the candles in exchange for the merchandise. The total value of the candles they needed for their other customers exceeded the sum of his purchases, so that they had to give him hard cash as well— 139 pesos, about one-fifth of the cost of a good slave.[149]

Many of the Monsanto brothers' transactions were in slaves— some for their own use, a few of whom they freed, but most, of course, for resale. Every person in Louisiana who could afford slaves owned them. By 1800 Angélica and Robert Dow had bought six and sold five; Gracia bought four and sold two; there is no record of Eleanora's purchases, but she sold six. The total of the brothers' purchases and sales, derived from the examination of thousands of pages of records in New Orleans and Natchez, but not in other Louisiana localities, is as follows: Benjamin bought nineteen and sold ten; Jacob bought two and sold thirteen; Manuel bought thirty and sold twelve; the brothers as a firm bought thirty-seven and sold eighteen. Because many of their business activities were in partnership, however, it must be presumed that Jacob sold some of those listed as Manuel's purchases, and that Benjamin sold slaves bought by his brothers, in addition to those he used on his plantation. Only three large transactions in slaves are included in the Natchez and New Orleans notarial records: twelve were bartered by Benjamin in 1785 for 3,280 pounds of indigo, which he probably had received in exchange for some other type of merchandise; thirteen were bought by Manuel in 1787 for 3,780 pesos from Hilaire Boutté; and thirty-one slaves were purchased by Manuel and Jacob from Daniel Clark the elder for 9,300 pesos "of the new Mexican mint," later in the same year.[150] No merchant of the time devoted himself exclusively to slave trading; this was a later development, when the number of farmers grew and the corresponding need for slaves increased. The Monsanto brothers therefore qualify as slave traders, in the manner of the times, although this was only one aspect of the exceedingly broad range of business activities in which they engaged.

18. BENJAMIN MONSANTO IN NATCHEZ

Although Benjamin had been in partnership with Fastio, this did not exclude a similar relationship with his brothers. But Benjamin aspired to be a planter. Although some of his purchases of land in the Pointe Coupee area were obviously for investment purposes—in less than a year, for instance, between April, 1784, and March, 1785, he made a ten percent profit on some acreage—he did run a plantation at the Pointe Coupee Post for a few years. But he was apparently not satisfied with that venture, and felt that he would do better in Natchez, where the brothers had already engaged in various business transactions, and which had replaced Manchac and Pointe Coupee as a center of trade. He purchased his first land there in February, 1785.[151] Shortly before this he had heard George Rapalie's boastful talk in Natchez about an imminent rebellion against Spanish rule, and had to testify as a witness in the long and involved trial which ensued.[152] Fortunately, no suspicion was directed against him, and some time after his marriage to Clara, he decided to undertake a planter's life in Natchez.[153] He had no difficulty in becoming accepted as a member of the Natchez community; his knowledge of French, Spanish and

English meant that he was equally at home with all of the settlers in the area. He not only enjoyed the social prestige to which Major Forman referred, but was accorded the trust and confidence of the Governor. Governor Manuel Gayoso de Lemos twice appointed him to teams of citizens who conducted inventories and appraisals of the estates of deceased neighbors, and in 1790 he was one of the men on a panel from whom arbitrators were chosen to compromise a dispute.[154]

Benjamin's plantation on the bank of St. Catherine's creek, next to David Williams' property (his daughter Mary Gayoso Williams later married Angélica's son David),[155] covered 500 arpents of land. The dwelling house, "planked and roofed with shingles," was, according to the inventory of Benjamin's estate in 1794, "somewhat decayed, feebly constructed and wanting repair." The outbuildings consisted of a kitchen of hewn logs, four small cabins serving as milk houses and slave quarters, and a well. Of furniture the main dwelling had little: "three beds and some trifles of furniture." Of animals there were two yoke of oxen, one hundred and twenty sheep, five work horses, about forty head of horned cattle, and some hogs in the woods. A cart and irons, three ploughs and seven spades, was the total of agricultural equipment. Benjamin owned seventeen slaves, but five were sold to a neighbor before his death, and four belonged to the partnership with Manuel.[156]

Benjamin had not succeeded too well in his farming venture—perhaps he had been draining cash from the business in order to support his ambition to become a planter. At any rate, whatever the reason, the firm was in trouble. On June 17, 1792, Benjamin had been compelled to borrow 1,000 silver dollars from his neighbor David Williams, using three slaves as collateral.[157] In early 1794, Benjamin joined eight other Natchez citizens in protesting to Governor Francisco Luis Héctor Carondelet against a formal moratorium on debts in the area—this would obviously put merchants like Benjamin and Manuel in a bind.[158] Four months before his death on September 30, 1794, Benjamin was in New Orleans with Jacob, negotiating with their creditors. On May 28, 1794, the creditors agreed to accept settlement over a period of three years. Some of the slaves would have to be sold immediately to raise cash. The complete list of assets and debits demonstrates that the Monsanto brothers should have had nothing to worry about. Customers in the Natchez area, and in New Orleans, Pointe Coupee, Galveztown, Natchitoches and Attakapas, were indebted to them for a total of $14,803. Added to this were their slaves: six already turned over to the creditors, worth $1,500, and ten more worth $3,200. They owed a total of only $6,610 to six creditors.[159] The difficulty was, as always, the scarcity of ready cash; and due partly to the moratorium on debts in Natchez, the brothers were in very narrow straits. Hence the need for time. Unfortunately, Benjamin's death intervened. Clara had to go to court for permission to sell some land in order to pay her overseer's salary and some other personal debts—only $300 was needed, but she could not do without it.

Not the least of the complications was the fact that Benjamin had made two wills. The first, dated January 25, 1792, when Benjamin was already ill, divided the estate between Clara and Manuel; Clara's dowry of 2,500 milled dollars was to be returned to her, but "if the present payment of the above sum should be attended with great inconvenience to my brother Manuel Monsanto, I desire that he may not be distressed, on giving good and undoubted security for the sum, and paying regularly and exactly the interest of the same, for the maintenance of my dear Wife." This will had been executed in Natchez, and was presented to the Natchez court and accepted for probate.[160] Then came the news from New Orleans that Benjamin had revoked this will and had written a new one, the day before his death. In the new will he left nothing to Clara, merely returned her dowry to her; he did not refer to "my dear Wife." Because of the "large sums of money we owe," Benjamin granted his executors an extension beyond the usual period of a year for the termination of his affairs. The surprise was that he designated his brother Joseph in Saint-Domingue as his residuary heir.[161] No wonder that Clara made claims on the estate, and created difficulties for Manuel, and for the creditors, upsetting the settlement which had been negotiated in May. It may be that Benjamin had been victimized by marital as well as financial and health problems—this might have been the reason for his decision to leave Clara out of his will, except for her dowry. Benjamin's estate was still in the courts in 1802–1803, when some of his debts had still not been discharged.[162]

19. MANUEL, JACOB, MAIMI AND SOPHIA

Manuel now had to struggle on alone; he survived Benjamin by less than two years. He tried hard, in his will, to help his executors to distinguish between his personal affairs and those of his distressed company: anything dated before Benjamin's death, though personal, was to be assigned to the creditors; anything dated thereafter belonged to him individually, as did the goods in his own home (which probably served as his storehouse). He bequeathed personal mementoes to Angélica's husband and sons, to Eleanora's children, and to Eleanora and Angélica. The estate as a whole was bequeathed to Angélica, Eleanora, Judith and Joseph. One of his most interesting bequests was a medicine box which he left to Dr. Dow. The portrait which emerges from Manuel's will is that of a scrupulously fair merchant—in a postscript he made special mention of two personal debts which he insisted be paid—and a fond brother, spelling out precisely which of his personal possessions he wanted each member of his family to have.[163]

Manuel made one further bequest: "fifty pesos to the quadroon named Sofia, daughter of the mulattress Mamy, another fifty to said Mamy, an identical sum to the free negress Rozeta, my former slave, all of which I want to be done." Manuel had freed Rosa on May 29, 1792. But Mamy, Maimy or Maimi William had not been Manuel's slave—she had belonged to Jacob, who freed her on August 4, 1783, when she was twenty-six years old, "in appreciation of her good service and for the payment of 300 pesos." Maimi did not have the money, then: Jacob gave her a year to secure it, but it was four years before Jacob acknowledged payment. Manuel made a point of referring to Maimi as a mulatto and to Sophia as a quadroon. The conclusion is inescapable that Sophia was Jacob's daughter, and that this was why Manuel remembered Sophia and her mother in his will. Manuel did not leave a bequest to another slave Jacob had freed in 1781. The deed of sale of a slave from Maimi to Sophia, dated February 9, 1795, is the first of many references to Sophia as Sophia Monsanto. By 1805, when both Sophia and Maimi had their own residences, or at least lived in different houses on Bienville street, Maimi too had adopted the name Monsanto. Maimi died in 1817; the heirs to her estate of $558 were Sophia and the pharmacist Philippe Zerban. There is no record of Sophia's passing. But it is natural to wonder if Madame Dow ever nodded to Sophia if she saw her while out strolling; Angélica must have known that Sophia was her niece.[164]

It is equally natural to wonder if Madame Dow ever greeted Judah Touro, after his arrival in New Orleans in 1802, with the information that she came of the same Sephardic stock as he, from the same Holland in which his father had been born.[165] If Manuel, Jacob or Benjamin had lived into the nineteenth century, they might have mentioned to Touro that they too were Jews, for they did not have Angélica's good reasons for identification with the non-Jewish community and with Christianity. But there had been no opportunity for them to associate with fellow Jews. It is therefore only in a more modern sense that the Monsanto brothers and sisters were Jews: they did not and would not abandon their Jewish identification; they would not become Christians; they remained conscious of their sense of being different—but only in this way were they Jews. They probably did nothing about being Jewish other than to resist the religious pressure of the environment—and part of the price they had to pay for this resistance was their expulsion from Louisiana. Had they adopted Catholicism formally, and become French subjects, after their arrival in 1757 or 1758, they would probably have been permitted to remain in Louisiana, would have preserved their hard-earned property. But this they did not do. Perhaps in this way alone did they reflect their origins in that Dutch community of Jewish refugees from Spain and Portugal—they would not turn against the memory of those fleeing ancestors.

The significance, then, of the Monsanto brothers and sisters is that of pioneers, who successfully tested and bested the

French prohibition against Jewish colonists, who were probably the only Jews ever to be expelled from territory now part of the United States partly because they were Jews, who successfully breached even the Spanish colonial barriers against Jews, and who were the first permanent Jewish settlers in a variety of localities: New Orleans, Baton Rouge, Pointe Coupee and Natchez.

20. OTHER JEWS AND SUPPOSED JEWS IN SPANISH COLONIAL LOUISIANA

For decades, the statement has been repeated that two Jews named Mendez and Solis were pioneers in the development of the sugar cane industry in Louisiana, during the 1790's.[166] There is no need here to discuss the complicated question of what contribution, if any, these men made to experimentation in the field of sugar cane refinement, but it must be noted that there is no evidence that members of Joseph Solis' family considered themselves to be Jews or that they were Marranos. The lineage of this family is known in some detail: they had come to New Orleans by 1771, after successive residence in Ireland (where Joseph Solis' grandfather, Manuel, was born), Boston (about 1717, where Joseph's father, also named Manuel, was born), and Santiago de Cuba (about 1755, where Joseph had married Barbara de Rosas). It is possible, of course, that some distant ancestor had been a *converso*, but no contemporary record has been located which refers to the Jewish background of the family.[167]

The question of the background of Joseph Solis' friend, Antonio Mendez, is more interesting and revealing. Born in Havana in 1750, Mendez was in New Orleans before August 16, 1784, when he petitioned the court for a *limpieza* certificate. The *limpieza* code, which had developed in Spain and was transferred to the colonial areas of the Spanish empire, was an antecedent of the Hitlerian "racial purity" laws. In order to safeguard the "blood purity" of Spanish "old" Christians, in contradistinction to "new" Christians, that is, former Jews

67

who had been converted voluntarily or through compulsion, it was required that genealogical data be presented to the courts which then certified that a family were "old Christians, pure of all taint of bad races of Moors, Jews, Mulattoes and Indians, and that they are not recently converted." In certain parts of the Western Hemisphere, of course, the emphasis was on the proof that Indians and Negroes did not appear in the family tree, but originally the reference to Jewish or "new" Christian forebears was of primary significance. Suits for the certification of family *limpieza* were entered in the New Orleans courts as early in the Spanish period as 1776. Apparently any Spaniard who possessed or aspired to social position wanted such certification, as did anyone who sought to play a role in the colony's official life.[168] The record of the hearing for Mendez' appeal is worth quoting in full:

"Proceedings brought by Antonio Mendez to prove his legitimacy, purity of blood, life and habits.

Court of Governor Esteban Miró.
Assessor, Juan del Postigo.
Escribano, Rafael Perdomo.

Antonio Mendez, a native of Havana and a resident of New Orleans, petitions to say it is convenient to him to have witnesses testify in answer to the following questions:

1st. Whether he is not the legitimate son born of the lawful marriage of Josef Mendez, a native of Pontevedra, in the Kingdom of Galicia, and of Ana Muñoz de Lara, born in the city of Havana?

2nd. Is it not true that his said parents always kept him in their house and called him their son and, he, in turn, called them his parents?

3rd. Is it not true that his said parents and maternal grandparents are and always have been old Christians, free from the taint of all impure races, such as Moors, Jews, mulattoes and Indians, and have not been recently converted and have never been prosecuted for infamous crimes, but on the contrary have always been employed in places of honor, have held high offices and have distinguished themselves by their personal qualities?

4th. Has he not always comported himself with dignity, has

68

his conduct not been correct, frequenting the Holy Sacraments often with the congregation of the faithful?

5th. Is not all that he has stated publicly and generally known?

Governor Miró, on Juan del Postigo's advice, decrees: Let the testimony this party requests be received, according to the tenor of the above interrogatorio, the taking of the said testimony to be entrusted to the Escribano, and done, bring the depositions to the Court.

Marcos Aragon is the first witness called. His testimony reads: In the city of New Orleans, on the 17th of August of the year 1784, the Escribano, pursuant to the foregoing decree, received the oath of Marcos Aragon, a witness presented by Antonio Mendez to give the evidence the latter has offered and the Court ordered taken. This oath was made according to law, and when examined upon the tenor of the foregoing interrogatorio, to the first question he answered: This is true in all its contents. The witness knows it [to] be a fact because for many years past he has been a frequent visitor in the home of Antonio Mendez' parents.

2nd. What has been stated is also true and well known to the witness through long years of acquaintanceship.

3rd. What is set down in this question is also true and well known to him, namely, that Mr. Mendez' grandparents have always been reputed to be white, people of distinction and free from any taint of impure races.

4th. It is true that Antonio Mendez has always conducted himself properly, and has never seen nor heard anything detrimental to him in the city of Havana, on the occasions the witness has been there, nor during his residence here. On the contrary he has heard everyone speak of him as an honorable man.

5th. All that he has stated is generally and publicly known and is voiced by everybody. What the witness has answered is the truth, under charge of his oath, he is 60 years of age, and he signed, to which Escribano attests. (Signed) Marcos Aragon, before Rafael Perdomo.

The other witnesses, Juan Francisco Romero, a resident of Havana, and Manuel Ramos, each in a separate declaration, corroborates the testimony of Marcos Aragon.

Then Governor Miró, on Juan del Postigo's advice, decrees: Considering the foregoing testimony produced for Antonio

Mendez, by which he has proven his legitimacy of birth, purity of blood and good conduct, His Lordship says that he must approve and does approve his claim, and for its greater validation and force he interposes his authority and judicial decree. He orders the certified copy requested, authorized in public form, given to the petitioner, upon the payment of all just and due fees."[169]

In 1785–86, Mendez was acting as the attorney for claimants on Isaac Monsanto's property. Later he served as a legal official of the Spanish colonial government. In 1790 he married Felicite Ducre in New Orleans.[170] Apparently a man of ability, he was called upon by the first American governor of the Louisiana territory, William C. C. Claiborne, to serve the new government in the area. Let Claiborne describe the ensuing experience in the words of his report to Secretary of State James Madison, from New Orleans, under date of February 13, 1804:

". . . I appointed a few days ago a Mr. Mendez, who had been represented to me an Honest Capable Man, Civil Commandant of a District [Terre aux Boeufs] about Six leagues below New Orleans. This District is inhabited principally by an humble, poor, indolent, ignorant people, emigrants from the Canary Islands, who Idolize their Priests, and feel little attachment for any one else. Mr. Mendez altho a Catholic; is said to be of Jewish extraction, and on this account (and for other reasons unknown to me) is by no means a favorite with his neighbors, who manifest disquietude at his appointment, and a few were imprudent enough to talk of not recognizing him as their Commandant. This Affair was represented to me as an alarming event, and strong measures on my part were advised. In pursuance however of that conciliatory Policy which I have adopted, I sent for some influential characters of the District, and on this day had an Audience with them; they professed attachments for the Government of the United States, respect for its Officers, and a determination to be obedient to the Laws; but as well for themselves as their neighbors they entreated me to nominate for them another Commandant. I determined to grant their request, and they have returned to their homes apparently well pleased.

"I have given you these particulars, since this Transaction has

70

been greatly misrepresented here, and should it reach (by way of report) the City of Washington, the exaggeration will probably be great. . . ."[171]

No other correspondence about the Mendez case has been located; this might imply that Claiborne was unduly anxious. Yet he was correct in feeling embarrassed by the affair, for Article III of the Treaty ceding Louisiana to the United States provided that

> "The inhabitants of the ceded territory . . . shall be maintained and protected in the free enjoyment of their liberty, property and the religion which they profess."

This provision was intended to protect the largely Catholic population of certain sections of Louisiana from any discrimination by the Protestant majority of the United States as a whole. But the Federal act which divided Louisiana into two territories, passed in 1804, did not refer to any one particular religion:

> ". . . no law shall be valid . . . which shall lay any person under restraint, burden, or disability, on account of his religious opinions, professions, or worship; in all which he shall be free to maintain his own, and not burdened for those of another . . ."[172]

Even if Mendez had been a practicing Jew, Claiborne would not have been bound to revoke the appointment, let alone on the basis of a rumor that one of his ancestors was Jewish. Certainly the Governor had no desire to perpetuate medieval Spanish prejudices; yet he interpreted his primary responsibility as being the establishment of American authority with a minimum of friction or controversy. He therefore followed the prudent course of giving in to the demand of the Canariotes for the time being . . . only to appoint Mendez to the position of Justice of the Peace for St. Bernard Parish three and a half years later. Claiborne had his way—gradually.

Even though there was no testimony about Mendez' paternal grandparents (perhaps because there was no one in New Orleans who could testify about the family's reputation in Pontevedra, from personal knowledge), he was regarded as an "old" Christian by the Spanish authorities; otherwise he would not have obtained the *limpieza* certificate, nor would he have held positions of legal responsibility under Spanish rule. Perhaps, as in thousands, perhaps hundreds of thousands of individual cases, since the establishment of the Inquisition in Spain and Portugal, the accusation of Judaizer was only a mask for other, less theological purposes; Claiborne hints at this in his report to Madison. At any rate, Mendez was surely not a Jew in terms of personal religious affiliation, conviction or knowledge, even if distant ancestors had been "new" Christians. But his experience points up one aspect of the Spanish colonial period, carried on into the years of the American regime, which demonstrates that there were areas of Louisiana and classes of its population which would have nothing to do with Jews, and which regarded a man's Jewish background with suspicion and hatred.

So far as we know, this was not characteristic of all settlers and officials of Spanish background, let alone of the larger French population. The French never did pursue Jews or former Jews with the same unrelenting fanaticism as the Spaniards. During the 1790's at least one family of Jewish refugees from Saint-Domingue appears to have settled in Louisiana. In early 1796, Sara López Pardo, surely a Jewess to judge by her name, applied in Bordeaux for a passport to leave for Louisiana with her two young children, together with her slave Martine and her daughter, "in order to arrange her affairs in Louisiana." Sara declared that she was thirty-two years old, and that she was a refugee from Saint-Domingue. Nothing further has been discovered about Sara or her fate.[173]

More suggestive, however, is Daniel Lopes Dias' application in Bordeaux, at about the same time, for a passport for his son Abraham to travel to Louisiana to be near his family. Nothing further is known of Abraham or his family; diligent searching in New Orleans notarial records and other manuscript sources has failed to uncover a single reference to any member of the family—but Benjamin Monsanto had died recently, and he and Gracia had left money to their Saint-Domingue relatives. Perhaps this Lopes Dias family was related to Rachel Lopes Dias, Judith's daughter-in-law. If all of the members of the

72

Monsanto family in Saint-Domingue had been wiped out, then members of Rachel's family could legitimately regard themselves as her heirs, with a justified claim on the inheritances from the Monsanto family. All of this is pure surmise—and the probability is that no members of this Lopes Dias family remained in Louisiana for a very long time, unless they lived in some rural area whose manuscript records have not been consulted.[174]

If, however, the Lopez Pardo and Lopes Dias families did settle in Louisiana, outside of New Orleans where their names do not occur in any census or directory, they were quietly absorbed into the dominant French Catholic environment without a ripple to mark their disappearance. This may offer additional evidence that, though there were Jews in colonial Louisiana, there was no Judaism.

II

Judah Touro—An Overview

New England-born Judah Touro was the first Jew known to have arrived in New Orleans after 1800, and the most famous for his contributions to the life of his adopted city. (Judah Benjamin's greatest renown was achieved through his service to the Confederacy; his residence was then in Richmond). When Touro died on January 18, 1854, lavish praise was accorded to the record of his life:

> "New Orleans has lost one of her best citizens, charity one of her sincerest devotees and humanity one of its truest friends.... Though earnest and successful in the prosecution of business, Mr. Touro was never a selfish or close man. On the contrary, he has for many years been the foremost of our rich men in all contributions to charitable objects. Some of his donations have been on a scale of magnificence and liberality scarcely paralleled in our country...."[1]

Seven years previously, however, the R. G. Dun and Company's confidential agent in New Orleans referred to him as "the old rat." That this agent envied Touro's wealth is obvious: "I sh^d like to have his note for a *million*," was his comment on his subject's financial standing.[2] This agent may well have been animated by antipathy against Jews. He almost invariably called attention to their ethnic background when he commented on the credit standing of Jews, and frequently made such a sneering reference as, for example, "stand well for Jews."[3] But it was not only so prejudiced an observer as this anonymous reporter who had negative reactions to Touro. His closest Jewish associate, an executor of his noted will, regarded Touro as an eccentric, indecisive, difficult, peculiar person: "Mr. Touro is the very impersonation of a snail, not to say of a crab whose progress (to use a paradox) is usually backward ... I must be very careful to humor him ... he is very *slow* ... You know he is a strange man...."[4]

The public acclaim granted to Touro following the publication of the terms of his munificent will, and the position of eminent philanthropist which has been awarded to him by hero-worshipping Americans, and particularly American Jews, have interfered with any earnest effort to comprehend the character of the whole man. This is a difficult task, in view of the destruction of his files, accounts and papers after his death, on his explicit instructions.[5] Without attempting to essay a full biography which perhaps can never be accomplished successfully, in view of the paucity of personal data, we shall try to underline some salient and revealing characteristics and experiences which have not previously been given their appropriate weight.

Touro was born in Newport, Rhode Island, on June 16, 1775, the son of Isaac Touro, the Dutch-born *hazan* (minister-cantor) of Congregation Yeshuat Israel, and his native American wife, Reyna Hays. The following year the elder Touro refused to take the oath of loyalty to the Revolutionary cause which was required by the Rhode Island Assembly, on the grounds that he was a Dutch subject, and that such an oath was also against his religious principles. That there was more to his feelings than he then revealed is indicated by his decision to remain in Newport after the town's capture by the British. He was given subsistence by the British commander, since most of the Jews had fled town and there was no way in which he could support himself. In 1780 he moved to New York City and petitioned "His Excellency Major General [William] Tryon Governor and Commander in Chief in New York" for relief, pledging "his loyalty and attachment to His Majesty's Government," and referring to the "persecution and distress" from which he had suffered. He was granted an annual allowance and daily rations by the British. On December 12, 1782, he requested and was given an advance on his stipend so that he might move to the island of Jamaica. Isaac Touro presumably officiated in Jamaica for a brief time prior to his death on December 8, 1783, after which his widow returned with her four children to New England, where she made her home with her brother, Moses Michael Hays, in Boston, until her death on September 28, 1787.[6]

Hazan Isaac Touro's decision to ally himself with the Tories is not recounted here to cast any stain on his son's patriotism, but rather to demonstrate one aspect of the stress and insecurity in which Judah's early years were spent. He had lived in four different places by the time he was eight years old: Newport, New York City, Jamaica and Boston. In Newport and New York City the family lived on military handouts; they had hardly established themselves in Jamaica before the father died and they were compelled to become refugees once again. In Boston they were poor relatives living on charity. Judah was fatherless when he was just past seven, and an orphan when he was twelve. These experiences with privation and grief must have left indelible marks on young Judah's character. No matter how kindly and generous Uncle Hays may have been, Judah cannot have helped feeling lonely, insecure and afraid.

Of Touro's youth in Boston, hardly anything is known. He probably received little formal education; years later, Gershom Kursheedt—who knew him very well—said that Touro's "great misfortune was in his want of education."[7] This probably meant, at the very least, that Touro evinced no interest in cultural matters. Moses Michael Hays was a prosperous merchant and insurance broker; Judah and his younger brother Abraham seem to have been apprenticed in their uncle's counting house at a fairly young age and to have learned there the ways of commerce which they followed for the rest of their lives. In 1798, according to report, Judah was sent as supercargo on a voyage to the Mediterranean. More significant, personally, is the legend of his falling in love with one of his cousins, and Uncle Hays's refusal of permission for the marriage. Stories about the romance were in circulation before Touro's death; Rabbi Isaac Leeser had heard them on visits to New Orleans. He thought that Touro had been in love with Rebecca Hays; other sources say it was Catherine. How much truth may underlie the legend cannot be ascertained at this late date. Certain it is that Judah did not leave Boston because of Rebecca's death; she died nine months after his departure. Nor is there any evidence that he maintained contact with Catherine throughout the years; a letter which Catherine's niece wrote to Touro two days before her death and which his own death prevented his receiving seems to imply that there had been little or no contact between them. One specific fact contradicts the romantic notion that Judah and Catherine languished for love of each other throughout their lives: Moses Michael Hays died in 1805—just four years after Judah went to New Orleans. If it was Uncle Moses' opposition which stood in their way, that was the time for Judah to have returned to Boston for his beloved, or to have sent for her to come to New Orleans.[8]

If we have no definite knowledge of Touro's motivation for leaving Boston, we are equally in the dark about his choice of New Orleans as his destination. He appears not to have gone South as a representative of his uncle's business; this may indicate that there was a falling out between them. There is no evidence, either, that he had received assurances from other New England firms that they would use him as a New Orleans agent, though naturally he must have solicited their shipments either before his departure from Boston or after his arrival in Louisiana. Touro certainly had no way of knowing, when he left Boston in October, 1801, that within a brief time Louisiana would be ceded by the Spanish to France, and then purchased from Napoleon by the United States. Whatever Touro's feelings and motivations, the kind of man who was adventurous enough to leave the familiar Yankee surroundings of Boston in order to seek a home and livelihood in so distant and exotic a clime as New Orleans was not the shy, retiring personality of later years. The story of his unhappy romance has been highlighted by writers who recognized how little color there was in Touro's life, but even if he was fleeing from a painful personal relationship, his choice of New Orleans as his future home reflected a positive strength in his character worthy of emphasis. New York, Philadelphia, Richmond or Charleston would have been more natural locations if he was only looking for another port in which to settle. But if he had really quarrelled bitterly with his uncle, who possessed important commercial connections in each of these cities, perhaps he chose New Orleans because Mr. Hays had no contacts there, although his uncle does not seem to have been so vengeful a man that he would maintain a vendetta with his nephew. But all this is surmise. The fact is that it took courage to move to New Orleans, still under Spanish domination, plagued by disease, riddled with commercial restrictions, peopled by citizens whose languages he probably did not know.

Fortunately for Touro and the economic future of the Crescent City, Louisiana came under American rule in a short time. There is no record of Touro's business life immediately after his arrival, but within a few years he was acting as a commission merchant—that is, he served as an agent for the sale in New Orleans of consignments of merchandise shipped from New England or from Europe, assisted the captains of ships in attending to their business, and solicited outgoing cargoes for his correspondents' ships. Touro's earliest printed advertisement which can be found dates from 1805; the wares which it lists are a good example of the variety of merchandise which he handled:

"Now Landing

From on board the Schooner William, Abraham Waters Master, From Boston, lying opposite the old Custom House, the following articles: 130 Boxes Cod Fish, 28 half barrels of 1st quality beef, 2 do [ditto] Neats Tongues, 10 Casks Cheese, 19 do Potatoes, 2 do French Hair Powder, 60 Boxes Mould Candles, 18 do Castile Soap, 60 do American brown Soap, 4 do Chocolate, 5 Cases Britannias, 2 do Platillas, 6 Kegs Butter, 2 Pipes Holland Gin, 6 Barrels Nuts, and a quantity of Pickled Fish in Kegs, in excellent order, consisting of Salmon, Mackeral, Herring, Tongues and Sounds, Soused Lobsters, &c.—ALSO—A few thousand Joice [joists] and Boards, which will be sold reasonable for cash. For particulars apply to the master on board, or to

J. TOURO"[9]

A few weeks later Touro advertised that his ship would soon leave for Antwerp, had half her cargo signed up, and had space for additional freight and for passengers.[10] The schooner *William* had brought a large assortment of foodstuffs and other products to Touro; possibly the entire cargo was consigned to him. Sometimes, however, only a few items on a ship were sent to him. His handling of a small order, sent to him in 1809 by the

Boston merchant, John Hancock, nephew and namesake of the Revolutionary leader, will indicate his role in miniature form. The consignment consisted of four pipes and two hogsheads of gin, which Touro sold for $484.75. From the proceeds he paid the captain of the Brig *Sally* $30 for freight charges; he also deducted $1.50 for cartage, $10 for storage of the gin for two months (probably in his own store), and a five percent commission of $24.25 for his services. He sent the net amount of the sale, $418.50, in Spanish milled dollars, to Boston, on the same ship which carried his report of the transaction to Hancock.[11]

Touro's report of a later transaction, on behalf of Christopher G. Champlin, the former Senator from Rhode Island, offers evidence of the difficulties which were involved in some consignments. On June 3, 1820, he wrote to Champlin that his ship had arrived, and acknowledged receipt of bricks and iron which had been consigned to him—"both of which articles, am sorry to say, have come to a very bad market—have only been able to sell about 15 m of the former at $5½—the iron have been obliged to store—considerable quantities has been imported here direct from Gottenburg, Stockholm &c this last season—so that the place is at present completely overstocked with it—you may however rely, I shall endeavor to do the best with both articles for your Interest... the Bricks are too small for this market—they will not work in with any other brick whatever, not even the Boston brick." Touro also reported that the ship's captain had been ill, justified his decision to ship a cargo of cotton rather than tobacco to the Liverpool market, and gave his estimate of the ship's probable date of departure.[12] A year later, on June 23, 1821, Touro had to admit to Champlin that he still had not sold the iron: "I am, my Dr Sir, as anxious as you possibly can be, to close the thing, in order that you might be enabled thereby, to wind up the concerns of the ship for that voyage—however as I think the market is now getting better for the articles, am in hopes to do something with it ere long—as soon as I do you shall be advised thereof—and you may rely that no exertions has been, nor shall be, wanting, to expedite the same as speedily as possible."[13] Champlin had obviously sent the bricks and iron to Touro without prior notification; Touro could not very well have rejected the consignment without losing the good will of this correspondent, and possibly of others. But it was not his capital which was tied up; Touro spent his time and energy, but the most he could lose in this sort of transaction was his commission. The client was responsible for storage costs.

In view of the destruction of Touro's business papers, and the absence of any substantial records of his correspondents, other than the Thwing Company's letter books in the Massachusetts Historical Society which date from the late 1840's when he was already an old man, it is impossible to present a fully detailed description of his commercial activities. He seems, however, to have restricted himself to a brokerage business, acting as the agent for New England, primarily Boston, merchants who sent consignments to him. Beginning in 1820, the *Louisiana Gazette* regularly printed itemized lists of ship arrivals and clearings, including the consignees of cargoes. During this and the following few years he received frequent shipments, but many other merchants were far busier than he. The cargoes which were sent to him included a wide variety of merchandise and foodstuffs: linens, glass, brandy, soap, olive oil, brandied fruits, almonds, wine, gunpowder, candles, beef, tongues, medicines, grass seeds, brimstone, paving stones, sulphur, lead, herring, furniture, dry goods, boards, mackerel, whale oil, codfish, rum, onions, cordage, cheeses, leather, salt and gin. Ships for which he acted as agent took on cargoes of sugar, tobacco, cotton, skins, logwood, molasses, books, beeswax and calcutta goods. He was also part owner of a number of ships, on and off throughout the years. In 1809 he purchased a one-third interest in the *Cabinet*. In 1815 he bought one-half of the *Highlander* for $4,500. Beginning in 1817, he invested in shares of various steamboats. He was not, however, a large-scale owner of shipping vessels; practically all of these ventures were in partnership with other merchants who probably took the major responsibility for these shipping activities.[14]

Most of Touro's business was in the wholesale consignment line; his customers in New Orleans were merchants, storekeepers and plantation owners, rather than the general public. One commodity which he did sell at retail was ice. He began to import this luxury from the North in 1828. In 1837, when rumors of an impending ice shortage were at large, Touro took the unusual step of sending a letter to one of the newspapers in which he assured the public that there was "sufficient ice now in the old and regularly established Ice Houses in Chartres, Conde and Commerce streets, and at the Pontchartrain R. Road; also at the house at the corner of Robin and Religieuse streets to satisfy the wants of the city and vicinity during the season, even should not another pound be received from the North." The 1838 *New Orleans City Directory* lists him as the owner of only two ice houses, those at 74 Conti and 23 Elysian Fields; he was, therefore, probably speaking for all of the owners of such establishments in his letter to the *Bee*.[15]

Touro was certainly not the most important businessman in New Orleans, nor even the most prosperous or successful Jewish entrepreneur. During the sixteen months beginning in January, 1818, for instance, Rochelle and Shiff, whom we will meet later, received twice as many consignments as did Touro, according to newspaper reports. Nor is there any evidence that Touro was a pioneer merchant venturer or high risk business leader comparable to the real-life Vincent Nolte whose story is told so dramatically in *Anthony Adverse*. But neither did Touro go bankrupt as Nolte and most of the other speculators did. He seems to have resisted the temptation of high profits and limited his transactions to conventional commission work, letting others take the high risks and suffer their consequences. He did not, so far as we can tell, buy or sell merchandise for his own account, except perhaps the ice. He invested very little of his money in the bank and other stock company ventures in New Orleans which collapsed during the panic of 1837–42. He did not speculate in the volatile cotton futures market as did most of his competitors, nor did he purchase a plantation in the style of prosperous Crescent City businessmen, and thereby fall victim to the economic ills of Southern agriculture and the slave system. In short, he held himself aloof from most of the dangerous aspects of New Orleans commercial life.

Touro's manner of living, to the end of his days, was simple and frugal, again in contrast to the usual New Orleans style of elegance and extravagance. At first, when he could not afford a home of his own, he lived with a number of other bachelors at 35 Conde street. Taking rooms in the same house in 1805 were the Chaplain of the Ursuline Convent and Vicar-General of the Diocese, the Very Reverend Jean Baptiste Olivier; the young merchant Richard Clague; and Alexander Milne, the Scots speculator who built the pleasure resort of Milneburg.[16] In later years, Touro lived in the same building as his store or warehouse; still later he lived, as we shall see, in a few rooms in the former rectory of Christ Church. But never did he build the sort of mansion which less successful men felt compelled to do in order to satisfy their social aspirations, let alone the kind of castle on which Alexander Milne lavished his fortune. It would be unfair to imply that Touro was a miser in the conventional sense, but it is instructive to observe that of the total assessed value of his estate of $928,774.74, probably a very low evaluation, only $1,960 was assigned to his personal possessions and furnishings—and this included silverware valued at $805 and about $600 worth of wines stored in his cellar. His carpets, chairs, hat stand, bedstead, crockery and glassware, and office furniture, were listed at $550 in the inventory. No books, jewelry or other valuables were included among his possessions.[17] It is not an occasion for surprise that a moderately successful businessman, who had no family and few personal friends, who indulged himself in no pleasures so far as we know, who was shrewd enough to invest his income wisely, should have accumulated the kind of wealth which Touro owned at the end of his life. Rabbi Isaac Leeser was writing from personal observation when he reported on Touro's style of living and saving:

"Mr. T. was not a man of brilliant mind; on the contrary, he was slow, and not given to bursts of enthusiasm, as little as he was fond of hazardous speculations; and he used to say that he could only be said to have *saved* a fortune by strict economy, while others had spent one by their liberal expenditures . . . he had no tastes for the wasteful outlay of means on enjoyments which he had no relish for. He [had] thus the best wines always by him, without drinking them himself; his table, whatever delicacies it bore, had only plain and simple food for him. . . ."[18]

Touro's wealth was not secured through commercial genius, or through skyrocketing profits, but gradually, through unremitting attention to his work, and through strict economies in his personal life. Perhaps he was always haunted by the private fear of a repetition of the penury in which his early years had been spent, when first his family existed on the meager dole provided by the British army, and when later he himself had to live on his uncle's charity.

Perhaps, too, it was his homeless childhood which led him to invest most of his savings in real estate. By 1812, he had already purchased a tract of land eighteen leagues below New Orleans. His earliest acquisition of a lot and building in the city itself which we have been able to discover in the notarial records took place in 1818. Property which he bought in 1821 was still among his holdings when he died. Confident in the future of New Orleans, he purchased lot after lot, virtually all in the commercial center of the city, paid cash, erected buildings, and collected rents. He appears not to have mortgaged any of his property; hence he was unaffected by the periodic economic slumps and panics which at one time or another drove most of New Orleans' businessmen into bankruptcy. Almost three-quarters of the assessed value of his estate was invested in these properties and buildings which he had bought and developed over the long years. He had indeed, as Leeser reported, "*saved a fortune*," and it in turn increased in real value because the growth of New Orleans continued throughout the years. His net assets continued to increase because he never retired from business activity, as the Thwing papers demonstrate; at the very end of his years he was still giving directions to his Northern agents about the ventures in which he was engaged, mostly far away from New Orleans by that time.[19]

During his early years Touro was an interested participant in matters of civic, political and business concern.[20] In 1804 he signed petitions which recommended candidates for the federal posts of port collector and port inspector.[21] In 1807 he served as a member of a grand jury which denounced military excesses in New Orleans, and criticized the city fathers for permitting too many taverns and gaming houses to flourish in town.[22] In March of the same year he joined one hundred and forty of the "most wealthy and respectable inhabitants of this city" in congratulating Governor Claiborne and General James Wilkinson on the discovery of the Aaron Burr plot, expressing confidence in Wilkinson's motives.[23] A month later Touro and forty-four other merchants petitioned Governor Claiborne to reappoint George T. Ross to the office of sheriff from which he had resigned during the Wilkinson-Burr controversy.[24] In 1812 Touro served on a special grand jury with some of the leading citizens of New Orleans including Angélica Monsanto's son David Urquhart, who acted as foreman, the banker Beverly Chew, Touro's former neighbor Alexander Milne, and his friend R. D. Shepherd. This grand jury submitted some very strongly worded presentments on such important subjects as the Baratarian smugglers and pirates, buccaneering vessels in New Orleans, and the neglect of patients in the local marine hospital.[25] In 1812 and 1813, Touro and Shepherd were elected to the board of directors of the Bank of Orleans.[26] But the Battle of New Orleans seems to have drawn a veil over his willingness or ability to participate in civic activities. Thereafter he appears to have withdrawn from positions of public responsibility; he did not again sign political petitions, serve on grand juries and public committees, or join the boards of commercial institutions.

Well known is Alexander Walker's florid description, in his book on Andrew Jackson and the Battle of New Orleans, which was published just two years after Touro's death, of Touro's service in carrying ammunition for the Louisiana Militia, his being wounded and left to die on the field of action, and his friend Rezin Shepherd's courage in carrying him off to New Orleans in order to secure medical care for him at the risk of being charged with desertion.[27] Touro was so grateful to Shepherd that he appointed him "the universal legatee of the rest and residue of my estate," identifying him as "my dear, old and devoted friend . . . to whom, under Divine Providence, I was greatly indebted for the preservation of my life when I was wounded on the 1st of January, 1815." Shepherd's share of the estate amounted to at least a half-million dollars and may have been as much as $750,000.[28]

Rezin Davis Shepherd (1784–1865), the great-great-grandfather of Senator Leverett Saltonstall, was a Virginian who came to New Orleans in 1802 as the representative of the Baltimore merchant William Taylor, whose niece he married a few years later. Rezin and his brother James were, apparently, more venturesome merchants than Touro, dealing in far larger sums than he, but this did not prevent Judah's participation in some of their transactions. The friendship which had been established between them in the early years was cemented by Shepherd's rescue of Touro. Although Shepherd was away from New Orleans for many years, during the period 1817–37, they remained close; Touro gave Shepherd his power of attorney in connection with the settlement of the affairs of both his brother Abraham, who died in Medford, Massachusetts, in 1822, and his sister Rebecca, who died in New York in 1833. When Rezin's brother, James Shepherd, died in 1837, the deceased was indebted to Touro for $138,752. James's estate was the subject of a bitterly contested suit which lasted beyond both Rezin's and Judah's lifetimes. Rezin's relatives accused Rezin of forgery, fraud, violation of confidence and utter rapaciousness. Nonetheless, Judah maintained his belief in Rezin's integrity, continued to take part in business dealings with him, and gave Shepherd rooms in his home from 1837 on. The relationship was not one-sided, motivated only by Touro's gratitude to Shepherd; Shepherd had many reasons to be thankful for his friend's confidence, hospitality, financial backing in business ventures, and his moral support in the controversies over James's estate.[29]

Was Touro's wound of any significance other than the strengthening of the friendship with Shepherd? Walker says that Touro was "struck on the thigh by a twelve pound shot, which produced a ghastly and dangerous wound, tearing off a large mess of flesh . . . Mr. Touro long survived this event, never marrying because of the wound." There is an oral tradition in New Orleans, supported by at least one published account, that the wound included damage to Touro's sexual organs, and that this was why he never married. But in 1815 Touro was already forty years old. Is it not more likely that he had already become accustomed to bachelorhood, and that the wound had nothing to do with his failure to marry? Perhaps the hardships of childhood days had implanted something in the emotions of Judah and his brother Abraham which denied both of them the warmth and comfort of marriage. Although tradition reports that Judah did participate in the gay social life of New Orleans prior to 1815, there is no record of his ever having served on the public ball committees which were so popular during the period. But we are still faced by the problem of his apparent withdrawal from public affairs after 1815: this might be explained by shame over the wound, if indeed it made him less than a man, or by a psychic trauma which resulted from his brush with death in the searing cauldron of battle—many another man has been emotionally crippled by the shock and fear of war. But all this is guess-work. We can only note that there was an apparent change in Touro's personality after the battle.[30]

Deferring a consideration of Touro's record of support for Christian churches, until we discuss his relationship to the establishment of a Jewish congregation, we shall now attempt to evaluate Touro's record as a philanthropist. It may well be true that he was secretly generous to individuals in need of help, as has frequently been asserted. Touro's pensioner, Parson Theodore Clapp, estimated that his patron gave away more than $20,000 in private charity.[31] One hopes that Clapp was more accurate in this report than in his assertion that Touro ordered his inheritance of about $80,000 from his sister Rebecca to be distributed to charity. No such instructions have been found among the legal papers relating to Rebecca's estate, nor in the powers of attorney which Touro gave to Rezin Shepherd. It is entirely possible that Shepherd was given private instructions to dispose of the money after the estate had been completely settled, but that was still going on seven years after Rebecca's death, and it seems unlikely that there would be no publicity attached to the contribution of so large a sum of money to public institutions.[32] Jewish tradition encourages the giving of charity in secret—but not as a substitute for the support of public institutions and agencies. If Touro was indeed a philanthropist, it is indeed strange that he was more than sixty years old before he made his first dramatic contribution to a public cause, the fund for the completion of the Bunker Hill Monument, about 1839, and that it was only two years before his death that he established the Touro Infirmary, his single significant contribution to the people of New Orleans during his lifetime.

The so-called Touro Free Library Society for which he was supposed to have offered to erect a building never became an actuality. Organized in 1824, perhaps to spite the directors of the New Orleans Library Society which had been in existence as a stock company since 1806, the Library was housed in Parson Clapp's Presbyterian Church and the books were available for use only for one hour on Saturday afternoon and for two hours on Sunday morning before services. One cannot escape the suspicion that the men who constituted the board of directors of the Touro Library—such leading citizens as Parson Clapp, Judge James Workman, Beverly Chew and Maunsel White— had named the institution for Touro in the hope of wheedling a large sum of money from him. It is peculiar that Touro's own name was not listed among the incorporators of the library, that he was not elected a director, and that no mention of his name was included in the public appeals for contributions of money and books. Touro seems to have been a victim of the library proposal rather than its benefactor or sponsor, to judge from the available information.[33]

New Orleans did not develop until quite late the philanthropic and social service agencies which were so characteristic of the Protestant-oriented cities of the North; its Catholic tradition tended to place responsibility for works of charity on the shoulders of priests and nuns. But there were occasional appeals in the press for support for worthy causes. During the 1830's, for instance, a number of campaigns for funds were publicized, to which other Jews contributed and for which they worked on committees. Among these were a fund for the assistance of victims of the July, 1830, Revolution in France; a subscription to help people who had lost their homes in a fire in Fayetteville, North Carolina, in 1831; a collection for the relief of the victims of the great cholera epidemic in New Orleans in 1832; and a fund for the victims of the Charleston fire of 1838. Touro's name did not appear in the newspapers even once in the lists of sponsors of these appeals, or in the tabulations of donors and their contributions; nor was he ever active in the work of the well-known Howard Association, organized in 1837 by a group of dedicated men (including some Jews) in order to render personal service to the victims of the periodic epidemics which made life in New Orleans so dangerous during the summer and early fall. Since the only anonymous contributions to these causes which were listed in the newspapers were of the five dollar variety, it is unlikely that Touro's retiring nature compelled the omission of his name from these lists; indeed, as in the case of the Bunker Hill Monument, the names of the donors of large anonymous contributions generally became known to the public—such news is too important to remain secret for very long.[34]

So far as can be discovered, the amounts which Touro contributed for public purposes, other than sectarian religious institutions and projects, which we defer discussing, were as follows:

1839–40: $10,000 to the Bunker Hill Monument

1843: $1,000 to the Redwood Library of Newport, plus whatever sum would be necessary to pave the sidewalk

1852: $40,000 as payment for the Paulding estate which he converted into the Touro Infirmary; he retained title to this property, however, until his death.[35]

It would be inappropriate to include in this list of philanthropic activities the check for $1,000 which Touro gave to the Firemen's Charitable Association in 1852 following a fire in which the prompt appearance of several volunteer fire companies saved "a considerable portion of my property;" this was more a reward than a disinterested beneficence.[36]

As we review the record, the conclusion seems inescapable that Touro's reputation as a philanthropist stems largely from the munificence of the bequests which were included in his will—approximately $483,000, incomparably larger than the sums he gave away during his lifetime.

Another aspect of Touro's philanthropic way of life is said to be revealed by his aversion to slavery. He is reported frequently to have purchased slaves "for the sole purpose of liberating them," and to have set some of them up in business.[37] A close search of the New Orleans notarial records and newspaper advertisements does indeed demonstrate that Touro did not deal extensively in slaves, unlike other commission merchants in New Orleans. He did own one slave at the time of the 1805 New Orleans census[38] but information about the disposition of that slave has not been uncovered. The very fact that Touro was in business in a slave society brought him into constant contact with the system. In 1809, for instance, fifteen slaves belonging to a bankrupt firm, of which he was a creditor, were sold at auction; some of the proceeds of the sale came to him.[39] More to the point, in 1812 he advertised rewards for the apprehension of seven Negro runaways from the planta-tion of one of his clients. If he was to serve his customers he had no choice but to participate in such activities as these.[40] Much of his merchandise was, of course, sold for use by slaves, including dry goods imported to New Orleans from the cotton mills of New England to be made into clothing for slaves.[41] Neither Touro nor any other New Orleans merchant could escape involvement in the daily workings of the slave system.[42]

Two very intriguing pieces of information have recently come to light, however, which relate to Touro's friendship with free Negroes. One was Ellen Wilson, a f.w.c. (free woman of color, in the terminology of New Orleans), for whom Touro purchased a home in his own name. Found among Touro's effects, after his death, was a note for $4,100 due to the same woman from J. G. Osgood. There is no way of identifying Ellen Wilson; she may have been one of Rezin Shepherd's slaves whom Touro is reported to have set free. Enough, however, to know that she is the only person for whose property and financial affairs Touro was willing to assume responsibility, so far as we can judge from the inventory of his estate. If we were dealing with anyone other than Touro, we would suspect that Ellen was his mistress; but all of the insight which we have been able to gain into his character contradicts such a suggestion. Just as little significance should attach to the presence in New Orleans of a John Touro during the period 1855–65.[43]

Far more significant is the fact that Pierre André Destrac Cazenave, one of the executors of Touro's will, and a bene-ficiary to the amount of $10,000 was a mulatto. In 1853, when he was thirty years old, Cazenave was a commission merchant. Identified in the R. G. Dun and Company records as the former confidential clerk and "pet" of Touro, he was reported to be worth $20,000 in 1854, and $100,000 in 1864, when he con-ducted an undertaking and livery establishment with his four sons. The 1866 R. G. Dun and Company report says that the Cazenave family were "Quadroons—Creoles, more properly now called colored persons." One of the Cazenave sons was Recorder of Births, Marriages and Deaths in 1875. Strange that none of the writers of the newspaper articles about Touro saw fit to comment on the fact that Touro had appointed a mulatto as an executor of his will, and described him, together with Rezin Shepherd, Aaron Keppel Josephs (a well-known Jewish attorney of New Orleans) and Gershom Kursheedt (Touro's adviser on Jewish affairs), as "my trusty and esteemed friends." Far more than any traditions or undocumented reports of Touro's interest in Negroes, does his regard for Cazenave demonstrate a remarkable spirit of dedication to the principle of human equality in an absolute and practical manner.[44]

Even if Judah Touro was not the heroic figure who has been glorified in order to feed American Jewry's well-known craving for "great men," he should still be recognized for what he was, a good, loyal, industrious human being. In a city like New Orleans, where simplicity was rare, Touro lived "a life remarkable for its monotonous simplicity."[45] He was not a leader of men in any sense, either communal or economic, but he was a decent man who pursued his own quiet, sober, moral way without participating in the extravagance, high fashion, conspicuous consumption and frenzied speculation which were so characteristic of life in New Orleans during his period of activity. Perhaps his noblest quality was his dogged loyalty—to Cazenave, the mulatto, to whom he offered a rare kind of friendship; to Rezin Shepherd, whom he supported in the bitter legal feuds over James's will and estate, despite Touro's aversion to law courts;[46] to the city of his birth, to which he was so generous in his will; to the memory of his brother Abraham, to whose three favorite charities he left bequests in his own will; to his cousin Catherine and the children of two other Hays cousins, whom he remembered in his will; and to the few close friends and supporters in New Orleans and elsewhere to whom he left token bequests in the will drawn up in the closing days of his life. These fine personal qualities should not be overshadowed by the heroic proportions of the philanthropic aspect of his bequests.

III

Jewish Settlers from 1803 to 1815

During the 1790's, as thousands of Americans poured across the Appalachians from the Atlantic seaboard, to establish farms in the Ohio and Mississippi valley areas, it became obvious that the swiftest outlet to the most desirable markets for their produce was down the Mississippi River and through the port of New Orleans. In 1795 the Spanish authorities reluctantly granted the right of commercial deposit to American citizens, but they were never happy about the arrangement and withdrew it in 1802. When Spain's cession of Louisiana to the French in 1800, at first kept secret, became public knowledge, some Americans became so agitated that they began to talk of war with France in order to secure American control over the port of New Orleans. President Thomas Jefferson's original intent in pursuing the more pacific course of undertaking discussions with the French was not to bargain for the vast Louisiana area, but only for New Orleans. Jefferson believed that the city would be the most important commercial center in the world: "with Boston, Baltimore, New York and Philadelphia on the left; Mexico on the right, Havana in front, and the immense valley of the Mississippi in the rear, no such position for the accumulation and perpetuity of wealth and power ever existed." Jefferson's instructions to James Monroe, who assisted Robert Livingston, the American Minister to France, in the negotiations, related specifically to the purchase of New Orleans and the assurance of free navigation on the Mississippi River. Napoleon's decision to dispose of the entire territory, on the other hand, was motivated by his fear that the colony would be seized by the British, upon the anticipated outbreak of war, and that British imperial resources would then be increased by the wealth of the productive Mississippi Valley. Napoleon preferred to sell the area to the inoffensive Americans than to permit it to fall into the hands of the British; the Americans for their part were willing to pay fifteen million dollars for this colonial empire because they regarded it as the key to the broader expansion of their commerce and trade.[1]

A similar dream of wealth and success drew thousands of Americans and Europeans, every year, to this Creole town which began its history under the government of the United States in 1803 with something less than 8,000 white residents. By 1810, ten thousand additional white inhabitants had swelled the population; new immigrants already outnumbered the French and Spanish Creoles. Later proportionate increases were equally large. New Orleans continued to exert the fascination of an El Dorado, an economic gold mine, on the imagination of bold, ambitious men throughout the ante-Bellum period. It was a boom and bust town, the most exciting, most cosmopolitan and exotic city in the United States. We shall, in this chapter, describe the background and experiences of those Jews who came to New Orleans and its environs in the period before the Battle of New Orleans.[2] Each one had his own personal emotional motivations for traveling so great a distance, whether from older settlements in the United States, or farther afield, from Europe. But all of them made their livelihood in some form of commerce. It was, therefore, the same lodestar of economic opportunity and personal success which drew them to the Crescent City in the years following the Louisiana Purchase, which had motivated the American government to acquire the city in the first place.

1. BENJAMIN S. SPITZER AND DAVID G. SEIXAS

By September, 1804, when he signed a petition which recommended a candidate for the position of Collector of the Port, Benjamin S. Spitzer had come to New Orleans to try his luck. Ben was probably the son of Barend Moses Spitzer, who arrived in America in 1770 and became a prominent Mason, a close friend of Haym Salomon, and a loyal member of Mikveh Israel Congregation of Philadelphia. The father died on Sullivan's Island, near Charleston, in 1796. Spitzer's partner in this New

Orleans venture was Israel Baer Kursheedt of New York City, who arrived in the United States the same year that Spitzer's father had died. So far as we know, Kursheedt did not himself come to New Orleans; he must have invested some money in the business, and may have been responsible for purchasing goods in New York City and supervising their shipment to Louisiana. But his interest in the business was represented on the spot by his seventeen-year-old brother-in-law, David G. Seixas, a son of the Revolutionary War patriot *hazan*, Gershom Mendes Seixas.[3]

Spitzer and Seixas lived at 21 Rue St. Louis; they owned three slaves, a woman who cooked their meals and kept house for them, and two males who worked in their store. B. S. Spitzer and Company, as the firm was called, dealt in dry goods, notions, foodstuffs such as coffee and sugar, liquor and other commodities. They also invested in the schooner *Nancy*, and owned the building on Condé street where the Public Baths were located. Their business was soon in trouble. Kursheedt dissolved the partnership in April, 1806, and Seixas tried to sell the Public Baths. He obviously failed to do so, because in September, 1806, suits were entered against Spitzer, and, eventually, everything—merchandise, furniture, the slaves, the ship and the Public Baths—was sold at sheriff's auction. Spitzer had not gone broke, however; in June he purchased the ship *Jane* for $6,000, and this ship was not seized for the creditors' benefit. How long Seixas remained in New Orleans is uncertain; the final notice of his presence refers to testimony which he offered at a trial in October, 1806. All of the firm's debts were not met by the sale of the property, and, as late as November, 1807, judgments were still being sought against Spitzer. Nothing further is known of him. Once he had done his best to straighten out his affairs, he probably left town for more promising horizons. On the other hand, David Seixas returned to town in 1829 and again in 1832 to sell the printers' ink he was manufacturing in Cincinnati. Three of Israel Kursheedt's children came back to the scene of this early failure, thirty years afterwards; one of them, Gershom, became the champion of Jewish vitality in the city during the 1840's, as we shall presently see.[4]

2. JACOB HART, WITH SOME INCIDENTAL COMMENT ON JEAN LAFFITE

Although they may have hoped to become permanent residents of the city, Spitzer and Seixas remained in New Orleans for little more than two years. So far as we can tell from newspaper and notarial records, Jacob Hart of New York City was probably the next Jew to come to New Orleans, in the fall of 1804 or the spring of 1805. Hart, who lived in New Orleans until his death on December 20, 1849, was born in Philadelphia on March 29, 1781, the son of Jacob Naphtali Hart and Leah Nathan.[5] The father had emigrated to America from Germany in 1775, stayed briefly in Baltimore, then moved to Philadelphia where he married, established himself in business, made financial contributions to the Revolutionary cause which were acknowledged by Congress, and took an active role in the affairs of Congregation Mikveh Israel. After the war he settled in New York City and held office in Congregation Shearith Israel, whose school young Jacob attended. The son was still in New York City in the summer of 1804, when he and his father attended services and made an offering.[6]

Young Jacob Hart was in New Orleans before June, 1805, when he shipped a cargo worth $3,600 to the West Indies on a schooner which ran into foul luck and was captured by a British man-of-war which in turn was taken by a Spanish ship. Hart's vessel ended up in the Mexican port of Campeche. In October, 1805, Hart accepted a settlement of $2,400 for his losses from the New Orleans Insurance Company.[7] It is probable that Hart's father and family were using their money and influence to help him get established, because his business grew much more rapidly than Touro's did. During 1806, for instance, the newspapers record the names of only two ships for which Touro was agent, but four for Hart; only one cargo was consigned to Touro, while Hart received eight. In 1806 Hart was already the owner of the schooner *President*.[8] Over the next few years, his own ships and those for which he acted as the New Orleans agent, made voyages to Kingston, Charleston, Baltimore, New

York City, Pensacola, Havana and Santiago, Cuba, and one was advertised as being available for any port in the United States or Europe. His cargoes included the usual variety of imports: dry goods, furniture, wines and liquors, brandied fruits, logwood, mahogany, gunpowder, bagging, playing cards, soap, paper, anchors, paints, candles, gigs, salt, codfish, vinegar, olives, raisins, sugar and coffee. A typical advertisement of Hart's goods appeared in the *Louisiana Gazette*, on February 10, 1807:

> "JUST RECEIVED AND FOR SALE,
> By the subscriber, at his store, No. 16, Chartres street
>
> Superfine red ground and fancy calicoes
> Brittanias and Dowlas
> Long lawns
> Checks and stripes, chintz shawls
> Printed pocket handkerchiefs
> Toweling, table cloths and napkins
> French broad cloths blue and black
> Crapes assorted colours
> Estopillas, French and English
> Men's beaver gloves
> Morocco skins, blue pulicat hdks.
> 45 Tons Campeachy logwood
> 22 Hogsheads Codfish
> 6 Pipes Madeira Wine
> 300 Boxes Marseilles Soap
> Brandy and Gin
>
> JACOB HART"

Hart bought and sold ships and real estate, advertised the availability of bills of exchange on New York, and fulfilled the usual responsibilities of a shipping agent and commission broker.[9] Hart had more to do with slaves than Touro. In July, 1808, he advertised three Saint-Domingue slaves for sale, a female cook and two fishermen; and, in November, 1808, he offered the public an opportunity to buy a twenty-four-year-old Negro who spoke English and French fluently, was a good tailor and also "has been accustomed to take care of horses." In 1810 he bought two slaves for 1,400 pesos from Captain Christoval de Armas of the Baton Rouge settlement in Spanish West Florida.[10]

Hart was the only Jew who was included in the directory of merchants which was published in B. Lafon's *Louisiana Yearbook* of 1809—but perhaps this was only because others were not interested in paying the fee which was required for the inclusion of a name.[11] At any rate, Hart was accorded some of those evidences of recognition which symbolized a man's acceptance into the mercantile community of New Orleans: during 1807–1808, he served twice as a representative of the creditors of bankrupt merchants; and in June, 1809, he was a member of the monthly committee of the New Orleans Chamber of Commerce. He took an active interest in the issues of the time: in 1807, he and Touro signed complimentary addresses to General Wilkinson and Governor Claiborne; on January 25, 1808, he was the only Jew who added his name to a petition which urged President Jefferson to appoint Captain Thomas Pollock to the command of the revenue cutter of the port.[12] Hart was also one of the young men who promoted the fancy balls which enlivened the social season: during the winter of 1806–1807 he served on the board of managers of the Tuesday night dances, and in 1807 he was one of four men who were in charge of the arrangements for the Washington's Birthday Ball.[13]

The strategic location of New Orleans made it a natural focus for a host of political and military plots designed to foment revolutions throughout the Caribbean area. The arrival of large numbers of refugees from Saint-Domingue, and of opponents of Napoleon's domination of Spain from Spanish colonial possessions in the area, stimulated a number of conspiracies during the first decade of the nineteenth century similar to the filibustering plots of later years. In 1809 the Mexican officials heard rumors from Louisiana that an expedition was being formed in New Orleans for the invasion of Mexico. An informer in New Orleans sent word to Mexico that Jacob Hart's schooner, the *Célestine*, which was cleared from New Orleans in the spring of 1809 for Laguna de Termión in Yucatán, was really one of the vessels being fitted out for participation in the invasion. Upon arrival in Mexico, the ship was confiscated and Hart's supercargo, Jean Robert, was arrested. Governor Claiborne protested to the Governor of Yucatán, in a letter dated July 17, 1809, that "there is no expedition preparing in this Territory against the Spanish Dominions . . . ," and denied that Robert and the others were "spies in the service of the American Government." Nonetheless, Robert and the officers and crew of Hart's ship were held in Yucatán for another six months. In November, Hart conferred with Claiborne and gave him a letter which the Governor sent on to Washington:

New Orleans 16th Novr. 1809

"His Excellency Wm. C. C. Claiborne
Governor of the Territory of Orleans.

Sir,

I honoured myself by addressing your Excellency on the 17th July last acquainting you of the seizure of the Schooner Celestine & her Cargo belonging to me & the Imprisonment of the Super-cargo Mr. John Robert Junr the Captain & Crew all Citizens of the United States of America, in consequence of a Letter received there & supposed to be written by a person in this City—purporting the arrival of an expedition here destined to act against the Spanish Possessions & I entreated your Excellency to address yourself officially to the proper authorities at Laguna— in contradiction of such nefarious reports & I had every expecta- tion that your representations would eventuate in the restoration of my property & the release of the Supercargo Captain & Crew of the Schooner but experiencing a disappointment (which may have arisen from the miscarriage of your Letters) I am again compelled to trouble your Excellency as an opportunity presents itself which may be depended upon for the carriage of any further representations which you may see fit to make upon this subject.—

I have the honour to remain

Your very obedt Servt

Jacob Hart"

Claiborne's second appeal to Yucatán was successful. The schooner returned to New Orleans, and, on April 14, 1810, Hart announced that Robert had become a partner in his business. In less than five months the partnership was dissolved;

97

the reason did not become clear until November 5, 1810, when Robert and his friend Ange Michel Brouard were charged by a grand jury with piracy. One of the writers on the Baratarian smugglers reports that Robert and Hart began a career of piracy in order to seek revenge "not upon French imperialists but upon their Spanish captors. They entered into the trade of French piracy that within the next four years gave a permanent celebrity to Barataria and its smuggler gangs." This historian is certainly mistaken in believing that Hart had been on the *Célestine* and had been imprisoned; and it has been impossible to find Hart's name mentioned anywhere in the records which concern Laffite's exploits. Of course, the New Orleans merchants who dealt with Laffite and bought his smuggled and pirated goods for resale in their stores were not likely to advertise the fact, nor did Governor Claiborne ever take any action against them. Still, consideration must be given to the fact of Hart's partnership with Robert. There are only two explanations for the sudden breakup: that Hart took Robert into his business, on his return from Mexican captivity, as a reward for his loyalty and as recompense for his unpleasant experience, but discharged him as soon as he discovered that Robert had become involved with Laffite; or, that Hart had known all along about Robert's activities, but, in order to protect himself, announced public dissolution of the partnership when he heard that Robert had been apprehended, while he continued secretly to participate in the profitable business end of Barataria. Either of these possibilities may be factual; unfortunately no further evidence has been discovered which may cast light upon Hart's relationship to Laffite's exploits. But he was the only Jewish businessman who seems in any way to have been connected with Barataria.[14]

This is probably a more logical place than any other to digress for a report on Laffite's Jewish antecedents and connections. Most authorities on Laffite accept as authentic the account that, after his mother's death, he was reared by his grandmother, and that his grandfather had been done to death by the Inquisition or, at least, had died in prison while in the custody of the Inquisition. One authority gives the grandmother's name as Maria Zora Nadrimal. Another says that she "planted a deep hatred of Spain in her grandsons."[15] A controversial document which purports to be Laffite's journal and autobiography refers to this grandmother's tales as the root of Jean's hatred of the Spanish:

"... My mother died before I can remember and my maternal grandmother, who lived with us, became a mother to me ... My grandmother was of Spanish-Israelite descent ... My mother's father had been an alchemist with a good practice and patronage in Spain. He was a free-thinking Jew with neither Catholic faith nor traditional adherence to the Jewish synagogue. But this did not prevent him from dying of starvation in prison for refusing to divulge the technical details which the Inquisition demanded from all Jews. Grandmother told me repeatedly of the trials and tribulations her ancestors had endured at the time of the Spanish Inquisition ... Grandmother's teachings ... inspired in me a hatred of the Spanish crown and all the persecutions for which it was responsible—not only against the Jews. ..."

Anyone who knows anything of the history of the Jews of Spain realizes that unconverted Jews could not live in Spain after 1492, and that synagogues ceased to function at that time. The grandfather could only have been a Marrano "new" Christian, a secret Jew who outwardly conformed to the Catholic faith while retaining his conscientious allegiance to Judaism; that he may have been an alchemist is possible, since such theories were still in vogue. But Laffite was not expected to be an historian on such matters; his garbled description of his family's Marrano background need not be regarded as evidence that the volume is a forgery.[16]

Another interesting Jewish reference in the alleged Laffite autobiography is the report of a discussion with the well-known Jewish merchant of New York City, Isaac Moses:

"I had a conversation with Isaac Moses about three years before his death. In 1815 he dissuaded me from trying to recover some of my profits. He states that he had never been reimbursed for his financial aid at the time of the Revolution against the English. He stated also that S. H. Solomon likewise had never been re-imbursed for the economical assistance which he gave to General Washington. That conversation with Mr. Moses in 1815 weakened my constancy of purpose in Washington at that time. ..."[17]

Isaac Moses, who was seventy-three years old in 1815, is not known to have been in New Orleans at that time. But he was indeed a patriot who had supported the Revolutionary cause with money and trade goods; he was one of that band of Jewish merchants which also included Haym Salomon (not S. H. Solomon as the "Journal" has it) who figure largely in Robert Morris' record of the new government's financial tribulations and transactions. But, if Moses had not been in New Orleans, and Laffite was never in New York, how would the latter ever have heard of Moses and Salomon? Some of Haym's children and grandchildren were in and out of Mobile and New Orleans in later years; one son, Ezekiel, as we shall see, died in New Orleans in 1821. But we know of no opportunity which they might have had to meet Laffite. The possibility suggests itself that Jacob Hart might have told Laffite about Haym Salomon and Isaac Moses, for he knew both families: Jacob's father and Isaac Moses were active at the same time in the affairs of Shearith Israel Congregation in New York City, and Jacob's sister Ella or Ellen married Haym Salomon's son, Haym M., in 1809. If, on the other hand, the diary is a forgery, its actual author must have had some special reason to be aware of Isaac Moses' financial support of the Revolution, and of his death in 1818. Isaac Moses' patriotic activities were far less publicized than Haym Salomon's; but in 1827, Jacob's brother-in-law, Haym M. Salomon, instituted a campaign to regain from the federal government the large sums of money his father is supposed to have loaned to Congress.[18]

Whether or not Jacob Hart gained added profits through participating in Laffite's illegal trade, he became quite prosperous. One after another, he brought his brothers to New Orleans from New York City to work with him. David, four years younger than Jacob, was in New Orleans by 1810, for the brothers were living together on Royal street when the federal census was taken that year; David, not Jacob, is listed in *Whitney's New Orleans Directory for 1811*. The youngest Hart brother, Joseph, died in New Orleans on August 19, 1817. Nathan must have joined Jacob and David no later than 1819, for in June of that year, before a trip to New York City, Nathan gave Jacob his power of attorney. Benjamin and Leon, two other brothers, may also have been there at that time. In the 1820 census, Jacob, living then on Chartres street, listed as members of his household two males between sixteen and twenty-six (Benjamin was twenty; Nathan and Leon, twins, were twenty-three); two males between twenty-six and forty-five (David was thirty-five and Jacob himself was thirty-nine); the two males over forty-five were probably relatives or clerks of whom we have no precise information. Also listed in the census report were seven male slaves.[19]

We would not have any precise knowledge of Jacob Hart's holdings and resources if he had not gone bankrupt in 1823, a catastrophe from which he seems never to have recovered. He was the first of the prosperous Jewish merchants of New Orleans to go through the wringer, a victim of overextension and speculation, high living and incautious investments. From what we know, he was probably worth more on paper, when he was sold out by his creditors, than Touro was. The auctioneers' advertisement of the sheriff's sale listed Hart's major possessions:

"One Half of the schooner Marsouin, measuring about 25 tons burthen.

A double Hydraulic, or Water [Cotton] Press, situated at the corner of St. Charles and Gravier streets.

A Horse Press and a Hand Press [also for cotton], situated at the same place.

A quantity of Sugar Pans, &c. viz:—40 sugar Pans, 2 Pivots and 1 Cylinder, at the corner of Custom-house and Rampart streets; 10 sugar Pans in the Fauxbourg St. Mary, on land belonging to Mr. [Millaudon].

Three Horses and two Drays.

An Admission Ticket to the French Theatre.

Three Lots of Land, situated in the Fauxbourg St. Mary . . . in front of Poydras-street . . . together with the Two Houses erected thereon . . . weather boarded, and covered with short pickets.

A Lot of Land, situated on the left side of the Bayou St. John, measuring about 120 feet, in front of the Bayou, and 132 feet on Mississippi street, together with the Buildings thereon erected, viz:—

A House on Sills, filled between the posts, measuring 50 feet front by 50 feet in depth, containing four rooms on the ground floor, with a front and back gallery, and two closets on the back gallery.

A Log Kitchen divided into two compartments.

Also the following Property on the joint accounts of the said Insolvent and Mr. Charles Parent, viz:—

The undivided half of a Lot of Land, situated on the further side of Lake Pontchartrain, in the parish St. Tammany . . . measuring superficially 2,657 arpents or thereabouts, together with all the Buildings and Offices thereon erected . . .

Together with a moiety of the Stock, consisting of 4 horses, 5 oxen, 10 cows, and 15 sheep.

Also the undivided half interest in [fourteen slaves listed by name and age.]

Also, one half of the crop of Cotton, and one half interest in the boy Adam, aged about 15.

Also, the undermentioned [thirteen slaves and a five-year-old slave child] employed in the Presses described above . . ."[20]

This inventory was incomplete in that it did not include Hart's cash assets, or the shares of stock of the Louisiana Insurance Company which he had purchased in 1820, or his personal effects.[21] But it does demonstrate the extent of his business activities and investments. In addition to the import-export business which he conducted with his brothers and which was not affected by this bankruptcy, he had built up one of New Orleans' indispensable cotton presses, was engaged in sugar refining, owned some income-producing property, and was half-owner of a plantation, of which his partner was probably the resident manager. Jacob had done well, indeed, for himself and for his brothers, but now eighteen or nineteen years' effort and hard work had gone down the drain. He had come to New Orleans to find his fortune, succeeded, and now had failed.[22]

Jacob Hart did not amount to very much after the 1823 bankruptcy. Shipments of merchandise came to him occasionally, but in 1831 and again in 1832 he was in such straits that sheriff's sales were conducted to dispose of some sugar kettles that he owned, and of a steamboat of which he was part-owner with his brothers Leon, Benjamin and Nathan.[23] He was probably supported by his brothers rather than through his own efforts. For many years, from 1826 into the 1840's, he held his brother Leon's power of attorney for investment purposes, and bought and sold slaves and part-interests in steamboats.[24] Meanwhile, Nathan and Benjamin conducted a cotton press business as Jacob's successors. Nathan, who in 1820 had been able to buy a slave only because of Jacob's countersignature and guarantee,[25] was listed in the 1830 census as owning fifteen male slaves (workers, probably in the cotton press), while Jacob owned none. The press and storehouse, constituting a number of buildings in the block bounded by Gravier, St. Charles, Common and Camp streets, burned to the ground in 1830. The estimate of the loss of the buildings, and of the twelve thousand bales of cotton which went up in smoke, amounted to three hundred thousand dollars, of which only forty thousand was covered by insurance. One newspaper reported that "the flames were discovered to burst out almost simultaneously on all sides of the square which leaves no doubt of its being the work of malicious design." There is no certainty that the brothers ever reestablished themselves in the cotton press business; within a few years they had left town. Only Jacob remained, continuing to manage affairs for Leon and Nathan; once in a while he conducted a little business for himself, as in 1839, when he advertised the availability of three houses for rent, but they too may have belonged to one of his brothers.[26]

Jacob was getting along in years, and was probably too tired and discouraged to undertake anything very substantial. It must have brightened his days, however, when he was joined by another member of his family after his brothers left. In the early 1840's his sister Hetty (Esther) and her husband Alexander Marks moved to New Orleans with their children and first grandchild. (Another granddaughter, named Ida, born in 1865, years after Jacob's death, eventually married Rabbi Max Heller of Temple Sinai in New Orleans. Their son, James, became one of the luminaries of the American Reform rabbinate, a distinguished leader in Zionist circles and gifted musicologist). Alexander and Hetty's son Isaac N. Marks was a well-known New Orleans civic leader in the ante- and post-Bellum years. It was Isaac Marks and another nephew of Jacob's, Ezekiel Salomon (son of Haym M. Salomon), who signed the invitation to Jacob's funeral in 1849. On balance Jacob's business career in New Orleans was fairly typical—ambition and success, disappointment and failure; it was illustrative of the high risk of commercial ventures in the town, of overexpansion, and of the danger of giving in to the temptation to invest in a plantation. But Jacob's career spanned the years from the early days of American occupation to the eve of the Civil War, when New Orleans had become the fourth largest city in the United States and its second busiest port.[27]

3. MAURICE BARNETT

Touro, Spitzer, Seixas and Hart were all native Americans; but hard on their heels came a number of foreign Jews who left Europe for a variety of personal reasons, yet all of whom were drawn to Louisiana by the promise of economic opportunity in their new home.

It is difficult to ascertain a specific date of arrival for most immigrants. The earliest references to them in local records may have been entered months or even years after their actual arrival. Maurice Barnett, for instance, first appears in the records of Baton Rouge, still part of Spanish West Florida, on April 13, 1806, when he witnessed the will of F. Bertin. But he may have been in the town somewhat earlier, for by July 30, 1806, he was sufficiently established to be married by Fray Juan Brady to Marie Céleste Trahan, daughter of Juan Trahan and Mara Josefa Le Jeune. Eight days prior to the wedding, Maurice purchased a lot of ground, twelve arpents below the fort, for 130 pesos; the document of sale does not refer to a building on the lot, but Barnett may have thought of erecting a home at that location.

This was probably not Maurice Barnett's first American experience. The likelihood is that he was the son of Lazarus Barnett, a Dutch broker, who settled in Philadelphia in late 1782 or early 1783, went into business with another Dutch Jew, Lyon Moses, joined Mikveh Israel Congregation, had business reverses and took off for London some time in 1784, leaving his

104

creditors with the impression that he had not turned all his assets over to the syndics. Bankruptcy in Philadelphia was not enough trouble for Lazarus; he had similar problems in London in 1785. It has not been possible to discover anything else about his life in Great Britain, other than the record of his death on March 26, 1797, in the burial register of the Great Synagogue of London. Maurice had been born in Amsterdam on September 22, 1776, and was therefore six or seven years old when the family moved from Holland to Philadelphia, and twenty-one years old when his father died. The Barnett family has preserved the tradition that Maurice served in Napoleon's Grande Armée before coming to Louisiana. But in view of the years of residence in London, it would seem far more likely that any military experience which Maurice had undergone was in the British army. Maurice probably brought to Louisiana his younger brother Edward, who had been born during the family's brief stay in Philadelphia; Edward later married Modeste Ledoux of Opelousas.[28]

In Baton Rouge, Maurice Barnett was a typical merchant of the time. He was willing to trade in anything that a customer might want to buy. His accounts with one neighbor became the subject of a dispute, and are, therefore, much to our edification, listed in a court record. They cover the period from November, 1808, to April, 1810. This customer, an innkeeper and merchant, purchased the following merchandise from Barnett: food-stuffs— cheese, vinegar, salted mackerel, cloves, cinnamon, nutmeg, salt, coffee; liquor—rum, gin, anisette, cider and wines; dry goods— three and a half ells of cloth, sewing thread, one-quarter ell of black velvet, one-half ell of another kind of velvet; miscellaneous—hardware, crockery, corks, buttons, furniture, cigars, nails, paper, pots, brooms and oars.[29] Barnett obtained most of his merchandise from suppliers in New Orleans, and sometimes fell behind in his payments to them; cash was always hard to find because much of his business was on the barter system.[30] Occasionally he was unable to collect any payment at all from a customer. One such recalcitrant was the fascinating Jean Fremont who had been teaching in Baton Rouge and left town suddenly; his effects were sold on December 19, 1806, and Barnett was one of the creditors who shared in the proceeds of the auction. Jean Fremont then found his way to Norfolk, Virginia, where he fell in love with a young married woman who divorced her husband, married him and became the mother of his son, the adventurer-explorer John Charles Fremont.[31]

On June 7, 1807, Barnett's first child, Maurice junior, was born. At this time, the Barnetts may have been living with Marie's family, but during the next year, Maurice bought and sold additional real estate, including a house which he purchased in June, 1808. It may have been this house which was repaired, or a totally new home which Barnett ordered Ralph Bell to construct for him. During 1807–1808, Barnett was employing a carpenter and brick-mason, buying and storing lime, and purchasing a pick-axe. All of this activity later became the subject of a greal deal of litigation but, presumably, resulted in the completion of Barnett's new home and store.[32]

Barnett had an excitable temper. In April, 1808, Frederick Arbour, the merchant-innkeeper at Fort San Carlos in Baton Rouge, came to court with the complaint that he had asked Barnett to work out an agreement for the settlement of their accounts, but Barnett "abused and insulted me, stating that he did not wish to settle any accounts with me." Governor Carlos Louis Boucher de Grand-Pré ruled that both parties should appoint representatives who would together compare the records of indebtedness and payment. Barnett's agent was given full and free access to Arbour's records, but when Arbour's arbitrator came to Barnett to examine his papers, Barnett "denied, without any reasonable excuse, the whole of the account . . . and moreover he flew into a rage, and it was impossible . . . to continue [the] work." Barnett was then compelled to come to court and to accept the recommendation of the intermediaries, namely, that he had to pay Arbour for one hundred stakes, four pots, a hoe, a quantity of lard, some empty bottles, and some wine and gin . . . everything else in both ledgers being cancelled out. We have already examined the record of Arbour's extensive purchases from Barnett. The latter, in turn, had been indebted to the innkeeper for sums of cash advanced to him, for meals, wine and liquor served at the inn, for the entertainment of guests at Barnett's expense (perhaps customers or business associates), for boarding the carpenter and bricklayer, and especially for meals, foodstuffs and even cash given to members of Marie's large family—"oranges . . . [and] apples given to your father [in-law];" "For the ball of his mother-in-law;" "For Joseph and Louis;" "Dinner for Louis;" "For account of David;" "For pancakes with Señor Trahan;" "For Young Trahan." The high cost of supporting his wife's relatives was reason enough for Barnett's temper, but he himself seems to have enjoyed fine food: he had a dinner for four "for the Mardi Gras," was a member of "la Société du banquou"—probably an eating club—for which he was host on occasion, and enjoyed crêpes and coffee at Arbour's many times. He was also indebted to Arbour for the rent of a pirogue, the hire of a skiff for eleven days and eight ferry passages. One fact worth noting is that Barnett was in greater need of hard money than Arbour; many guests at the inn must have paid cash for their rooms and meals, but Barnett's customers bought his merchandise on credit, or paid him in kind.[33]

Barnett was evidently not only a man of hot temper, but also of some strength and capacity for leadership. In August, 1808, the Governor was told by an informer of the projected scheme of three deserters from the United States Army, who were lurking in the area, to rob a New Orleans merchant who was coming upriver to Baton Rouge. Grand-Pré appointed Barnett leader of a posse to apprehend the criminals. Although his detachment included only four Negroes and a white man, Barnett swiftly located the deserters, and "I had the three of them tied together and delivered them at three in the afternoon in the Fort of Baton Rouge without any further happening worth mentioning." Barnett is described in the record of the ensuing trial as "commandant of the military expedition." This title was a trifle high-sounding, perhaps, but Baton Rouge was a frontier post without a military establishment. The Governor had to depend on a civilian militia, and who better to call upon than this British or French veteran?[34]

Barnett may have farmed some of the land he acquired, but since he did not invest heavily in slaves—there is only one slave purchase on record—it is unlikely that he had any serious intention of becoming a planter. Most of the records of his activity in Baton Rouge concern purchases at auction, and investments in

107

and sales of real estate. In 1811, he joined eight neighbors in forming the first corporation in the area's history, a company whose sole purpose was to erect buildings on four lots which had been purchased at the auction of an estate. The investors probably had little faith in the future of the venture, for they named their corporation "Société de la Folie."[35]

The "Société de la Folie" was supposed to last twenty years. If it still flourished in 1831, Barnett had long since moved away from Baton Rouge. According to young Maurice's recollections in later years, the family was in New Orleans by 1812. The father had been, until then, the only permanent Jewish resident of Baton Rouge, probably its first, although the Monsanto brothers had lived and worked and traveled in and out of the area for a number of years, and, as we shall see, other Jewish merchants came to Baton Rouge, and one even may have had a branch store there. But Barnett was the only one who actually lived in the community for an extended period of time. Now he left for the big city, probably for economic reasons. A merchant would have far more opportunity in New Orleans than in Baton Rouge, especially since Baton Rouge no longer possessed the economic advantage of being a Spanish colonial outpost; in 1810 the local settlers had revolted against Spanish rule and established their own "Republic of West Florida," but the area was quickly annexed by the United States. If Barnett was to be an American, he probably thought he would be a more prosperous one in New Orleans.[36]

What the elder Barnett did for a living between the time of his move to New Orleans and 1830 is a matter of doubt. His name does not appear in newspaper advertisement or reports; if he was in business in New Orleans he was very quiet about it. His name continues to appear in a few Baton Rouge records, but these offer no evidence of his residence or full-time occupation.[37] It is possible that he worked for another merchant, or that he was learning the auction business in someone else's employ, or that he was traveling on the frontier. Young Maurice gives no clue, in his reminiscences, of his father's activities during this period. He reports only that he himself attended the College of Orleans when he was ten or twelve years old (it was really not even a high school), but left because of hazing by older boys, and was enrolled at Visigne's private school, where he was a student from 1817 to 1822. Maurice, Jr., was not the only son to receive a good education; two other sons— Edward (born in 1816) and Alphonse (born in 1823)—were trained to become members of that elite group of New Orleans notaries who were held in as high esteem as attorneys because Louisiana still followed the French system of legal practice.[38] In 1822, after he left school, young Maurice was apprenticed to a local merchant, then clerked with the dry goods firm of Solomon Soher and Daniel Goodman, whom we shall meet later, and, in 1825, opened his own retail store. Five years later the elder Maurice Barnett's name appears in the newspapers as a ship agent and as recipient of a shipment of specie from Mexico.[39] That same year, according to the son's recollections, "my father and I went to San Antonio, in Texas, on a trading expedition which proved to be a very profitable one, as we sold all the stock of nankeen, platillas, silks, satins, large silk shawls, etc., that we took with us. That region was, at that period, without stores." Perhaps this was what the elder Barnett had been doing throughout the years, traveling in the hinterland. Whatever his business, he had prospered. The 1830 census credits the family with eight slaves, five male and three female. Maurice's daughter Hélène, who was married to Sol Audler by then, had three female slaves and one male.

In 1831 the father opened an auction business which in time became one of the best-known in New Orleans. His sales were advertised in the newspapers almost every day. He was particularly active in the marketing of Louisiana and Texas real estate. In addition, he sold furniture and other household equipment, ships, houses and almost everything else imaginable. He was especially noted for his slave sales. The slaves were not his own property, of course; he was the agent for their owners. But, in time, his auction mart at the St. Louis Hotel—with his sign above it—"M. Barnett./ Office 40 St. Louis St."—came to be pointed out to visitors as a relic of slave days; and picture postcards of "The Old Slave Block," as it was called, were sold to the tourists who flocked to the exotic French quarter.[40]

Between 1836 and 1849, the Maurice Barnett father and son team conducted the auction business together, while Alphonse and Edward shared offices as notaries. After 1850, the elder Maurice retired from business, but young Maurice continued auctioneering, in association with his brother Lewis, with dry goods as a sideline.[41] Longevity was a distinction of the Barnett male line. The elder Maurice died just after his eighty-ninth birthday. The newspaper said that he had "enjoyed remarkably good health, and retained his mental powers until within a very short period of his death." Maurice the younger lived past his ninety-first birthday; "up to the very day of his death," reported a journalist, "his mental faculties were in nowise clouded, and his wonderful memory enabled him to recall the reminiscences of this city and state when this century was still young." Lewis, the youngest son, who was born in 1828, lived to the age of ninety. It was strong stock which Maurice Barnett Sr. had brought to Louisiana to merge with the French Catholic Trahans of Baton Rouge.[42]

4. Samuel Hermann

Much as Maurice Barnett first established himself in the Baton Rouge area before moving permanently to New Orleans, so Samuel Hermann made his earliest home on the German Coast, in St. John the Baptist Parish. The precise date of his migration to Louisiana is not given in any document, but it was some time before April 21, 1806, when he was married to Marie Emeronthe Becnel Brou in the St. John the Baptist Church at Edgard. Marie Emeronthe was a young widow whose first husband, Pierre Antoine Brou the younger, had died in April or May of 1802 after a marriage that lasted less than three years, but produced two sons. Samuel's first child, Samuel Edmond Hermann, later referred to as Samuel Hermann, Jr., was born on January 9, 1807. The elder Hermann was a native of Roedelheim, near Frankfurt-am-Main, Germany, the son of Louis Hermann and Eva Hirsch.[43]

The Becnel and Brou families had been in the German Coast area for several generations. Marie Emeronthe's great-grandfather, Ambrose Haydel or Heidel, had come to Louisiana as

110

early as 1721, from the German Electorate of Mainz. The
Becnel family arrived from London in the next generation.
Thomas Becnel married a Brou girl in 1742; they were
Emeronthe's grandparents. Her parents, Pierre Antoine Becnel
and Madeline Haydel, were married in 1772. These people
were modest farmers. We have no information about the reason
for Hermann's decision to settle there, rather than in New
Orleans. Perhaps he peddled among them, and thus met
Emeronthe. She and Pierre had lived with the Brou family,
so there was no farm for which Samuel had to take responsibility
after their marriage. Since the German Coast is not too distant
from New Orleans, it is possible that Hermann acted as agent
for some merchant in New Orleans, perhaps Hart Moses Shiff,
at whose wedding in 1813 Hermann acted as witness, and with
whom he was on close personal and business terms for many
years, or R. L. Rochelle, Shiff's partner, who served as godfather
at the baptism of Samuel's second son, Louis Florian, who was
born on February 27, 1810. When the 1810 census was taken,
Samuel was living on the right bank of the German Coast,
with four male children under ten years of age—Florestan and
Valsin Brou, Emeronthe's two sons by Pierre Brou, and Samuel
Edmond and Louis Florian,—in addition to four slaves. The
only extant records of Hermann's early commercial transactions
are slave sales in 1809 and 1811—these, together with his later
banking and financial operations in New Orleans, lead to the
conclusion that he was in some kind of trade during his residence
on the German Coast.[44]

Samuel Hermann's earliest appearances in the notarial records
of New Orleans also relate to slave trading. On May 14, 1813,
he purchased a slave for $400; on April 19, 1814, he bought
eighteen slaves from George Weinbrenner of St. John the
Baptist Parish, for $10,000. In the latter bill of sale, Hermann is
described as a "merchant, of this city." The previous year,
Weinbrenner had borrowed $5,000 from Rochelle and Shiff,
giving them a mortgage on his plantation as security for the
loan. Plantation owners were always notoriously short of cash;
only merchants and bankers could have five or ten thousand
dollars available for loans. Hermann had probably begun his
life on the German Coast as a petty trader, saved some capital,

perhaps conducted a store in the area, and then moved on to New Orleans where there was greater opportunity for business expansion.[45]

Emeronthe and Samuel lost an infant in New Orleans on February 25, 1814. A third son, Lucien, was born late in the Edgard years or early in the New Orleans period of the family's residence, but no baptismal certificate can be located in either place. A daughter, Marie Virginie, was born on September 28, 1816. One of the witnesses at Virginie's baptism in St. Louis Church in New Orleans was Asher M. Nathan, with whom Samuel was in partnership from 1818 to 1823.[46]

Samuel Hermann concentrated on finance more than the typical import-export business of the time. He dealt extensively in loans, mortgages, bank stocks, bills of exchange and real estate. He acted as a broker for planters who needed advances on their future crops, and arranged for shipments of merchandise to them, but he appears to have been less concerned with wares and commodities than with credit. He was a merchant banker of the period, a private banker, who engaged in financial transactions locally and throughout the world. But at one time or another he owned ships, two of which were named the *Hermann* and the *Florian*. His field of operations ranged from Lisbon to Hamburg and Gothenburg, from Liverpool to New York City, and from Tampico to the islands of the Caribbean. Hermann managed the affairs of other merchants, and, while Hart M. Shiff was away from town, took care of his interests. As quickly as he could, Hermann trained his sons and set them up in business. In 1828, when young Samuel was twenty-one, his father made him a partner; in 1833 they enlarged their operations by taking in two additional partners, F. W. Schmidt and John F. Oetzman. In 1834 the firm imported large amounts of specie from Mexico, $45,000 in June and $50,000 in November. By 1833 Lucien had become a partner in John Hagan and Company and earned $18,750 his first year; he later became a partner in the successor to Hagan's, Thomas Barrett and Company. Florian was a partner in Byrne, Hermann and Company, which made over $100,000 profit in 1833; in 1836, Florian was a member of a new firm, Hermann, Briggs and Company.[47]

112

The Hermann family was extremely prosperous. Already, in 1820, according to the federal census, ten slaves had served the household. In 1831, Samuel tore down the house at 820 St. Louis street in which he had lived since 1823, and built one of the showpiece homes of New Orleans. This mansion still stands today, and is used by the Christian Women's Exchange as a residence hall for single girls. It followed Yankee architectural patterns, rather than those of the French-Spanish Creole tradition. The elaborately carved Georgian doorway opens on a broad center hall which reaches back, beyond several high-ceilinged parlors on either side, to a gracefully curving stairway leading to the second floor. Past the stairs are doorways which lead from a broad veranda to an open courtyard, planted with shade and fruit trees and formal gardens. Among the out-buildings are a narrow, three-story structure which was used for bachelor visitors, the usual slave habitations and a large stable, the latter used now as a gift shop. Characteristic New Orleans galleries appear in front of the home over the entrance way, and at the rear of the second floor. Hermann paid $15,205 for the construction of the home, and an additional $5,000 for the three-story quarters in the rear. In this luxurious home, Carl Kohn, the nephew of Hermann's friend, Samuel Kohn, attended a party which he described in a letter dated March 7, 1833:

"... By the by I must not forget to tell you of a most magnificent soiree M. Hermann gave last week, but was unfortunately very much thwarted by the weather, which that day, and that only one for a fortnight before and after proved most wretchedly bad, he was thus prevented of illuminating his court, and showing his Fireworks, which had already been prepared. But nevertheless out of three hundred and fifty persons invited, very few failed to come—it was no doubt the finest party that had ever been given here, his commodious house, splendid Furniture, and Mr. Hermann's own good *nack* giving him every facility of making it as agreeable as it could possibly have been made. ... ."[48]

A few weeks later Carl complained to his uncle Samuel, who was then living in Paris, that Marie Virginie was showing great coolness toward him. Samuel had sent Carl some music from

Paris, in response to Carl's importunate request, and Samuel sent two sets.

"... I have communicated to Miss Hermann, that you wished her to play a duet with me, which you chose expressly to do in which she *acquiesced*, but only acquiesced—the fact Miss H. behaved most unaccountably cold to me ever since my return from Mobile, which rather startled me in the beginning and made me think that I must have made myself guilty of some gross neglect toward her. However I am now convinced that I could never have given Miss Hermann any serious cause for treating me with such marked coldness ... Were [she] a man, I would long have asked for an explanation but with a lady it is a delicate business. I may however yet question her about it, should I have an opportunity to play that duo with her. Mr. & Mrs. H. are as kind to me as ever, but you may well think that I can not visit the house as frequently and with as much pleasure as I otherwise might do. ...."

If the Hermann and Kohn families were hoping for a match between Carl and Virginie, they were disappointed. Virginie married Dr. Joseph Ursin Landreaux in St. Louis Church on January 28, 1835. Less than three weeks later, Samuel, Jr., married Eugénie De Buys, widow of Henri Hypolite Tricou. Florian had already been married, on December 25, 1830, to Adèle Longer, whose mother was a De Buys.[49]

A number of surviving portraits enable us to study members of the Hermann family at close hand. Dr. George de Tarnowsky of Wilmette, Illinois, owns a portrait of young Samuel which was painted by Vaudechamp in 1833; it portrays a handsome, cultivated, sensitive man. Dating from about the same time is a portrait of Emeronthe, dressed in the height of fashion, the property of another great-great-grandson, Mr. Pierre A. de Tarnowsky, president of the Armour Pharmaceutical Company of Chicago. Emeronthe stares with a sour frown at the stranger who stands before her; there is no grace or charm or warmth in her glance. Perhaps she had been beautiful when Samuel Hermann married her, but there is no touch of loveliness in this portrait, nor, indeed, in another which is in the possession of Mr. James Reiss of New Orleans, which probably dates from the late 1840's, after havoc had been wreaked in the family fortune; here, Emeronthe is an old, frowning woman, somewhat sad, resigned and weary. Her appearance makes one wonder if she ever felt any joy or love. Mr. Reiss's portrait of the elder Samuel, on the other hand, brings the onlooker into direct contact with a strong, virile, masterful man, who has worked and played hard, who grins at the world and its follies and pitfalls, and probably at his own illusions as well.

The Hermann men were fairly active civic leaders. In 1830, Samuel, Sr., was a member of a committee which raised a fund for the widows and orphans of the victims of the July revolution in France; his firm gave the highest amount, $100. In 1832, Samuel Hermann and Son contributed $50 to the cholera epidemic relief fund. In 1838, Samuel, Jr., served on a committee which solicited donations for the relief of those who were rendered destitute by the disastrous fire in Charleston. In 1833, Lucien was a manager of the Washington Birthday Ball which was held at the Orleans Ball Room, and the following year he served as one of twelve masters of ceremonies of a parade in memory of Lafayette, a cherished hero of the New Orleans population. In 1839, Lucien was appointed an aide-de-camp for military affairs by the Governor, but this was largely an honorary position which recognized social prestige rather than military training; the following year he served as a member of the Central Committee of Correspondence of the Louisiana Whig Party. In 1836, young Samuel was a member of a special grand jury which concluded its deliberations by recommending the construction of a new custom-house, and the establishment of a permanent military force in New Orleans to stand guard against the possibility of an abolitionist uprising. Florian's social and equestrian interests resulted in his election as a steward of the New Orleans Jockey Club in 1837. The elder Samuel does not seem to have taken any role in such matters, other than his membership in an anti-duelling society in 1834—probably more for the sake of his sons than for himself.[50]

Such public activities as these were clearly of secondary significance to the Hermann men. Business was their major concern. Despite their comparative youth, all three of the sons served as directors of banks and other financial enterprises. In

1832, Samuel, Jr., was nominated for a seat on the board of the City Bank; in 1834–36 he served as a director of the New Orleans Gas Light and Banking Company, and, in 1837, both he and Florian were members of its board. Lucien was nominated to the board of the Western Marine and Fire Insurance Company in 1832; in 1836 he served simultaneously on the boards of the Carrollton Bank, the Orleans Navigation Company and the new Exchange and Banking Company of which he was an organizer and commissioner. The Governor appointed Lucien to the board of the Union Bank in 1835, and in 1836, he and another Jew, Joachim Kohn, were elected directors of the Louisiana State Marine and Fire Insurance Company—two out of seven. Each of the brothers took his turn on the Arbitration Committee of the New Orleans Chamber of Commerce. Samuel, Sr., does not seem to have been interested in offices; those honors he turned over to his sons. But we may be certain that he enjoyed the uses of power.[51]

This prestige, prosperity and popularity did not erase the memory of his European family from Samuel's mind. In 1835 he returned to Germany to visit his relatives and to make provision for their maintenance. This is the report of a German magazine about his wealth and generosity:

"RICHES—AN ORNAMENT OF THE RIGHTEOUS.

Grand Duchy of Hesse, Sept. 3. A young Israelite, native of Roedelsheim, near Frankfurt, had gone to America as a commercial clerk 31 years ago, as the circumstances made it very hard for him to get on at home. Though arriving utterly destitute in the New World, he succeeded in amassing a great fortune by diligent industry, so that at present he finds himself at the head of the first commercial firm in New Orleans, Herrman [sic] & Co., and in possession of several million dollars. Some weeks ago he paid a visit to his old home for the purpose of providing for his numerous relatives. He has transferred to them each a sum of as much as 150,000 florins as capital so that they may expand their business activities, and in addition has made arrangements for those of his family's members, who need a rest on account of advanced age, to be given a considerable allowance regularly during their lifetime by a Frankfurt banking house. He has now gone back to New Orleans."[52]

Let us hope that all of Hermann's gifts were in cash, rather than promises, for soon he had no surplus funds to distribute to admiring German Jewish relatives. The financial excesses of the early years of the decade gave way, in 1837, to panic and depression; stability did not return to New Orleans' economy until 1842. Land speculation, the enormous increase in the state debt, an unreasonable expansion of the number of banks and the availability of banking credit, and the precipitous fall in the cotton market in England, conspired to make New Orleans one of the hardest hit of all of the financial centers of the United States. The shock waves of fiscal crisis began in England, traveled swiftly to New York, and then shook the foundations of wealth and commerce in New Orleans, foundations which were at least as insecure as those of London and New York. Lucien's firm, Thomas Barrett and Company, was one of the first to collapse; it was shattered by the bankruptcy of the New York City Jewish bankers, J. L. and S. Josephs, who in turn were destroyed by the tightening of their credit in London. S. Hermann and Son, and Hermann, Briggs and Company (Florian's firm) suffered some losses in the Josephs debacle, but both had worse problems. Theirs had been the only New Orleans firms to enjoy open credits of £10,000 with Barings for the purchase of cotton; this credit was withdrawn in 1837. In addition, the two firms had endorsed each other's notes, and had overdrawn their credit with the Gas Light and Banking Company, the most notoriously manipulated bank in the city, in which all four of the Hermann men wielded influence. Florian was in deeper trouble than his brother and father. The elder and younger Samuel Hermanns had liabilities of only $5,592.67 on their own notes, and $23,289.03 on notes which they had endorsed; but Florian's company had a deficit of $428,640.71 on its own notes, and $74,922.67 on notes which carried its endorsement. Both young Samuel and Florian had used their position in the Gas Light Bank to join everyone else in milking its resources.

It is not possible, because of the paucity of reliable information, to discover how much money each member of the family lost in this upheaval. Hermann, Briggs and Company, in which Florian was a partner, was in debt for six million dollars when

117

it suspended payment in 1837. Their paper assets amounted to more than that figure, but the partners refused to drive their own customers into bankruptcy by pressing for payment. Month after month, Florian and his partner gathered in whatever funds they could, and transmitted them to the creditors; by June of 1839 they succeeded in reducing their indebtedness to two million dollars. But that September the bottom dropped out of the New Orleans financial structure again, and all of Florian's hopes disappeared in the ruins. He lost everything he possessed. The elder Samuel had reorganized his company in 1837 in an effort to stave off the plague of bankruptcy, but by 1840 he was in such dire condition that some of his real estate and stock holdings had to be sold at auction, for only a fraction of their value, and, in 1841, his beautiful home was also sold to satisfy his creditors. He had given some money to Emeronthe; she bought the home at a price far below its value, but it was too expensive to maintain, so she and Samuel decided to let it go. It was purchased by the notary Félix Grima, in whose family's possession it remained until 1921.[53]

The Hermann family's experiences following this financial disaster are difficult to trace in any detail. The elder Samuel and his wife probably had to live on the little they had saved from the debacle. Young Samuel and Florian must have gone to work for relatives or friends; they never again occupied business positions of importance or responsibility. Lucien became a notary, and used his knowledge of finance in his office of secretary of the Board of Presidents of Banks, which attempted to reorganize the shattered economic life of the city. Lucien remained active in Masonry, and served two terms as Grand Master of Louisiana, 1849 and 1850. Emeronthe died on March 11, 1851; the elder Samuel on June 3, 1853. It has not been possible to locate Samuel Hermann's will anywhere in the New Orleans area; perhaps his possessions were so few that he saw no point in framing any legal document. Virginie's husband died a few months after her father. She and Florian remained in New Orleans, Florian making a living in the cotton brokerage business. Lucien and the younger Samuel and his family moved to San Francisco about 1854—perhaps they had only been waiting for their father's death. Both of them worked as notaries

118

in San Francisco. Lucien was a bachelor, but young Samuel's family grew from generation to generation. Two of his grand-daughters married men who matched their great-grandfather in dynamic vigor, intellectual perception and personal charm: Chauncey Depew, Senator from New York, 1899–1911, and President of the New York Central Railroad, and Francis Griffith Newlands, brilliant attorney and Senator from Nevada, 1902–1917.[54]

5. SAMUEL KOHN, INCLUDING REFERENCE TO THE HEINE BROTHERS

We possess more information about the precise circumstances of Samuel Kohn's departure from Europe than about any other European Jew who came to New Orleans in this early period; this good fortune is due to the fact that Samuel's sister Resie married an uncle of Lucien Wolf, the distinguished British Jewish historian, who wrote about Samuel Kohn in one of those intimately personal essays which historians so rarely publish. The Kohn family lived in the village of Hareth in Bohemia; Sam, says Wolf,

> "was known all over the country side as a good-hearted, hare-brained ne'er-do-well, fond of the tavern and the lassies, and fonder still of a game of cards . . . One day the news ran through Hareth that Samuel Kohn had disappeared. He had last been seen drinking and gambling with strangers in the *Gast-haus*, and, after some high words, had tramped off . . . a picture of abject misery . . . It seems that he had been cheated of everything he had in the world by a gang of cardsharpers. When he left the tavern with empty pockets, he felt he could not again go home to the poverty-stricken cottage in the wood and confess his follies to his long-suffering mother, so he turned his steps in the direction of the county town, and thence tramped northward all the way to Hamburg. He worked his way on a sailing vessel to New Orleans. . . ."[55]

It was not auspicious that Samuel's earliest appearance in New Orleans was as co-owner of an inn at Bayou St. John, in July,

1806, where the public was promised "the best of liquors." Sam and H. Labruère, his partner, announced that "separate rooms may be had for private parties" in their "house of ENTERTAINMENT," and that "every care and attention will be observed to render the house agreeable to those who may visit it." But perhaps this was the only thing that Sam knew how to do—and instead of frittering away his time with boon companions in drinking parties and gambling sprees, he had determined to earn his living by putting his experience to work in an establishment in which others could enjoy such pleasures.[56]

But Kohn must have been in Louisiana for a number of months and even possibly years to have accumulated enough capital to have become Labruère's partner. No information is available about his prior activities in the area, and nothing is known about his life during the next few years other than that by 1808–1809 he had earned enough money to purchase property in Rapides Parish to the northwest of Baton Rouge. Two parcels of land which he had bought at that time brought $1,200 and $1,600 when he sold them in 1816. Even allowing for a dramatic rise in the value of land, the young Bohemian had done very well during his first few years in Louisiana. Unfortunately the parish records have been destroyed, making any investigation of Kohn's other transactions in the area impossible; the only surviving notation of these land investments of 1808–1809 is the record of their subsequent sale in the New Orleans notarial archives. Kohn's next appearance in the archives is in 1810, when he contracted with a builder to construct two houses in the Faubourg Marigny of New Orleans, of a design similar to that of the adjacent structures which Kohn had recently purchased. Kohn was to pay the contractor $1,200 and transfer to him a lot in Alexandria. Later in the same year Kohn loaned out $1,112 in exchange for a mortgage on a house and lot on Bienville street. In 1812 his name appears in the records as the endorser of two notes for a total of $402.[57]

These early transactions established the pattern of Kohn's role in the commercial life of New Orleans until he moved to Paris in 1832. He was a banker—money lender—investor—real estate promoter—financier. He lent money on interest, but frequently had to sue to get it back, or had to put his creditors in the hands of receivers. The courts often designated him as the trustee of the property of bankrupted merchants. He endorsed notes for clients, and thereby earned a commission for himself. He built dwellings and business structures throughout New Orleans, and was one of the major promoters of suburban construction. From a penniless Bohemian immigrant, a wastrel in his village, he became, through wit, grit and acuity, one of the wealthiest financiers in New Orleans, worth more than $400,000 at the time of his death in Paris on May 18, 1853— and this was the residue after more than twenty years of retirement, and the sharing of his substance with his many relatives. Whether it was the humiliation of being unable to face his family, or the hardship of coming to a strange new country as a friendless immigrant, Sam had learned his lesson well. He was obviously a man of native talent; once he made up his mind that he would not again bear the burdens of shame and privation, he promptly found the road to success. Kohn's portrait on wood, now in the possession of his great-great-grandnephew, Maunsel White Hickey of New Orleans, reveals a strong, firm, determined countenance—that must, of necessity, have been his personality. Kohn was single-minded in his pursuit of fortune; only a few records point to his participation in community affairs. He served as treasurer of a Masonic lodge in 1823, and acted as a member of the committee of arrangements for a political dinner in 1831. His name appears in a published list of philanthropists only once, but on that occasion, when a fund was being raised to assist families whose bread-winners had died during the cholera epidemic of 1832, he gave more than any other citizen, $1,000. In 1829 he served as president of the Orleans Navigation Company; but this was primarily business, because he was the leader of a group of stockholders who voted the incumbent officers out of power and supported the idea of selling the business to the state. These are the only references to Samuel Kohn's public interests which we have been able to discover.[58]

Lucien Wolf did not record when Samuel first notified his family that he had come to New Orleans, and succeeded in establishing himself on a firm footing, but it was probably fairly early in his career. In view of what we know about his generosity towards his family in later years, he probably began sending funds to them as soon as he could. When his brother Joachim was nineteen or twenty years old, in 1819 or 1820, Samuel brought him over to New Orleans. Either because Joachim was not interested in finance as much as in mercantile pursuits, or because Samuel wanted him to obtain experience in various forms of commerce, Joachim was set up in the commission brokerage line with a series of partners, ending up with J. A. Bordier in 1826.[59] Kohn and Bordier was a characteristic business of the time. It was the New Orleans agent for some shipping lines, owned a number of ships in its own name, and handled cargoes to and from ports near and far, on the Mississippi River, in the Caribbean area, on the Atlantic seaboard and in Europe. Among its imports were wines, coffee, cigars, beeswax, dry goods which were "suitable for the Mexican market," mahogany, logwood, tobacco, straw hats, beef hides, deer skins and specie. Trade between Mexico and New Orleans, during this period, was basic to the city's economy: in exchange for consumer goods of every sort, ships brought back mahogany, logwood and Mexican coinage in huge amounts. Kohn and Bordier did not have to grow as gradually as other firms; although Samuel was not a working partner in the business, he undoubtedly invested large sums of money with Joachim.

After Samuel Kohn moved to Paris in 1832, Joachim held his power of attorney and acted as his agent, buying and selling property, building more homes and stores, suing debtors; he also seems to have continued Samuel's business, although, in 1835, he organized a new firm. Joachim represented Samuel's interest in the expanding suburb of Carrollton, of which Laurent Millaudon, Touro's one-time associate, was also a major developer. During the booming thirties Joachim was a member of more boards than any other Jew; he was a director of the New Orleans and Carrollton Rail Road Company, the Carrollton Bank, the Louisiana State Marine Fire Insurance Company, and the Mechanics' and Traders' Bank. Obviously Joachim did not need to follow in his brother's footsteps; he began life in New Orleans without having to undergo any of the hardships which stood in Samuel's way. His portrait by Vaudechamp, painted in 1836, which Mr. Hickey has presented to the Louisiana State

122

Museum, reveals little of Samuel's rugged strength; Joachim's face is handsome and sensitive; his eyes are thoughtful and compassionate; his appearance is that of the romantic dreamer, or a scholar.[60]

On June 22, 1834, Joachim was married to Marie Thalie Martin, the nineteen-year-old daughter of a fashionable French physician. The wedding was solemnized in St. Louis Church by Abbé Moni, "with the dispensation of the impediment of mixed religion given by Msgr. Antoine Blanc, Vicar General Administrator of this diocese."[61] Joachim and Marie had three children. Little is known of the eldest, Samuel Arthur (probably named for Uncle Samuel), other than that he was born on November 13, 1835, although he was not baptized until May 9, 1838, and that he lived most of his life in Paris where he died in 1909 or 1910. The second son, Joseph Gustave (March 18, 1837–September 7, 1906), was a distinguished student of Louisiana natural history who gave Tulane University his magnificent collection of more than 6,600 specimens of birds, fish, reptiles, mammals, crustaceans, mollusks, insects and plants. The third child, Amélie, married Armand Heine (a cousin of the poet Heinrich Heine), who came to New Orleans with his brother Michel in 1842 to open up a commission and banking business which was, in 1854, estimated to be worth as much as $600,000.[62]

Armand's brother Michel also married a New Orleans girl, Marie Céleste Amélie Miltenberger, who grew up in a home on Royal street next to Joachim Kohn's—perhaps it was in Joachim's home that they met. They were married in St. Louis Church on April 5, 1853, "dispensation obtained from ecclesiastical authority for the difference of worship." Both Heine families moved to Paris about 1866. In 1875, Michel's daughter, Marie Alice Heine, married the Duc de Richelieu; after his death she married Alberto, Prince of Monaco, Duke of Valentinois, Marquis of Baux and Baron of Bois and Calvinet, to name a few of his titles. This marriage of Grace Kelly's predecessor on the throne of Monaco lasted from 1889 until 1902, when it was dissolved by divorce. Marie Alice, one of the first American-born women to marry into European nobility, was a Catholic, not a Jewess, but her father remained a Jew all his life and, even after he moved to Paris, maintained his interest in the Jewish Children's Home of New Orleans.[63]

Samuel Kohn left New Orleans before the panic of 1837; most of his funds seem to have been safely invested in real estate. Joachim's business survived the worst of the storm, but his firm was in some difficulty in 1842. After his wife's death the following year, Joachim seems to have abandoned business pursuits in his own name, and to have devoted himself mainly to the conduct of his brother Samuel's affairs in New Orleans, and to the education of his children. He moved back and forth across the Atlantic between New Orleans and Paris, and died in France in 1886. Whatever Joachim had to give his children, Uncle Samuel left each of them $66,500. Samuel died in Paris on May 18, 1853, and was buried there, although his name appears on the family tomb in New Orleans. He also left money to three other persons of interest.

One of these was Delphine Blanchard Marchegay, formerly of Saint-Domingue, who was Samuel's housekeeper in New Orleans, and probably his mistress. She remained in New Orleans for a little while after his move to Paris, then joined him there. His bequest to her was an annuity of $800 a year, which Marie Amélie Kohn Heine undertook to pay each year so that the property in New Orleans could be sold, and the estate distributed. Delphine lived to the age of eighty-five; she died in Paris on January 8, 1877, twenty-three years after Samuel.[64]

Another important heir mentioned in Samuel's will was Edouard Kohn, son of Samuel's brother Simon, whom Samuel brought from Bohemia to Paris in 1847, at the age of twenty-two, and helped establish in the banking business. Edouard became a distinguished Frenchman, a member of that remarkable circle of Parisian Jews—wealthy, cultured and philanthropic—led by the Rothschild family, of whose hospital he was a director. Edouard himself married into the powerful banking family of Von Embden (who were also related to the Heine family), and his children married into the Weisweiller, Meyerbeer and Bischoffsheim families—one almost feels required to refer to them as dynasties, although all of them originally began much as the Kohn family did, in abject poverty. Edouard was the only member of the Kohn family to become a leader in Jewish and nonsectarian philanthropies; these activities were one reason that the French government conferred the Legion of Honor upon him in 1873.[65]

A third heir of Samuel Kohn carried on the family tradition in New Orleans. He was Carl Kohn, another nephew, who was brought to New Orleans by Samuel in 1830 or 1831. Maunsel White Hickey, his great-grandson, owns Carl's letter book, from which we have already quoted; this manuscript volume contains fair copies of letters which Carl wrote to his Uncle Samuel in Paris from June 10, 1832, to December 18, 1833. They reflect the bright, eager, ambitious and attractive personality of this youth of sixteen or seventeen who had grown up in the crude, unsophisticated environment of a Bohemian village where, he says, his "younger years were passed unworthily and in ignorance." Apparently without any secular education before he was brought to New Orleans, in a very brief time he became conversant with English, French and Spanish, learned to play the flute and fire the pistol, developed the social graces of an old-line New Orleans aristocrat, and voraciously devoured everything he could discover about merchant banking and commission brokerage. In the style of the time, he went to work for Merle and Company as a junior clerk, and spent long hours at tedious tasks, but when summer came, unlike other young men who had to earn their living, he was able to take a vacation in Bay St. Louis, Mississippi, for several months, so that he could escape the heat and the ever-threatening epidemics. He developed a strong interest in politics and included information about important public events in his letters to his uncle. Because of his Uncle Joachim's social position, he gained entree into the finest homes, but it was his own gift of warmth which secured for him a host of friends among younger and older people alike, and constant invitations to the fashionable balls and parties.

Carl took himself very seriously, for all his desire to taste every aspect of the social life of New Orleans. He admitted that his ambition could be regarded as selfish, but he believed that it was his primary responsibility to take advantage of every opportunity "of getting along in the world." And get along he did. In 1835 Joachim dissolved his partnership with Bordier and took Carl into his business. In 1839 Carl was elected to the board of directors of the Atlantic Insurance Company, the first of a series of steps which brought him, ultimately, in 1871, to the presidency of the Union National Bank. During the intervening years, he engaged in a variety of enterprises which involved trade with Mexico, the marketing of western produce, cotton, sugar and molasses, and diverse forms of investment. He was an example of the nineteenth-century capitalist who sought opportunities for profit in many forms of raw materials. Through depression, panic and war, he continued to build his fortune; there was always a place in the economic scheme of things for this clever, personable man.

On June 27, 1850, in a ceremony performed by the famous Parson Clapp, Carl married into one of the "finest families" of New Orleans; his bride was Clara White, the daughter of Maunsel White, a wealthy commission broker turned planter, and Héloïse de La Ronde, daughter of Pierre Denis de La Ronde II, a distinguished Creole who had been a major general at the Battle of New Orleans. When Carl died on August 27, 1895, the newspaper reported that he was "one of New Orleans' most respected citizens . . . a man of fine intelligence, thoroughly educated, widely read, and transparently honest." After his retirement from business, the reporter said, he had spent his time in his "elegant home on the corner of St. Charles and Julia streets, surrounded by the best and most cultured society, and in the companionship of his beloved books." The emphasis on learning, culture and books is worthy of comment; Carl had come a long way from the untutored origins of the Bohemian village in which he was born and spent his early years.[66]

Samuel Kohn returned to that village in 1833, after he had established his residence in Paris. His father had died on January 18, 1831, but his mother may still have been alive. There were large numbers of relatives to greet him on his arrival. Carl responds ecstatically, in his letters from New Orleans, to his Uncle Samuel's description of his generosity to the members of the family, and to every detail of the visit: "I take a lively interest as you may well think in all your details about our dear relations, your dispositions with regard to them, & that they are now comfortably settled." Lucien Wolf's description of Samuel's arrival, probably interlaced with some fancy, reflects some of the feeling of wonder which the former "ne'er-do-well" created in the village:

> "One morning in the 'thirties the whole of Hareth was thrown into a paroxysm of the most intense excitement by a story which a peasant had brought into the village. Late in the preceding night he had been passing the widow Kohn's cottage, when there suddenly drove up to the door a capacious travelling carriage drawn by six horses, and attended by four black servants in gorgeous liveries. A 'gentleman of noble presence'—so said the peasant—had alighted and entered the cottage, and the black servants had followed with the baggage, which included a mysterious hogshead. The yokel had afterwards peered through the window and had seen—so he averred—the hogshead opened in the presence of the widow, and—he swore it by all the saints— it was full to the brim of newly-coined gold. . . ."[67]

Even if there was no hogshead full of gold, there could have been one, or for that matter, several. Whether Samuel Kohn dazzled his mother and relatives with real gold, or merely made arrangements for regular payments of cash to them, so that their need for food, clothing and shelter would be met, really makes no essential difference. Some happiness was brought to his poor Jewish family eking out its life in that remote Bohemian village through the opportunity for wealth and success which New Orleans had offered to Samuel Kohn.

6. RUBEN LEVIN ROCHELLE AND HART MOSES SHIFF

On October 19, 1807, the *Orleans Gazette and Commercial Advertiser* carried the following notice:

> "Received by the late arrivals from Philadelphia, and for sale by the subscribers, An Assortment of black silk velvet Ribbons, figured, striped and plain, suitable for the Spanish market. Also VIOLINS and VIOLIN STRINGS, assorted.
>
> R. L. ROCHELLE & CO.
No. 9, Bienville street."

Rochelle had been in New Orleans for at least four months, probably longer, for on June 16, 1807, he had sold a slave to two French Louisianians. Rochelle was a peppery fellow. In 1810, the report was circulating that he was about to go bankrupt. He demanded to know the name of his slanderer from Mossy, the auctioneer who was quoted as having repeated the story, but Mossy refused to divulge it. Rochelle thereupon wrote an advertisement for the newspaper, and publicly denounced "the person acting in this base manner" as "a wretch devoid of feeling" and "a scoundrel." "The epithets of a liar and a base man are justly his attributes," said Rochelle, "and the midnight robber, is innocent when compared to him, who, under a mask stabs a man's character." To prove to his creditors that he would not leave them in the lurch, he invited them to present their bills to him for immediate payment. Rochelle also had an opportunity to demonstrate his courage in personal combat. The newspaper reported, in 1810, the details of this event:

"PROTECTION!

"Last night one of the City Watch was using very insolent language to a gentleman's family, Mr. Rochelle was passing, and on hearing such outrageous abuse, he ordered the fellow to be silent and to go away; in place of obeying Mr. R. he turned his abuse upon him. Mr. R. provoked at his insolence, gave him a gentle chastisement and sent him off; soon after, Mr. R. having returned to his own house, the same fellow and another of the City Watch, both armed with *dirks* and *swords*, knocked at his doors and demanded admittance, threatening him with *death*—he fastened his doors and armed himself with a sword—they forced open the gate and attacked him—he defended himself against them both, until his neighbors flew to his assistance . . . Had Mr. R. been a weakly small man, in all probability, he would have [fallen] by the hands of these assassins."

The next issue of the paper retracted the statement that the attackers were city guards; all the more did Rochelle have reason to be grateful that he was not a "weakly small man," if they were just ordinary ruffians.[68]

How does a Jew in the first decade of the nineteenth century

come to have a name like Rochelle? Every sort of possibility
had occurred to this writer: that he was a Sephardic French
Jew; that he had passed through La Rochelle on his way from
Europe to America; that it was his wife's maiden name. Rochelle
never married, however, and with the first name Ruben could
not have been Sephardic. Had he not left bequests to his brothers
in Europe we might have known nothing of his origins. His will
presents us with enough information to hazard a guess about
his change of name; his brothers were "Maritz & Bernahard
Rothschild now Residing in the City of Hamburg in Germany."
According to his estate papers, Ruben himself was born in
Hamburg on August 15, 1780, the son of Levin Jacob Rothschild
of the "English Plank in this City, merchant," and his wife
Handel, daughter of Joseph Heilbut, who were married on
June 1, 1775. The name Rothschild is very difficult for French-
speaking people to pronounce, unless it happens to be the name
of a family of wealthy bankers who are elevated to the aristocracy.
But Ruben came to Louisiana too early for people there to have
heard of the financial wizardry of *the* Rothschilds; they must
have pronounced it "Rochelle" so often that he decided to
change it for convenience' sake. This is all supposition, of course,
and the change of name may have taken place in France, if
indeed Ruben worked there for any period of time before
coming to New Orleans.[69]

At the time of Rochelle's first business activity in New Orleans,
it was standard commercial procedure for a firm's public name
to be that of its owner; if he had an active partner, both names
were used. But if he had a silent partner, or had secured the
financial support of someone in another town, the words "and
Company" would be added to his name. We do not know who
Rochelle's partner or partners were. Perhaps his father and
brothers had invested in his venture. Perhaps it was the "Worthy
old Friend Charles H. Rodbertus, now a residence near Rostock
in Mecklenburg," to whom he left ten thousand Spanish dollars
in his will—although this man may not have been a merchant
at all, but the professor of Roman law whose son Johann Karl
became a famous economist. Perhaps it was a relative or friend
in Philadelphia where he had many suppliers and where he

129

died on September 1, 1824. This partner may even have been the man who, in 1810, became his publicly known associate, Hart Moses Shiff.

Shiff was in New Orleans by February 17, 1810, at the latest; on that date he and Rochelle paid off a debt to Leonard Wiltz.[70] Shiff was a member of one of the most distinguished Jewish families of Europe; its lineage is traced back, in Frankfurt-am-Main, to Jacob Kohen Zedek Schiff, a fourteenth-century rabbinical judge. The name "Schiff" probably came from the German word for "vial," possibly used as a sign for the shop of an apothecary. The family was renowned for its rabbinic scholarship—the greatest merit in European Jewish life. Among its men of note were Rabbi Meir Schiff, known as Maharam, author of a widely used Talmudic commentary, who lived from 1608 to 1644; David Tevele Schiff, who was Chief Rabbi of England from 1765 to 1792; and David Tevele's nephew, Nathan Adler, another Chief Rabbi of England. The Schiff family lived in the house in the Frankfurt ghetto which had the sign of the "Green Shield" on it; they sold their half of the building to the Rothschild "Red Shield" family as late as 1784. Our Hart Moses was born in Frankfurt, probably in that "Green Shield" house, in 1779 or 1780, some little time after the death, on March 15, 1779, of his grandfather Herz Joseph Schiff, for whom he was named. Hart's parents were the merchant Moses Herz Schiff and Brainle Schwab. Moses Herz Schiff, the father, had a brother named Jacob Schiff, who died on October 20, 1843, for whom a grandson was named Jacob Henry Schiff. This Jacob Schiff emigrated from Frankfurt to the United States after the Civil War, and became the outstanding American Jewish leader of his time. Grown wealthy through the success of Kuhn, Loeb and Company, the banking firm which he headed, he gave lavishly of his means to the Hebrew Union College, the Jewish Theological Seminary of America, Temple Emanu-El of New York City, and the Jewish Publication Society of America, whose first English translation of the Bible was endowed by him.[71]

All of that, however, was past or future. Family relationships, traditional Jewish scholarship, and strong religious values obviously had no hold on a young man who was willing to travel so far as the Louisiana frontier to make a new life. Hart Shiff's anglicization of his last name was probably symptomatic of his impatience with the past and his determination to find a more rewarding life than that of the crowded Frankfurt ghetto with its still galling restrictions on its Jewish inhabitants. In New Orleans, Shiff and Rochelle swiftly established an active and prosperous business. From the time their partnership began, they were altogether inseparable in business—no independent ventures or interests are recorded in their names. They followed the sort of commission brokerage-merchant banking pursuits with which we have already become familiar: ship agencies; mortgages on property; advances to planters; cargoes of imports for retail and wholesale trade; shipments of Louisiana cotton, sugar and tobacco to the Atlantic ports and Europe. They endorsed notes, represented European merchants, erected their own tobacco warehouses, bought and sold real estate, and owned shares in steamboats, banks, insurance companies and other capitalist ventures. Their cargoes came to New Orleans from Liverpool, Hamburg, Altona, Bremen, Amsterdam, Rotterdam, New York and Philadelphia. They were prosperous and respected enough to hold a seat on the board of the Louisiana State Bank between them.[72]

The partnership might have gone on for many years, but Rochelle fell ill in 1824, and, in hope of regaining his health, retired from business and left New Orleans. Whether he intended to return to Europe or to live in Philadelphia cannot be ascertained, but it was in the latter city that he died on September 1, 1824. When the news arrived in New Orleans, the newspaper made haste to transmit it to the public:

"DIED—At Philadelphia, on the 1st of September, MR. R. L. ROCHELLE. He was buried from Mrs. Carr's, and every requisite honor paid to his remains. The Exchange of New-Orleans will miss him much—on all public exigencies his purse was open—active and industrious in business, his acquirements enabled him to contribute to public amusement—and there were none who contributed more freely. We shall leave it to his particular friends

131

to write his obituary. We only express the feelings that his loss excites at the moment."

What contribution he made to public amusement was never described in any detail, nor did any friend offer a more personal tribute. Perhaps Rochelle had been a violinist or pianist—he advertised an inordinate number of musical instruments in his early business years. The names of his closest friends are revealed in his designation of three of the most prosperous Yankee merchants in New Orleans as his executors—William Montgomery, Stephen Henderson and Judah Touro. To "my Old and worthy Friends Wm. Montgomerys youngest son August," he bequeathed $10,000. Perhaps he was particularly attached to this boy because he had no children of his own.[73]

The main burden of settling Rochelle's estate fell on Shiff's shoulders, because so little time had elapsed since their decision to divide their property. The reports of Rochelle's assets in the probate papers were drawn up in Shiff's countinghouse. It was several years before everything could be wound up; one debt which took years to collect involved the bankrupt Vincent Nolte of *Anthony Adverse* renown, the French firm of Charles Martineau and Son, and Senator Josiah Stoddard Johnston. Rochelle's brother, Maritz Rothschild, was forced to sue in the Louisiana courts for the settlement of other outstanding accounts. When Rochelle's affairs were finally brought to a conclusion, the estate was valued at $147,283.91, and included some slaves, a brick house and four lots on the Batture at the Faubourg St. Mary, and $127,980.41 worth of stocks and notes for loans. In that period before the frenzied speculation of the 1830's, Rothschild/Rochelle had amassed a modest fortune in New Orleans in less than twenty years, and he was spared the misery and humiliation which were the lot of so many of his friends who were destroyed by the thundering financial crisis which began in 1837.[74]

Shiff had been married on December 11, 1813, in St. Louis Church, to Marguerite Basilique Chessé, daughter of Jean Jacques Chessé and Marie Madeleine Plauché. They had at least eleven children, of whom four died in childhood. After Rochelle's passing—although he continued the business for some time—Shiff gradually withdrew from daily commercial activity, and began to travel with his wife and children. They were in New York City and Philadelphia in the summer of 1827, and in Europe in 1828. In May, 1830, they again went to Europe by way of Baltimore, stayed in Frankfurt until the following May, and then moved on to Paris. Shiff and Evariste Lauve were partners in a plantation in Iberville Parish, but Hart never worked at farming. His interests tended more in the direction of the North and beyond, to Europe. Perhaps it was Ruben's early death from the debilitating effect of living too long in the New Orleans climate; perhaps Shiff had owned a larger share of the business and therefore did not need to give his constant attention to business matters; perhaps it was Basilique's yearning for the glamor of life in Paris; perhaps it was Shiff's desire to take advantage of the educational opportunities which France would afford to his children; perhaps it was simply that all wealthy Creole families in New Orleans regarded France as their true homeland. It may have been a combination of these factors which led Hart away from New Orleans and helped him escape the debacle of 1837. Carl Kohn wrote to his Uncle Samuel, on December 18, 1833, that "Mr. and Mrs. Shiff have taken rooms at the American Hotel—I do not think Mrs. S. will enjoy much her residence in this place again, separated as she is from her children & the amusements and excitements of Paris." At any rate, by the early 1840's, Hart's son Edward, now become a notary, had assumed total responsibility for his father's affairs. He held his power of attorney and bought and sold property in his name; in 1844–45, after the economic life of New Orleans was again on an even keel, Edward, acting for his father, and Joachim Kohn, on behalf of Samuel Kohn, sold so much real estate which the two men had owned jointly, that they used specially printed notarized forms to save the work of filling in all of the details in the usual documents.[75]

Hart Shiff died in New York City on February 26, 1851; he and his wife had probably chosen that city for their home because it was a half-way point between New Orleans and Paris, in both of which cities their children lived. Shiff was worth more than $800,000 at the time of his death. His estate listed $86,141.34 in cash; $383,125 in real estate, mostly in New Orleans and vicinity; and $225,387 in stocks and bonds. This was all quite aside from many thousands of dollars worth of uncollectable notes from bankrupted friends and associates, and worthless shares of stock in companies and banks which had collapsed during the late 1830's and early 1840's. Unfortunately, his affairs were so complicated, and his children and children's children so numerous, that the estate had still not been settled when the Civil War began; this, of course, reduced its value in many ways.[76]

The Civil War created other problems for Hart Shiff's family. His son Henry volunteered for service as an Assistant Surgeon with the 10th Regiment of Louisiana Infantry, and was captured at the Battle of the Wilderness. He was taken to the old Capitol Prison in Washington, and, after he took the oath of allegiance, was given his parole, and joined his mother in Paris. By October, 1864, Basilique had somehow prevailed upon Orville Browning, the former Senator from Illinois, to intercede with President Lincoln to permit Henry to withdraw his oath. Browning wrote up the problem in his diary:

> "Henry's father, who is now dead, once lived in New Orleans and had invested in Southern stocks, and loaned money on mortgages, and there is a large indebtedness from the rebels to the family, who are now in Paris. Shiff himself is in Paris with his mother. She is afraid if the rebels find out that her son has taken the oath of allegiance to this government they will confiscate her large interests in the South, and that she will be unable to collect any portion of the debts due the family there, and, therefore desires leave for him to withdraw his oath. . . ."[77]

Lincoln favored going along with Basilique and Henry; Secretary of State Seward was violently opposed to the accommodation. Browning records that Seward was "very much excited and was boistrous and profane." But Lincoln insisted that the request be granted, and so it was done. But there was trouble in New Orleans anyway. Henry's sister-in-law, Edward Shiff's widow, was accused of disloyalty to the Union. Her plantation was so close to Confederate territory that it was constantly raided by rebel bands, and the Federal officials suspected that she was encouraging the Confederate marauders to seize her harvested crops. After a lengthy trial, Emilie Shiff was cleared of the accusation.

Fortunately, Hart Shiff had not lived long enough to be compelled to decide whether he was really a European, a Southerner or an American. Nor did he leave any personal papers which might give us a clue to his feelings. He had spent close to thirty years in Frankfurt; less than twenty-five in New Orleans making his fortune; more than twenty years moving between New Orleans, New York and Europe. Although he was an American citizen in a technical sense, and probably never wished to be considered a German, the cosmopolitan atmosphere of New Orleans encouraged him to feel that America was too provincial, and that the real capital of the civilized world was Paris. He and Basilique would have felt a close affinity to the members of today's jet-set who move so freely from one continent to another and participate in a culture of wealth and pleasure which transcends national boundaries.[78]

7. SALOMON S. DE JONGE

Some of these personalities registered their activities and experiences in hundreds of newspaper advertisements, notarized deeds and personal documents. Others left only the briefest record of their passage. One of these was Salomon S. De Jonge, a Dutch Jew who first appeared in the New Orleans press in 1808 as a constable, signing a notice that he was about to seize some property, and would sell it at auction to pay its owner's debts. The work of a constable was only one aspect of the "Commission and Collection Line of Business" that De Jonge advertised. On July 13, 1808, he listed some of his stock as "200 barrels of coarse Salt, first quality, 100 of cargo Beef, 500 barrels of Rice, first quality, 65 fine Flour, 60 Pork, good quality." He also had for sale a "smart Negro wench, 17 years of age, warranted, with her child." He made his office at the Public Baths which Spitzer and Kursheedt had owned. "Through the medium of a respectable mercantile house of Philadelphia," he announced, he was able "to procure every article not to be found in this place," and solicited orders for all types of merchandise. He did some trading in Baton Rouge in 1812, which

135

may indicate that he was busy traveling in the country as well as keeping his store in New Orleans.[79]

De Jonge's name does not appear in any of the census records; he apparently never owned a home where he would be listed as head of the household. He is listed, however, in the 1822 *City Directory* as a commission and exchange broker at 22 Toulouse street. The same year, J. S. De Jonge, who was probably his brother, died at the age of twenty-three, and was buried in the Protestant Girod Street Cemetery.[80]

In 1823 De Jonge was in business with Solomon Soher, a Jew from New York City whom we will meet again; this association did not last very long. De Jonge's next appearance in our sources was in 1838, when he became an incorporator of the New Orleans Philharmonic Society. The following year he signed an advertisement offering for sale a two-story home, a summer residence in Carrollton, a "fine young servant girl . . . handy at everything," and a French piano.[81]

We lose sight of De Jonge again until his death on July 7, 1852, at 229 St. Philip street. One friend testified that De Jonge was seventy-two years old, and was a native of Amsterdam; another reported to the Probate Court that Salomon had said about three years previously that he had not heard anything from his mother for a while. The friend guessed that De Jonge's mother had been dead for some time; this information was necessary before the estate could be settled. It amounted to about $7,000 and was divided into equal portions among the three heirs: the executor, Richard Fear Nichols; Alfred Hennen, a well-known attorney; and a woman named Rosalyn Eleanore. Salomon De Jonge was buried next to his brother.[82]

8. ASHER MOSES NATHAN

The available source materials are not very enlightening about the business activities of early country merchants like Maurice Barnett, Samuel Kohn and Samuel Hermann. Luckily for us, but unfortunately for him, another Jew, Asher Moses Nathan, in partnership with Alexander Hart, was unable to pay his creditors in 1810. The papers relating to his case include a meticulous inventory of his property. Nathan and Hart had come up the Mississippi River to Baton Rouge from their headquarters in New Orleans, in early 1810, loaded with merchandise for sale in the surrounding rural area. They had with them twenty-eight trunks, seven bags, six boxes, five chests and some additional merchandise including a bolt of cloth. Once in Baton Rouge, Nathan sought out Maurice Barnett, and arranged for transportation to Bayou Sara in a pirogue which belonged to Barnett. Nathan or Hart, together with a number of clerks and helpers, stayed for twenty-two days in Bayou Sara in a building owned by Barnett, and then returned to Barnett's place in Baton Rouge. It was there, in March, 1810, that all of the merchandise was seized by the sheriff on the claim of the creditors, and sold at auction. They had begun this trip with $8,083.93 worth of goods. This traveling stock included a wide assortment of dry goods and notions to attract the attention of the farmers and their wives: blankets, flannel, cotton shawls, handkerchiefs, Madras, linen, cambric, muslin, towels, remnants, bombazette, cassimere, gingham, nankeen, gauze, cotton shirting, blue cloth, black velvet, brittany cloth, corduroy, worsted binding, calico, muslin robes, silk handkerchiefs, dimity, bed ticking, Marseilles cloth, silk suspenders, platillas, cotton hose, lace, night caps, silk gloves, cotton shirts, silk shawls, silk hose, ostrich feathers, ribbon, ticklenburg, red flannel, bagging, chambray, printed muslin, hats, parasols, umbrellas, wicks, looking glasses, shoes, ornamented combs, horn combs, metal and silver buttons, pins, needles, pocket books, watch seals, perfume, penknives, razors, fans, razor cases, and gold watches.

Whether the value of $8,083.93 which was placed on this tremendous quantity and variety of merchandise was wholesale or retail is unclear, but it was probably wholesale, since the goods were being inventoried for auction in quantity. Nathan and Hart's bills payable, dating back to May, 1809, amounted to a total of over $16,000. But with this great amount of merchandise in their possession, plus goods worth $6,052 in their store in New Orleans, and over $2,200 in accounts receivable, they were in no real difficulty. What had probably happened was that the partners had begun their ambitious operation with too little capital—some of their debts were simply loans of money—and too much merchandise to sell in a brief time. They therefore lost all their investment of money and time and energy. Not so Maurice Barnett: he did not have to wait for his payment, like the other creditors, until well into 1811. He was on the spot, and collected the $108 owing to him for services rendered to Nathan and Hart during the venture to Bayou Sara, as well as the $97 expense of conducting eight days of auctions at his store: the expense included two cases of gin, fourteen bottles of wine and two flasks of rum, which were dispensed to the prospective customers to stimulate their bidding.[83]

Asher Nathan had been born in Amsterdam about 1784, the fourth of seven children of Moses and Milko Nathan, on his father's side a descendant of that Nathan Nathan who was known as the *sofer*, the ritual scribe, of Amsterdam. Asher may have come to the United States about 1800 with his sister Catherine and her husband Hyam Harris, who were married in London in 1799. Asher was with them in Charleston no later than 1804. It may have been there or in London that he met his partner Alexander Hart, who was born in Portsmouth, England, in 1777. Hart and Nathan's accounts with their creditors in New Orleans go back only as far as May, 1809. We do not know how much earlier they had arrived there. Hart must have been frightened and dismayed by the failure, because he disappeared from view immediately. Nothing is known of his life until 1831, when he began his service as the cantor of Congregation B'nai Jeshurun of New York City. By then he had been married and widowed, and had at least one child, a son named Isaac. On July 26, 1836, in New York City, Hart was married to a New Orleans woman who was known as "the widow Kokernot," Betsy Levy Kokernot, who had come to New Orleans no later than 1820. Alexander gave his Hebrew name, to be inscribed on the religious certificate, as "Alexander the son of Master Yehudah who is called Hart," and Betsy, as "Billah the daughter of Master Nachman." Two officers of the New York congregation witnessed the wedding, which Alexander presumably conducted for himself. The couple set out for New Orleans, the scene of Alexander's disastrous venture of twenty-six years before, where, with Isaac's help, they enlarged Betsy's dry goods business. At the time of their marriage, Alexander was fifty-nine; the bride was forty-six. But New Orleans was not a lucky place for Alexander. He died in less than three years, on February 12, 1839, leaving Betsy a widow once more. We shall have reason to refer to Betsy later.[84]

Asher Nathan was less easily discouraged than Alexander. He continued to do business in and around Baton Rouge. Perhaps he stayed there because he had fallen in love. On March 24, 1811, he was married by Fr. Juan Brady (who had already married Maurice and Marie Barnett) to Margarita (or Marguerite) Dalton, the twenty-three-year-old daughter of Ana Burke and Valentine Thomas Dalton. Dalton first appears in the Spanish West Florida records in 1799 as a part-time interpreter and minor governmental functionary. A farmer and petty storekeeper at the time of his death on February 6, 1807, he owned three tracts of land to which the title was not clear, a few cabins, some merchandise of a trivial character (rolls of paper, padlocks, pencil cases, fans), an eighty-year-old slave and some livestock. Maurice Barnett had been appointed an appraiser for the estate. The livestock (eleven hogs, six cows and four bulls) and farm implements brought 167 pesos at auction; the other property went for 1,627 pesos. There was no purchaser for the sick, old slave. Dalton's debts ate up the proceeds of his estate.[85] But Marguerite had apparently been left some money by her mother. The day before she and Asher were married, they went before the Parish judge to record Marguerite's dowry of $5,000, and Asher promised that the sum would always be kept separate from his own property. In the record of Marguerite's estate, after her death on July 15, 1854, in Pass Christian, Mississippi, this amount was still listed as her own.[86] Antonio Gras, who had been chosen by Marguerite as her guardian after her father's death, sold her a lot of ground on July 26, 1811, for $300 and "in consideration of the natural love and affection" which he bore her. During the period from May, 1811, to August, 1812, Asher was busy buying and selling land and merchandise in the Baton Rouge area, but he was also traveling to and from New Orleans.[87]

Nathan had not lost everything in the venture with Hart,

or he was using money provided by his Charleston relatives to reestablish himself. How else explain the fact that by December, 1812, accounts due to him totalled $2,354? We know this because his store in Baton Rouge was robbed, and, in his notice offering a reward for the return of his property, he listed, in addition to two damask table cloths and a piece of checked goods, a "Red Morocco Pocket Book" which contained business papers of that value. Among the notes, due bills and accounts were the following: notes for $202 and $200 executed by one Major Milton in favor of Samuel Kohn, endorsed by Rochelle and Shiff, who in turn endorsed them over to Nathan; an account of Maurice Barnett in favor of Jacob Hart for $56; a note from Maurice Barnett for $12; an account of David Hart against some merchants for $353, endorsed to Nathan; and a due bill from S. S. De Jonge for $54. Only Judah Touro and Samuel Hermann, among the early Jews in the area, are missing from this list of Nathan's commercial contacts, which includes, also, many non-Jewish merchants and customers.[88]

Beginning no later than 1813, Nathan's major interests were in New Orleans, although he continued to make business trips to Baton Rouge, where he kept a branch store, over a period of years. He set himself up as a commission and exchange broker, in partnership with D. C. Williams for a year or two, alone after Williams took a post with the state government. Nathan's office was in Chartres street. There he conducted the sort of business which was characteristic of the time; he loaned money on interest, gave advances to planters, listed property for sale and auction, bought and sold slaves and shares of stock, took merchandise on consignment, and accepted responsibility for the affairs of ships which docked at New Orleans. During the early 1820's he was, for a time, in partnership with Samuel Hermann. He did not rival Hermann or Samuel Kohn in the height of his success, but, like Hermann, he did go into bankruptcy during the depression of 1837–42.[89]

Asher's sister Catherine and her husband Hyam Harris, together with their ten children, or at least most of them, moved to New Orleans about 1825. Asher probably supported them in whole or in part during their stay in New Orleans, because when Hyam died on June 1, 1828, the value of the furniture and stock

140

of his small store amounted to just $463; his only other possession was a seventy-year-old slave, Lucretia, who brought $72 at auction. At the inventory of Hyam's estate, Catherine reported that the silver plate in their home was her own private property, a gift from her brother Asher. The children, Levy Judah, Alexander, Isabelle and Aaron Harris, were still minors who required a male guardian; Henry M. Hyams, who had recently come from Charleston and had known the family there, agreed to act in that capacity. Rebecca, Abraham Hyam and Moses Harris were already adults, as was Amelia, who had married Daniel Goodman just a few months previously, on February 26, 1828. Asher Nathan set Moses Harris up in business in Mobile in 1837; sometimes Moses represented his uncle's interests, sometimes he acted on his own account.[90]

Asher Nathan's losses during the depression of 1837–42 were not serious. In the R. G. Dun and Company report of 1853, Asher was described as "an old resident & one of the most respectable Brokers in the city belongs to the old school. Is rich and a sup[erio]r bus man." Alexander Harris, his nephew and partner, was called an "intelligt yg man." The firm was said to be worth $50,000. In 1854 Nathan and Harris put in the successful bid for marketing $600,000 worth of 1857–58 bonds of the New Orleans, Jackson and Great Northern Rail Road Company. In 1859 Nathan retired and the business was named Alexander Harris and Company, but Nathan continued to give his financial support to Alexander and two of his brothers who were in the firm with him. Marguerite's estate, probated in 1854, listed $12,000 in real estate, $3,900 in slaves owned jointly with her husband, and $2,000 worth of furniture. Asher's will, written in 1862 and probated after his death on December 18, 1864, included charitable gifts of $11,000, and personal bequests of $5,000 to Amelia Harris Goodman and $3,000 to Alexander. He also left portraits of himself and his wife to Alexander. The remainder of the estate, which was apparently quite large, although the succession records cannot be located, was bequeathed by Asher to Achile Lion, a young man whom he adopted as his son by a special act which the Louisiana Legislature passed on March 12, 1859. To Anna Lion, about twenty-seven years old in 1862, "who resides in Paris now under the Protection and care of Madame De Blimère," Asher Nathan left the income from a fund of $8,000; after her death this additional amount was to go to Achile.

Who were Achile and Anna Lion? Achile was presumably a grown man, or he too would have required the designation of a guardian. Was Anna mentally incompetent, therefore requiring "Protection and care?" A French Negro artist named Jules Lion was active in New Orleans as a lithographer beginning in the late 1830's; one Achille Lion appears in a notarial record in 1844 as Jules's son. But there may not have been any relationship at all between Achile and Anna Lion and the artist. The feeling is inescapable that Achile and Anna were Asher Nathan's mulatto children who had been sent to France for their education. Why else would Asher leave them his fortune, in view of the tremendous number of his nieces and nephews who lived in New Orleans? Why else would Asher have waited until after Marguerite's death to adopt Achile? Why, indeed, unless Achile was a mulatto, would Asher not have his "adopted son" with him in New Orleans? Asher Nathan was not a unique figure if he had fathered these two mulatto children; such occurrences were frequent in ante-Bellum New Orleans.[91]

9. ALEXANDER PHILLIPS

In Baton Rouge, the Carmelite priest Juan Brady performed almost as many ritual ceremonies which involved Jews as did Père Antoine in New Orleans. On December 10, 1811, Brady married Alexander Phillips to seventeen-year-old Rosina Thomas, who had been born in Natchez, the daughter of John Thomas and Elizabeth Macough. Phillips, a native of Amsterdam, had come to the United States at the age of sixteen, about 1791, perhaps as an indentured servant. A report which was published in the first decade of the twentieth century, but which was probably based on Alexander's recollections of his early experiences, describes his wanderings:

> "After having received the trade of a whitesmith [tinsmith], and enduring the numerous privations always attendant upon poverty, he emigrated to the United States ... He settled at first in the

State of Pennsylvania. There he was obliged by necessitous circumstances to take employment in the capacity of a farmer's boy. For two years he served in that humble capacity. In 1794 . . . he enlisted under Gen'l Anthony Wayne, to quell the 'Whiskey Insurrection.' . . . He then secured employment from Gen. Hennen of Harrisburg, Pa. With this gentleman he remained until 1799, when, removing to the city of Philadelphia, he procured, under the advisement of a friend, a small quantity of merchandise, and thus equipped, girded up his loins and marched through the country as an itinerant, always finding a ready market . . . [A]t the end of a few years he became master of his own establishment and settled in the Quaker City . . . [H]e, in the year 1808, removed [to] the city of New Orleans, and immediately entered into the mercantile business."

The only record of Phillips' stay in Philadelphia annals is the mention of his partnership in 1804 with two other Jews, Lyon Cadet and Abraham Gumpert. He went first to Baton Rouge, however, rather than to New Orleans; in her will, written in 1876, Rosina said that she and Alexander remained in Baton Rouge for about one year after their marriage, "when we removed to this city where I have remained ever since." In December, 1811, Alexander Phillips, Maurice Barnett and Asher Nathan, the only Jews in the area, joined their neighbors in signing a petition of the inhabitants of Feliciana County (part of the territory formerly known as Spanish West Florida), which asked for special favors from the federal government in order that they might be integrated into Louisiana.[92]

Phillips' business ambitions were more modest than Samuel Kohn's and Samuel Hermann's. While he began his activity with shipping agencies, part ownerships of vessels and real estate dealings, he gradually restricted himself to wholesale and retail trade in groceries. An active Mason, he also participated in politics and served three terms as an alderman, in 1826 and 1827, and again in 1836; he was probably the first Jew to hold elective office in New Orleans. Phillips was prosperous, but he was not a wealthy man; in the 1820 census he is listed as owning four slaves; in 1830, ten. In 1824 he sold his home on Bienville street for $13,000, and built a more elegant one on Chartres.[93]

Alexander brought two brothers to New Orleans from Amsterdam. The first to come over was Isaac, who was in New

Orleans by 1814, when he purchased a slave. Isaac's wife, Martha Cline, was probably a Methodist. In 1817 he was managing a "house of entertainment" in the Baton Rouge Hotel, but he spent most of his life in New Orleans, where he later conducted a clothing store. His only daughter, Rosina, probably named for Alexander's wife, died two years after her marriage in 1839 to Nathaniel Jewett Merrill.[94]

The third brother, Asser or Asher, arrived in New Orleans about 1819. He and Isaac probably were in the clothing business together, although each had other separate commercial interests. Asher named one of his sons Alexander in honor of his brother; Alexander did not return the compliment, but did name one of his sons for Isaac. Asher was the first of the brothers to die. Alexander signed the death certificate on March 5, 1839, and reported that Asher was sixty years old, while he himself was sixty-three. Asher's estate was valued at $11,674, and included three slaves worth $900. Asher's wife was Johanna Marie Debott, a native of Rotterdam; she was single, twenty-six, when she arrived on the brig *Planter* from Amsterdam, on January 1, 1820. Perhaps they had already been engaged in Holland, and he came ahead to establish himself before sending for her.[95]

Several of Alexander's eight children occupied significant places in the life of New Orleans. One, Alfred, became a prominent attorney. John B. Cotton, a well-known judge in the middle years of the nineteenth century, first married Alexander's daughter Sophia, and after her death, her sister Rosina, the widow of Nathan Haber. Elleonora was married to Simon Newburger, a successful merchant.[96]

10. BENJAMIN LEVY[97]

An advertisement in the *Louisiana Gazette* of April 8, 1811, marked the beginning of the career of a pioneer New Orleans stationer, bookseller, bookbinder, printer and publisher:

"The subscriber having opened a Book and Stationery store in Chartres street opposite Mrs. Fourage's boarding house begs leave to inform the public that he will always have on hand a large and general assortment of Stationery of every description, together with an extensive assortment of Law and Miscellaneous books, which he will dispose of on the most reasonable terms: he will also keep Blank Books of every description or can rule and bind to any pattern with Spring Backs, Russian Bands or plain on the shortest notice. From his knowledge of the business in general and the unremitting attention he intends bestowing thereto, he hopes to meet with a share of their patronage.

B. Levy"

Born in New York City in 1786, Levy had gained experience as a bookbinder by the time he was twenty-two; two years later he became the partner of James Olmstead in a New York stationery store. He was a third-generation American, named for his grandfather who had emigrated from London to Newport, Rhode Island. Benjamin's father, Simeon (1748–1825), left that famed Jewish community, where Judah Touro's father officiated as *hazan*, and moved to New York City, where he became the teacher of Hebrew, English, arithmetic, and other subjects in the school of Shearith Israel Congregation; David Seixas and Jacob Hart were no doubt among his many pupils.[98]

It was probably his family's penurious circumstances which sent young Benjamin on the venturesome voyage to New Orleans, so far from home. There were five or six other children, and the father earned little from school-teaching, and had failed in business when he tried that. But the education which he had received from his father, and the bookish atmosphere which he absorbed in their home, marked him for life as one who would always be involved with books. Benjamin's departure from home did not signify a break with his family. He visited them several times before and after his father's death; he later brought his sister Mary to live with him in New Orleans; and he remained in contact with his sisters Hannah and Julia, mentioning all three in his will as his "Dear Sisters."[99]

In 1817 Benjamin married Emilie Prieur, daughter of Prosper Prieur and Marie Jeanne Casenauve. His bride, who had been born on November 2, 1799, was thus almost nineteen when she gave birth to their first child, Alexander, on September 7, 1818. Alexander was baptized in July, 1819, by Père Antoine, who

145

also baptized the second child, Isabel Mathilda, who was born April 2, 1820. Although his children were reared as Roman Catholics, this seems merely to have been a matter of convenience. Isabel married a Protestant, the notary Albert Childe Ainsworth.[100]

Levy was not, of course, the first bookseller in New Orleans, but he was one of the first to concentrate his energies on this cultural-commercial field, and was certainly the first to remain in it for an extended period of time—more than forty years. Within a few weeks of his first business announcement, Levy formed a partnership with Michael Reynolds, but this relationship lasted only about three years. In August, 1814, the firm's creditors entered suit, and bankruptcy proceedings resulted. But that did not deter Levy; in 1815, he opened another store under the name of "Benjamin Levy & Co.," advertising books, stationery, binding and subscriptions to the popular literary journals. It is entirely possible that his silent partner as early as 1815 was his old New York associate, James Olmstead, for after the latter's death on September 9, 1823, Levy announced that their partnership was now dissolved and that he would continue the business alone.[101]

Throughout his years as an active bookseller, Levy advertised profusely in the New Orleans and Louisiana newspapers, taking as many as nine separate notices to announce the receipt of new novels, biographies, literary annuals and gift books, volumes of history, memoirs, classical literature, home-remedy guides, works of drama, law and politics. But beyond the more general stock he carried and constantly replenished, he specialized in law books; this appears to have been a major personal interest—catering to the needs of attorneys. Other aspects of Levy's work were the sale of various types of stationery supplies, and the printing of business forms and the like. The range of his wares was as varied and extensive as today's stationery stores': pens, pencils, writing paper, notebooks, ink, knives, albums, writing desks, and all of the other odds and ends which a business man or housewife would want. In addition to the stock of "Books, Pamphlets, Cards, Checks, Bills of Lading, Bills of Exchange, Steam-Boat Bills, Posting Bills, Hand Bills, Labels, Custom-House and Notarial Blanks, &c, &c, &c."

which he printed and had for sale, he also sold theater and lottery tickets.[102]

But bookselling, stationery printing and selling, and bookbinding (Levy's first occupational proficiency, which he continued to advertise throughout his career), were less unique than his pursuits in the publishing field. He was one of the most active and productive publishers in New Orleans during the period 1822–41, and was probably the first Jewish printer-publisher not only in the South, but in the entire country. Jews had been active in bookselling and publishing in New York City for a number of years before Levy's first imprint appeared—Benjamin Gomez and Naphtali Judah were well-known booksellers and publishers during the 1790's, but their volumes were farmed out to professional printers, while they devoted their activity to selling, and most of their publications were ordered jointly with other booksellers. Levy was the first American Jew to combine printing, publishing and selling.

Levy's name first appeared on the title-page of a book in 1817, when Olmstead published the second edition of William Darby's popular *Geographical Description of the State of Louisiana*, and listed "B. Levy & Co. Booksellers, New-Orleans," as the sole distributor of the volume. This was in the Gomez–Judah tradition. Levy first announced his new venture as a printer-publisher in 1821, and, characteristically, advertised the publication of a legal volume, one of François-Xavier Martin's *Louisiana Term Reports . . . Cases Argued in the Supreme Court of the State of Louisiana*. In 1822 he published three volumes by Martin, another legal imprint, an almanac and the second New Orleans city directory (the first in eleven years). Throughout the following nineteen years, he continued to publish a wide variety of books and pamphlets. The largest proportion of the one hundred and thirty-three identifiable imprints of his press were of a legal character. If we count each of the eleven parts of Edward Livingston's *Penal Code* as a separate entity (which is justified because they were printed and distributed at different times over a five-year period), the legal items constitute almost half of his publications. These were compilations, reference volumes, appeals, briefs, and attorneys' courtroom pleadings. A few were published at the expense of the state or city—but Levy was never

147

an official governmental printer despite the fact that his wife's brother, Denis Prieur, served seven terms as Mayor of New Orleans, more than any other chief officer of the city. The interesting point is that Levy was the first New Orleans printer to publish legal treatises. Legal scholars probably turned to him because he took a particular interest in the practice of law, maintained a good stock of legal texts, and got along well with attorneys. A list of the authors of legal volumes published by Levy reads like a roster of the outstanding legal talent of the city: François-Xavier Martin, James Workman, Edward Livingston, Louis Moreau-Lislet, Pierre Derbigny, Samuel Livermore, John Slidell, Meinrad Greiner. (How ironic that Levy did not publish anything by the two leading New Orleans attorneys of Jewish birth, Judah P. Benjamin and Myer M. Cohen—but both were involved in his bankruptcy in 1842–43, Benjamin as assignee, and Cohen as United States Commissioner!)[103]

Approximately a quarter of Levy's publications were of a business nature, including acts of incorporation of banks and other institutions. Only twelve were political; ten were of literary or general interest; five were almanacs, and two were city directories. Because of New Orleans' diverse population, many were printed in French, or in both French and English, and one was printed in Spanish. Only three were printed by other firms, the 1817 Darby volume, and the 1841 *Louisiana Digest*, the first and last to bear his name, and, in addition, a book on *The Law of Slavery*, by Jacob D. Wheeler, published in 1837.

Comparatively few of the products of Levy's press were of permanent general interest and worth, although the *Term Reports* of the Louisiana Supreme Court decisions, and some of his other legal volumes, have a reference value which has required their reprinting throughout the years. Among the exceptions are J. C. Beltrami's *La Découverte des Sources du Mississippi et de la Rivière Sanglante* (1824); Charles Gayarré's *Essai Historique sur La Louisiane* (1830–31); and especially Edward Livingston's *Penal Code* (1822–27) which, while never adopted by the Louisiana Legislature, has had an enduring influence on concepts of criminology here and abroad. It was reprinted a number of times, both in the United States and in France, and is still the subject of frequent comment and evaluation.[104]

Another of Levy's publications which was of great utility in its time was the *New-Orleans Price-Current and Commercial Intelligencer*, the first business journal to appear in the city, which Levy established on June 27, 1822, and continued to publish on a weekly basis until December 28, 1839, the final issue to bear his name. This newspaper, which Levy printed for seventeen years, and even seems to have edited for a brief time in its early years, listed wholesale and retail prices not only for New Orleans, but also for Mobile, New York City, Philadelphia, Baltimore and other cities; it was a business man's guide to the present and the future. Associated with it was a *Price-Current Letter Sheet*, with the printed matter on two pages, leaving the last two pages blank for correspondence and comment; this handy business report seems to have been published by Levy from 1822 on. These publications and other commercial imprints demonstrate that Levy's connection with mercantile interests was second only to his relationship to attorneys.

Perhaps it was these same contacts which brought about Levy's business failure. It is difficult to make sense out of the many reports and listings of debits and assets compiled for Levy's bankruptcy proceedings in 1842–43, but this much is certain— it was neither his book and stationery store nor his printing business which drove him into court, but a combination of mortgaged real estate investments, bank debts, and bad notes which he had endorsed. Had he been content to manage his thriving business, in which he had prospered, he would not have run into trouble. But his intimate acquaintance with business growth and speculation undoubtedly enticed him into risks and associations beyond his competence. In 1835 he became a Commissioner of the Ocean Insurance Company, and around the same time was elected a director of the Mechanics' and Traders' Bank. This was a bad time for anyone to become involved in these reckless and unbridled financial operations. The panic of 1837 was soon upon the town and Levy was trapped. Although he owned only 245 shares of Mechanics' Bank stock, less than any other director, he had borrowed $8,530 and endorsed notes amounting to $4,605.62. In addition, he owed $3,640 to the Louisiana State Bank. He had made other investments, too: 130 shares of Union Bank stock; 400 shares of Nashville Railroad stock; 5 shares of Merchants' Exchange stock;

5 shares in the Barataria and Lafourche Company; and a number of heavily mortgaged parcels of real estate, some of which he owned in his own right, or in his sister Mary's name, others jointly with Francis Cook, who had been the foreman in his printing plant since about 1831. Had he maintained a liquid cash position, he might at least have weathered the storm and kept his business intact.[105]

In 1839, in an effort to retrench, Levy leased his printing plant and the *Price-Current* to his son Alexander and to Francis Cook, and moved his store from Chartres street to the corner of Camp and Gravier, but this only helped to stave off disaster until 1842. According to a declaration of credits and debits which he drew up on December 20, 1842, he owed a total of $75,347.20 in unpaid bills and $37,588 in notes. The first sum was owing to suppliers and publishers in New York City, Baltimore, Philadelphia and Cincinnati; the second included $18,000 to Francis Cook, $17,000 to Levi Pierce, a wealthy New Orleans attorney, and $863 to his son-in-law. His assets amounted to $56,465 in stock and $14,799 in bills receivable. The stock in his store, his store lease, his real estate and even his home at 15 St. Charles street, which he had purchased in 1831 for $14,500, were sold at auction for bargain prices. The final imprint bearing Benjamin Levy's name, of which no copy seems to have survived, is the catalogue of the auction sale of his merchandise, printed by Alexander. The text of the bill which Alexander Levy presented to Judah Benjamin for his services read as follows:

"Alexander Levy—
19th April 1843—

Printing 500 Catalogues of Books and Stationery for Sale at Auction, B. Levy's Estate, on Best Royal Paper 78 Pages made up into Pamphlets, for	$218.50
My Services, with a Clerk, to make the above Catalogue and to arrange Stock for the Auction	$100.00
Paid Cash for Negro Hire, in Hoisting Up and Down, Carrying, &c. &c.	$23.50
Three Weeks extra services, for myself and one Clerk, in attending the Auction, promoting Sales, Collection &c &c	$150.—
	$492.00"

We may be certain that Benjamin Levy preferred that if this Auction Catalogue had to be printed at all, it be printed by his son.[106]

Benjamin Levy never reestablished himself in business following his bankruptcy, but he did take an active role in Alexander's business ventures. During the period 1839–42, while Alexander and Cook were partners in the printing business, their firm issued ten publications under their imprint. After that partnership was dissolved, Alexander went into business as Alexander Levy & Company, under his father's guidance and assistance, but it was no longer the flourishing, successful operation of old. The firm concentrated on stationery and lawbooks, and published only nineteen items, all in pamphlet form, none big enough to be called a book, or of any literary or historical significance. One, however, is the fascinating license form which was issued by the New Orleans city government in 1857 to prostitutes who observed the law which prohibited their occupying ground level quarters. The firm went bankrupt again, in 1858. Ben simply had no luck at all.[107]

Within a period of seventeen months in 1851–52, Levy had suffered great sorrow. Emilie died on February 21, 1851; A. C. Ainsworth on May 5, 1851; and Mathilde (she used that name rather than Isabel) on July 22, 1852. Benjamin's grandchildren, Aline Mary, Annie Elizabeth and Martin Luther, were only eleven, seven and five when their mother died. We do not know whether they were reared in Benjamin and Alexander's home, which was tended by Benjamin's sister Mary, but they were his moral and legal responsibility—a heavy one for a sixty-six-year-old man. Fortunately he lived until 1860, and Mary seems to have remained in New Orleans for a few more years before crossing through the Confederacy to Washington, where she made her home with her nephew, Adolphus Solomons, another printer-publisher.[108]

What kind of man was Benjamin Levy? Gullible and attracted by the vision of quick profits, certainly, to judge from his ambitious investments. But modest also; note his comment about the value of his household possessions: "Much of this furniture I bought when married in 1817. It is almost impossible for me to name its true value now." One catches a glimpse of

151

his affectionate, tender nature in the provision of his will which related to his grandchildren; he bequeathed to them his "whole Library & Book Case, hoping they will profit by this, my only Legacy to them. I wish it was in my power to leave them more Substantial proofs, of my strong & tender Affection, but indeed it is not, I hope they will be enabled by their own industry, and ability, to not regret this bequest So very small." Efforts to locate this "Library & Book Case," if indeed it is still in existence, have been unavailing. What further imprints it might contain, and how many other indications of Levy's nature and character! The children had no doubt inherited something from their parents' estates, and probably also had received gifts from prosperous Prieur relatives, for most of Levy's possessions and cash assets (amounting to a total worth of only $1,760, including the value of a slave) were divided between his son and his sisters. Touching were his comments about slaves:

"Item, I give and bequeath to my Dear Son, Alexander Levy, my Black Slave Man, Richard or Dick White, a Barber, for his use During Life, unless the Slave Richard or Dick White can buy his Freedom, for the amount of Five hundred Dollars in cash. But in case the afore said Slave cannot buy his freedom during the Life of my Son, as afore said, the said Slave Richard shall be sett [sic] Free, in the usual forms by Law,—

"From the tenor of the foregoing, My Wish and direction is, That the above named Slave Richard, is never to be sold, Mortgaged, or hired out for a Longer term than one Year at a time, and never to be hired out of the State of Louisiana . . .

"I should like (if it is possible,) to give to each of the coloured people, Born into my family, viz, Richard[,] Harry[,] Samuel, Ellen, Joseph, Martha and Horace, and Millee likewise (belonging to my Dear Grand Children,) Some Small Memorial of their old Master, and to whom I have always been strongly attached, this wish, my family will carry out, in the best way, they may choose to adopt.—"

Benjamin Levy devoted more words in his will to these slaves than to the members of his family: indication enough of a warm and kind spirit.[109]

Not many deaths warranted newspaper editorials in those days, any more than in our own. The editors of the *Daily Crescent* got some of the facts twisted in their sketch, but they expressed respect not only for a journalistic colleague who had printer's ink in his veins, but for the man Benjamin Levy, in their eulogy of January 11, 1860:

"DEATH OF AN OLD CITIZEN.—Benjamin Levy has been called hence; he departed this life yesterday morning at his residence on Canal street, in the 74th year of his age. Mr. Levy was a native of Long Island, New York, and arrived in this city about the year 1812. His profession as a book-binder and printer led him to be largely concerned with the art preservative of all arts—printing. In the year 1818 he opened a large and extensive book and stationery store on Conti street at about the inter-section of Exchange Alley ... In the year 1822 he established the New Orleans Price Current, which has attained so high an eminence in the commercial world, and now located on Camp street. His connection with the Price Current was of many years' duration. He was one of the pioneers of journalism in our city ... For a long period of time—over a quarter of a century—Mr. Levy stood the highest of the high in his vocation. Like thousands of others he had to undergo the viscissitudes [*sic*] and revulsions of commerce and trade. He met the adversities and disasters with courage and rectitude. In the many relations of life and as a good citizen he stood high and unblemished. Over forty years ago he became connected, by marriage, with the old, respected and ancient family of Prieur. His descendants enjoy high social position in our community. In fine, our departed friend was emphatically a good man; he was universally respected by all our citizens. And thus, one by one, the men of other days are called from this sublunary sphere."

11. JEWS IN THE BATTLE OF NEW ORLEANS

We have thus far traced the personal, familial and business careers of all but two of the Jews who had settled in New Orleans by the time of the battle that saved the city from capture by the British. One of these two was Manis Jacobs, whose story we defer until later. An obituary at the time of his death in 1839 said that he had lived in the city for thirty years, but the earliest reference to him which we have discovered is a newspaper advertisement of 1812.[110] The other person unmentioned thus far was Simon M. Cohen. These two round out to fifteen the number of Jewish men definitely known to have been in New Orleans by 1814–15. Of these, at least ten, and possibly eleven, served in the armed forces under Andrew Jackson on the fields of Chalmette Plantation on January 8, 1815. Two-thirds of any group is a large proportion, but it is important to recall that all of these Jews were comparatively young men, some of them single, who were not only willing but able to take part in the defense of their new home.

The records of the military units which took part in the campaign, particularly the home guard, the Louisiana Militia, are scanty and incomplete. In addition to Touro, whose service we have already noted, a contemporary roster, dated December 20, 1814, lists four of our men: S. Coh[e]n, a member of the Compagnie des Dragons, Plauché's Battalion of the Louisiana Militia; another "Cohn" who served in the Compagnie des Carabiniers, and who is probably to be identified with Samuel Kohn; Maurice Barnett, listed as a Dragon in the Compagnie des Francs; and J. Hart, of the Compagnie des Dragons (à pied). These are the only early references to military service by our men which we have been able to uncover.[111]

With a number of men named Jacob Hart in New Orleans at the same time, two of whom were known to be military figures, and the third a policeman, it would be difficult to state with any assurance that it was our Jacob Hart who served as a private in Plauché's Battalion, were it not for a list which was published at the time of the 34th anniversary celebration of the Battle of New Orleans, on January 8, 1849, designating those who were still known to be living at the time. So far as we know, our Jacob Hart was the only man bearing that name who was still alive and in residence in New Orleans—he did not die until December of that year. Another name on that list was Maurice Barnett's. When he died in 1865, an obituary in the *Picayune* said of him: "A veteran gone. We are once again called on to announce the demise of one of the small but highly honored class of our old citizens, the veterans of the Battle of New Orleans, so few of whom remain to us. Mr. Maurice Barnett, Sr. died yesterday. . . ."[112]

Of the others, the evidence is less conclusive. An obituary of Isaac Phillips which was published in 1851 reports that he "fought in the Battle of New Orleans, January 8, 1815—defended his adopted country. A Jew by birth."[113] Our other men are listed in a recent compilation of the names of men who served under Jackson, which was painstakingly assembled from various sources, including those in Baton Rouge and in the National Archives in Washington; unfortunately, sources are not cited for each specific individual. The following names are of particular interest to us: Rochelle and Shiff (no first names), both privates in Dejan's First Regiment; Samuel Hermann, a private in De Clouet's Regiment; Dejonge, Sergeant of Musicians and Chief Musician, Plauché's Battalion; Alexander Phillips, 2nd Lieutenant of Dejan's Regiment.[114] All of these pieces of information, although far from definitive, mesh well with facts already at our disposal. It would be natural for Rochelle and Shiff to have enlisted together in the same regiment, since they were partners; we would expect Rochelle to have served, in view of what we have already learned about his physical courage and prowess with the sword. S. S. De Jonge was so interested in music that he was an incorporator of the New Orleans Philharmonic Society in 1838; as Chief Musician he may even have conducted a band. Alexander Phillips, we recall, was a veteran of the military forces which were assembled to quell the Whiskey Rebellion. In view of the tremendous amount of effort which has been expended on research on this subject, it seems unlikely that any new, dramatic sources of information will be discovered to give further details about the activities of these men. We shall have to be content with the meager evidence at our disposal, sufficient to indicate that this small number of Jews shouldered their share of responsibility, accepted the burden of fear and danger, and achieved whatever of glory and satisfaction were in store for those who followed Jackson to victory. Of only four of our men is there a total absence of evidence of participation in the battle: A. M. Nathan, David Hart, Benjamin Levy and Manis Jacobs.[115]

Only one of these citizen-soldiers maintained an interest in military matters. Simon Cohen's name occurs frequently in the newspaper advertisements which the New Orleans military units utilized, beginning in 1829, to announce their drills, reviews and parades. From April, 1829, to May, 1830, he was Sergeant Major of the Artillery Battalion. In October, 1830, he was elected 2nd Lieutenant, and another Jew, Joseph Lasalle, replaced him in his former post. Cohen held this rank until 1833.[116]

Little is known about Cohen's earlier years in New Orleans. His obituary in the *Bee* reports that he had come to the city from Amsterdam about 1810. In 1818 he bought a slave and her two-month-old baby, but the sale was annulled when it was discovered that they were mortgaged to someone else. That same year Cohen leased all of the rooms in his house, other than his tobacconist's shop and his living quarters, to two men who apparently set up a billiard parlor; when they failed to pay the specified sum of $1,200, he confiscated the billiard tables. In the 1820 census, Cohen is listed as the owner of four slaves.[117]

After a long illness, Cohen died at the age of fifty-five, on August 21, 1836. A friend wrote a long and emotional tribute to him for the French section of the *Bee*; he berated Cohen's former friends who had neglected him during his illness, when he was in need of funds as well as good cheer, and criticized the Artillery Battalion for its failure to provide military honors at Cohen's funeral. Jews were apparently not among those friends. Less than four months before Cohen's death, he was baptized a Roman Catholic by Abbé Moni, who also gave him the last rites and conducted his funeral. But it would seem as though this deathbed conversion may simply have been the result of the insistence of his importunate and loyal friend. He had been in New Orleans for twenty-six years, or thereabouts, without feeling any need to renounce Judaism and adopt a new faith. The last words of his anonymous friend's French tribute are full of pathos:

> "Adieu Cohen! . . . adieu! puissent ces faibles lignes, tracées avec la plus vive émotion, adoucir l'amertume des chagrins de ceux qui le chérissaient sur cette terre, et attester le souvenir d'un ancien ami."[118]

IV

From the Battle of New Orleans to the
Formation of the First Congregation

French settlement of the site of New Orleans had begun in 1718, but the city did not enter its American period until 1803. The early years of the nineteenth century were late in the day for old American cities like Boston, New York and Philadelphia, but they were just the beginning for New Orleans. French-Spanish Creole influences have persisted to this very day; New Orleans is still a different kind of American city. But the period from 1803 to 1815 was a pioneering age, and those European and Yankee immigrants who came to the city then were participants in the living drama of the transformation of a colonial port into a vibrant, dynamic, enterprising, though still Creole, metropolis. Our Jews who settled in New Orleans before the battle which saved the city from British conquest (even though the peace treaty had already been signed before the first shot was fired) were forerunners in the same sense as all others who immigrated to this new frontier. During the second decade of the nineteenth century, for the most part after 1815, another 10,000 white settlers swelled the population—that was larger than the entire number of residents at the time of the Louisiana Purchase. Almost 20,000 more entered the city during the 1820's, but the 1830's were the years of greatest growth; the white population more than doubled from 46,082 in 1830 to 102,193 in 1840. A large proportion of these were European immigrants, quite aside from at least an equal number of foreigners who landed in New Orleans, stayed for a brief while, and then fanned out through the South and up the Mississippi. New Orleans was so popular a port of debarkation partly because the fare was cheaper than to New York City—ships which transported cotton to Europe did not always fill their holds with cargo for the return voyages to New Orleans; human cargo was better than none. But not all of the newcomers were

Europeans. Many were native-born Americans who left cities like New York or Philadelphia because they believed fortunes were to be made in New Orleans, or who forsook the states of the "old" South, like Virginia and South Carolina, because business conditions in those areas had become stagnant. New Orleans, regarded by Europeans as an American city, was to Americans themselves a city on the frontier of the "new" South, or, rather, the Southwest as it was known in that day.[1]

To establish the precise number of Jews in any location at any specific time is extremely difficult. No questions relating to religious affiliation or preference may be asked by census-takers. We are therefore dependent on the use of names and other identification indices if we are to reach even an approximate number. But the manuscript census returns are hard to use: the handwriting is frequently difficult to decipher; names are spelled incorrectly; information is inaccurate. In the case of New Orleans, two separate and independent studies reflect some of the problems inherent in the utilization of the census records. Ira Rosenswaike, who has spent much time on the examination of the census records of 1820 for information about Jews in various cities, located a total of ten Jews in the New Orleans returns; this writer identified an eleventh Jew. But altogether missing from the census data are the names of seven other men whose experiences we have already sketched.[2] The 1822 *New Orleans City Directory* includes the names of seven additional Jews, but omits a number of those whose presence is confirmed by other sources. The *Directory* listing is quite helpful, however, because of the occupational data which it reports. With twenty-five Jews listed by name, the occupational distribution is as follows: six merchant-bankers and brokers; three commission merchants; two traders; one liquor dealer (who dealt more in slaves than in liquor); six clothing and dry goods storekeepers; one hotelkeeper; two brothers in the Hart cotton press; one grocer; one bookseller; one watchmaker; one cigar manufacturer. Those names omitted from the *Directory* belong largely to petty shopkeepers whose business activities were probably so limited that they did not consider it worthwhile to enter their names. The most exhaustive list of Jews in New Orleans during this time was published in the constitution of the first congregation, in 1827; it includes thirty-five members and thirty-three contributors—but some in both categories lived outside of New Orleans, and a number were in town only for a brief time and then left for other horizons. Thirty-five Jewish heads of households are listed in the 1830 census, as best we can read them, but probably more than that number are omitted.

At any rate, it is not our intention to compile a list of every Jew who resided in the city temporarily or even permanently during the period following the Battle of New Orleans. The pioneers, as we have called them, were a special breed, and we have studied them exhaustively for reasons which will become more apparent in another chapter. We have made no effort, however, to trace every Jew who came to New Orleans in the years after 1815. But some of these American and European migrants to New Orleans are especially interesting or important, and it is to these that we now turn.

1. Visitors, Transients and Victims

Any port like New Orleans was bound to have a large transient population. People were forever coming and going, because ships were the fastest and most convenient method of transportation. Anyone traveling from the Atlantic seaboard or from Europe to the lower and middle Mississippi Valley areas was more likely to go to New Orleans by ship and then up the Mississippi, than to undertake the arduous journey across the Appalachians. But there was yet another reason for so much traffic in and out of the city: the climate made New Orleans so uncomfortable during the summer, and the summer epidemics made it so unhealthy, that many permanent residents, let alone transients, left the city for long months at a time.

There were probably dozens of Jews like Samuel Mordecai, of Warrenton, N. C., who stopped in New Orleans for a brief time. He was in the city in May of 1815, while his ship was unloading and taking on cargo. This was only one stop on a trip which he was making from New York City to Europe. Sam bemoaned his lack of letters of introduction to local people;

time rested heavily on his hands while he was waiting.[3] Sam's brother Solomon, the physician, made a similar stopover in New Orleans in 1823 on his way from Virginia, via Baltimore, to Mobile, where he intended to open his medical practice. But he was in too much of a hurry to send his impressions of the town back to his family in North Carolina.[4]

A visitor who stayed longer, and returned several times, was the actor Aaron J. Phillips, the son of the well-known Jewish leader of Philadelphia, Jonas Phillips, and the uncle of the dramatist-politician, Mordecai Manuel Noah. Aaron Phillips arrived in New Orleans in March, 1819, fresh from the "Theatres of New York, Philadelphia, Baltimore & Charleston," and announced that he would make his first appearance on the stage of the Orleans Ball Room in a program of monologues. The featured piece, "for the first time in this city," was "Sterne's Celebrated LECTURE ON HEADS." The first part included the following:

> "No. 1 Head of Sir Whiskey Whiffle. 2. Comical Fellow. 3. Hamlet's Soliloquy on Death. 4. Head of Jonas, or the Card Playing Conjurer. 5. Head of an Apothecary. 6. Clarence's Dream. 7. The London Blood, going to keep it up. 8. The London Blood, after he has kept it up. . . ."

The second part of this hodgepodge highlighted Antony's oration over Caesar, and Collins' "Ode on the Passions." A reviewer expatiated on his pleasure at the performance, praised Phillips as "an actor not inferior to any of the stars now playing with such boasted honor at New-York and Philadelphia," and chided the population of New Orleans for their unresponsiveness to the opportunity to hear Phillips, regretting that this "amusement of the most chaste refinement and intellectual character, was not honored by the attendance of more of the fashion and beauty of New Orleans." But he said that the people of the town would be given another chance—Phillips was going to repeat the performance, and was even making plans to open his own theater with a company that would specialize in performances of Shakespeare. Aaron joined the company of the St. Philip Street Theater (Phillips of St. Philip) and took the lead in three plays before returning to the East. Aaron did come back to

New Orleans for the winter season of 1819–20 with a repertoire which included *Romeo and Juliet*. But James Caldwell's company had taken the city by storm, and there was no room for a rival. On March 3, 1820, Phillips announced his imminent departure, but he probably stayed in town long enough to watch the Caldwell company's performance of his nephew Mordecai Noah's patriotic play *She Would be a Soldier, or, The Plains of Chippewa*, which was enlivened by the participation of a local detachment of regular Army troops. A reviewer reacted enthusiastically to the Noah drama. "This is the best American Play which we have ever seen," he said. "When our country can boast of such writers as Mr. Noah, we see no necessity of our importing 'British Literature' and British plays 'by the bale and by the hogshead.' " Noah's dramas continued to evoke a lively response from the theater-goers of New Orleans for many years to come, but his uncle Aaron Phillips had not hit it off so well—he paid only one more visit to the city, in 1823.[5]

Reports of passenger arrivals and cargo receipts in the New Orleans newspapers frequently refer to Jews who came to town on business, stayed for a little while, and then moved on. G. Cohen was in and out of New Orleans with trunks and boxes of merchandise, during the business season of 1825–26, on his way from Philadelphia, then up the Mississippi River, and then finally through New Orleans again bound for Havana. At about the same time, S. Levy arrived in New Orleans from Charleston, but his name does not appear again in the records. John B. Levy came to town in 1828 with thirty-seven slaves for sale; he did not even land them, but sold them at the dock from the schooner *Transport*.[6]

These people were, obviously, transients who had no intention of remaining in New Orleans. There were others, however, who intended to become permanent residents, but luck ran out on them, and they died in New Orleans. Among these were Henry Hartman, a commission merchant, and Benjamin Levine, a watchmaker, both of whom died in 1818. Hartman said in his will that he thought his mother, Julia Hirsch, might still be living, in Hamburg, but if not, his executors should make every effort to find his heirs and distribute the proceeds of his estate equitably.[7] Levine had kept in closer contact with his family.

He left $300 to George Levine of Petersburg, Virginia, and $200 to Mary Levy of New York City, probably his brother and sister; the remainder of the estate was to be sent to Moses Levy of Gloucester, England, probably his father.[8] On December 23, 1820, Ezekiel Salomon, Haym Salomon's oldest child, arrived in New Orleans on the steamboat *Car of Commerce* from Louisville, to assume his new position as cashier of the New Orleans branch of the Bank of the United States. He signed notices of checks and drafts available, bank closing dates and similar advertisements in the newspapers until his death on September 27, 1821. One summer in New Orleans was too much for forty-three-year-old Ezekiel.[9] Another casualty was Baruh Jonas, who came to New Orleans from England about 1819–20. He was born in Teignmouth, Devonshire, on January 18, 1798, and may have been related to the Jonas brothers, Abraham and Joseph, who were among the earliest Jewish settlers in Cincinnati. Baruh was married to Teresa Barbarin on November 25, 1820, by the Reverend James Hull. A Protestant ceremony was probably the best compromise this Catholic girl and Jewish man could make. Jonas died on January 4, 1822, a little more than a year after his wedding, and was buried in the Protestant Girod Street Cemetery. Presuming that he was one of the twenty-two children of Benjamin Jonas and Annie Ezekiel of Exeter, it was his brother George and nephew Benjamin Franklin Jonas who brought great distinction to their family's name in New Orleans in later years.[10] Another Jew who died the same year as Baruh Jonas was Louis Levy, thirty-four, of Pennsylvania, one of a large number of "strangers" who died in the yellow fever epidemic that fall.[11]

2. DEALERS IN SLAVES AND INDENTURED SERVANTS, AND MANY MEN NAMED JACOBS

We have no way of knowing how many young Jewish men came to the New Orleans area as indentured servants or "redemptioners," as they were called. It would be surprising if there were none. They may, as a matter of fact, have been among

162

those advertised by other Jews. A. F. Strauss, listed in the 1822 *City Directory* as a grocer at 36 Gravier street, below Tchoupi-toulas, was the agent for the brig *Mississippi*, which arrived at the port from Bremen in November, 1819, with a shipload of indentured craftsmen and farmers, some with their families, who now had to work for several years to repay their fare, as Alexander Phillips apparently had done when he arrived in Pennsylvania. "They are all remarkably healthy," said Strauss' advertisement, "exclusively Germans, and of good character." Levy Jacobs, with headquarters first at 4 Conti street, then at 29 Toulouse street, was another Jew who got a commission for his activity in selling contracts for the repayment of the $70 ship passage money of redemptioners. During 1820 he advertised a number of shipments of these people, as many as a hundred at a time; they included blacksmiths, brewers, bricklayers, butchers, barbers, carpenters, joiners, upholsterers, millers, painters, ropemakers, shoemakers, coopers, gardeners, tailors, tanners, wheelwrights, and masons, and women who had been trained as laundresses, dressmakers and domestic servants.[12]

Levy Jacobs had begun business as an exchange and commission merchant by 1819 at the latest, with a non-Jewish partner named George Asbridge. They offered to "sell or purchase goods at private sale; buy goods at auction; procure freights and vessels for freight; buy and sell Negroes; exchange foreign bills; execute instruments in writing." After they dissolved their partnership, Jacobs seems to have concentrated on liquor sales and slavetrading. He came as close as any New Orleans Jew to specializing in this business. During the late 1820's large shipments of slaves came his way. In September, 1828, he notified the public that he was expecting about 100 "prime, Virginia slaves, selected expressly for this market [slave-dealers always said that, because planters were suspected of shipping their unwanted, sick or rebellious slaves to the expanding areas in the South where more slaves were needed]:—among which are, Ostlers, Carriage Drivers, Mechanics, Field Hands and Cooks, House Servants, seamstresses and washer women." Jacobs was indignant when he was accused of foisting inferior Kentucky slaves on his customers instead of the superior Virginia ones he advertised:

163

"NOTICE—A report being circulated that I have for sale no other than Kentucky slaves, I beg leave to state to the public that all the Negroes which I have on hand, and shall hereafter keep for sale are and will be Virginia born Negroes, of good character; that the person who has stated to the contrary, with the view of injuring me, I call upon in this public manner to come forward and support this charge if he can, or hereafter hold his peace. All Negroes sold and bought by me from traders (excepting at my own house) will be free of commission.

L. JACOBS"

The social position of a slave trader in Jacobs' time was not inferior to that of other merchants of a similar success. Levy Jacobs even called himself "Esq." in an advertisement. We may be certain that no one lifted an eyebrow when Levy's daughter Isabella was married, on May 5, 1832, to T. G. Joans, a young printer-journalist. If any eyebrows were raised, it was not because Levy was a slave trader or a Jew, but two years later, when Joans, editor and publisher of the *Mercantile Advertiser*, the *Price-Current's* competition, absconded with the proceeds of some forged notes.[13]

There were many men in New Orleans at this time whose last name was Jacobs. One was Manis Jacobs, the jeweler and trader whom we have already met briefly. Another was Ralph (Raphael) Jacobs, whose nephew, Dr. Joseph Bensadon, became the first medical director of the Touro Infirmary. Ralph was in New Orleans by 1822 at the latest, conducting a ship brokerage business at 3 Custom House street. At that time his partner was one J. W. Melder, who left Ralph and then went bankrupt still owing him some money. Ralph himself was in business difficulties in 1832, and his property had to be sold to satisfy his creditors. Back in business again, he sold some real estate, bought shares in a ferry company, and guaranteed the captains of ships that he would be able to provide seamen, on bond, for ships' crews. He had two offices for those in a hurry to reach him, one at 84 Gallatin street at the foot of the vegetable market, and the other in the rear of a grocery store on the levee. Ralph died on April 23, 1845, at the age of sixty-three.[14]

Ralph was not related to Levy Jacobs, so far as we can discover, but Levy did have a brother named Jacob Jacobs. Perhaps Samuel Jacobs was another brother. We know very little about Sam other than the public ventilation of his domestic troubles. On August 24, 1824, he announced to the readers of the *Louisiana Gazette* that he would no longer be responsible for his wife's debts:

> "CAUTION. Whereas my wife Rosette has left my house without any just cause whatever, this is to caution the public not to trust her on my account, as I will not pay any debts contracted by her."

A month later, Jacobs printed a retraction. The previous notice had been issued, he said, "merely through a mistake"—"now I have the pleasure to let the public know that we live in perfect harmony." But the "perfect harmony" did not last very long. Before the year was out, the court approved the couple's legal separation. In 1834 Sam went bankrupt and his property was sold at sheriff's auction for $16,200; his possessions included 24 lots of unimproved ground, a building on the levee, and a slave with her six-month-old child. Sam's possessions were still being sold in 1839, the last time his name was mentioned.[15]

3. SCANDALS AND DUELS

Samuel Jacobs' legal separation was an unusual occurrence, but not so his marriage to a local non-Jewish woman. Intermarriage continued apace as the newcomers arrived, and their children were invariably reared in conformity with the Christian environment. On October 18, 1822, Lise Augustine, the daughter of J. M. Cohen, a native of Holland, and Marie Victoire Leboulh of Louisiana, was baptized at the St. Louis Church.[16] The following year, Victor Souza, the son of Antonio Souza and Marie Pereira of Bordeaux, was married in the same church by Père Antoine, to Rose Bourdeaux, the daughter of Pierre Bourdeaux and Anne Marcely of Saint-Domingue. Nineteen days before his wedding on December 23, 1823, Victor underwent Roman Catholic baptism; he is the only Jew during this period, other than Simon Cohen, whose name is included as a convert in the baptismal books of the St. Louis Cathedral.[17] But this did not prevent Victor's being identified as an "Israelite" contributor to the newly founded congregation in 1827, under the name "Souza, Jr.," along with "Souza, Sr.," who we presume was his older brother, Mardochée. The older brother went bankrupt soon after the congregation was organized, in 1828. Victor Souza and his partner Decadie Baiz underwent the same unpleasant experience in 1834, but "absconded and defrauded their creditors, whom they have shamefully deceived," according to a notice which offered $1,000 for their apprehension, or $500 for either. Despite his conversion to Catholicism, Victor was described as a Jew:

"Victor Souza, a Jew, is about 4 feet 11 inches high, has a large face, large nose and a small mouth; his face is red, and his beard strong and black. D. Baix, a jew, [sic] about 5 feet 3 or 4 inches high, full face and pock marked, strong black beard . . ."

Newspapers in Mobile, Louisville, Baltimore, Philadelphia and New York City were instructed to copy the notice and to bill the syndic for the creditors, for whose benefit four slaves and three lots of ground were sold at auction. Baiz was probably identical with the Abraham Baiz whose name appears in the Bordeaux records as traveling to New Orleans in 1827 and returning home in 1829, but nothing further is known of his New Orleans career. Victor Souza was apprehended, tried for fraud, convicted, and sentenced to prison. After his release he kept store in Texas and New Orleans, but success continued to elude him. Despite his formal conversion to Christianity and the fact that his children were reared as Catholics, everyone, including the R. G. Dun reporter, thought of Victor as a Jew.[18]

Not all scandals involved a convert. Two Jews got into one of the worst name-calling feuds imaginable, over an absolute trifle, in 1836. These men were Solomon Audler and L. A. Levy, Jr. Audler, who was in Charleston in 1824, and in New Orleans by 1827, was probably a brother of the Dr. E. M. Audler whose "Asiatic Lenitive" for the cure of toothaches, headaches and other "diseases" was a widely advertised patent medicine. Sol married Maurice Barnett's daughter Hélène; they are listed as owning four slaves in the 1830 census. In June of that year he went bankrupt, and two years later, Myer Audler, probably another brother, took the same punishment. L. A. Levy, Jr., has eluded precise identification; there were more than a dozen Levys in town in the early 1830's. It is possible that he was a son of the Levy Andrew Levy who married into the Simon family of Lancaster, Pennsylvania, or that he is identical with the Lewis A. Levy who was buying property in Houston in 1842, but neither suggestion is more than a guess.

The occasion for the trouble between Audler and Levy was a linen coat. One of the Phillipses in town, probably Asser, was auctioning off a lot of linen coats. Phillips promised Levy he could have one at the same price as those which were sold at auction. The coat Levy tried on did not fit, so he exchanged it for one in the batch that Audler bought. Audler billed him for it, but since he had already paid Phillips for it, Levy saw no reason to pay Audler. Sol sued for the cost, but lost the case; pursuing the matter still further, he went to the auction store where the coats were sold, and called Levy a thief. In a rage, Levy sent friends to challenge Audler to a duel, but Audler refused on the ground that Levy was not a gentleman and, therefore, was not entitled to satisfaction. Levy promptly issued a handbill denouncing Audler as a coward:

> "*Notice to the public* . . . S. Audler having gravely insulted me this morning at the auction store of Mr. J. B. Blache, I deem it my duty in justice to my reputation, to state to the public, that my friends called upon the said individual for satisfaction, which he did not grant, I hereby proclaim him to the public, as a coward, and no gentleman, and beneath the notice of the community.
>
> May 28th 1836
> (Signed)   L. A. LEVY, JR."

Audler immediately took an advertisement in the newspaper, told his version of the entire matter, and asked the "impartial public" to decide "whether an individual guilty of an act of this description, should be entitled to the satisfaction due a gentleman. I have been required to give gentlemanly satisfaction, to whom? I would ask—to a man? a gentleman? No! it is to one who cannot prove himself a gentleman, for the act of which he stands charged by me cannot be termed the act of a gentleman. A man he is not; it needs but a glance to perceive it; he was well aware at the time he wrote the challenge that he could not obtain a gentlemanly satisfaction from me, otherwise he would not have demanded it. . . ."

Audler asked the editors of newspapers in New York City and Philadelphia to reprint his long description of the dispute, probably so that relatives and suppliers in both cities might thereby be informed about it. Levy went Audler one better and added the Charleston papers to the list when he published his reply to Audler's attack. Levy's denunciation was a masterpiece of invective:

"This self same Audler—this vendor of worn out harness—this wash-tub dealer has with the impudence and characteristic daring, inherent in triflers called me that which in the hearing of our most respectable citizens and in a most public place (New Exchange) he himself was called—"a Thief" Audler!! Ay Audler! Sol Audler!!! and who does not shrink at the very letters of his name. He *has* been *is* and *ever will be* the detestation of the honest man, the land mark for the Coward, the beacon for the Insolvent debtor, the light house for the smuggler—he dares to speak of intrusion on the public! well may he do so. Oznaburgs, Italian silk cottonades, old swords and belts, &c. &c. groan loudly a requiem for the ledger of his poor creditors—As to an enlightened public to which he thrice appeals I will but say that it is too 'enlightened' ever again to trust this blackened lump of infamy . . . the public must condemn him for calling *me* a Thief when he himself is so notoriously known as an adept in the business. . . ."

Audler simply reiterated his innocence and asserted his assurance that "after a long residence in this city (I flatter myself without reproach) that my reputation cannot suffer in the opinion of an impartial public, by the slanderous and unfounded accusations of such a worthless fellow as Levy." Here the newspaper notices cease. Whether Audler and Levy were ever reconciled is not known. But it must have been a source of merriment to many readers, and of embarrassment to many Jews, that these two men vented their spleen at each other in public over so trivial a matter.[19]

The challenge to a duel which Levy hurled at Audler is an example of how thoroughly the Jews of New Orleans had adjusted to the temperament of their neighbors. We have uncovered two examples of such affairs of honor in which Jews took part in the 1830's. In both episodes, the Jews involved were not permanent residents of New Orleans. Matthias Gomez, the son of the New York City bookseller, and a third-generation American, was killed in a duel on June 19, 1833. Carl Kohn tells his Uncle Samuel about it in his letter of July 7:

"We had a duel here again between Mr. Bosqui, the same that killed his cousin Marchand, and an American Gomez by name. The cause was quite a trifling one, nevertheless they were determined upon the destruction of one or the other—they fought with muskets at forty paces, and fired four times without effect, the fifth time however Gomez fell dead, and Bosqui was wounded severely in both his legs. The Physicians thought it incumbent upon them to have one of his legs amputated, but he, fluttering as he was between life & death, preferred rather to die than to be maimed, & would not permit his limb to be amputated—now he is almost able to walk again to the great disappointment of every orderly & quiet townsman—."

How long Gomez had been in town is unknown, but it was long enough for him to have purchased some property from Samuel Hermann; that November, the nineteen lots were sold at auction for the benefit of his heirs in New York City.[20] The other Jew involved in a duel, Major Leon Dyer, was more fortunate than Gomez. In 1836, on his way from Baltimore through New Orleans to serve in the army of Texas, Dyer took the side of a friend in a quarrel with a New Yorker, resigned his commission, and met his antagonist at the usual early morning hour of seven a.m. Both missed on the first shot. Their seconds regarded this as satisfaction enough for wounded honor. Dyer proceeded on to Texas.[21]

169

4. Boys and Family Men

Most of the Jews who came to New Orleans had no mind for pretensions to such an aristocratic privilege as dueling. They came to New Orleans with little more than the clothing on their backs and a willingness to work hard. Some of them were young enough to be thought of as boys rather than men. One of these was Jacob Bodenheimer, who ran away from his home in Speyer, Germany, at the age of fourteen, because he could not get along with his stepmother. He arrived in New Orleans aboard a sailing vessel in 1822, worked for storekeepers only a little better off than he, and in 1827 left for Moscow Landing in northern Louisiana, where he cleared a farm, opened a country store and operated a ferry. His years in New Orleans went totally unnoticed in press and public records; we know of them only because his son, who became the mayor of the Louisiana town of South Highlands, wrote down some stories his father had told him, at the urging of a local student of history.[22] Another such boy was David L. Kokernot, who arrived in New Orleans in 1817 with his father, Levi Moses Kokernot, at the age of twelve. David's mother and brother remained in Amsterdam, probably just long enough for the father to establish himself in business. David was meanwhile apprenticed to a Mississippi River pilot for a few years, then shipped out for Amsterdam, Bremen and New York on various vessels. His mother, Betsy Levy Kokernot, and his brother Louis were in New Orleans by 1820 at the latest, so David could then have stayed at home. But adventure and the sea were in his blood. David went back to the sailing life, was shipwrecked in Haiti where he worked on a mulatto's plantation, took ship for Hamburg where he did some buying for the family's store, worked for the United States government on a revenue cutter, was shipwrecked again, this time on the Texas coast, and, after taking part in the battle of Anahuac and other campaigns of the Texas War for Independence, settled in Texas as a storekeeper and rancher.[23]

David's mother and brother led more prosaic lives. After

170

Levi's death, his widow and son operated a retail store at the corner of St. Louis and Levee streets, bought and sold property, and built some structures along the railroad in the Faubourg Marigny. In 1832 the sheriff seized part of their stock to pay some bills. Betsy and Louis seem to have caught an inordinate number of runaway Negroes, or stopped Negroes carrying money without the proper identification; probably much of their trade was with slave-owners. Betsy brought some relatives over to New Orleans from Holland in 1831; her family was increased even more after her marriage to Alexander Hart, whose story we have previously described. When Alexander and his son Isaac joined her business in 1836, her son Louis became a partner of his brother-in-law, Benjamin Van Ostern, another Hollander whose family had been in town since before 1820. Ben's father, Levi, another dealer in dry goods, had gone bankrupt in 1828. One hopes that the partnership between Louis and Ben worked more smoothly than Louis' marriage to Nancy Van Ostern; they were divorced in 1839, probably the first divorce in New Orleans in which both husband and wife were Jews. There was financial trouble in the family in 1839, too, over the division of property among all these in-laws: Isaac Hart, Louis Kokernot, Betsy Kokernot Hart, and Benjamin Van Ostern. Whether it was just a family disagreement enlarged to include three diverse interests, or one more result of the crisis which began in 1837, we cannot make out from the records. Louis and Nancy's children died very young, so the Kokernot name did not survive in New Orleans as it did in Texas, but the Van Ostern name was carried into the Christian community through David—Nancy's other brother, who married Mary Chapman Thayer.[24]

If Levi Moses Kokernot brought Betsy and their sons to New Orleans as early as 1817, or even 1820, they may have been the first Jewish family to settle in New Orleans as a household. All of his predecessors whom we have been able to trace, with the possible exception of Manis Jacobs, seem to have been bachelors who established families, if at all, after their arrival in the area. But the number of Jewish families increased swiftly after 1820. Aaron Daniels, who arrived about 1822, at the age of forty-six, brought his wife along with him; whether they came

171

directly from Prussia or stopped somewhere else on the way, is not known. Daniels was another dry goods shopkeeper of whom there were, eventually, dozens. He kept his store at 17 Chartres street. In 1834, he went into partnership with Daniel Goodman, Hyam Harris' son-in-law. Goodman, another Hollander, was in New Orleans no later than 1824, when he was twenty-three years old. He was an active Mason and was highly regarded by his lodge brothers. In 1837 he was appointed a commissioner in New Orleans for the sale of stock of the Vidalia, Harrisonburg and Alexandria Rail Road Company. The same year he was elected secretary of the Young Men's Howard Association, the society of rescue-workers who rendered public service during the annual yellow fever and cholera epidemics. In 1840 Goodman and Daniels went bankrupt. If they had been content with the vast quantities of dry goods which they bought and sold at wholesale and retail, concentrating especially on the plantation market, they would have survived the depression. But Goodman's penchant for joining every organization in sight led him to purchase stock in a number of flimsy enterprises; he and Daniels also speculated in paper money and invested in Tennessee and Kentucky land. All of their property was sold at a sheriff's auction in 1840. Goodman's will cannot be located, so we have no knowledge of how well he recovered from these losses, but Aaron Daniels' estate was worth only $674 at his death on February 6, 1862.[25]

5. New Yorkers Come and Go

Goodman had another partner before Aaron Daniels: Solomon Soher of New York City, who came down to New Orleans about 1822 to try his luck. He was in business with S. S. De Jonge for a while, but was Goodman's partner by 1824. They had a dry goods store on Chartres street, but were also actively buying cotton and peltries. Together with Goodman's brother-in-law, Abraham Hyam Harris, they owned shares in a number of steamboats during 1828–1830. Harris left the firm in 1830, but Soher and Goodman maintained their partnership for another four years. How much of this time Soher spent in New Orleans is uncertain. Some time in 1828 he married Haym Salomon's granddaughter, Miriam Andrews, whose brothers had set up a store in Huntsville, Alabama, in 1827, and eventually became wealthy factors and merchants with branches in Mobile, New York City and New Orleans (1835). Miriam seems never to have accompanied her husband to New Orleans; her children Rosalie, Zipporah and Moses were born in New York City in March, 1829, May, 1831, and June, 1834, respectively. Soher probably wanted to protect his wife from the discomforts and dangers of the New Orleans climate, or he may have spent much of his time in New York City as the buying agent for his firm's retail merchandise and as the salesman for the cotton and furs they bought in New Orleans. By 1834 Soher had left New Orleans; his son W. Andrews Soher was born in May, 1836, in England. Perhaps he had already made whatever money he thought he could amass in New Orleans; or he may have been so unsuccessful that he lost hope and went to England to work there for Miriam's brothers' interests which soon assumed international proportions.[26]

Other New Yorkers came to New Orleans to cash in on the prosperity, too, but they did not stay as long as Sol Soher. Rowland and John Myer Davies, and Rowland and Monroe Cromelien were in business in two different locations during the period 1822-1826. One store, at 24 Canal street, was called R. and J. M. Davies, while the other at 59 Canal was known as Cromelien, Davies & Company. Their interests were the same: both firms handled wholesale and retail dry goods, acted as agents for ships, bought cotton and sugar, imported specie, advertised for the plantation trade, and sold merchandise sent to them on consignment from the North. Both Davies brothers were married to Cromelien girls, but since they traveled back and forth between New York and New Orleans, it would appear that their wives did not want to settle in Louisiana. Or perhaps the brothers and cousins-in-law did not do as well as they thought they should. Both firms closed down in 1826. But if the four men sold everything they advertised, and made a profit out of it, they must have made enough to retire on.[27]

173

6. THE GOTTSCHALK CLAN

Edward Gottschalk came to New Orleans from London at about the same time as these New Yorkers. Born about 1795, the son of Lezer (Lazarus) ben Gottschalk Levi and Shinah (Jane) Harris, Gottschalk first appears in the New Orleans records in an 1823 advertisement of a reward for the return of some cheap jewelry stolen from his rooms at 36 Conti street. In 1825 Gottschalk was working for Hart Shiff, but by 1827 he had entered into a partnership arrangement with a man named Reimers. They set up the sort of commission brokerage business which was so common in New Orleans: they dealt in shares of stock, sold exchange on other cities, bought and sold slaves, liquor, dry goods, notions, cotton, rope, and so forth, and acted as ships' agents. Their trade was primarily wholesale. During the period 1827–1830, they seem to have been one of the largest commission houses in the city.[28]

On May 26, 1828, Père Antoine married Edward to Marie-Aimée Bruslé, the twenty-year-old daughter of a wealthy refugee from Saint-Domingue. Their first child, Louis Moreau Gottschalk (named for his granduncle, the scholarly attorney Louis Moreau Lislet), who was to become the first great American-born composer-pianist, was born on May 8, 1829.[29] Just a few weeks before the baby was born, Edward took his brother James into his business. James had been in New Orleans since 1825 at the very latest; another brother died in the yellow fever epidemic of 1824, at the age of twenty-three.[30]

Perhaps Edward Gottschalk expanded his business too swiftly, or speculated too freely. In 1830 he became a bankrupt. His office equipment and the goods stored in his warehouse were sold at sheriff's auction; countinghouse desks, book presses, chairs, railings, a stove and pipes, barrels of snuff, boxes of cigars, bitters, cordials, sauces, crayons, cases of liquor, a medicine chest, and a shipment of napkins, were among the property which was sold. Three years later he sold some land, nine slaves and the contents of his home. Among the parcels of real estate were two hundred and eleven lots of ground in the town of Magnolia and along the railroad, one hundred and sixty acres in Illinois, a similar number in Missouri, and some lots in New Orleans. The furnishings of his home at 88 Rampart street, between Bienville and Conti, are an interesting index of the luxury with which he had surrounded his wife and children:

> "beds and bedding, cradles, sofas, sideboards, clocks and vases, card tables, a dining table with six additional pieces, round table with marble slabs, looking glasses, toilettes, wash stands, chairs, an elegant glass English chandelier, plated ware, cut glass, carpets and rugs, fenders and irons &c, crockery and kitchen utensils . . . Also, one second handed elegant upright piano forte of German manufacture, three new d[itt]o English manufacture, also a collection of books, in English, French, German and Spanish, and a handsome saddle horse, with saddle and bridle . . . Also a superior and excellent Harp. . . ."

Whether this sale of his household possessions and personal property was related to his prior bankruptcy is not clear; nor can we tell why Edward's wife had to sell a great deal of her own property during 1834–1837. Aimée and James had a small fortune invested in real estate in the suburbs of New Orleans and in Mississippi, Illinois and Florida. The members of the family were clearly involved in speculative ventures and in financial problems; with many mouths to feed—a child was born to Edward and Aimée almost every year—Edward must have felt hard pressed.[31]

It may be that Edward was not himself involved in the sale of his wife's holdings; beginning in 1835 he once again seems to have become an important commission broker, if we can judge his success from his newspaper advertisements of shares of stock, Texas lands (sixty-five thousand acres at one time), slaves, houses, and coffee. He seems not to have been ruined by the panic of 1837. Louis Moreau, who showed every sign of being a musical prodigy very early in his life—the harp and all of the pianos had undoubtedly been purchased for him—was sent off to Paris in 1842 to continue his musical education, and Aimée, with her four younger sons and two daughters, joined Louis there in 1847. Edward stayed in New Orleans, trying to make enough money to support two households, but he was close to bankruptcy at the time of his death on October 23, 1853.

Aimée seems to have been excessively ambitious for herself and her children; Edward was a victim not only of his own speculative nature but also of his wife's inordinate expectations of wealth, luxury and social recognition.[32]

7. Physicians, Dentists, Quacks and Military Men

How many members of his family Edward brought to New Orleans is uncertain. At least one more brother came to Louisiana; he was Dr. Joseph Victor Gottschalk, who arrived in 1836 from Prussia, and tendered "his services to the public, as Physician, Surgeon, Oculist, & Accoucheur." Dr. Gottschalk had his office at his residence on Conti street, between Chartres and Levee. But he was dead within a year; he fell victim on July 10, 1837, at the age of forty, to the perennial New Orleans menace, yellow fever. Joseph left his wife, Marianne Charlotte Wagner, a native of Stargart, Pomerania, her son by a previous marriage, and his own four children. The inventory of his modest estate, which was worth about $3,000, included the typical medical equipment of the time: a large case of amputation instruments worth $120; a pocket case of instruments valued at $50; some instruments used in midwifery, dentistry and the like, together with a medical saw, all worth $60; and another portable case inventoried at $50.[33]

Other Jewish medical people were in New Orleans at one time or another throughout the years. One Michael Solomon notified the population of the city, in 1823, that he had just arrived from Surinam "where he has long and successfully administered relief to those affected with corns; and offers his services to the public for the effectual cure of that distressing complaint. He also flatters himself to have in his possession the very best medicines useful for that purpose."[34] A better trained man was Dr. Gerson Adersbach, a graduate of the Prussian State University in Halle an der Saale, who served as a contract physician with the United States Army at Forts Jackson and St. Philip, at the mouth of the Mississippi, below New Orleans, from 1826 to 1829. Adersbach also spent some time in private practice in New Orleans. He died from the effects of a bout with yellow fever, while on his way North in 1829.[35] Dr. G. Eichhorn arrived in New Orleans in 1828, convinced that his experience in the West Indies and Mexico had qualified him to treat tropical diseases, especially yellow fever. He had also, he reported, "made some successful operations on eyes, & tenders services in this branch of medicine." In 1833 Eichhorn decided to leave New Orleans, and notified the public that bills for his services might be paid at Samuel Hermann's counting house. Carl Kohn wrote the news of Eichhorn's departure to his Uncle Samuel and commented sarcastically that he supposed that "Dr. Eichhorn has gone to Tampico to astonish the world there."[36]

Dr. Zachariah Levy Florance, who advertised his prowess at every sort of dental work and sold toothpaste and a tincture for sore gums, moved to New Orleans from Charleston in 1827 or 1828. His sons Jacob and William had already come to town and established themselves in business in 1825. By the early 1830's, two more sons, Benjamin and Henry, were also in New Orleans. They were a big, busy, bustling family. William and Henry were both active in the Louisiana Militia; Jacob ran for the office of alderman twice, but lost both elections. The family's fortunes rose and fell. William went bankrupt in 1838, and Jacob's "elegant mansion," the Florance House hotel, at the corner of Camp street and Lafayette Square, was sold at auction in 1839 and converted into a boardinghouse. But several of the brothers became wealthy men before they moved North in the late 1840's or early 1850's.[37]

Another Jew who was active in the Louisiana Militia was Joseph Lasalle, who served as Acting Adjutant of the Second Regiment in 1829, and was elected Sergeant Major, then Lieutenant, of the Tirailleurs, in 1830–31. Lasalle was also interested in politics. In 1828–30, he served as clerk of the fourth ward elections; in 1833 he was a judge at the polls. His name was placed in nomination for the office of enrolling clerk of the state legislature in 1833, but he received only three votes. Lasalle ran what he called a "Cheap Store," where he sold dry goods, liquor, glassware and china, jewelry, firecrackers and other odds and ends first on St. Philip street, then at the corner of Condé and Dumaine, finally at 237 Royal. He went bankrupt in 1834, at which time he was in debt to Manis Jacobs for $1,628. His creditors finally accepted settlement in 1837, but it is uncertain whether he was still in New Orleans at that time. Lasalle faded from view as silently as he had appeared in 1827.[38]

8. A DIFFERENT KIND OF COHEN

Lasalle was probably not a Frenchman, despite his name, but rather a German who, like others, adopted the name under French influence during the Napoleonic period. There were, however, a number of French Jews in New Orleans at this time. Two were the brothers Sacerdote, Salomon and Simon, natives of Bordeaux, who were in New Orleans by 1818 at the latest. Sacerdote is, of course, a Latin/Romance translation of Cohen, the Hebrew word for priest. Simon was an ordinary sort of person, with a dry goods store, who made fairly frequent buying trips to France. His wife was Sipora, daughter of Jacob Delvaille and Rachel Cardose of St. Esprit, near Bayonne, a famous old Sephardic community; one of Sipora's brothers, Abraham, lived in Jamaica.[39] Simon's brother, Salomon Sacerdote, was a different kind of fellow from his brother. During the early 1820's he was sole- or part-owner of the Frascati Hotel, located in the Clouet suburb of New Orleans. This establishment was a warm-weather resort, which featured family dinners, rooms for private social functions, lawn bowling, and bar rooms. On holidays there were fireworks, balloon ascensions and other forms of entertainment. Salomon went broke in this venture, ending up with debts of more than $19,000—$3,000 to Simon—and, in desperation or out of personal inclination, turned to the demimonde. He opened a gambling house, the license for which cost him $5,000—the state used its income from licenses for such establishments to support schools and hospitals. This gambling house may have been located in the St. Philip Street Theatre which Sacerdote and a partner bought and converted into the Washington Ballroom—the scene of the notorious quadroon balls for which New Orleans was so well-known during this period, and which have been romanticized from occasions for assignation into formal coming-out parties for sheltered quadroon maidens. Sacerdote's partner in this under-taking seems to have been the wealthy "free man of colour," Antoine Jonau, a man of some mystery, who took over the property after Sacerdote's death in August, 1834. Salomon's estate was estimated to be worth $39,177. His wife, Aimée Dauqueminil de Morand, and his brother Simon were his heirs.[40]

9. The First Warburg and his Sons

One of the most unusual of all the early Jews who came to New Orleans was Daniel Warburg, the first member of that distinguished German-Jewish clan of bankers, scientists and philanthropists to establish residence in the United States. The Warburg genealogy can be traced back almost as far as that of the Schiff family. Daniel's earliest known forebear was one Simon of Cassel, an exchange broker, moneylender and grain merchant in Warburg in the middle of the sixteenth century, who died about 1566. The family was in Hamburg and nearby Altona from the early years of the seventeenth century. Daniel's father, Samuel Abraham Warburg, was first a merchant of Dutch-made wares in Altona, and then a commission merchant in Hamburg; he died in the latter city in 1834 at the age of seventy-five.[41] Daniel, who was born in Hamburg on October 10, 1789, was in New Orleans by 1821, when he was in the commission business with Henry G. Schmidt, a friend of Samuel Hermann. During the 1830's Daniel was especially active in the real estate line, buying and selling property; he was a founder of the Company of Architects, a development firm. He also served as secretary and director of the Levee Steam Cotton Press, and was on the board of the Citizens' Bank. His property holdings during this period appear to have been tremendous, but he apparently went broke in 1839–41; in 1853, he was still being dunned for more than $12,000 in unpaid notes.[42]

Warburg had political aspirations. In 1835 he was a candidate for alderman of the fifth district of New Orleans. After he lost this election, the *St. Francisville Journal* jocularly listed him as a potential gubernatorial candidate. He had other ambitions as well. On July 9, 1836, he made the startling announcement in the *Bee* to the "Captains and Seamen of the Shipping in the Port of New Orleans" that he knew and possessed "the true knowledge of what is termed the quadrature of the circle, and can prove it by a figure, true in its demonstration and true in its calculation." After twelve inches of tightly-printed, closely-reasoned geometrical and philosophical ratiocination (which included the statement, "I deny all belief in religion whatever be its name or ceremonies") he named his price for the revelation of his discovery:

> "I demand of the American nation and government the payment to me of Ten Millions of Dollars, or of the British nation and government Five Millions pounds sterling, if either of them desire to be in possession of the knowledge the truth of which I declare to possess.
>
> "I consider it but a trifling sum, *for if the genius that governs me*, should teach me the secret art of ship building, according to the laws of nature, the nation I shall instruct in that secret will govern on the seas of the world.
>
> "I know the true meaning of the philosophers stone, and can form the cross. . . ."

Warburg signed his statement with his motto, "The Lion and the Serpent." Neither the American nor the British government made any effort to purchase Warburg's secret. Three years later, in the midst of the economic disaster which affected him as well as others, Warburg was still laying claim to mathematical and scientific knowledge denied to other men. In 1839 he published two pamphlets of a mathematical nature. The first was entitled, "*The Goddess Eve.*" *Two Tables, Constructed to Demonstrate by Numbers The True Mode for Extracting the Square Root out of all entire numbers above 1000, and the Cubic Root out of all entire numbers above 1000. Besides: Multiplication and the Rule of Three with Entire Numbers. (These Tables may be carried to endless extent.)* This twelve-page item, printed by E. Johns and registered with the Clerk of the District Court on January 2, 1839, was dedicated to the former President, John Quincy Adams. This gem was followed, on September 16, 1839, by another tabled work, *Buy a Lottery Ticket; or A Chance to Get Rid of Money.* *"Table and the necessary explanation, to shew the combination of a Lottery Scheme composed of 75 Numbers, three Numbers in a Row on each Ticket, and 12 Numbers drawn to determine the Prizes."* A professor of mathematics who has examined these communications thinks that Warburg was an early member of "the International Clan of Assorted Nuts." Perhaps his family was aware of his ambition to become recognized as a mathematical genius and therefore shipped him off to the United States where he would not embarrass them; or he may have slipped beyond reason after losing his way in the speculative quagmires of New Orleans. We have no way of telling whether he was eccentric only in this one way, or in many others.[43]

Warburg has another claim on our interest. He was the father of two mulatto sons, Eugène and Daniel Warburg, who have some significance in the history of artistic endeavor among American Negroes. Their mother, Marie Rose, was apparently a Cuban Negro, still a slave when Warburg first cohabited with her. In March, 1830, Warburg took the requisite legal step of making public announcement of his intention to free his slave Eugène. He must also have freed the mother, although we cannot locate the relevant documents, because their other children, Henri Arthur, Elizabeth Eulalie, Marie Françoise, and Joseph Daniel, appear to have been born free. Marie Rose Warburg, f. w. c., was free by 1837 at the latest, for she herself purchased a slave named Mary early that year. The younger Daniel was active as a stonecutter, tomb designer and engraver, and spent his entire life in New Orleans. Eugène, apparently more ambitious, temperamental and talented, left the city about 1853, after having studied with a French artist named Garbeille, and studied and worked in England, France and Italy. In England he is said to have been commissioned by the Duchess of Sutherland to design bas-reliefs illustrating the story of *Uncle Tom's Cabin.* In 1855 he did a bust of John Y. Mason, the United States Minister to France; this sole surviving example of Eugène's work is now in the Virginia Historical Society in Richmond. Two further pieces, *Le Pêcheur* and *Le Premier Baiser*, are men-

181

tioned by a biographer, but are not known other than by title. Another piece is known only from an extensive description in the *Bee*, December 13, 1850:

> "A CREOLE SCULPTOR—We paid a visit to Hall's gilding establishment in Canal street yesterday, and examined with some attention a marble statue chiseled by a young Creole of our city, EUGENE WARBURG, a pupil of GARBEILLE. It represents, we presume, GANYMEDE, Jove's cup-bearer, kneeling and presenting a flowing beaker of Nectar to the King of Gods and Men. The design is beautiful, and the execution reflects infinite credit upon the taste and talent of our townsman. The statue is offered for raffle, and is estimated to be worth $500. Every patron of art, and admirer of native talent should gladly take a chance on this exquisite specimen of sculpture. If Mr. WARBURG will bestow proper study on his models and labor assiduously at his profession, he will doubtless attain deserved excellence."

Eugène Warburg died in Rome on January 12, 1859, when he was about thirty-three years old. His father may still have been alive, but the mother had apparently died some years before.[44]

10. A JOURNALIST AND A DRAMATIST-EDUCATOR

Eugène Warburg's sculpture of Ganymede and Jupiter was probably reviewed for the *Bee* by its English-language editor, Dr. Samuel Harby. A physician and journalist, son of Isaac Harby, the distinguished dramatist, educator and pioneer of religious reform in Charleston, Samuel was in New Orleans by 1834, when he was twenty-one years old. Whether he practiced medicine in New Orleans is uncertain. He was working for the *Bee* by 1838, and in 1844 became one of the four owners of the newspaper. He continued to be a major factor in the paper's management and editorial staff until his death on June 11, 1862. Sam's first wife was Frances Levy, L. A. Levy's sister, whom he married in March, 1842. She died in November, 1850; a year later he married her sister Sarah, a widow. Dr. Harby was an acknowledged intellectual leader in New Orleans; his opinions and taste were highly respected.[45]

Young Sam Harby had been brought to New Orleans by his uncle George Washington Harby, who was only sixteen years older than he was. George became a well-known educator, dramatist and cultural leader in New Orleans. He was in the city before November 28, 1828, when he was married by Parson Clapp to Mary Olivia Lucas, formerly of Louisville. He probably opened his private school immediately after his arrival, serving as headmaster and senior teacher. (In an advertisement in 1834 he wrote of having served as an "English and Classical Teacher" for the past eight years.) Harby employed a number of assistant teachers as well as instructors in various specialized fields. The courses of study which Harby's Academy offered to its pupils included the following:

"Orthography, Reading in Prose and Poetry;
Grammar;
Penmanship, on the Caretarian principle;
Ancient and Modern Geography;
The use of the Globes;
The construction of Maps;
Arithmetic, Geometry;
Plain Astronomy, Mythology;
Logic, Constitution United States;
Universal History;
Botany, and all useful and polite learning.
LANGUAGES.
English, French, Spanish, Latin."

School hours were from eight in the morning until three in the afternoon. Tuition charges amounted to four or five dollars a month, with additional fees for foreign language instruction. By 1839, the fees were between $4 and $8 a month for day pupils, and $25 a month for boarding students, the latter charges including tuition, room, meals and laundry. Harby's philosophy of education was simple and clear:

". . . Oral Instruction and Conversational Lectures are the only sure methods of teaching rational beings. Pupils must have explained to them the meaning of all their studies—they must be made to comprehend what they are doing. Long tasks may improve memory, but cannot instruct the understanding. The thinking powers must be brought into operation. The curiosity must be excited—then search commences; the preceptor aids the student— the truth is discovered—the boy is delighted—the task has been a pleasant one; and the utile cum dulce is combined. This causes powerful excitement in the breast of youth, and ends [leads?] to a noble emulation, and a virtuous ambition.

"In fact, in order to instruct youth three things are essentially requisite:—Easy tasks—certain advancement—and pleasant occupation . . ."

In order to demonstrate how effective his methods of pedagogy were, Harby invited interested persons to visit the school and quiz the pupils who, he felt sure, were prepared to answer questions at any time, not just in scheduled examinations. As a matter of fact, George's educational system was an old fashioned one, stressing classical learning and formal knowledge; he was probably following the same approach which his brother Isaac had used in his Charleston institution. When the school building at Tivoli Circle burned down on January 11, 1840 ("supposed to be the work of an incendiary," said the *Bee*—not, let us hope, the "work" of a disgruntled student), Harby's private venture came to an end. His institution was transformed into a public school of the third municipality, and began to admit girls. Of a total of 110 students in 1842, divided into four grades, seventy-six were boys and thirty-four were girls; only twenty-three of them were enrolled in the French class. Meanwhile, Yankee teachers were being imported from the North; Horace Mann's influence was being felt throughout the country. New educational techniques were being developed, predicated on the needs of the middle class—education was no longer to be the privilege of an elite caste trained in the classical manner. George Harby, apparently, could not adjust to the new day. By 1855 he had been demoted from principal to teacher, and was working in a school in the first district of the city.[46]

Mary Harby died in Louisville while visiting with her family in the fall of 1834. A year later Abbé Moni married George to fifteen-year-old Marie Ulalie Pouillot, an orphan who had been born in France.[47] This young lady had probably been attracted to George, who was twenty-two years older than she was, far

184

more by virtue of the glamor of his theatrical interests than the intellectuality of his profession as an educator. George was the heir to a family tradition of literary and dramatic interests. His brother Isaac had written and produced plays of a classical character in Charleston during the 1820's. George's earliest theatrical effort, a melodrama on an American theme, *Tutoona, or The Battle of Saratoga*, was presented at the New Orleans American Theatre on February 22, 1835—in honor of the celebration of Washington's birthday anniversary. James Rees, George's friend and colleague, who published a number of books on the contemporary drama in America, thought that *Tutoona* "is the best national drama we have—greatly superior to 'She would be a Soldier' of Major Noah." The *Louisiana Advertiser's* reviewer praised *Tutoona* for "a score of hair breadth escapes, a great deal of action, and interesting incident," but thought that its "many trivial passages . . . its many extravagant tirades . . ." and an excessive number of "scalping, whooping, trotting Indians," detracted from its success. Another reviewer dwelt more on the author's character, and the issue of native American drama, than on the play itself:

"TUTOONA OR THE BATTLE OF SARATOGA.—This play was performed on Saturday night to an overflowing and delighted audience. At the end of the piece the author was universally called for when he appeared and addressed the auditory in a most feeling and beautiful manner . . . This Drama . . . possesses spirit, vivacity and sentiment, which proves what we have always heard of our fellow-townsman—that with a generous and noble philanthropy, he has a heart and a spirit, one would think too great for so small a compass. He has for a very long time been among us, one of the most arduous laborers in the cause of literature.—His oration— his essays in the cause of education, his beautiful address when he received a standard for the Louisiana Guards are now ripe in our memory:—and his general probity, and moral qualifications have proved him a man of more than ordinary talents and literary acquirements. He is a native of our soil . . . let us not cast a mist before our eyes because this play is not transatlantic . . . We sincerely hope this production may prove a source of satisfaction and *profit* to the author. . . ."

185

Tutoona was repeated three times, the final performance being a benefit for the author; it was revived in 1841. In 1835, George also delivered the address at the cornerstone ceremonies of Caldwell's new theater.[48]

James Rees, for whose periodical *Dramatic Mirror and Literary Companion* Harby wrote New Orleans news in 1841–42, gives us the names of other dramatic pieces which Harby wrote: *Minka, or the Russian Daughter; Mahommed; Stephania; The Robber Girl; Azzo; Abou Hassan; The Gentleman in Black;* and *Twenty Years' Life of a Courtesan.* None of these dramas is recorded as having been produced in New Orleans. But a local color farce by Harby, *Hard Times in New Orleans,* was given twice in 1837—one hopes that some of the bankrupted merchants and bankers had enough money to buy tickets to find out what was so funny about their troubles. Harby's "domestic drama," *The Deceived,* was presented in 1838. His most successful work was a dramatization of Robert Montgomery Bird's novel, *Nick of the Woods.* After a trial performance or two in Natchez, it was given its premiere in New Orleans on March 20, 1838. The *Picayune* reported that *Nick of the Woods* was received with "deafening applause;" the critic marveled that Harby had so successfully "dove-tailed the language of the author with his own, that his drama comes before us as a perfect whole." He pleaded with the public to support the play, because Harby was in financial trouble, "arising from his too free disposition to aid and assist his fellow creatures. We could enumerate an hundred instances of his generous open hearted kindness, manifesting itself diametrically to his disadvantage. To recover some portion of these losses, he has had recourse to his pen." The author's benefit, on March 23, 1838, included a potpourri of other pieces (the trial scene from *The Merchant of Venice;* a German song in seven parts; and the operetta *No!*) added to *Nick,* in order to attract as large an audience as possible. *Nick of the Woods* was performed in St. Louis, Philadelphia, and other cities, and Rees seems to have done everything possible to popularize Harby's work throughout the country—he was convinced that Harby's version of *Nick* was the "most popular" of the many stage adaptations of the novel—but the time was not propitious for anyone to aspire to become a professional dramatist in America. Although there is no question but that Harby was the only successful New Orleans dramatist in this period, it was discouraging that some of his works were never even performed, and those that were, lasted only a few days. At the time of his death in 1862, hardly anyone remembered his early prominence as a stagecrafter.[49]

11. THREE CHARLESTONIANS

George and Sam Harby were not the only Jews who came to New Orleans from the cultured environment of Charleston. Others came, too, similarly motivated by the zest for adventure and the longing for fortune, but also bringing with them the proclivities for intellectual pursuit, professional excellence and service in public life which were so characteristic of that famed Jewish community. One Charlestonian newcomer was the seventeen-year-old college dropout, Judah P. Benjamin, who arrived in New Orleans in 1828, with no visible assets other than the wit, charm, omnivorous mind and boundless energy with which he would find his place in the sun. When Benjamin arrived in New Orleans, he stayed with and probably worked for Jacob Levy Florance, the dentist's son, who must have known him in Charleston. On the eve of the Civil War, when Benjamin was publicly accused, in the North, of having been expelled from Yale because he had been caught in a theft, Florance wrote the following to his daughter Lavinia:

> "It [the charge of theft] has shocked me and all his admirers Christians and Jews. Whether the charge is true God only knows. As the present political troubles has brought it out, after slumbering so long it may be untrue. But the signer and the collegeates are named and most of them are living. All that I know is that about 1827 when he arrived at New Orleans and entered my family (then about 18 years old) he said that he had been to Yale college. Had not finished his studies and left because his father could not support him."[50]

If Benjamin did not work for Florance, then his employer prior to the time that he learned the rudiments of law while working for the notary G. R. Springer, must have been Samuel Hermann, for that wealthy Jewish merchant-banker was a witness at Benjamin's marriage to Natalie St. Martin on February 16, 1833.[51]

It would serve little purpose for us here to attempt to summarize Judah Benjamin's meteoric rise to wealth, political power, professional prestige and national prominence. The reader is referred without apology to Robert Douthat Meade's splendid biography of the man which offers penetrating insight into Benjamin's life, particularly his career as Attorney General, Secretary of War and Secretary of State of the Confederacy. Benjamin will always be worthy of study in depth.[52] We shall later refer to him as an example of the process of assimilation, but it is interesting here to note that he was married not as "J. P. Benjamin," the name he always used in public, or as "Judah Philip Benjamin," his full name, but as "Philip Benjamin." Was it the priest who bridled at entering the name "Judah" ("Judas?") in the church's marriage register, or did Natalie refuse to call him by his first name? We shall never be able to discover why neither his first name nor even his first initial was used in the wedding document, but perhaps this occurrence was symptomatic of a problem with which he had to deal all through his life as a public figure.

Judah Benjamin, according to report, came to New Orleans with his older cousin, twenty-two-year-old Henry Michael Hyams. Hyams was not only searching for opportunity for himself, but was exploring the area with a view of moving his entire family—his father, three brothers and three sisters—to Louisiana. Benjamin's grandmother and Hyams' mother were sisters, and the families appear to have been very close. Henry is said to have been admitted to the New Orleans bar in 1830, but there is no record of this in the city. He did not, at any rate, remain in New Orleans very long, but secured a position as cashier of the Donaldsonville branch of the Canal Bank. Members of his family joined him in that town. On January 16, 1833, his sister Eliza was married there to Joseph Benzaken

Marks. The wedding was probably conducted by their father, Samuel Hyams, who had performed a number of such ceremonies in Charleston. Marks was another Charlestonian who moved to New Orleans. He served as a notary in New Orleans until his death by drowning in 1851.[53]

One William Hull denounced Henry Hyams in the press in 1834 as a *"mean, despicable* coward," and challenged him to a duel. Hyams answered very calmly that after Hull "shall have cleared his character from the suspicion of having stolen One Thousand Dollars from the brother of the undersigned, no satisfaction due to a gentleman, shall be withheld from him." He referred any answers to his two seconds, one of whom was his cousin Judah Benjamin. In 1835, Henry was a leader at an anti-abolitionist mass meeting in Donaldsonville and was appointed a member of a vigilante committee to thwart anti-slavery propaganda and quell any servile rebellions which might take place. This activity foreshadowed his active participation in the Democratic Party after he moved to New Orleans in the 1840's. In 1855 he was elected to the state senate, and in 1859, became Lieutenant-Governor of Louisiana—the first Jew known to serve in that office in any state in the Union.[54]

It will do no harm to go beyond our self-imposed time limit of 1828 in order to include a third Charlestonian who practiced law in New Orleans, Myer M. Cohen, who arrived in Louisiana somewhat later than Benjamin and Hyams. Cohen conducted a Charleston "English and Classical Academy," very similar to George Harby's, from 1824 to 1828, until he passed his bar examinations. He practiced law and entered politics; in 1835 he was a justice of the peace, and a member of the South Carolina legislature. As an officer of the Washington Guards of Charleston he spent three and a half months in the Seminole War, and wrote one of the most popular books about it, entitled *Notices of Florida and The Campaigns. By M. M. Cohen (An Officer of the Left Wing)*, published in Charleston in 1836 by Burges and Honour. Late in 1836, when he was thirty-two, and had not yet made his fortune, he decided to move on to the broader, more exciting opportunities of New Orleans, and on March 16, 1837, opened a law office in the Banks Arcade; he also secured an appointment as Commissioner (legal representative) in New Orleans for the state of South Carolina. He immediately threw himself into the political and cultural life of his new home. In December, 1837, he delivered an ornate address on the relationship of literature and commerce at the annual meeting of the New-Orleans Commercial Library Society. In 1838 he was a leading spokesman at the meeting which was organized to raise funds for the victims of the great Charleston fire, and George W. Harby joined him in collecting contributions in the second municipality. Cohen was a typical American "joiner." He was constantly active on committees: for the relief of the people of Natchez; for the establishment of a German theater in New Orleans; for the reception of the Governor of South Carolina when he visited the city. Despite his literary pretensions, and his variegated activities, he was also a brilliant, industrious attorney who specialized, as Judah Benjamin did, in commercial law. He was active in the New Orleans Law Association, and served as a member of the Administrative Board of the University of Louisiana, of which he ultimately became secretary. His practice brought him into constant contact with business interests; he was attorney for the Mutual Benefit Life and Fire Insurance Company, chairman of the permanent committee of the New Orleans, Algiers, Attakapas and Opelousas Rail Road, and president of the South-Western Industrial Fair of 1854. Cohen was frequently embroiled in political activities. In July, 1851, he presided at a riotous mass meeting after the news reached New Orleans of the execution of some of the Southern filibusterers who had invaded Cuba under the leadership of Narciso Lopez. At the age of sixty-nine, in June, 1873, Cohen himself was tried for taking part in an assassination attempt on the life of the Reconstruction governor of Louisiana, William P. Kellogg, but was acquitted of the crime! He was still active in the practice of law, and was teaching admiralty and commercial law; as late as 1883, he wrote a scholarly treatise on admiralty law. A man of many interests, both scholarly and activist, was Myer Cohen, who, because he had once declined a federal judgeship, was still called "Judge" Cohen when he died on February 23, 1887, at the age of eighty-three. His enterprise, hot temper, militant spirit, local "booster" qualities make him seem as much a man of our times as of his own.[55]

* * * * * * * * * * * * * *

So we come to the end of our description of this mixed multitude of Jews who came to New Orleans in this early period in search of fortune, adventure and happiness. They came from New York City, from Charleston, and from England, France, Holland and the German-speaking lands, drawn by the promise of wealth, success and personal fulfillment, driven, too, by personal failure or lack of opportunity in their old homes. They were individuals all; no generalizations can accurately characterize them as a group. Some found permanent security, prosperity and fame; others ended in bankruptcy, defeat or death. Some made a high mark, wrote their names large in the economic and political life of the city; others left a bare record of their passage. Most of them were engaged in the hectic commercial pursuits of the city—the business emporium of the Southland—but there was a sprinkling of attorneys, medical men, cultural leaders. Drama there was in the lives of many, duels, divorces, public conflicts; others lived quietly. They were people, and people are always interesting. But they were Jews, too. . . .

V

Judaism Finally Comes to New Orleans:
The Organization of a Congregation

We have found no evidence to justify a very late report that
Jewish services were conducted in New Orleans in 1750; indeed,
we have not located any Jews in the town until 1757–58, and
there is not the slightest hint in documentary form, either
friendly or hostile, that they attempted to meet for worship.
Surely Rochemore would have added that fact to his denunciation of the presence of Jews during the *Texel* affair.[1] Rabbi
James K. Gutheim is reported as having said in 1850 that formal
Jewish life in New Orleans began with the "assembling in a
small room of twelve persons, in 1824."[2] But this was probably
a misprint or a slip of the pen. There is nothing to suggest that
"The Israelite Congregation, of Shanarai-Chasset, (Gates of
Mercy,) Of the city of New-Orleans, State of Louisiana," traced
its origins back to 1824. Indeed, when the Jews of Cincinnati
were soliciting contributions for their building fund in 1825,
they made a point of asserting that "there is not a congregation
within 500 miles of this city and we presume it is well known
how easy of access we are to New Orleans, and we are well
informed that had we a Synagogue here, hundreds from that
City, who now know and see nothing of their religion would
frequently attend here during the holidays."[3] Whether there
were so many "hundreds" of Jews in New Orleans at this time
is open to question, but so far as the leaders in Cincinnati knew,
no form of organized Jewish communal life existed in New
Orleans in 1825. That development was delayed until the arrival
in the city of one of those determined, creative leaders upon whose
shoulders the fate of the faith of Israel has always rested.

1. JACOB S. SOLIS

This man was Jacob S. Solis, who was born in the Sephardic
community of London on August 4, 1780, and was in the
United States by the fall of 1803. Solis almost immediately

192

associated himself with the Spanish-Portuguese Shearith Israel Congregation of New York City, the congregation of Hart, Seixas and Benjamin Levy. Following his marriage on April 24, 1811, to Charity Hays, daughter of a Westchester County farmer and brother of a future High Constable of New York City, Solis became adept at *shechitah* (the ritual killing of animals) so that he might provide kosher meat for his family while they were living in Mt. Pleasant, N. Y. In 1814 or 1815 Jacob and his brother Daniel opened a store in Wilmington, Delaware, and solicited the trade of local customers with the promise that they would save not only time but also money by making their purchases in Wilmington, rather than in Philadelphia where they were wont to do their buying. The Wilmington venture lasted for five or six years, and then Jacob returned to Mt. Pleasant. In 1822 he applied to Mikveh Israel Congregation of Philadelphia for the position of official *shochet* (ritual slaughterer), but was told by Simon Gratz that the position had been taken—Jacob's brother Daniel served in that capacity in later years. Although little is known about Jacob's financial situation, it is apparent that he had not done very well in Wilmington, or he would have remained there; and if he was willing to accept the poorly paid position of a congregational *shochet*, he had little expectation of doing very much better. In 1826 he was attempting to promote the establishment of an academy for Jewish boys and girls where farming, crafts and domestic skills would be taught in addition to the Jewish traditions; the school and its attendant workshops would be supported by prosperous Jews because the institution was designed particularly for the benefit of Jewish orphans. Solis was obviously concerned with Jewish welfare and public service, but he was just as obviously in search of a way of supporting his growing family.[4]

Solis must have been desperate for a livelihood to go as far as New Orleans without his family; perhaps he had heard of the booming conditions there from a fellow-member of Shearith Israel like Sol Soher. Tradition has it that he first came to New Orleans to open a store in 1826, but the year was more likely to have been 1827. His family has preserved the story that, once in New Orleans, he found himself unable to purchase *matzos* (unleavened bread) during the Passover festival, and, appalled that no one else was interested in baking any, he himself ground the meal and made his own; this experience led him to the determination, runs the tale, to lead a campaign to found a congregation. But Jacob's youngest child, Phoebe, was born on March 30, 1827, when Jacob was still probably in the North, and the congregation's *Constitution and Bye-Laws*, published in 1828, reports that it was "Founded February 2d, A. M. 5588, BY JACOB S. SOLIS, of the State of New-York, December 20th, 1827." Despite the confusion of dates—he could not have founded the congregation twice—it is apparent that the congregation had not been organized for the High Holy Days of 1827. If Solis had already been in New Orleans in early 1827, and if he had felt challenged by the absence of any celebrations of the Passover holiday, he would undoubtedly have conducted services for the New Year and the Day of Atonement, and the congregation's inception would have been identified with those services.

Whether or not Solis intended to remain in New Orleans is unclear; only a few indications of his business activity have been located: the purchase of some property and receipt of some merchandise, both in March, 1828. He left New Orleans in early June and returned to his family via Louisville and Cincinnati; he appears to have gone back to New Orleans some time in the fall of 1828 or the winter of 1828–29, but was in Mt. Pleasant by December 29, 1829, when death struck him there. After the news of his death reached New Orleans, the secretary of the congregation wrote to Jacob's widow; he told her that "as soon as the sad tidings came to this place the Board of Trustees held a meeting on account of the Death of their Beloved Member and first founder...." It is obvious from the congregation's acknowledgement on the title-page of its *Constitution* and from the resolutions which were adopted by the officers and trustees that Jacob Solis alone was responsible for the successful campaign to create the congregation:

"OBITUARY

"Died at Mount Pleasant, (N. Y.) on the 29th December last, Mr. JACOB S. SOLIS, aged 49 years, a native of London, (England,) and for the last twenty-five years, a respectable citizen of the United States. It is so common to praise after death, that

I am almost detained from mentioning the virtues of a truly good man. Mr. Jacob S. Solis will be long lamented by his family and friends, particularly remembered by the members of the Israelite Institution of New Orleans, for his indefatigable exertions in establishing it on the principles to protect the widow and the orphan from the cold charity of a hard world; and insure the latter an education and support. Such men merit the highest eulogy.

"He who wipes one tear from the widowed cheeks or protects one orphan from the allurements of a wicked world, cancels a thousand sins at Heaven's chancery.

"At a stated meeting of the Trustees of the Israelite Institution of this city, duly assembled according to notice, the following Resolutions were unanimously adopted.

"1. Resolved, That in consequence of the death of our much lamented member *Jacob S. Solis*, and in consideration of his many virtues, and the effectual services rendered to this Institution on its formation, the officers wear crape on their left arms for the space of thirty days from the date of this meeting.

"2. That the Secretary of this Institution do write a consolatory letter to the widow and orphans of the late Jacob S. Solis.

"3. Resolved, That the above Resolutions be published in two papers of the city.

By order of the Board.

SOLOMONS, Secretary pro tem.

"New Orleans, Feb. 7th, 1830."[5]

2. THE CONSTITUTION AND BY-LAWS

The printed pamphlet which the congregation published in late May or early June of 1828 is a fascinating source of information and insight. It includes the following:

a) English and French versions of the act of incorporation, approved March 25, 1828, which authorized Manis Jacobs,

Aaron Daniels, Isaac Phillips, Souza "senr," Abraham Plotz, J. S. Solis, Bernard Lejeune "and all other white Israelites living in this city," to form the congregation and to engage in appropriate activity for a period of twenty-five years. The officers were to be two *Parnassim* ("senior wardens") and three *Gabaim* ("junior wardens"); all of them were required to be residents of New Orleans and over twenty-five years of age; at least one *Parnas* and one *Gabai* had to be married, and a property-owner. The funds of the congregation were to be used only for "erecting or repairing Temples, relieving the unfortunate, and . . . establishing schools for the education of Israelites." The final provision of this charter, an indication of the excessive amount of intermarriage in the community, stipulated that "no Israelite child shall be excluded, either from the schools, from the Temple, or the burial ground, on account of the religion of the mother." This was in direct opposition to the judgment of Jewish law that the child always follows the religion of the mother; in the absence of a formal act of conversion to Judaism, the children of non-Jewish mothers would automatically be considered to be gentiles.

b) The by-laws, in English and French, which related mainly to business matters, elections, charges for funerals, and similar subjects. These rules returned, again and again, to the question of the status of intermarried members. Article 21 provided that a "strange woman," i.e., a non-Jewess, married to a Jew, might be buried in a special section of the cemetery, but "it is well understood, and forcibly regarded, that they shall be buried after the Israelite custom." Article 23 guaranteed, once more, that "all children born of an Israelite, and not having abjured the religion of the father, shall be entitled to burial." Article 25 offered "members married to strange women" the privilege of burial next to their wives (in the special section) or children. Article 31 gave Jewish women "married to strange men" the right to be buried in the cemetery, if they had not been converted to another religion, and if a designated sum of money were contributed to the congregation . . . but the authors of the by-laws showed what they thought of such women by including this permission in the same article which specified that "All adulteresses shall be buried apart." Suicides and prostitutes were also to be interred in a special section of the cemetery. These provisions relating to intermarriage offer vivid testimony of the extent of marriage out of the faith, and demonstrate how strongly the congregational leaders tried to keep these men from feeling alienated from their ancestral faith, and how profoundly they hoped that the children of these marriages might be saved for Judaism.

One further by-law required that "all prayers offered shall be after the custom of the Portuguese Israelites." This was certainly inserted on the insistence of Jacob Solis, himself trained in the Sephardic ritual, although most of the members of the congregation were of Ashkenazic background. Perhaps several other factors entered into the decision—the majority of the congregations in the country still maintained the Sephardic rite; many of the wealthiest and most successful Jews of the country were identified with Sephardic congregations; some of the New Orleans Jews who had been established longest in town, men like Touro and Hart, although inactive in the organization of the congregation, had been reared in a Sephardic environment; and, finally, the affinity of the population of New Orleans for French culture might have led the Jews of New Orleans to identify with French Judaism, largely Sephardic in places like Bordeaux. Nonetheless, if the strongest leader of the congregation had been an Ashkenazic Jew, there is little question but that his preference would have been followed.

c) A list of the officers, members, Jewish contributors and non-Jewish contributors. This is a unique source of names of New Orleans Jews. We print it here, with data in the notes about those persons not hitherto identified in our narrative; those noted with the # sign are altogether unknown.

Officers for this year—Officiers de cette année:

Manis Jacobs, Esq. *President.*
Aaron Daniels, Esq. *Vice-President.*
A. Plotz, Esq. *Junior-Warden.*[6]
A. Green, Esq. *Junior-Warden.*[7]
A[sher] Phil[l]ips, Esq. *Junior-Warden.*
Isaac Phil[l]ips, Esq. *Treasurer.*
S. Audler, Esq. *Secretary.*

197

Members of the Congregation—Memb. de la Congrégation:

Jacob S. Solis
Abs. Goldsmith[8]
Bernard Lejeune[9]
Nathan Hart
A. H. Dejong[e]
L. S. Levy[10]
A. S. Emmony#
David Lewis[11]
Samuel Jacobs
Moses J. Hart[12]
Marx Myers[13]
Ralph Jacobs
Levy Prince[14]

A. P. Levy[15]
Solomon Ferth[16]
Myers S. Ellis[17]
Lewis Kokernot
J. La Salle
Marton P. Levy[18]
Solomon Hunt[19]
Charles Myers#
L. Jones[20]
Aaron Kirkham[21]
Joseph Solomons[22]
Abr. Block[23]
E. Stern[24]

Doct. Z. Florance

Names of the Israelite Donors, who are not Members of the Congregation—Noms des Donateurs Israélites qui ne sont pas membres de la Congregation.

Judah Turo [sic]
H. Florance
Daniel Depass[25]
Daniel Goodman
L. Jacobs[26]
John Marks#
Edward Gottschalk
Benedict Solomons#
L. Morange[27]
Jacobs L. Workum[28]
L. Solomons[29]
L. Jacobs, Jr.
Souza, sen.
Joseph De Pass[30]
S. Sacerdote[31]
Souza, jnr.

Samuel De Pass[32]
Edward Engelhart#
Hyam Harris
William Hardcastle#
S. Silverberger#
A. H. Harris
M. Joseph[33]
A. Lange[34]
Moses Harris
D. Kokernot
Isaac Lyons[35]
Jacob L. Florance
Israel Solomons[36]
M. Milone#
Wm. Florance
L. B. Baruck[37]

Myer Barnett, senior

Names of the Honorable donors who are not Israelites.
Noms des honorables donateurs non-Israélites.

George W. Morgan	Jno. R. Grymes
Wm F. Saul	L. Pilié
J. H. Holland	Joshua Lewis
J. J. Mercier	John Woolfolk
J. Peillon	John M. Baity
	Carlile Pollock[38]

d) A twenty-four-year calendar of Jewish festivals, transliterated in accordance with the Sephardic pronunciation of Hebrew, undoubtedly prepared by Jacob Solis.

3. Manis Jacobs, the First President

We have deferred until now a detailed consideration of the life and career of Manis Jacobs, the man who accepted the responsibility of directing the affairs of this new congregation. Born in Amsterdam about 1782, Jacobs arrived in New Orleans some time between 1809 and 1812. The first precise reference to his presence in town was a newspaper advertisement in May, 1812, in which he offered a reward of fifty dollars for the apprehension of Solomon King, whom he accused of stealing a large quantity of jewelry. Jacobs described King as "a native of the state of New York, who professes to be a Doctor, and sometimes a clerk . . . has been but a few days in this country [Louisiana], and is known in Natchez as a swindler." At that time Jacobs had a partner named J. Calker, and made his headquarters at 13 Custom House street. The only early references to Jacobs are to a lawsuit against one Cholros in 1814, and the purchase of slaves in 1817 and 1822.[39] The notarized records of Jacobs' slave transactions reveal a fascinating and, for New Orleans, unique habit: he always signed his name in English with his Hebrew name "Menachem" in Hebrew letters as a cachet or seal. Of all the Jews in New Orleans during this early period, he was the only one to express his personal

199

identification with Judaism through his signature on business papers. This was his way of saying, through all those long years when there was no formal Jewish life in New Orleans, that he still considered himself a Jew in a positive sense.

Jacobs may have brought a wife with him from Amsterdam or elsewhere when he first came to New Orleans, but we know nothing about her. She was probably Jewish, and, if so, was the only woman of Jewish birth in town other than Angélica Dow, Clara Scott and, possibly, the Lange sisters. All we know is that Manis had a daughter named Irma who was about twenty-eight years old in 1843, when her husband, Bernard Hart, died. Since Irma had married a Jewish man, it is a reasonable assumption that she herself was Jewish. Jacobs married a second time, probably between January and July of 1826. His bride was the widow Angélique-Charlotte Jacinthe Verneuille, who had been born in Paris in 1781 or 1782, married Denis Verneuille there and bore him a son named Louis-Alexandre. Angélique and Denis may have lived in Saint-Domingue before they came to New Orleans. Angélique was already a widow in 1812 when she lived in New Orleans with her uncle, Jean-Baptiste Le Sueur Fontaine, a refugee from Saint-Domingue and a well-known actor-editor-businessman. It is worth noting that Manis' wedding to Angélique was probably the first marriage of a Jew and a Christian not to be performed in a church. Angélique was a French Catholic. St. Louis Cathedral was the only Catholic church in New Orleans at the time of their wedding, and there is no record of their wedding in its marriage registries. The conclusion is inescapable that Manis would not submit to a Catholic ceremony. He may have asked some Jew in town to conduct the wedding, or may even have performed it himself, since a rabbi is not required to take part in a Jewish marriage service. But it would have been interesting to see the Hebrew letters for "Menachem" in the marriage register of St. Louis Cathedral! By the spring of 1828, Manis and Angélique were the parents of two children, Thérèse and Félix.[40]

Little is known about Manis' business career. In the 1822 *City Directory* he was listed as a trader at 232 Dumaine, corner of St. Claude. He was delinquent in paying taxes in 1823, gave a mortgage on some property in 1826, and was curator of the estate of a watchmaker in 1832. By 1833–34 he appears to have become fairly prosperous. He endorsed notes for Joseph Lasalle for $1,628, and for Samuel Jacobs for $400—these, together with other notes amounting to at least $1,275, were unpaid at the time of his death. In 1834 Manis made substantial investments in real estate, and was one of seven men who established the construction and development corporation named the Company of Architects. But within a few years the speculation bubble of New Orleans had burst, Manis was taken to court by the Architects Company, and some of his property was sold at sheriff's auction. He was a partner with S. S. De Jonge and Lewis Levy in several of the investments listed in his inventory, but these and other holdings had to be sold for the benefit of his creditors, after his death. These sales included thirteen lots of which he was sole owner, twelve lots in which he had a share, his own home at the corner of Royal and Barrack streets, another house, and three of his eleven slaves. The estate was in litigation for some years. Angélique and Irma kept trying to hold on to their interests by purchasing each other's property at sheriff's auction, but how well this succeeded is not shown in the records.[41]

When Manis Jacobs died on September 24, 1839, six days after Yom Kippur, he was eulogized as the "Rabbi" of New Orleans:

"OBITUARY.

'Tis now oh! death! thy poignant sting we own,
'Tis now oh! grave! thy victory is shown!

"The conflict is o'er; the struggle is ended, the king of terror has declared and sustained his prerogative, and another worthy member of our community is '*gathered unto his fathers*.' On the 28th inst. resigned his spirit to the hands of his creator, in the 60th year of his age, the Reverend MANIS JACOBS, Rabbi of the Hebrew Congregation of this city, a native of Amsterdam, (Netherlands) but for the last thirty years a resident of New Orleans. In the demise of the subject of this obituary, society has to deplore the loss of one of its most valuable members; as a *philanthropist* his name will ever be deeply engraven upon the hearts of the indigent

201

and distressed; the couch of disease will have to mourn the bereavement of one whose daily solace was to administer to the comforts and necessities of those who had been overtaken by the iron hand of stern adversity. He had indeed

..................................'A tear for pity
And a hand open as day for melting charity.'

"In the social walks of domestic life an afflicted widow and three orphans have to bemoan the transit from this earth of an affectionate father, a kind and loving husband; yet as an alleviation of the family's affliction under this great loss, it pleased divine providence in some degree to prepare them for the shock by the gradual progress of his disorder to its fatal termination. His remains were conveyed to the sepulchre of his FATHERS, surrounded by a numerous concourse of friends and citizens, where the funeral rites according to the Hebrew religion were performed in a most solemn and impressive manner, the requiem chaunted and the body consigned to its earthly bed, amid the regrets and tears of many. 'May his soul rest in peace. Amen.' "[42]

This tribute was signed "M"—one would wish that it had been written by "G.W.H." or by almost anyone else. George or Solomon Harby would surely have avoided the sick-sweet flavor of death so apparent in this and other obituaries that "M"—probably A. J. Marks—wrote. But now, at least, we know the identify of the early "Rabbi" about whom so much legend has clustered over the years. In a well-known description of American Jewish life written in 1842 by Dr. M. Wiener for a German-Jewish periodical, following an extensive trip throughout the Western hemisphere, some stories were told about "Rabbi" Jacobs:

"The deceased rabbi was by birth a Hollander with a Catholic wife who only with difficulty could be prevented from putting a crucifix into his coffin. Wondrous stories were told about this spiritual leader, who died six years previously. Thus, a short time before his death, he delivered in the synagogue, on the Day of Atonement, an address in which he demonstrated to his congregation that fasting on that day was damned nonsense. . . ."[43]

Dr. Wiener was an Orthodox Jew who objected to any relaxation of the tradition; perhaps Manis Jacobs had been propagandizing on behalf of the Reform movement, still almost unknown in the United States. But Wiener demonstrated no understanding of the courage which was displayed by a man like Jacobs who, without any training as a rabbi or Jewish scholar, did his best to give some Jewish leadership to his coreligionists. Rabbi Max Heller, writing in 1922, reported that Manis' Catholic descendants believed that he had been buried in a Catholic cemetery; it was probably to discredit any such supposition on the part of Angélique's friends that "M" referred to Manis' Jewish burial in so insistent a manner.[44]

4. A Charter, a Wedding and a Cemetery

The early months of the congregation's existence were hectic. After the meeting on December 20, 1827, at which Jacob Solis persuaded his fellow-Jews to organize a congregation, many steps had to be taken. First the application for a charter had to be prepared for approval by the two houses of the legislature and by the Governor; it was probably ratified at the meeting which was held on February 2, 1828.[45] Manis Jacobs must meanwhile have consented to serve as president; he was probably elected at the February meeting, together with the other officers. The next assignment was to locate a property which could be used for a cemetery—the indispensable requirement of an organized Jewish community.

But before the cemetery could be found, another event took place—the first documented Jewish wedding in New Orleans. On February 26, 1828, Daniel Goodman was married to Amelia Harris, or in terms of their traditional Hebrew names, Naphtali the son of Yom Tov took Malkah the daughter of Hayyim as his bride. Samuel Hermann and Samuel Kohn were the official witnesses who signed the Hebrew marriage document, the *Ketubah*, but their names are in English, not in Hebrew; they may have come as guests of Amelia's uncle, Asher Nathan, who, as a relative, was forbidden by Jewish law to act as a witness. Judging from Manis Jacobs' Hebrew script in his

203

signature seal, he probably could not print the Hebrew text of the *Ketubah* as beautifully as it appears in this document; Jacob Solis must have been the *sofer* (scribe) for the occasion. He may, however, have instructed Manis Jacobs in the wedding service, if he did not already know how one was conducted.[46]

Once this festivity was concluded, Manis Jacobs and Jacob Solis could continue their search. They finally found an appropriate site in the Lafayette suburb in Jefferson Parish, at Jackson avenue and Saratoga street. This was fairly distant from the center of things in those days. Because the congregation was not yet a corporation, and therefore could not legally own property, Manis purchased the lot on March 13 for $361.25. Once the charter had been approved by the legislature on March 25, and, presumably, some money was collected, Manis turned the property over to the congregation; this took place on April 26.

The choice of a name for the congregation must have been made very early in this chain of steps. Solis' was probably the decisive voice in the selection of Shanarai-Chasset but he could not have recommended any Hebrew words more difficult to transliterate or pronounce. Through the years Shanarai-Chasset was written in a variety of forms, even by the officers—"Sharri Haset," "Sharei Shisset," "Shangarai Chasset," "Shangarai Chassed," "Shaarai Chesed." It was a good thing that the congregation ultimately came to be known as Touro Synagogue!

Meanwhile the act of incorporation, and an exchange of complimentary letters between Solis and Jacobs, appeared in the newspapers; an official meeting was held to elect the officers authorized by the charter; and the constitution and by-laws were drawn up for printing. All of those men in town who had promised to join the congregation (and pay their dues!) were asked to go to Aaron Daniels' store at 17 Chartres street to sign the constitution, under threat of forfeiting one hundred dollars in addition to accrued dues if they delayed beyond June 14. But the officers must have had a difficult time collecting both signatures and contributions, because the printed notice which summoned the Jews of New Orleans to do their duty was repeated in the newspapers day after day into August, well beyond the deadline.[47]

Jacob Solis left New Orleans for Louisville and home some time in May or June of 1828. Manis kept him informed of the welfare of his new baby, the congregation:

New Orleans   June 4th 1828

Mr. Jacob S. Solis

I have the honor to forward you by the present your umbrellas, [   ][48] pamphlets of our Consti[tu]tion and by laws[49] which you will be So good and dispose of, one to the president of the Hebrew Congregation of Sincinaty two to New York, two to Philadelphia, one to Baltimore one to Richmond, one to Charleston, one for yourself one to Luries[50][,] Myers[,] Jacobs, Lyons, Workum[,] Joseph, Goldsmith, near Louisville. My dear Sir Since you been gone I had hard work, to do, that is to Say, to Say prayers every Evening in the house of the mourners, and you know that I do not know much about the portuguaise minhag [rite] Still we come on pretty well. I have been yesterday in the afternoon on horse back to the burial ground and the Sons of the demise have made already a tombstone at over the grave; when you will write me from New York inquire how a corpse must lay. For Some think yet that the feet ought to lay in the East,[51] write me also how you came on at Natchez, and write another letter from Louisville and one from Cincinaty.[52] I hope you may succeed in all your good undertakings. I have the honor to be Your most humble

Manis Jacobs

Madame Jacobs and her
Children send their compliments
Mr. Marks goes every Evening with me to prayers
But Complains that I keep him too long there
I send you one more for Mr Salomon of New York and for
the president to Savana
one for Salomon Hunt and one for Baruk[53]

This report reveals how sincerely and conscientiously Manis Jacobs was attempting to lead the congregation—distributing the *Constitution*, conducting services, inspecting the cemetery. It was Hyam Harris who had died on June first, and whose grave site Jacobs had inspected. This funeral was followed swiftly by two others: Emanuel Stern died on July 25, and his wife, Jeanette Hunt Stern, died on July 28. Stern had been in New Orleans since 1824 at the latest; he went bankrupt that year. The Sterns had two sons: a younger boy named Isaac, who went to live with his aunt Mrs. Van Ostern, and an older son, Adolphus Sterne.[54] Adolphus was the well-known Texas pioneer who smuggled weapons and ammunition into Nacogdoches for the Fredonian Rebellion in 1826. From 1831 to 1833 he held various offices under the Mexicans, and was a secret emissary for Sam Houston in New Orleans, equipping an entire company for the Texas Revolution of 1835. Sterne kept a store in Nacogdoches, practiced law, bought and sold land, was an active Mason, and served several terms in the Texas legislature, before his death on March 27, 1852. He is said to have lived and worked in New Orleans from 1817 to 1826, but we have found no record of his activities; he was probably like many other young men, clerks and apprentices, who grew up the hard way before they decided on their future. While he was active in business in Nacogdoches, he kept in contact with some Jewish businessmen in New Orleans, Alexander Phillips among them. Adolphus was represented in the proceedings in New Orleans connected with his father's estate by Edward Gottschalk.[55]

There were other funerals to take care of, holiday and Sabbath services to conduct, meetings to arrange, and a myriad of responsibilities to keep Manis busy. On August 26, 1829, he wrote a long report to Jacob Solis about the congregation's progress: Alexander Phillips had contributed fifty dollars; "old [Jacob?] hart Doct A Costa and L. Levy in making apology for you and the Congregation before the board, put in the minute book was at last received."[56] One of the members had lost a child; Levy Prince and Leopold Jones of New York had died; Solis' cousin Solomon sent his regards (but there were too many Solomons for us to try to figure out who this might have been). Manis asked Solis to order "two holy books" (Bibles?) from London, and to try to raise some money for the congregation among his friends in New York City. He also reported the exciting news that the congregation had paid $205 at an auction

206

for a lot of ground 70 by 80 feet at the corner of St. Louis and Franklin streets. This was to be used as the site of a synagogue, if the necessary five or six thousand dollars for construction could be raised. "Now Sir," wrote Manis Jacobs,

"we have to beseech you a favor knowing that there exist in New York Several rich Israelites, who walk in the ways of God, and particular one who all ready has Shewn to the congregation of New York his charitable heart to ask a loan of them or him of the amount of five thousand or Six thousand Dollars for wich we will pay them or him a Small interest and give him or them a morgage on the property until final payment. Sir we all know that there is no greater Mitzva [good deed] among Israel than to Save the life of an Israelite, and in helping to build temples that the name of the great god of Israel may be propagated in the whole Globe. . . ."

That Manis meant Harmon Hendricks, even though he did not remember the name, was immediately recognized by Solis, who wrote on the overleaf of the address sheet, "H. Hendricks, Esqr./ New York."[57] Hendricks (1771–1838) had advanced thousands of dollars to Shearith Israel so that the congregation could pay its debts and remain solvent. The letter itself reported the background of the congregation to the prospective donor:

"Having heard of your Noble action and your magnanimity, towards our brethren, therefore, we the officers of the Israelite Congregation, Sharei Shisset of New Orleans, take the liberty to address ourselves to you, hoping that you will not reject our request. New Orleans had always the reputation by Israelites, Gentiles, &. to be the last place in the union for religious Societies, it is but 17 months ago that there was not here, the least iot of an Ysraelite Congregation. Since that the time they have a place of interment a Metaher House [at the cemetery for the preparation of the dead for burial] and a lot to build a temple on, and all that through your worthy fellow Citizen Mr. Jacob S. Solis, we now pray you to advance the Said Society the Sum of Six Thousand Dollars, with a Small Interest and Morgage on the property till final payment for wich we have authorize Mr. Jacob S. Solis to

207

make arrangements with you. In So Doing the blessings of the God of Israel will never cease to come on you and your family for ever and ever, and will never Cease from your descendants, we remain for ever

Your most humble servants:

MANIS JACOBS, pres.

AARON DANIELS, vice-presed."[58]

That Manis Jacobs had to ask Solis to try to obtain a loan for the New Orleans congregation from a wealthy New Yorker, when there were so many wealthy Jews in New Orleans, spoke volumes. It is to a review of that problem that we now turn.

208

Prinsessegracht (*van de Kerkweg*)

1. Home of Sir Salomon de Medina (David Monsanto's Employer), The Hague
(Right half of third building from right)

2. The Hague Synagogue in which the Monsanto Family Worshipped

RÉPONSE

Du Sieur MONSANTO & Compagnie, Armateurs du Senault le St. Jean-Baptiste, Demandeurs.

Au Mémoire du Sieur RAOULT, Capitaine Commandant ci-devant ledit Navire, Deffendeur.

LA foibleſſe apparente des moyens allégués par le Sieur Raoult dans le Mémoire qu'il vient de faire paroître pour ſa défenſe, ne doit pas faire préſumer favorablement de ſa cauſe. C'eſt en vain que l'on y cherche les préſomptions ſi fortes, qu'il y annonce en commençant. Loin de ſe diſculper des Griefs qu'on lui avoit imputés dans le Précis du 29. Mai 1765, il ſemble prétendre cauſe d'ignorance ſur la plûpart; & ceux deſquels il ſe défend, ſont ſi foiblement réfutés, qu'on pourroit demander à quelle fin, il fait paroître une Réponſe ſi vague, & ſi peu motivée.

Le glaive dont il veut que s'arme la Juſtice, au ſoutien de ſa Cauſe, n'eſt pas encore déployé. Ses droits mis dans la Balance de l'impartialité ne paroiſſent pas encore prépondérans. Les procédés du Sieur Monſanto ne ſembleront indignes, qu'autant

---

4. Angélica Monsanto Dow

Portrait by José de Salazar

5. Angélica's Husband, Dr. Robert Dow

Watercolor by Unknown Artist

6. Angélica's Elder Son, Thomas Urquhart

Portrait by José de Salazar

7. Angélica's Younger Son, David Urquhart

Bust by Hiram Powers

8. Judah Touro

Daguerreotype

9. Judah Touro

Portrait by Solomon Nunes Carvalho

10. Touro's Friend, Rezin Davis Shepherd

Portrait by Gilbert Stuart

11. Maurice Barnett's Old Slave Block

SALES AT AUCTION.

BY M. BARNETT, Sen., Auctioneer.

Cornelius Hurst vs. His Creditors—*Syndic Sale.*

ON Monday, the 2d Dec, 1839, at 12 o'clock noon, at the City Exchange, St. Louis street between Chartres and Royal streets, by order of Alexander Grant, syndic of said estate, and by virtue of an order issued by the honorable the first judicial district court of the state of Louisiana, dated the 26th day of October, 1839, the following slaves surrendered to his creditors by said insolvent, viz:

DICK, about 28 years of age, a well disposed man.

OSBORN, about 26 years of age, mulatto; a good carriage driver and waiter, active and handy at any thing he is put to.

LUCINDA, about 22 years of age, Osborn's wife, very intelligent, good cook, washer and ironer.

COMMODORE, about 6 years of age, ⎫
JOSEPHINE, about 4 years of age, ⎬ Lucinda's
HENRY, about 2 years of age, ⎪ children.
OSBORN, about 1 year of age, ⎭

NED, about 19 years of age, accustomed to work in a brick yard.

LOU is about 17 years of age, accustomed to work in a brick yard.

MINGO, about 28 years of age, brick moulder, stout able bodied man.

WINNEY, about 37 years of age, worked in a brick yard.

PRISCILLA, about 24 years of age, stout able bodied woman.

SERENA, about 21 years of age, a good off-bearer in a brick yard, and her child.

MATILDA, about 25 years of age, cook, washer and ironer, and her three children, viz:

THOMAS, about 10 years of age.

TONEY, about 6 years of age.

WILLIAM, an infant.

SALLY, about 22 years of age, mild and well disposed woman; cook, washer and ironer.

JULIANNA, about 21 years of age, and her child; accustomed to work in a brick yard.

MARY, about 23 years of age, also accustomed to work in a brick yard.

JACOB, about 25 years of age, stout man, accustomed to work in a brick yard.

Terms—Six months credit for all but Jacob, who will be sold at six and twelve months, for notes drawn and endorsed to the satisfaction of the syndic, who reserves to himself the privilege of refusing names as endorsers, until he is satisfied therewith, without assigning any cause therefor; the notes to bear an interest at the rate of ten per cent. per annum (if not met at maturity) until paid—without this however giving the parties thereto the right of prolonging the payment after due. The purchasers will be allowed forty-eight hours after a notification from the notary that the titles are completed, to arrange the settlements, and if not effected within that period, the slave or slaves to be resold at auction, for cash, on the account and risk of the said original purchasers, without delay or public notice; and said parties held responsible for any loss that may accrue thereon, with all expenses, costs, &c. Acts of sale before Edward Barnett, notary public, at the expense of the purchasers. The slaves not to be delivered until the terms of sale are complied with.

New Orleans, 29th October, 1839.

12. Maurice Barnett Sells Some Slaves

SATURDAY 12th NOVEMBER, 1836.

BY M. BARNETT Sr.

At 11 O'clock, at Hewlett's Exchange,

Corner of Chartres and St.-Louis streets,

Will be Sold

The Beautiful Town Called

JEFFERSONVILLE,

DIVIDED INTO LOTS.

This Town is situated at less than a mile distance from Madisonville, and on the Tchefoncta River, and is one of the prettiest spots in the State of Louisiana. The land is generally very high, covered with handsome trees, and for health unsurpassed by any on the borders of the Lake.

A more suitable place for country seats could not be found, and the increase of the Lake trade and settlement of the back country premise ere long to make of Jeffersonville a town that will rank higher than any in that section of the country.

Fish and game abound there, the marketing can be had from the neighborhood very cheap, lumber and bricks for building can be procured at low prices, add to which, the military road to Nashville, passes in the vicinity, a good carriage road leads to Covington, and other places, and the steamboat of the Amelioration company will take passengers there daily for $1. A distance of about two hours sail only from town, advantages which must in less than one year form a considerable settlement there.

From Madisonville to the Lake a shelled road is about being made, which can easily be continued to Jeffersonville. The distance between the nearest points of the two places being less than half a mile. A good road leads also to Mandeville, Lewisburg, Springfield, and various other places.

It is rarely such an opportunity offers to speculators, for although the Proprietors are fully aware that in a year or two, this property would command ten times the price they may realise at present; yet they have determined to sell every lot without any kind of reserve, and on the most liberal credit.

TERMS—6, 12, 18, 24 and 30 months for notes endorsed to the satisfaction of the vendors, bearing mortgage until final payment. The purchasers to be put in possession at their own expense.

Acts of sale to be passed before Wm. BOSWELL, Esq. Notary Public, at the expense of the purchasers. Those who wish to pay cash will be allowed 10 per cent, per annum discount, and those paying the two first instalments in cash will be dispensed giving endorsers for the remainder.

The plan will be shortly exhibited at the Exchange.

SAMEDI 12 NOVEMBRE 1836,

PAR M. BARNETT Sr.

Il sera vendu, a 11 heures du matin, a la Bourse Hewlett, encoignure Chartres et St.-Louis,

La Belle Ville Appelée

JEFFERSONVILLE,

DIVISEE EN TERRAINS,

Cette ville, situee a moins d'un mille de distance de Madisonville, et sur les bords de la Riviere Tchefoncta, est reconnue pour l'un des plus jolis sites de la Louisiane.

La terre est generalement haute, couverte de beaux arbres, et n'est surpasser par aucun endroit sur le developpement du Lac pour sa salubrité.

C'est l'eslipacement le plus convenable pour former des etablissements et residences d'été, et l'augmentation progressive du commerce avec l'intérieur du pays promet avant long-temps de placer Jeffersonville au premier rang des villes de cette partie de l'état.

La pêche et la chasse y abondent. Les vivres, à tres-bon marché sont fournis par le voisinage, le bois et les briques pour les constructions au prix le plus mediocre. On peut ajouter à ces avantages que la route militaire de Nashville passe à 20 arpents de là, de bons chemins conduisent à Covington et autres places de l'intérieur, et que le bateau à vapeur de la C°. des Ameliorations prendra les passagers chaque jour pour $1. La distance de la Nouvelle Orleans à Jeffersonville peut etre parcourue en 2 heures on peut penser qu'au moins d'une d'une ville, nombre d'etablissements y seront deja formés.

De Madisonville au Lac, un chemin de coquilles doit etre fait, et peut alsement etre continue jusqu'à Jeffersonville, la distance entre les points les plus rapprocha, étant de moins d'un demi mille. Une bonne route mène à Lewisburg, Mandeville, Springfield et autres endroits dans les environs.

C'est vraiment une occasion offerte aux speculateurs, car quoique les Proprietaires soient persuades que dans un an ou deux cette propriété decuplera sa valeur presente, ils sont determines a vendre sans reserve aucune, et aux termes les plus avantageux.

CONDITIONS: 6, 12, 18, 24 et 30 mois, en billets endosses à satisfaction des vendeurs, portant hypothèque jusqu'à parfait paiement. Les acheteurs se feront mettre en possession a leurs frais; les actes de vente seront passés chez M. Wm. BOSWELL, Notaire public, à la charge des acquereurs. Ceux qui paieront comptant auront droit a un escompte de 10 pour cent par an, et ceux qui effectueront les 2 premiers paiements comptant seront dispenses de donner des endossements pour le reste de leurs billets.

Dans peu le plan sera exposé à la Bourse.

Imprimé par GAUX et Cie., Rue de Chartres, No. 108, entre Conti et St.-Louis.

13. Barnett Real Estate Auction Broadside

14. Samuel Hermann, Sr.

Portrait by Vaudechamp

15. Marie Emeronthe Becnel Brou Hermann

Portrait by Vaudechamp (?)

16. Samuel Hermann, Jr.

Portrait by Vaudechamp

17. The Samuel Hermann Home in New Orleans

18. Garden Patio of the Hermann Home

19. Samuel Kohn

Portrait by Unknown Artist

20. Joachim Kohn

Portrait by Vaudechamp

21. Carl Kohn

Portrait by Jacques Amans

22ₐ Alexander Hart — The Widow Kokernot's Second Husband
Portrait by Unknown Artist

SYSTEME

DE

LOI PÉNALE

POUR

L'Etat de la Louisiane,

COMPRENANT

LES CODES,

1. *Des Délits et des Peines,*   3. *De Discipline des Prisons,*

2. *De Procédure,*   4. *Des Preuves :*

Ce dernier applicable au Civil comme au Criminel

ET

UN LIVRE

CONTENANT

Les Définitions de tous les Mots techniques

DONT IL EST FAIT USAGE DANS CE SYSTEME.

Préparé en vertu d'une Loi de l'Etat,

PAR EDOUARD LIVINGSTON, D. EL. L.

Nouvelle-Orléans :

DE L'IMPRIMERIE DE BENJAMIN LEVY,

Rue Conti, No. 56,

1825.

---

23. A Levy Imprint: Title Page of a Section of
Livingston's *Penal Code* in French

24. Louis Moreau Gottschalk

C-302

NOTICE.

Daniel Warburg

Inhabitant of the Parish of Orleans, having intention to emancipate *his slave a mulatto named*

Eugene aged four years

Every person having any legal opposition to said emancipation, are required to file said opposition in the office of the Parish Court of the said Parish, within forty days from the date of the present notice.

New-Orleans,
February 9th 1830

[signature] Sheriff.

AVIS.

Daniel Warburg

Habitant de la Paroisse d'Orleans, étant dans l'intention d'affranchir *son esclave mulâtre nommé*

Eugène agé de quatre ans

Toutes les personnes qui pourraient avoir des oppositions légales à faire audit affranchissement, sont prévenues d'avoir à les présenter à la Cour de la susdite Paroisse dans le délai de quarante jours, à dater de celui de la présente déclaration.

Nouvelle-Orleans,
(9 février 1830)

[signature] Sheriff.

25. Daniel Warburg Frees His Son, Eugène

"THE GODDESS EVE."

TWO TABLES,

CONSTRUCTED TO DEMONSTRATE BY

NUMBERS

THE TRUE MODE FOR EXTRACTING THE

SQUARE ROOT

OUT OF ALL ENTIRE NUMBERS ABOVE 100,

AND THE

CUBIC ROOT

OUT OF ALL ENTIRE NUMBERS ABOVE 1000.

BESIDES:

MULTIPLICATION AND THE RULE OF THREE
WITH ENTIRE NUMBERS.

(These Tables may be carried to endless extent.)

BY

DANIEL WARBURG, Author.

NEW-ORLEANS.
PRINTED BY E. JOHNS & CO., STATIONERS' HALL.
1839.

26. Title Page of Warburg's *The Goddess Eve*

BUY A LOTTERY TICKET;

OR

A CHANCE TO GET RID OF MONEY.

————◦◉◦————

"A Table and the necessary explanation, to shew
"the Combination of a Lottery Scheme, com-
"posed of 75 Numbers, three Numbers
"in a Row on each Ticket, and 12
"Numbers drawn to determine
"the Prizes."

BY

DANIEL WARBURG,

Author of "The Goddess Eve."

NEW-ORLEANS.
PRINTED BY E. JOHNS & CO., STATIONERS' HALL.

————

1839.

27. Title Page of Warburg's *Buy A Lottery Ticket*

28. Eugène Warburg's Bust of John Y. Mason

Tutoona, or

The Indian Girl.

A Drama in 5 Acts.

By Geo. W. Harby

Persons.

Gen. Gates.
Major Scott
Col. Thomas
Capt. Davis
Serg't Griffith
Old Doyle ———— Officers and Soldiers ————
Miss Mary Scott, ———— daughter to Major Scott.

Indians

Coppersnake ———— a chief — Tutoona's father
Mantogo ———— a Warrior. ————

Indian Warriors, &c.

Tutoona, the Indian Girl. ————

Time. "On the 18th October, 1777. at Saratoga, the British army, nearly ten thousand men, including Indians, surrendered to Gen. Gates." American History.

Performed at the New Orleans, American Theatre, for three evenings. ————
1835.

29. Title Page of Manuscript of G. W. Harby's *Tutoona*

30. Judah P. Benjamin

31. Manis Jacobs' Signature, with Hebrew Name, on a Legal Document, 1823

THE
CONSTITUTION
AND
BYE-LAWS,

OF THE

ISRAELITE CONGREGATION,

OF

SHANARAI-CHASSET,

(GATES OF MERCY,)

Of the City of New-Orleans,

STATE OF LOUISIANA.

Founded February 2d, A. M. 5588,

BY JACOB S. SOLIS,

OF THE STATE OF NEW-YORK,

DECEMBER 20th, 1827.

———

NEW-ORLEANS:

PRINTED BY F. DELAUP, PRINTER OF THE CONGREGATION.

1828.

32. Title Page of the 1828 *Constitution*

במזל טוב

בארבא בשבת באחד עשר יום לחדש אדר שנת
חמשת אלפים וחמש מאות ושמונים ושמונה לבריאת
עולם למנין שאנו מנין כאן בארליאנס אנך נפתלי
בר יוסטוב אמר לה להדא בתולתא מלכה בת
חיים הרי לי לאנתו כדת משה וישראל ואנא אפלח
ואוקיר ואיזון ואפרנס יתיכי כהלכות גוברין יהודין
דפלחין ומוקרין וזנין ומפרנסין לנשיהון בקושטא
ויהבנא ליכי מהר בתוליכי כסף זוזי מאתן דחזי
ליכי מדאורייתא ומזוניכי וכסותיכי וסיפוקיכי
ומיעל לותיכי כאורח כל ארעא וצביאת מרת
מלכה בתולתה דא והות ליה לאנתו ורי נדוניא
דהנעלת ליה מבי אבוה בין בכסף בין בדהב
בין בתכשיטין במאני דלבישא ובשמושא
דערסא חמשין לטרין וצבי נפתלי חתן דנן
והוסיף לה מן דיליא חמשין לטרין סך הכל מאה
לטרין דכסף רבך אמר נפתלי חתן דנן אחריות
שטר כתובתא דא ותוספתא דא רין קבל עלי
נפתלי חתן רשל כנכסי בחיים ובלמות מן יומא
דנן ולעלם ואחריות שטר כתובתא התנך דנן
כחומר כל שטרי כתובות ותוספות דנהגין
בבנת ישראל העשוין בתיקון חכמינו זל דלא
כאסמכתא ודלא כטופסי דשטרי וקנינא מן
נפתלי בר יוסטוב חתן דנן למרה מלכה בת
חיים בתולתא דא בכל מה דכתב ומפורש
לעיל במנא דכשר למקניא ביה הכל שריר
וקים

34. Isaac Leeser

35. Gershom Kursheedt

Portrait by Unknown Artist

36. Christ Church (extreme left) Before Its Transformation into
Nefutzoth Yehudah Synagogue

VI

Why Had It Taken So Long?
Assimilation or Continuity?

When Manis Jacobs wrote to Jacob Solis, asking him to try to borrow five or six thousand dollars from New York Jews so that the New Orleans congregation might undertake the building of a synagogue, he was reminding him of something that both of them knew: the wealthiest and most successful Jews in New Orleans could easily have contributed that amount of money if they had wanted to participate in the project. Samuel and Joachim Kohn, Samuel Hermann, Asher Moses Nathan and Hart Moses Shiff would neither join the congregation nor contribute to its support; Judah Touro and Edward Gottschalk both made contributions, probably very small ones, but had no interest in joining or helping the congregation in any substantial way. Any two of these men could probably have built a synagogue out of their own funds without missing the money at all. But they did not. What was different about them as Jews? Why had they who were among the earliest Jewish settlers in New Orleans—all but Gottschalk—never undertaken the establishment of a congregation themselves, in the early years? Why did it take so much longer to found a synagogue in New Orleans than in any comparable location?

1. The Kind of Jews They Were

Difficult as it is to generalize about men whose personalities and characters were vastly different and complex, it is surely obvious that the men who came to New Orleans in the early years, before 1815, were strong and courageous individualists. They arrived alone, without a relative or a friend; they dared to confront the challenge of a new life without any help. Each of them was poor, armed only with a willingness to work hard. They were independent men. All this is to their credit; it demonstrates something admirable about their inner spirit—they were the stuff of which pioneers are made, hardy, determined, self-reliant. New Orleans needed their kind of imaginative vigor desperately. They contributed greatly to the city's growth and prosperity. But this quality of mind and spirit also tells us something about their feelings towards Judaism and the Jewish community. They simply did not care if they were distant from the heritage of their families. They were willing to leave the protective shelter of a full Jewish life at home, in Frankfurt, Hamburg, Amsterdam, London or New York City, in order to find fortune and success on a frontier where Judaism did not exist. They did not need the security of fellow Jews, of kosher food, of synagogue services, of holiday celebrations, even of memorial prayers for their departed. They knew in advance that they could do without the warmth and the familiar customs of Judaism. Touro could have gone to Charleston where there was a congregation, a community, and economic opportunity; Asher Nathan had even been there before he came to Louisiana; Alexander Phillips could have remained in Philadelphia. The Europeans could have immigrated to one of the cities of the Atlantic seaboard where there were established Jewish communities. That they did not settle in any of those cities, but decided to come to New Orleans, is primary evidence that Judaism was not very important to them.

As early as 1807, it was apparently well known that the Jews who had settled in New Orleans were not particularly loyal to their faith. The sensitive, intelligent Rebecca Gratz had already heard this, and sent a warning to her brother Joseph, before he took a trip to New Orleans:

"... At New Orleans, there are many who call themselves Jews, or at least whose parentage being known are obliged to acknowledge themselves such, but who neglect those duties which would make that title honorable and then respected—among such my dear Jo, I hope you will never make one; be assured the worthy & the thinking part of the community will ever estimate a man, by his attention to the serious, domestic duties which speak more truly his character than the external forms in which he presents himself to the world; who would depend on a man's engagements with his fellow men, if he violates his more important engagements with God?"[1]

The Jewish community of the United States in 1807 was very small. News traveled swiftly. Those Jews who observed the traditions knew each other well. It did not take long for Rebecca Gratz in Philadelphia to hear from some traveling merchant, or perhaps from David Seixas' family in New York City, that men like Judah Touro and Jacob Hart paid little or no attention to the observances of the Jewish faith. After all, Jacob Hart's father had been a congregational leader in two cities, and Judah Touro's father had been a cantor and teacher. And here were their sons, in New Orleans, neglectful of their religious obligations. But Rebecca Gratz did not and could not understand that the ambition which drove these men to the entrepreneurial center of the South did not leave much room for feelings of religious devotion. Nor did New Orleans judge a man's worth by his "engagements with God," as Rebecca would have preferred. It judged him by the success of his enterprises. If he made good, he was a man of worth. These men had come to New Orleans because they thought that this was a city in which they would find fortune.

But perhaps it was not only indifference to Judaism which permitted these men to go so far from home or any place resembling home. The late years of the eighteenth century and the early years of the nineteenth century were a period of rapid disintegration of the traditional modes of Judaism. The old hold was being loosened. The rigid restrictions were no longer accepted without question. Jews who moved into the modern world beyond the strict bounds of the Jewish community were wondering if there was really any aspect of Judaism that was worth retaining. The first stirrings of what was to become Reform Judaism, the effort to help the Jew to adjust to life in the new world of constant contact between Jews and Christians by "modernizing" Judaism, had not reached the ears and hearts of very many young Jews. Not until 1824 did the first attempt to modify traditional practices lead to the formation of a new kind of congregation in Charleston, under the leadership of

George Harby's brother Isaac. There was as yet no alternative to traditional Orthodoxy for men who asked any sort of questions. But it may have been something even more personal than this generalized dissatisfaction with traditional Judaism. We do not know enough about the individual experiences of the European immigrants to evaluate their response to the ritual of their childhood days. But it is possible that men like Judah Touro and Benjamin Levy, whose fathers were so closely identified with the synagogue and its life, had been repelled by the rigid insistence on observance, by the inevitable separation from non-Jews, by too great a concern with religious matters. It is not only self-reliance and self-assurance that send a man far from home to a strange new world, all alone. It may also be alienation and rebellion against the past. Perhaps it was with relief that some of these early Jews came to New Orleans to find a life that would be free of the restrictions of Judaism.

There was another factor which motivated the Europeans more strongly than the American-born men: escape from the degradation associated with being Jewish. Nowhere on the European continent were Jews treated with true equality or were they granted true freedom. Always there were reminders of disability and inferiority. All of these early settlers must have been grateful to be far away from a Europe that still despised Jews. Only Carl Kohn left testimony of the anguish and resentment that a young Jew felt at the treatment accorded to Jews in Europe, but we may be certain that he was expressing something that all of them understood. Written in 1833 to his Uncle Samuel who had visited the Kohn family in rural Bohemia, these words of Carl's are worth pondering:

"...The accounts you give of our relations are indeed sorry enough but alas! what can we expect otherwise—it is a sad thought, that those who are so near & dear to us, in spite of your exertions & sacrifices for them can still not succeed to better their situation—It is indeed a miserable country they live in—New Orleans with its ... fevers & cholera is by far a preferable place—there at least a man inclined to labour can gain a livelihood, not only for himself, but also for his children, and can amass sufficient means, to exempt him from want in his old age; but in our wretched country, an honest man with a large family to support,

212

despised and trodden-under-foot as he already is by religious prejudice, is still not allowed to enjoy in quiet the fruits of his own limited industry; continually preyed upon by an oppressive & partial government, it is no wonder that the word Jew has become proverbial for s[ala]ud. . . ."[2]

Here is a sort of helpless anger that has to be choked down, because there is no hope for the future, just more pain for Jews. But it spills over, this anger, against the Jews themselves. Even though he indulged in sentimental recollections of his childhood, and wrote with longing of the *"Kichlach* [little cakes] on the table" in his home, Carl could not help speaking with some scorn of his fellow Jews in the Bohemian village:

". . . I can well imagine the inconvenience you were subject to during your stay in our native country—but in a country where ignorance reigns to such a degree, where all information is banished from our class, and where no change takes place . . ., a man like you, so nearly related to the family [,] an American, and particularly a 'richard' will always collect crowds of the curious, who stare at him with surprise, in seeing nothing supernatural about the man, who had resolution enough to raise himself thus high above his cast, and as to the crowd of beggars, that astonishes me less, for ours is a land of beggars, where an honest man cannot but be a beggar, & the only land, where a man like my poor dear father, whose ideas of honor are a little more elevated than those of others, cannot, in spite of hard labor, bodily & mental exertions advance himself beyond the humble limits, which fate has set for him . . ."

Jews are a "class," and a "cast[e]." And Carl will not identify himself with the class and the caste, nor can he speak of his uncle as one of them—he "had resolution enough to raise himself thus high above his cast." Carl was undergoing a struggle that had been characteristic of ambitious and sensitive young Jews since the first glimmering of hope for escape from the Jewish "fate" appeared with the Enlightenment—the struggle between resentment against anti-Semitic prejudice and oppression, and alienation from the Jews themselves, as though they were partly responsible for their condition. Carl was delighted to know that Samuel planned to help his father "find himself a

213

place of refuge from persecution & trouble in some other part of Germany," but advised against it; one difficulty he foresaw was that

> ". . . should he settle elsewhere, he will then be among strangers, the odium of being a Jew will yet be upon him, & among them it would require a long time, before the qualities became known, which distinguish him from the common class. . . ."[3]

Carl had already become something of a snob. Freedom, opportunity, affluence, knowledge, had drawn him away from his Jewish identity; Jews were a "common class" with whom he no longer associated himself. Jews, in his mind's eye, represented suffering, degradation, beggardom, poverty, ignorance. Perhaps these were feelings that most of these early European Jewish immigrants had about Judaism: they wanted to establish themselves as human beings, not as Jews, for Jews represented something they had been compelled to regard as contemptible.

The extent of intermarriage during the early years is yet another point of reference from which we can measure the distance of their drift away from Judaism. Of the fifteen Jews who established permanent residence in New Orleans between 1802 and 1815, seven remained bachelors, seven intermarried, and one, Manis Jacobs, married a Christian woman after his first, Jewish, wife died. There is no evidence that any one of the bachelors remained single because he would not marry a Christian. Even after larger numbers of Jews, including whole families, arrived in New Orleans, a high degree of intermarriage continued, probably as much as fifty percent, well into the 1830's. While it is sometimes suggested that intermarriage leads to the disintegration of Jewish loyalties, it is more likely, at least in this New Orleans experience, that the decision to settle in Louisiana, and therefore to marry a Christian, stemmed from a weakening of consciousness of Jewish identity. These men had already, to some degree, abandoned their Jewish nature and become secularized. Practically all of the children of these intermarriages, as we have seen, were reared as Christians. Alexander Phillips had two daughters who married Jews, but it is not known whether they considered themselves to be Jewesses. Their feelings may have been similar to those of Maurice Barnett's daughter Hélène, who married Sol Audler, the secretary of Shanarai-Chasset, but who had her children baptized in the St. Louis Church, and was buried in the same Catholic cemetery as her mother. While it is true that there was not a Jewish girl within hundreds of miles of New Orleans whom one of these men might have married, it is at least equally significant that none of them seems to have made any effort to preserve his children from absorption into the Christian population. Although in some cases there was a delay of a few years, baptism was the inevitable rule. The fathers were just not interested in bearing any responsibility for the perpetuation of Judaism. The extent of intermarriage was not lost on Jacob Solis; when he and his co-workers drew up the constitution and by-laws of the congregation they broke every Jewish law in their formulation of rules and regulations which concerned "strange" wives and the children of intermarriages. To have forbidden intermarried men from joining the congregation or contributing to it, to have refused any recognition of Christian wives or unconverted children of Christian mothers, would have been tantamount to rejecting a large proportion of the Jews in town. As it was, they need not have worried; many of the intermarried men would have nothing to do with the congregation. None of their children, even Manis Jacobs', identified themselves as practicing members of the community.

Yet it is equally important to emphasize the fact that of all the men who married Christian women, only one, Victor Souza, formally abandoned Judaism and adopted Christianity. All of the others, with the exception of Simon Cohen, alone and fatally stricken at the time of his baptism, remained what they were, secularized Jews, unaffiliated Jews, estranged Jews, but still Jews. Some were buried with Christian rites, but not because they had become Christians—this was the decision of their families. Perhaps it was pride, perhaps some primitive feeling of stiff-neckedness that made them resist baptism. But if they had wanted to become Christians, to endure the indignity of adopting a religion which was meaningless to them, in order to secure

215

acceptance by their neighbors, if they had wanted to pay the price of baptism for the "ticket" of admission to Western culture, as Heinrich Heine called it, they could have done that in Europe. Perhaps many another might have sent the message back home, which Dr. Gerson Adersbach did, in his will, that despite everything, he "died without quitting the religion into which he had been born."[4]

Paradoxically enough, some of these men were even willing to give financial support to Judaism elsewhere, if not in New Orleans. It was almost as though they were saying that they had no objection to the perpetuation of Judaism in other places—just so long as it made no personal claims on them. When Ruben Rochelle was in New York City in 1819, he gave an offering to Shearith Israel. He also contributed $250 to the building fund of Mikveh Israel Congregation of Philadelphia early in 1824; at the same time Asher Nathan sent $250, Samuel Hermann and Hart Shiff $100 each, and Judah Touro $300. In 1827, Hart Shiff donated some money to the building fund of B'nai Jeshurun Congregation of New York City. The New York Jews of whom we have written, Sol Soher, and the members of the Cromelien-Davies clan, also made contributions to Shearith Israel and B'nai Jeshurun, and later, in 1845, to another New York congregation, Shaaray Tefila, but perhaps their situation was different, because they may never have intended to stay in New Orleans. Samuel Hermann, on a visit to Germany in 1836, gave one thousand gulden (the equivalent of about $2,500 today) to his old congregation in Roedelheim . . . but he appears not to have given even one dollar to the New Orleans congregation. It is apparent that these men had no dislike for Judaism; they simply had no interest in personal identification with a congregation.[5]

Perhaps historians have underestimated the cluster of complex meanings which these immigrants associated with the concept of freedom. Freedom from reactionary political controls, economic deprivation and anti-Semitic prejudices, yes; but perhaps also the freedom to be whatever one wanted, including the freedom not to be Jewish. Even intermarriage was an expression of freedom from parental and traditional authority—for it would not and could not occur in most European countries, where state churches regulated such matters as marriage and family life, where intermarriage without a Jew's conversion was unacceptable.

2. JUDAH TOURO AND JUDAISM

When Shanarai-Chasset was organized in 1827–28, Judah Touro made what was probably a token contribution, but refused to join as a member. This must mean that he did not want to worship at its services. Prior to this he had been the recipient of at least three appeals for funds for new synagogue buildings, from Shearith Israel of New York City in 1817, from Mikveh Israel of Philadelphia in 1824, and from Bene Israel of Cincinnati in 1825. The only request to which he responded was the one from Philadelphia, and it would appear as though it was Rochelle who solicited his fellows in New Orleans, even though Touro sent the draft to Philadelphia. Rochelle probably had closer, friendlier contacts with the foreigners Hermann, Nathan and Shiff than Touro did.[6] As we shall see, it was not until about 1847 that Touro took any genuine interest in Jewish life. Rabbi Isaac Leeser said, after his death, that "it was late in life when Mr. T. became impressed with the necessity of being an Israelite in more than in mere words."[7] Touro's magnificent philanthropy to Jewish causes in his will has been read back into earlier years. But there is no evidence to justify the assumption that he was always interested in giving of his substance to institutions which strengthened and perpetuated Judaism. As a matter of simple fact, he was far more interested in supporting Christian than Jewish religious institutions. As early as 1816 or 1819, he purchased a pew in Christ Church, the Episcopal church which Dr. and Mrs. Dow attended, and of which Touro's friend Shepherd had been a founder and warden.[8] In 1822, when there were more than enough Jews in New Orleans to form and benefit from a congregation, Touro bought the First Presbyterian Church for $20,000 so that the

217

building would not be torn down and the land sold to pay the church's debts. This deed of generosity, together with the $25,000 received from the sale of a legal lottery for the benefit of the church, enabled Parson Theodore Clapp to stave off ruin. Touro was the legal owner, the landlord, of the church, but he did not charge any rent for the use of the edifice. According to Parson Clapp, Touro

> "incurred an additional expense of several thousand dollars for keeping it in repair. For myself he professed the strongest personal regard, and showed it by giving me almost the entire income of the church—the pew rents—for about twenty-eight years. He might have torn the building down at the beginning, and reared on its site a block of stores, whose revenue by this time would have amounted to half a million dollars at least. He was urged to do so on several occasions, and once replied to a gentleman who made a very liberal offer for the property, that there was not money enough in the world to buy it . . . Most of my friends are not aware of the magnitude of the benefits which he was actually pleased to confer on me . . . he gave me in small sums, from time to time, not less than twenty thousand dollars."[9]

It was well known in New Orleans and elsewhere that Touro owned the church; Isaac Leeser quoted Touro as saying, "I am a friend to religion, and I will not pull down the church to increase my means."[10] This was indeed an unusual procedure, even an unprecedented one, for a Jew to own a church building, but perhaps no greater anomaly has ever existed than the request of a Jewish community for a loan of five or six thousand dollars from someone a thousand miles away in order to help them to build a synagogue, while in their own midst at that very time a co-religionist owned a Christian church building for which he had paid twenty thousand dollars!

Touro's interest in and contributions to Christian institutions continued for many years. In 1840, during the depression, when Christ Church was in financial difficulties, he paid $25,000 for the church's rectory on Canal street; he lived in this home until his death. The price he paid for the building was very generous. It was really more a contribution than an investor's purchase of a property—the inventory of Touro's estate included six parcels of property on Canal street, including this home. Altogether they were appraised at only $54,150. Even if the home was far more valuable than the other lots, it could still not have been worth as much as all the others put together, back in 1840, when the price of real estate was very depressed. Touro's purchase of the rectory was probably arranged by Rezin Shepherd, who also served as the intermediary in 1847 when Touro traded a lot of ground which he owned at the corner of Canal and Dauphine for the outmoded Christ Church sanctuary—which was then remodeled into a synagogue for the use of the Dispersed of Judah Congregation. Shepherd loaned his church $14,000 at interest so that it might proceed with its new building plans. Touro not only made an outright contribution, but also bought a $1,000 bond at the same time.[11]

In 1851, the new St. Louis Cathedral was finally completed, after almost two years of construction, at a cost of $139,238. At the time of his death, Touro's papers included $14,000 in St. Louis Cathedral bonds, about ten per cent of the total cost. No list is known to be available which includes the names of the purchasers of bonds and the amounts of their holdings, but it would be interesting to know whether any Catholic resident of New Orleans invested as much in the bonds as Touro did.[12]

In 1850 or 1851, Parson Clapp's church burned to the ground. It was now a Unitarian, no longer a Presbyterian, church. Clapp appealed to other Protestant churches for permission "to hold meetings . . . occasionally," in their buildings, but "the favor was denied on the alleged ground that by showing such a kindness, they might encourage the dreadful heresies which we were laboring to promulgate." Touro again came to Clapp's assistance; "he purchased a small Baptist chapel for us to worship in, free of charge, till he could put up a larger building for the use of the congregation." The inventory of Touro's estate notes that the First Baptist Church's land and building had been bought by Touro, on June 25, 1851, for $12,000.[13]

It seemed as though Touro was a friend to every religion except his own. He helped Presbyterians, Unitarians, Episcopalians and Roman Catholics. It may have been true, as Clapp quoted Touro as saying, that "although an Israelite to the

219

bottom of his soul, it would give him the sincerest pleasure to see all the churches flourishing in their respective ways, and that he was heartily sorry they did not more generally *fraternize with*, love, and help each other," but Touro was demonstrating that he was "an Israelite to the bottom of his soul" in a very peculiar fashion.[14]

In the next chapter, we shall attempt to evaluate the influences which finally led Touro to build a synagogue, and to make contributions in his will to a large number of congregations and other Jewish causes. But this is surely the place to wonder what kind of inverted and perverted thought and feeling led him to such consistent support of Christian churches, while neglecting the need for a synagogue. We do not pretend to have a satisfying answer to this question, because Touro himself never explained this curious facet of his character. Clapp seems deliberately to have avoided discussing it. There is the suggestion of an answer in an oblique comment by Isaac Leeser that ". . . for a period of more than thirty years . . . but few Israelites resided in New Orleans, and with the greater proportion of the few Mr. Touro held no intercourse, if we are correctly informed." Leeser referred to what he thought was Touro's waiting until "respectable men" came to New Orleans to take the lead in Jewish affairs.[15] But this was a description of a situation, rather than an explanation of Touro's feelings. If the implication was that Touro had nothing in common with Hermann, Kohn, Phillips, Jacobs, Nathan, Barnett, Shiff, because they were uncouth foreigners, how explain the fact that he was close enough to Rochelle, another Ashkenazic immigrant, to act as an executor for his estate—unless the reason is that Rochelle, like Touro, was friendly with the leading Yankee merchants in New Orleans? But if Touro did not want to have anything to do with foreign Jews, what of native-born men like Jacob Hart and Benjamin Levy, who stemmed from backgrounds similar to Touro's? And in the 1820's, many more men of similar experience had come to New Orleans: Harby, the Florance brothers, other Charlestonians and New Yorkers, and especially Jacob Solis, determined that the new congregation should follow the Sephardic pattern in which he and Touro had been reared. It makes little sense to think of Touro as a snob, holding himself aloof from Jews with whom he had nothing in common in 1827, but building a synagogue for some of these very same people in 1849. Leeser's information about the paucity of Jews in New Orleans was, of course, quite wrong—there were several hundred by 1830. Perhaps the truth is that Touro did not want to have anything to do with Jews or Judaism during most of his life. We admittedly end up with more questions than answers: Was Touro so thoroughly ashamed of his father's Tory preferences that he associated the Tory-father with the rabbi-father image, and atoned for his father's lack of Americanism by his own support for "American" (Protestant, Anglo-Saxon) religion? Was it guilt over his disloyalty to Jewish tradition which prevented him from helping to found a congregation? Was it self-hatred for himself as a Jew which drove him to attempt to buy friendship and good-will by supporting Christian institutions? Could it have been an ever-present fear of anti-Semitism which pressed him to outshine Christians in "Christian" philanthropy and generosity?[16] We will probably never really comprehend this peculiar quality in the character of a man who was otherwise quite consistent and coherent. It may well be that he himself never saw the contradiction, never perceived the paradox. All the more strange and incomprehensible.

3. THE INFLUENCE OF NEW ORLEANS

Whatever attitudes to their personal identity as Jews Touro and the other Jewish immigrants may have brought with them, New Orleans itself exerted a profound influence on their self-perception.

There is, for instance, the undeniable fact that religion was quite unimportant in the lives of most of the inhabitants of the city. The French and Spanish Creoles were not devout Catholics. Most of the men acted as though religion was a formality designed only for women and children. Roman Catholic leaders believed that New Orleans had been infiltrated with the libertarian ideas of the French Revolution; certain it is that there were numerous and influential French-speaking Masonic lodges in the city—and the Catholic hierarchy always conceived of Masonry as a source of danger to faith and morals. An official report on conditions among Catholics in New Orleans, sent to Rome before the Battle of New Orleans, though perhaps somewhat exaggerated, indicates some of the impressions which churchmen had gathered about the religious life of the city:

"Many Catholics die without the sacraments, many children are unbaptized; others scarcely see a priest once in a lifetime; marriages are contracted without a blessing; Christian doctrine is not taught, and such a decay of Catholic life is to be observed, that within a few years the Catholic faith will be entirely obliterated . . . There is rife in the city of New Orleans, a spirit of unbelief, or rather of godlessness which is gradually corrupting the whole mass. This plague is to be attributed to the coming of a great number of free-masons and hucksters of every description, to the spread of French maxims, to infrequent preaching of the Gospel, to love of lucre and pleasure, so much intensified by the climate and the number of female slaves; above all to the scandals given by the clergy."[17]

We need not accept every word of this hostile view as true— nor those of the Protestant clergyman, Joel Parker, in 1834, who believed that Catholic "men are, almost without an exception atheists [who] regard religion as intended only for women and servants, and they do not give themselves any trouble on the subject"—to recognize that religion was not a major factor in public and private life in New Orleans.[18] Business, success, wealth, property, pleasure, excitement, were far more important. A young Jewish college graduate wrote in his diary in 1835 that he planned to leave Charleston, and go to "that emporium of wine, women and segars, etc., etc., New Orleans. . . ."[19] If the Jews had found in New Orleans a devout and pious society, they would have felt impelled to identify themselves religiously— either with the environment or with their ancestral heritage; they would not have remained in the middle-ground of indifference and disinterest.

The only other factor which could have forced these Jews to organize a congregation and establish a semblance of Jewish life would have been a general antagonism towards them. But all available evidence indicates that anti-Jewish prejudice was notable for its absence. A careful reading of the New Orleans newspapers from the very beginning of their publication until the early 1840's has uncovered only one vicious attack on Jews as Jews that is of local origin. In 1824, a resentful friend of one John Clay launched this tirade against Samuel Hermann and Ruben Rochelle or Hart Shiff, when they foreclosed on Clay's mortgage:

"COMMUNICATED.

To the Editor of the Louisiana Gazette.

Sir—Be pleased to insert the annexed in your respectable Gazette; it is the commencement of the memoirs of *Levy Smile Chops*, who has his nefarious and corrupt office in Chartres Street, and the *memoirs* are dedicated to *Mordecai Turtleface*, who must necessarily figure in some future & more enlarged additions of Levy's Memoirs, which I am now preparing for the press, and which will be promulgated through the medium of your paper and finally be in pamphlet form.

Should *Levy* or *Mordecai* cut any capers and wish to know my real name, you are hereby at liberty to come out and afford it to them, but to no other person.

Levy, is a German or Holland Jew, and keeps his office in Chartres-street, near the New Exchange, and *Mordecai* keeps his *speculation* office in St. Louis-street, also near the New Exchange, and is also a Jew, whether from Holland, Germany or Denmark, it is still the same, he is a *Jew* and not a Gentile.

Yours Respectfully,

HENRY INTREPID PERSEVERANCE.

June 24th, 1824.

"To LEVY SMILE CHOPS,

SIR,—You have chosen to be the *cats paw* for others who do not or dare not wish to shew themselves. You even bring suits for your principals and take your solemn oath that the debt is your own, when you know at the time that such an oath is false. Where is your conscience? Is there not a God who looks down upon you? You have attacked a gentleman in this way who resides in Royal-street; you, under your invidious name, persecute him, and even want to sacrifice his property to oblige your *principal*, when you knew that there was no necessity for it; you know that your *Principal's* debt was safe, and you know also, that this unfortunate, though worthy and honorable man, was in the act and doing all he could to raise funds, the first object of which was to pay the very *debt* in question; but to foster your *Principal's interest*, and to emit your own spleen and perhaps both of your spleens are emitted to persecute this gentleman. You let the dogs of war loose upon him by bringing suits, and to distract his credit and endeavoring to prevent his procuring funds—appal his exertions and to get his house, which your *Principal* wants upon your own terms, you even employ one of your ungodly band to appraise his property—but Sir, you will not succeed, your ends will not be met.

Beware then Sir how you sport with yourself! the dark ages are passing by and a Messiah is coming; the day of retribution will arrive, when all evil doings will be ripped up—it behooves you then to be circumspect, and I beseech you to stop at the mark you have advanced in treating my friend amiss, else, you may be called upon to answer for your own sins;—a thousand leaves are folded away ready for you.

Do you recollect the cotton transaction, T. M., foreman of the Jury?—*mark* the sugar speculation, M.R. & P. at Richmond. Pause! don't make another step:—there are pens ready dipt in *gall* for you, not to be used by my friend in Royal-street—his lofty mind has no such guile: he is like Job, suffering under his pains and looking forward for better days. But there is a host of honest souls who are watching your motions and ready to join in your downfall.

HENRY INTREPID PERSEVERANCE"[20]

This was the only nasty attack on Jews which was ever published in a New Orleans paper during this period. Occasionally the columns of the papers included news of Jewish activities throughout the world; mostly these were pieces of exotic information used as filler. Sometimes they had reference to the persecution of Jews abroad, or to the activities of distinguished Jews. Mordecai Noah's attempt to create a Jewish colony on Grand Island in New York aroused more than passing attention. In New Orleans, as elsewhere, the Rothschild fortune was a subject of fascinated interest. One such story, quoted from some other newspaper, gave an unkind characterization to banking families like the Rothschilds and Goldsmids: "They settled exchanges, and put up or put down stocks at their will. But, except in the business of turning and making, what is called money, these 'great dignitaries' are very common and indifferent men. Indeed, some of them are extremely ignorant and stupid, though always prompt as to what they think the summum bonum—the getting of money."[21] While this sort of scorn for rich Jews may have been current in New Orleans, too, and hatred such as John Clay's friend expressed may have seethed in other breasts, there is no evidence that such feelings were widespread.

To the contrary, every indication points to a broad-scale acceptance of Jews by both the Creole and Yankee societies of New Orleans. The frequency of intermarriage is one measure of the welcome which was accorded to Jews. Even the church, until sometime in the 1830's, ignored the religious problem. The difference of religion was not even noted in the church registers which recorded their marriages. Apparently it did not matter very much to anyone that these men were Jews. We may be certain that the men who remained bachelors did so out of choice, and not because they were rejected or deprived of the opportunity for social contact with non-Jewish families. It is difficult for us to judge the social position of all of the families into which these early Jewish men married. Certainly none of them made any pretense of being aristocrats, nor was any of them wealthy; but the young men themselves had little to offer other than the hard work they were willing to perform. Wealthy, upper-class Creole families would hardly have considered accepting into their midst even young men of French or Spanish Catholic background who could not bring wealth, land or family prestige to their daughters. If the earliest Jews were cut off from relationships with families on the highest level of society it was not because they were Jews, but because they were poor. Once they had established themselves on a firm financial foundation, however, the sons and daughters and nephews and younger brothers of these earliest Jews were accepted everywhere—in homes, in schools, in social circles that matched their own wealth and position. Edward Gottschalk,

Joachim Kohn, the Hermann sons and daughters, and Carl Kohn went to the very top of the social ladder, because they or their fathers or brothers had achieved affluence and social prestige.

Judah Benjamin's marriage to Natalie St. Martin seems to be an exception to our general rule. He was still poor, just beginning to establish his career. Although Natalie brought with her a dowry of $3,000 and two slaves, the young couple had to live with her parents for three years before they could move into their own home. The reason for Benjamin's acceptance into a family of high social caste will always be as inexplicable as the nature of his relationship to Natalie throughout all the years of his life. Perhaps the ugly rumors about Natalie's premarital escapades which still persist in New Orleans today had some factual basis. Certainly she never displayed any of the customary signs of love or even affection for Judah once they were married. She maintained a separate household in Paris throughout most of the years which he spent in Washington, Richmond and London. At any rate, it was a very unusual marriage from the very beginning.

Worthy of note, too, is the fact that non-Jews were involved in intimate, personal occasions in the lives of these Jews, as witnesses at weddings, as godparents at baptisms, as friends and executors of the signing of wills and the settling of estates, and at family meetings in connection with the guardianship of children and the like. It was far more than a pleasant business relationship which led Ruben Rochelle to leave a bequest to William Montgomery's son, and to ask Montgomery and Stephen Henderson to serve as his executors. Equally impressive is the evidence that Jews were willingly accepted into the Masonic lodges and fancy military units which were apparently the most prominent social organizations in town; that they served on the committees which conducted the balls that flourished during the social season, and on civic as well as business boards of every sort. Families of prominence sent their children to Harby's school, and the most intelligent men in town flocked to "Professor" E. A. Cohen's New Orleans Chess Club.[22] When the New Orleans Histrionic Association was organized in 1848, Joseph Soria was the leading man in most of the early productions, Isaac N. Marks took many comedy leads, and the ever-present "organization man" of New Orleans, M. M. Cohen, was legal advisor.[23] Whatever their interests, abilities, wealth and occupation, the Jews of New Orleans seem to have had no trouble in finding non-Jewish friends and associates to enrich their lives and share their leisure as well as their business hours.

There was probably less prejudice against Jews in New Orleans during the ante-Bellum period than in any other important city in the country. It takes us beyond these early years which we are considering in such detail, but it is worth emphasizing that Louisiana elected Jews to high political office earlier than any other state in the Union. At one and the same time, just before the outbreak of the Civil War, Judah Benjamin was serving in the Senate of the United States, Henry M. Hyams was Lieutenant-Governor, and Dr. Edwin Warren Moïse—who had already served as Attorney-General of the state—was Speaker of the legislature. All three of these men were originally Charlestonians, but no matter how cultured the Charleston Jewish community was, South Carolina showed no sign of electing Jews to such high office. During the secession crisis, Salomon de Rothschild, the twenty-four-year-old scion of the Parisian branch of that noted family, was on a grand tour of the United States; from New Orleans he wrote back home about these Jewish men of consequence:

> "What is astonishing here, or rather, what is not astonishing, is the high position occupied by our coreligionists, or rather by those who were born into the faith and who, having married Christian women, and without converting, have forgotten the practices of their fathers.
>
> "Benjamin, the Attorney General of the Confederate States, is perhaps the greatest mind on this continent. Hyams, the [lieutenant-] governor of Louisiana, Moyse . . . And, what is odd, all these men have a Jewish heart and take an interest in me, because I represent the greatest Jewish house in the world. . . ."[24]

Carl Kohn's reports to his Uncle Samuel reflect his acceptance into the highest society of New Orleans. Despite the many references he made to anti-Semitic prejudice in Bohemia, he wrote not even one word that was suggestive of rejection in New Orleans. He and other Jews, and sons of Jews, were later welcomed into the two exclusive clubs of New Orleans, clubs which today are closely associated with socialite Mardi-Gras organizations and which are reported to exclude persons of Jewish birth. Carl and his nephew Gustave were members of the Boston Club, as were Judah P. Benjamin, Isaac and Samuel Delgado, Benjamin Franklin Jonas, Charles, H. O. and J. M. Seixas, Adolph and Victor Meyer and Julius Weis, among others. Jonas was a member of the Board of Governors and Vice-President during the period 1894–1904. Armand Heine was a founding member of the Pickwick Club; he and his brother Michel actually owned the clubhouse from 1884 to 1894, long after they had gone to live in Paris. Edward Barnett and Cohen M. Soria were presidents of the Pickwick Club. Not all of these people were practicing Jews, but they were all born Jews or their fathers were. What an ironic commentary on manners, mores and morals that folk who are welcomed in one generation should be scorned in another. Thus New Orleans eventually turned its back on the open society which was one of its happy characteristics in this early period.[25]

This large-scale acceptance of Jews into almost every nook and cranny of social, political and cultural life, in addition to the more obvious opportunities of the market place, meant that there was no negative pressure upon Jews to create a congregation or to develop an intensive Jewish life. Their energies were directed outward rather than inward. Certain social and economic factors made New Orleans an exceptional American city in this regard, during this period: the turbulent growth of the city, bringing into its midst people of every kind of background and heritage, and turning it into the most heterogeneous city in the country; the strong rivalry of Creoles and Yankees, both sides eagerly seeking both Christian and Jewish recruits; the absence of a tradition of hide-bound, narrow evangelical Protestantism on the one hand, and of defensive, separatistic and suspicious Catholicism on the other; the constant need for men of talent and ability to take leadership in a society where many young men were unambitious, effete dandies; the tremendous economic potential of the city, never really exploited to its

228

fullest, constantly in need of rich imagination and strong direction; the periodic financial crises which shook out the incompetent and the incautious, and made room for new risk-takers. All of these aspects of the city's growth made it possible for Jews to be accepted as human beings, rather than Jews; as a result, they did not feel compelled to consider themselves Jews in any primary sense, unless they wanted to—and most of them did not.

But this distinctiveness of New Orleans society should not be exaggerated. It is possible that most frontier areas into which Jews moved as separate individuals, rather than as groups, offered similar opportunity for acculturation and assimilation. Jewish historians have, somewhat understandably, been reluctant to evaluate this negative aspect of the American Jewish experience in precise detail. Jacob Rader Marcus has forcefully demonstrated, however, that every Jew who settled and remained in colonial Connecticut ultimately merged into the overwhelmingly Christian environment which surrounded him. It would be worth investigating the first generation of Jewish settlement in every geographical frontier area—before mass immigration—to discover whether the experience of Jews in New Orleans was characteristic, rather than unusual.[26]

4. An Irreducible Residue of Jewishness

Despite the centrifugal forces which drew these people away from their Jewish identity—their own disinterest in Judaism and an environment which offered them a warm acceptance into the general community—these early Jews should not be regarded as conscious, deliberate assimilationists who wanted to have nothing to do with Jewishness. To the contrary, most of them gravitated toward each other, especially the immigrants, as though drawn by a magnet, and established friendships with each other that flourished throughout the years. Ruben Rochelle and Hart Shiff shared a business partnership which was severed only by illness and death. A. M. Nathan had commercial relations with almost every Jew in Louisiana as early as 1811.

229

Touro, Hermann, Rochelle and Shiff were co-owners of a steam-boat in 1817. Nathan and Hermann were partners for a few years during the 1820's and remained close friends afterwards. Jacob Hart's cotton press was located in buildings which Rochelle and Shiff owned. As soon as Aaron Daniels came to New Orleans, he seems to have become acquainted with almost every Jew in town; many times he testified at probate hearings that he had known such and such a man since 1822. Solomon Soher was in partnership first with De Jonge, then with Daniel Goodman. Maurice Barnett sent his oldest son, Maurice, Jr., to Soher and Goodman, so that he could learn business procedures from them. Edward Gottschalk worked for Rochelle and Shiff. Shiff and Samuel Kohn owned a great deal of property together. Edward Shiff for a time held Kohn's power of attorney. Samuel Hermann took care of Shiff's business while he was out of town. And so it went from one business and family to another: a constant interplay of partnerships and friendships.

This "irreducible residue of Jewishness," this affinity of Jews for each other, did not stop at the door of a store or counting-house; these men established deep and abiding friendships which involved the most important events in the life-cycle. Ruben Rochelle and Samuel Hermann were two of the five witnesses at Hart Shiff's wedding. Rochelle was the godfather at the baptism of Shiff's daughter Luisa who was probably named for him—his middle name was Louis or Luis, and that was the way he was listed in the religious record of the event. A. M. Nathan was a witness at the baptism of Shiff's daughter María. This ceremony was held on the same day in 1824 as the baptism of Edward Shiff, for which event Samuel Kohn was asked to be a witness. Samuel Hermann and Samuel Kohn were witnesses at the Jewish wedding of A. M. Nathan's niece in 1828, and a few months later Samuel Hermann performed the same role at Edward Gottschalk's Catholic wedding. In 1830, Samuel Kohn was a witness at Florian Hermann's wedding. Both Samuel Hermann and his son Samuel, Jr., were witnesses at Joachim Kohn's wedding in 1834, and Hart Shiff's wife was the godmother for Joachim and Marie's son Arthur's baptism in 1838. It was almost as though their common background in a Jewish world they had left behind still bound them together in a day when the formal ceremonies of birth, marriage and death took place within a Catholic cathedral. If Catholicism had no spiritual meaning for them, the presence of their Jewish friends did.

This same intimacy prevailed in the area of wills, executorship, and the like. When Henry Hartman, of whom so little is known, died in 1818, his will said that if his executor was out of town, he was certain that his "good friends Abraham [*sic*] M. Nathan and Mr. Samuel Kohn" would accept the responsibility—was it just because they were Jews, even though he did not know Asher Nathan's correct first name, that Hartman called these men his "good friends?" Alexander Phillips was a witness at the signing of the will of Benjamin Levine, who died the same year as Hartman. When Louis E. Cohen died of yellow fever in 1826, Emanuel Stern acted as the executor and took the inventory of the estate; even though there was yet no congregation, Stern was fulfilling the religious duty of caring for the effects of a coreligionist—he was not a creditor, and Cohen's little stock of jewelry and dry goods was worth only $95.62, but Stern went to the trouble of taking care of matters, and even complained to the Probate Court that one of the Kokernot boys had taken some books from Cohen's place before the effects were sealed.[27] When Joachim Kohn's young wife died, A. M. Nathan and Armand Heine were present at the formal meeting to discuss the welfare of the children, as required by law. Armand Heine, Joachim Kohn, Edward Gottschalk and A. M. Nathan joined members of the family in administering the affairs of their old friend Hart Shiff. Carl Kohn was one of the executors of the will of A. M. Nathan. Carl was also involved in the settlement of Edward Shiff's estate—this was carrying the relationship into the second generation. And so it went. These people felt close to each other and depended upon each other. They may have believed that they understood each other better because they were Jews.

Perhaps there was even some nagging feeling of regret for what had been left behind, some longing for Jewish warmth. The formation of the Association for the Relief of Jewish Widows and Orphans in 1854, the first agency of its kind in the entire United States (because mortality rates in the area were so much higher than elsewhere, and because New Orleans continued to

231

be a port of high immigration) seems to have offered some of these people an opportunity to demonstrate their concern with Jewish needs on a humanitarian rather than a religious level. Alexander Phillips, Asher Nathan and Edward Shiff made contributions to the Association at its very inception. Joachim and Carl Kohn were elected honorary members, along with such distinguished American Jewish leaders as Rabbis Isaac Leeser, David Einhorn and Isaac Mayer Wise. Armand and Michel Heine were honored with the same life membership which was extended to Alfonse de Rothschild. Henry M. Hyams, who gave $100 to the building fund, was a vice-president of the Home from 1855 to 1857. When Asher Nathan died in 1864, he bequeathed $5,000 to the Jewish Widows' and Orphans' Home, in addition to $3,000 to each of two Catholic institutions. Carl Kohn also remembered the institution in his will; among charitable requests of $1,000 he left $250 to the Jewish Home, and $100 to Touro Infirmary. One has the feeling that even though he was a member of "high society" in New Orleans, Carl did not want to be too far away from his Jewish background. His daughter Eveline, reared as a Christian, married a Jew, Victor Meyer, the brother of Adolph Meyer, a Louisiana congressman from 1891 to 1908. Eveline and Victor were married in Christ Church. But by that time social prejudice against Jews was rising, and Carl may have viewed with some satisfaction the marriage of his daughter to a man who had been born into the same heritage in which he himself was reared. Carl remained close to his European cousins; he had business dealings throughout the years with Edouard's banking firm, Kohn, Reinach and Company, and was its agent in New Orleans during the 1870's. He must have been aware of Edouard's intense interest in the activities of the Alliance Israélite Universelle, and perhaps derived some pride from it. Without any documentary evidence to prove such a conclusion, we sense in Carl's life some of the ambivalence which frequently characterizes the inner life of a sensitive, intelligent Jew who assimilates into the non-Jewish environment, some yearning, perhaps only a silent sigh of regret.[28]

The support and encouragement which Carl Kohn and others gave to the Widows' and Orphans' Home stand in stark contrast to Judah Benjamin's total indifference to Jewish life. While he was quite willing to accept Jews as clients in his law practice, and probably had a few social friends among Jews, Benjamin took no part at all in Jewish religious or philanthropic activities. Even when a matter of Jewish significance was brought before the United States Senate, as for instance, the question of discrimination against American Jews by the Swiss cantons, Benjamin continued to follow what can only have been a conscious policy of aloofness. The vicious attacks which were directed against him as a Jew during the trying years of his leadership in the Confederate cabinet did not evoke from him any expression of pride in or warm memory of the heritage into which he was born. There was no ambivalence in Judah's decision to ally himself with the larger world in which he played so conspicuous a role; he was a Jew only in the sense that he was born one, and that he was not converted to another religion, at least not until he was on his deathbed, and, in all likelihood, probably unconscious.[29]

But the stirrings of Jewish affinity which all of these men other than Benjamin felt were no substitute for a vigorous determination to preserve one's Jewish identity intact. So long as the poorer, less successful Jews, who had to struggle to make a living, to learn the language, to adjust to the ways of this bewildering country, received no positive Jewish leadership from men who were already established, even they, who wished to remain loyal Jews, were rudderless. What they required was a catalyst, an insistent, knowledgeable leader who would set an example for them, who would show them the way, who would help them. It was unfortunate that so much time had to elapse before a man like Jacob Solis arrived in town and helped them to organize a congregation. But they could be grateful that they did not have to wait even longer, until 1840 perhaps, when the next committed, affirmative Jewish leader, Gershom Kursheedt, came to New Orleans.

VII

Toward a More Normal Jewish Communal Life

The organization of a congregation, in 1827–28, did not mean the automatic solution of the problems of Jewish existence in America in personal or communal terms. It was only the beginning of the confrontation of the challenges and dilemmas implicit in the very life of Jews in a free and open society. The long delay in the founding of Shanarai-Chasset masked the real problem: whether Judaism was to find the means to survive and flourish in this new environment where many of the old assumptions could not stand up to reality. Without a congregation there was not even the effort; with a congregation, for the first time, the inherent difficulties became evident.

1. A Congregation's Role and Functions

New Orleans Jewry now had to endure what many another community had already experienced, a long period of false starts, difficult practical problems, unrewarded efforts and uncertain direction. The congregation was in existence, but it was frail and weak. Lay leadership changed constantly; professional, trained rabbinic leadership was altogether missing. Since neither Hendricks nor Touro nor anyone else was willing to lend enough money to the congregation to make the building of a synagogue possible, a structure at the corner of St. Louis and Franklin streets, across the street from the St. Louis Cemetery, was rented or purchased, and remodeled for use by the congregation.[1]

Some insight into the inability of the leaders to provide even a modicum of ritual guidance to the congregation, and the length of time that it took them to obtain the basic tools of

Jewish worship—prayer books, lists of the traditional Scriptural readings for services, Torah scrolls, a ram's horn—is derived from a letter that Manis Jacobs and Isaac Phillips sent to the officers of Shearith Israel of New York City in 1833, five years after the organization of the congregation:

New Orleans May 31, 1833

To the Presid^t & Governing Rulers of the
Israelite Congregation Shearith Israel of New York

Gentlemen—

Having now commenced in a Country where no more than 33 years ago the name of an Israelite was an abomination to establish a small place to Worship the God of our Fathers and Wishing to read in the holy written Book his command every Saturday We therefore have accepted the offer of Mr. Jacob Luria and are willing to pay you what he may owe you on it you will be so kind and have it sealed with your Seal, and send it by the first Packet with his Bill in the hands of the Captain, which will be paid to him on delivering the Sephar [Torah scroll], you will also be so kind and send us a list of all the [Sidras] and Maftarim [Torah and prophetic readings] to be read every Sabbath and holy days.

We remain for ever and ever your affectionate brethren.

Marius [Manis] Jacobs Treasurer
Isaac Phillips Vice Presid^t

Address

Isaac Phillips Vice Presid^t of the
Israelite Congregation of New Orleans
Sharri Haset, New Orleans Louisiana

P.S.—If you can send us a few Setts of Detuska Machzerim [Ashkenazic prayer books] in Hebrew and translated in English and also a few Daily praying Books they will be paid for with the greatest thanks but they must be after the Minhag [rite] of the Teduskai for we have no holy days praying Books here after that Minhag which are translated into English neither praying Books for every day, neither have we a Shofar [ram's horn] if you will send us these articles at the same time the Vice President bonds himself in behalf of the Congregation to pay the said Bill to the Captain who may be the bearer thereof.

235

Know all men by these presents that I will at delivery to the Bearer of four Setts of Prayer Books of our holy days, in hebrew and translated in English and Six Daily praying Books also translated in English all after the Minhag of the Teduskas and two Shofars whatever the regular charge may be of them and again if the said Society were to send a spare Sephar at a reasonable price I also will pay for it at their estimation signed by me and Sealed with the Seal of the

Congregation Sharri Haset New Orleans—Isaac Phillips Vice Presid[12]

The Shearith Israel trustees agreed to forward the scroll to New Orleans, if the Shanarai-Chasset people would pay the $14.90 that Luria or Lurie owed for pledges he had made, and directed their president to take care of the other requests. If Solis had lived, we may be certain that he would have moved much more swiftly in gathering together these ritual requisites for worship, and that he already had enough reference volumes in his library to provide the guidance that the congregation needed. But at least Manis Jacobs and Isaac Phillips were trying to provide the essential paraphernalia for their congregation's ceremonial life. Two other references in the communication to New York require comment. The first is the very strong statement that under Spanish domination "the name of an Israelite was an abomination." Manis Jacobs had come to New Orleans no later than 1812. Was it his impression that the Creoles had hated Jews? Or had he perhaps met Angélica Monsanto Dow and heard from her some description of the experience of 1769? To have reported that there were very few Jews when he came to New Orleans would have been one thing; to say that the very name Jew was "an abomination" was another. The second interesting piece of information in this letter is the emphasis on Ashkenazic or, to use the word for German that Sephardim used, Tedesco, prayer books. Solis had presumably provided Manis Jacobs and the congregation with Sephardic volumes of prayer. Surely the four sets of Ashkenazic Holy Day prayer books and six volumes of prayers for daily and Sabbath services which he requested were insufficient for the entire congregation's needs. This order ought therefore not be interpreted to mean that the congregation had decided to adopt the Ashkenazic rite, not yet—but it was an augury of things to come. Some members were undoubtedly complaining that the Sephardic rite was unfamiliar to them, and wanted prayer books they could use. Manis was probably attempting to keep them loyal to the congregation by supplying them with these volumes; he may have feared that otherwise they might not remain members. Precisely when the congregation abandoned the use of the Sephardic rite and shifted over to the Ashkenazic is not revealed in any record, but it may possibly have been after Manis' death.

Shearith Israel presumably did not have an extra Torah to send to New Orleans. A second scroll was not obtained until 1837. Strangely enough, the dedication of this new Torah was not held in the synagogue, but in the home of a former president, Louis Levy, at 119 Bayou road. The reason may be that Levy was the donor of the scroll. Jacob Bensadon, the father of the future medical director of the Touro Infirmary, was the chairman of the committee on arrangements for that occasion.[3]

Manis Jacobs probably conducted most of the weddings and funerals. On March 12, 1837, he married a future president of the congregation, L. A. Gunst, to Jeanette Nathan, the widow of J. B. Broome. He continued to perform such ceremonies until shortly before his death. But he was probably not Orthodox enough for the taste of one Moses B. Reas, otherwise unknown, who conducted three weddings on April 29, 1835. Two of the brides were Moses' own daughters, Jeanette and Minette. The third was Adele Lam. The grooms were, respectively, Jacob Myer, Penel Levy and Leopold Dalsheimer.[4]

Unfortunately no congregational minute books survive from this period. We have therefore to piece our information together from various sources. Occasionally, the newspapers reported the names of the congregation's officers. In 1834, Benjamin Van Ostern was secretary. In 1835, Louis Levy was president; Isaac Phillips, vice-president; A. M. Plotz, treasurer; A. J. Marks, secretary; and Joseph De Pass, Asher Phillips and Solomon Ferth, trustees. The following year the officers were shuffled around again: A. M. Plotz was president; Joseph De Pass, vice-president; P. Hart, treasurer; A. J. Marks, secretary; S. Hyams, L. A. Levy and B. Voorsinger, trustees. In 1838, Plotz and Marks held the same offices, but Hart became vice-president, and Manis Jacobs returned to office as treasurer; three new men became trustees, A. De Jonge, Daniel Levy and J. Mayer. Plotz and Marks were reelected in 1839, but J. Mayer moved up to vice-president and L. A. Gunst became treasurer, while S. Jacobs and F. Hearnsheim joined S. Hyams as trustees.[5]

The most important service which the congregation extended to its members, and to the itinerant Jews who died in their midst all too frequently, was in connection with funerals. A committee of members prepared the corpses for burial in accordance with the prescriptions of Jewish tradition, and made all of the arrangements for the services. In 1839 the estate of David Lewis was charged with the following costs: $10 for a coffin and hearse; $25 for five carriages; $3 for digging the grave—these are the normal expenses connected with a funeral. In the case of the death of a pauper, the president was authorized to draw on congregational funds for as much as $25 to pay for the ritual shroud, a coffin and hearse, two carriages, and the opening of the grave. Members of the congregation who had contributed toward the purchase of the cemetery, and who paid the regular dues of $40 a year (a very large sum of money at that time), were entitled to graves without further payment. In addition to accepting responsibility for funeral arrangements, the congregation also seems to have undertaken to fulfill the role of surviving family for Jews who died in financial difficulty or who had no immediate family. Thus in 1833, for instance, Joseph Lasalle and Manis Jacobs seem to have performed a congregational duty when they witnessed the will of Sarah Jessurun Cohn, who had been married only two days previously to Salomon Cohn; she died a week after her wedding. In 1836, when Marius Cohen, a forty-two-year-old immigrant from Amsterdam, died, Plotz made the official certification of death to the probate court, as the president of the congregation, and the vice-president and secretary reported the inventory of Cohen's effects to Plotz. It was a brief list, showing how small the stock of a petty trader or peddler might be: a trunk of old clothing (his own?); a basket containing four glasses, one pair of glass fruit dishes, four flower pots, nineteen glass and china cups, and seven wine glasses; and one "lot" of gilt jewelry, consisting of earrings, finger rings, breast pins and beads. This was all that Marius Cohen owned at the age of forty-four. David Lewis, who died in 1839, was a little better off—his possessions were worth $460.98. In Lewis' case, A. J. Marks and Isaac Phillips made the report of the death to the office of the Recorder of Births and Deaths, and Phillips acted as curator of the estate. After Alexander Hart married the Widow Kokernot and moved to New Orleans, he may have taken some role in the congregation's life, but the only reference to his activity which we have been able to discover is a funeral which took place at his home on August 29, 1837; the deceased was an artist named J. E. Levie, thirty-seven years old, a native of England, more recently a resident of New York City, a victim of yellow fever. Hart probably conducted the funeral services.[6]

Dire emergencies must have arisen frequently in a port city like New Orleans. Death struck new immigrants more frequently than older settlers. Many a needy widow and orphan were thrust upon the community's charity. Without specific records, it is possible to judge the extent of the need for help only from the frequency of death notices, and the importunate references to concern for the widow and orphan in the printed obituaries of such men as Asher Phillips, Manis Jacobs and Alexander Hart. The new by-laws adopted by the congregation in 1841 authorized the president to give $10 to anyone in need of help; "but in case of extreme necessity the President and Vice-President may increase the sum to fifty dollars, provided they jointly agree to do so." It was not until 1844 that a Hebrew Benevolent Society for the relief of the aged, the sick, the poor, the widow and the orphan, so characteristic of other Jewish communities, was organized in New Orleans.[7]

That the officers of Shanarai-Chasset attempted to create a program of relatedness to the larger world is demonstrated by two surviving reports. In 1831, the congregation passed a resolution of tribute to the memory of Abbé Grégoire, the champion of Jewish emancipation in revolutionary France in 1789, as soon as news of his death reached New Orleans, and sent it to the leader of French Jewry, Adolphe Crémieux. Because his reply expressed so well the feeling of gratitude for the Abbé's humanitarian principles which animated Jews throughout the world, Crémieux' letter was printed in the New Orleans news-paper. It is interesting that the Jews of New Orleans felt that they had a special relationship to the orbit of France, and that the communication from Crémieux was printed in the *Bee's* French section, but not in the English portion. In terms of local community relations, Shanarai-Chasset appears to have been the first congregation in the history of American Jewry to invite non-Jews to come to the synagogue for a lecture on the cere-monies of Judaism, and the foundations of Christianity in Judaism. Manis Jacobs made two such public presentations— one in English and one in French—during successive weeks in October, 1834. The public announcement said that these lectures were offered "at the request of many French Israelites and of other persons of different religions." So long ago did Manis Jacobs and his colleagues anticipate the "open house Sundays" which the Catholics, Protestants and Jews of New Orleans conducted with nationally acknowledged success during the 1960's.[8]

2. ALBERT J. "ROLEY" MARKS

Even though Jacob Solis was not an ordained rabbi, he would have been able to give learned, firm direction to the congrega-tion's religious program, had he lived to return to New Orleans. He was sufficiently knowledgeable about the basic traditions— the conduct of services, the observance of the holidays, the laws of kosher food, weddings, funerals and other rites of pas-sage—to have guided those who knew far less than he. Alexander Hart, too, might have given this sort of leadership to the Jews of New Orleans, but he was probably too busy making a living during his few years in town. Manis Jacobs certainly did the best he could, but his background was far from satisfactory; no matter how hard he tried to fulfill his responsibilities, he was a pale substitute for a rabbi. Once he had died, the leadership of the congregation passed to even weaker hands—those of Albert J. Marks, who was the secretary of Shanarai-Chasset, probably

the only paid officer, from 1834 on. Following Jacobs' death in 1839, and until about 1842, Marks officiated at most weddings and other religious events and services. The congregation printed a special volume for its wedding records, which included formal authorization for "Mr. A. J. Marks of the Hebrew Congregation to join in the bonds of matrimony Mr.....................
and .... in compliance with the formalities required by the laws of the state of Louisiana," and signed by the parish judge. Marks's Hebrew name was given as "Israel the son of Tzvi the righteous, Rabbi." On the certificate which was presented to the bride and groom, Marks signed his name opposite the printed title Rabbi, and the president, secretary and another officer of the congregation countersigned the document to make it official.[9]

Marks was an actor by profession. Born probably in England, he first appeared in a theatrical performance in New Orleans in 1826. When he actually established his residence there is not known, although he was in and out of town from then on. He must have been the Mr. Marks who complained to Manis Jacobs, in 1828, that the mourners' services were too long. Albert appeared with local theatrical companies in New Orleans, and with the well-known troupes that toured to Mobile, Natchez, Nashville and St. Louis. At one time he was with Samuel Drake, George Harby's friend, in Kentucky; he was also a member of companies which were led by Noah Ludlow and Sol Smith, the two leading impresarios of the South. In Ludlow's reminiscences, we are told how Marks received his nickname "Roley":

"He was generally known among his professional brethren as 'Rowley Marks,' having obtained this *sobriquet* from having, in Charleston, South Carolina, gained some credit by performing old *Rowley*, in the 'School for Scandal,'—the only character he had ever been given credit for in the public prints, and which he was very fond of showing and bragging on; but he was old *Rowley* in every thing. 'Rowley' Marks was a short, fat, round-faced, good-natured little Jew, and was somewhat a favorite with the public, inasmuch as that he contrived to make the people laugh, which some seemed to think was all that was required of a comedian. He had a wife, a pretty little woman, without much talent, but much respected by all who knew her. In New Orleans, in after years, I believe Mr. Marks occasionally officiated as a rabbi, being of the tribe of Levi, and a lineal descendant from Aaron, the ancient high-priest."

Sol Smith described Marks at greater length, and in more humorous vein:

"Rowley is a character. I first became acquainted with him in 1830, but his fame had reached my ears as early as 1826, when he formed a part of Mr. Alexander Drake's traveling company in Western New York and Kentucky. Rowley is an Israelite, and has been for many years high-priest of the Jews in New Orleans and parts adjacent, receiving a handsome income from the chosen people for the performance of marriage ceremonies, funeral rites, and other *little* operations indispensible to the proper starting of young Jews of the male sex into their second week's journey of life.

"Rowley is an actor of no inconsiderable talent—that is to say, of a peculiar kind—*very* peculiar, I might say. Comic old men are his hobby, and it would do your heart good to see one of his laughs. I say *see* one of them, for nothing particular is *heard* when he laughs; a sort of turning up of his eyes, a filling of his cheeks with wind, and suddenly letting it burst forth, at the same time giving himself a half turn, stooping as if to spit, indulging in a sly wink at the public, and swinging his cane about—and it is done."

Smith had a knack for descriptive narrative. His readers throughout the generations since his book was first published in 1868 have been amused by his vivid portrait of Marks's comic antics:

"Rowley was once stage-manager in a traveling company under the direction of my brother, and during the whole of a very hot summer he luxuriated in the performance of *Gov. Heartall, Old Smacks,* and *Andrew Mucklestane*. Andrew Mucklestane! Ah! how often have I witnessed his impersonation of this character, which is nothing more or less than a sentimental Scotch fisherman, very benevolent in his feelings, and ever ready to rescue runaway countesses and drowning children! And to see Rowley sweating through the 'business' of this character is a treat to all lovers of the romantic drama. Rowley introduces thirteen *falls* in this

242

performance, and more than once has it been found necessary to *prop* the stage before subjecting it to his energetic manoeuvres . . .

"In appearance Rowley Marks is a little *below* the middle size, measuring in his stockings, about four feet and some inches. A gleam of good humor is always beaming on his countenance, except when he experiences a twinge of the gout (unfortunately pretty often), and he is one of the best-natured fellows in existence."

Roley was obviously not much of an actor. Bit parts were all he could fill. The traveling theatrical life was a hard, unremunerative one. Not being able to make much of a living at acting alone, he had to supplement his income in all sorts of ways. He became a jack-of-all-trades, served as paid secretary and "rabbi" of Shanarai-Chasset (hardly at the "handsome income" reported by Sol Smith), and also as a part-time inspector at the custom house and a fireman. He began his activity in the Washington Fire Company, No. 4, in 1834. In 1836 he was elected its (paid) secretary; four years later he became second assistant foreman of the company, and was made a director of the Firemen's Charitable Association. In 1841, when he was president of the fire company, he opened a business as a custom house broker, and, during the summer months, conducted some theatrical entertainments out in the country; these were burlesques, more of the sort of nonsense in which he specialized, a different title every day of the week, but virtually the same melange made up of miscellaneous bits and pieces.[10]

More in keeping with Marks's role as part-time rabbi was his secretarial service to the Young Men's Philanthropic Association, a group which was organized in 1839 in response to one of the recurrent yellow fever epidemics. He also took part in theatrical benefits for charitable purposes, and composed "A Fireman's Song" for presentation at a fund-raising performance for the Fireman's Charitable Association, which led him to be called the "Poet Laureate of the Firemen."[11]

In the description of New Orleans Jewish life in 1842, to which we have already referred, Dr. M. Wiener described Marks as a "stain on the Jewish clergy," and reported that he did not observe the dietary laws, did not have his sons circumcised, and

sometimes was too busy with his many other activities to conduct services—on the festival of Purim, for instance. One Rosh
Hashonah, when an observant member of the congregation
commented that it was a shame that a man should act as rabbi
who did not have his sons initiated into the covenant of Abraham,
and who got "beastly drunk on the day when his two sons died,"
Marks, "beside himself with rage, pounded on the pulpit and
cried out, 'By Jesus Christ! I have a right to pray!' " Wiener
also reported that in only four Jewish homes in town were
forbidden foods avoided; in only two was the Sabbath strictly
observed; two-thirds of the Jews did not have their sons circumcised; not even fifty of the Jewish boys could read Hebrew;
the synagogue could accommodate only fifty persons, but was
thinly attended even on the High Holy Days; the one Torah
scroll was "so shot through with holes that even ten years ago
no one would have ventured to read it." But whatever Marks's
failings as a "rabbi," and they were obviously many, the neglect
of religious duty in New Orleans could not be blamed on him.
To the contrary, he was a symptom of the problem. Indifference,
ignorance and impiety permitted a man like Marks to take the
pulpit by default. Roley Marks never pretended to be more
than a makeshift, a fill-in. He was a bustling comic, attempting
to make a living in a profession that offered few rewards to any
but the most accomplished of dramatic actors. To help fill the
gap, he joined any organization that could use his services as a
paid secretary, and served as rabbi because the congregation
had no member capable of leading its services better than he,
and its members were not sufficiently interested to offer enough
salary to attract a *hazan* to New Orleans from some other
American city or, perhaps, England. Whatever Marks did for
the congregation was apparently more than anyone else was
willing or able to do. His reputation in New Orleans as a family
man was quite respectable, and his colleagues in the theater
found him likeable, if somewhat ludicrous. But, ultimately,
resistance to Marks's service as spiritual leader of the congregation seems to have mounted, and he drifted back onto the stage.
During the 1840's he rejoined his friends on the road, and
appeared once more in Natchez and Mobile. He took part in a
large number of productions at the Olympic Theater in New

Orleans during 1848 and 1849, and then faded from view. We have been able to find no record of his death, any more than of his birth—perhaps he died while on tour away from New Orleans.[12]

3. ISAAC LEESER AND GERSHOM KURSHEEDT AND JUDAH TOURO'S RETURN TO JUDAISM

Because New Orleans was so distant from the major centers of Jewish population, it had to put up with the worst of the lot of amateur, untrained, uncommitted, uninspiring religious leaders upon whom most American Jewish communities were dependent until the 1850's. Congregations in Philadelphia, New York City, Baltimore and Charleston, during the 1840's, were making a major effort to enhance their religious program, to bridge the gap between the old world and the new, between need and reality, between license and authority. As early as 1824, George Harby's brother Isaac had attempted to create a new, liberal approach to Jewish traditions in Charleston, but his departure for New York City in 1828 doomed "The Reformed Society of Israelites" to slow disintegration. But Reform congregations were founded in New York City and Baltimore during the early 1840's and continued this experimentation with a modernist approach. Meanwhile, rabbis with stronger educational qualifications began to come to the United States from England and Germany, men who were willing to devote all their time, energy and imagination to the solution of the problems of Jewish living in the new American society.

Characteristically, however, the first great religious leader of American Jewry was not an ordained rabbi who had been fully trained in Europe, but a self-motivated and inner-directed young man named Isaac Leeser who was only eighteen years old when he came to the United States. Born in Westphalia, Germany, in 1806, Leeser had received a sound, traditional Jewish education in Europe before he came to Richmond to work in his uncle's store. Leeser had not been trained as a rabbi, nor had he ever thought of entering the profession. But within a few years of his immigration to the United States, he had so thoroughly demonstrated the superiority of his own knowledge to that of the average Sephardic or Ashkenazic cantor or minister, that the old Sephardic congregation of Philadelphia, Mikveh Israel, invited him to become its *hazan*. Leeser had continued to study, had begun writing about Judaism, and had already perceived the great need of American Jewry for a broad range of educational media and institutions. During the first twelve years of his ministry in Philadelphia, he instituted regular weekly preaching in English and published many of his sermons for broader distribution; produced and published a well-edited Sephardic prayer book with an English translation; published the first of a series of basic religious school textbooks on Jewish beliefs and the Hebrew language; issued the first of a number of volumes on Judaism designed for the instruction of adults; created the first Jewish Sunday School Society in the land with the help of Rebecca Gratz; and attempted to organize a national conference of representatives of American Jewish congregations. Leeser was serious, creative and stubborn. He knew full well that a large number of educational and other institutions had to be developed if American Jews were to remain Jews in any meaningful sense.[13]

Leeser became, directly and indirectly, a major influence in the transformation and maturation of American Jewish life. New Orleans was one of the many communities which were profoundly affected by the impact of his personality and labors. Jews in New Orleans, as almost everywhere else, were stimulated and edified by his prayer book translations, his collections of sermons, and other published volumes, as well as by the monthly issues of the journal, *The Occident and American Jewish Advocate*, which he began to publish in April, 1843—a creative milestone in the development of American Jewish communication and articulation. The pages of the *Occident* brought the texts of sermons, and articles on Jewish religious problems, to the eyes of people throughout America who had never seen anything about Judaism in print before; it conveyed news about congregational life in various communities to the attention of people everywhere, and gave them a sense of cohesiveness. The *Occident* aroused a feeling of urgency among some of those who had previously been utterly indifferent to anything Jewish, and

established the earliest foundation for a sense of national relatedness among those scattered Jews who did care about the future
of Judaism in America. The *Occident* was perhaps the greatest
contribution which Leeser made to American Jewish life. He
edited it single-handedly, and always lost money on its publication costs. If he had married, and needed to support a family,
he could never have carried it off.

Leeser's strongest influence on New Orleans Jewish life was
through his disciple, Gershom Kursheedt, who moved to town
from New York City in late 1839 or early 1840. Gershom's
father, Israel Baer Kursheedt, a learned Jew who had studied
for the rabbinate in Europe, had met Isaac Leeser on the
latter's first day in Richmond, May 5, 1824, and the Kursheedt
family and Leeser were extremely close from then on. His
father transmitted to Gershom a passionate love for Jewish
learning and a profound concern with Jewish causes, which
were also nurtured by his mother, the daughter of the Revolutionary War patriot rabbi, Gershom Mendes Seixas, for whom
he was named. Gershom instinctively responded to Leeser's
remarkably creative ideas and activities, and gave him his full
support and encouragement. Leeser had other followers in New
York City, but Gershom became his first in New Orleans. It
was probably his sister Rebecca's husband Benjamin Florance
who drew Gershom to New Orleans, where he went into business
as a broker. From 1845 to 1849 he was co-editor and publisher
of the *New Orleans Commercial Times*, a paper that was similar to
Levy's *Price-Current*. After an unpleasant break with his erstwhile
partner, he returned to the brokerage business. Kursheedt was a
Mason, a member of the Howard Association, the philanthropic
society which rendered splendid service during the recurring
epidemics, and an active Whig. But his greatest love was
Judaism.[14]

Kursheedt was one of the earliest subscribers to the *Occident*,
and probably solicited subscriptions for the journal in New
Orleans as soon as its publication was announced—a total of
fifteen men signed up during the first year, including Judah
Touro. Kursheedt probably also sold Leeser's prayer books and
other publications in New Orleans. He was active in Leeser's
1845 venture to create the first American Jewish Publication

Society. Although he must have corresponded with Leeser from the very beginning of his stay in New Orleans, the only letters which survive in the Leeser manuscript collection at Dropsie College start in 1847. It would be interesting to know Gershom's opinion of what had been happening to Shanarai-Chasset. Some time during the late 1830's the congregation had discarded the Sephardic ritual and adopted the Ashkenazic, probably because of the large influx of German-born Jews, and the inability of any leader to conduct the Sephardic ritual. Kursheedt had joined the congregation when he came to New Orleans, and was one of the fifty-one members who signed the new by-laws of 1841 which, among other changes, noted that the services should be "in conformity with the rules and customs of the German Israelites," and henceforth banned the membership of any man who had intermarried. When the Hebrew Benevolent Society of New Orleans was established in 1844, Gershom became its first treasurer.

Shortly after the High Holy Days of 1845, Kursheedt organized a new Sephardic congregation, called the Dispersed of Judah— Nefutzoth Yehudah; in the year and a half prior to its receipt of a charter from the state, Kursheedt succeeded in persuading forty men to join the congregation. The reason for the formation of the new group may not have been only ritualistic, but also social. Native-born Jews like the Florance brothers, members of the Labatt, Harris, Hyams and Harby families, as well as men with such Sephardic names as Soria, Rodrigues, Bravo, De Pass, Mendez, Da Vega, and Peixotto—possibly including recent immigrants from the West Indies—must have felt much happier with each other than with newcomers from Germany. There is no doubt, also, that Kursheedt and others must have been altogether appalled at the antics of a man like Roley Marks. But perhaps there was a clever—not to say almost diabolical— reason for the organization of the new congregation: Gershom Kursheedt's hope to secure Judah Touro's cooperation, at last. Shanarai-Chasset had undertaken a campaign for building funds in 1843; an appeal was printed and circulated throughout the country, signed by four men, Benjamin Florance, Leopold Levy, S. Ries, and, of all people, Alexander Phillips, now apparently willing to take leadership in communal activities.

When Kursheedt discovered that Touro still would not do anything for the congregation, he must have decided to organize a new one in the hope that he could arouse Touro's interest. How else explain the name, Dispersed of Judah, but in honor of Judah Touro, or in recollection of the original name of the Newport congregation? There is evidence in Kursheedt's later reports to Leeser that he had already, in the early 1840's, been seeking, unsuccessfully it must be noted, to gain Touro's support for some of Leeser's pet projects—a Jewish high school and college in Philadelphia, a national congregational union, and the Publication Society.[15]

Although Touro would not consider joining the Dispersed of Judah Congregation, he was somehow persuaded to accept the financial responsibility of providing it with a synagogue. How Gershom accomplished this is an "enigma wrapped in a mystery"—unless it was not Gershom who was the successful advocate, but Rezin Shepherd. It is surely more than a coincidence that Touro finally bestirred himself to do something concrete for the Jewish community of New Orleans at the very same time that Shepherd's church had outgrown its building and was planning a new structure. Our best judgement is that Shepherd—according to Kursheedt, the one man who knew how to deal with Touro—told Touro of Christ Church's plans and suggested that it would be a good idea for him to trade some desirable land that he owned in exchange for the Church, and then to remodel the building into a synagogue. But, even so, it may have been Kursheedt who suggested the idea to Shepherd.

Shortly afterwards, Touro took another step to identify himself with Judaism. He gave $500 to the president of the University of Louisiana to endow a gold medal which would be presented annually to the student who demonstrated excellence in the cultivation of the Hebrew language.[16] It would almost seem that some crisis or new development had sent Touro back to Judaism. Perhaps it was so simple a thing as a frightening illness or the onset of old age, with accompanying fears of death and retribution—but we will probably never learn precisely what it was that made him amenable to Kursheedt's pleadings.

Kursheedt, as the president of Dispersed of Judah, had the headache of securing designs for the renovation of the church building, which had to be approved by Touro who, a good deal of the time, could not make up his mind. As Kursheedt reported to Leeser in December, 1847:

"Mr. Touro is the very impersonation of a snail, not to say of a crab whose progress (to use a paradox) is usually backward. My patience is well nigh exhausted with him and I am interrogated by so many concerning his intentions that it is not unusual for me to dodge a corner in order to avoid meeting certain parties who seem to think that I am making a mystery of the matter.

"Your advice to me to urge Mr. Touro is also very good & I have profited by your counsel but the only answer I get is 'well we will see' 'there is time enough' &c &c. I can not order the man and as Mr. Shepherd tells me I must be very careful to humor him or in one instant all may be lost . . .

"Our people here with very few exceptions are a strange set. I am as honorable as I can be and they are incapable of understanding me. Mr. Touro keeps me in hot water with them all the time & I sometimes wish myself anywhere but in N. Orleans. . . ."[17]

The people undoubtedly thought that Kursheedt had found the way to appeal to Touro, and now expected Kursheedt to get everything done in a hurry, but it was months before he secured Touro's approval, and then he had to negotiate with the carpenters and builders who were to do the work:

"I am about to contract for finishing the inside of our new Synagogue & what with Mr. Touro on the one hand with his peculiar notions, & the mechanics on the other, with their attempts to make a good bargain I assure you I am not a little perplexed. . . ."[18]

The workmen labored all through the spring, summer and autumn of 1848, and then, when Kursheedt and Leeser were discussing the liturgical appurtenances and furnishings which were to be ordered in Philadelphia, disaster struck. Kursheedt discovered that the roof of the building "was so defective as to be really dangerous & after some weeks lost in convincing Mr. Touro of this he acceded to my wish to have it taken down." Kursheedt kept reporting to Leeser that Touro was "dreadfully slow" . . . "very *slow*"—but probably no slower than the carpenters and other workmen. The building was not finished until the spring of 1850—three years after Touro had first agreed to the conversion of the church into a synagogue. Nowhere in the correspondence does Kursheedt mention the amount of money that Touro was spending on the building, but it may have been more expensive, in the long run, to renovate and convert the old building, than to put up a totally new one.[19]

In January of 1849, Kursheedt, Leeser and Touro began to review the names of possible candidates for the ministry of the congregation—Kursheedt presumably had been conducting services himself. The most prominent candidate, and the successful one, was Moses N. Nathan, who had been serving congregations in St. Thomas, in the Virgin Islands, and in Kingston, Jamaica. This clergyman was, coincidentally, the nephew of Asher Moses Nathan, and the cousin of the Harris brothers and sisters. Rev. Nathan reached New Orleans only a few days prior to the dedication of the new building. Joining him in the conduct of the services on May 14, 1850, was Isaac Leeser, who came down from Philadelphia at Touro's expense, and stayed with Kursheedt, in whose kosher home he could safely eat. Also participating in the service of dedication was Rabbi James K. Gutheim, who had recently been called to New Orleans by the Shanarai-Chasset Congregation, now stimulated to renewed, or new devotion, by the competition offered by Kursheedt's congregation. A private service was held in the morning, when Judah Touro sealed a commemorative stone in the portal; a very small number of people was invited, it was reported, because of Touro's shyness. Late in the afternoon the public ceremonies were conducted; the building was thronged with Jews and non-Jews who were admitted by ticket only. It was a day of triumph for Kursheedt, who had made all of the arrangements for the dedicatory program, even to the training of the choir. Everyone expected that this new synagogue would give the kind of lift to New Orleans Jewish life for which it had been waiting these many years. On Touro himself, it did have a profound influence. He seems to have returned to Judaism in a most determined way. He attended services regularly, built a schoolhouse next to the synagogue in 1851 and provided rooms there for Gershom Kursheedt to live, and gave regular contributions to the congregational treasury. He also became a strict observer of the Sabbath. In a letter which he wrote to the Firemen's Charitable Association after a fire which destroyed some of his property, the major portion of which was rescued, however, through the efforts of the local fire companies, he said that he would not write on the Sabbath:

New Orleans, January 5th, 1852.

"H. Bier, Esq.,
President,
Firemen's Charitable Association:

Sir:—

Having been made aware of the exhausted state of your treasury, and knowing the usefulness of fire departments, as exhibited on Saturday morning last, when through the activity of several companies, a considerable portion of my property was saved, I beg to present the enclosed one thousand dollars and hope that it may temporarily relieve the widows and orphans dependent on the association for support.

Saturday, on which the fire occurred, being my Sabbath, has prevented me from sending this until this morning.

Very respectfully,

J. TOURO"[20]

The Dispersed of Judah Congregation did not, however, prosper as had been anticipated. Everyone expected Touro to do everything, or rather Kursheedt to do everything, and Touro to pay for it. Moses N. Nathan was miserable; he felt as though he were altogether dependent on Touro's charity. In early 1853 he left New Orleans in disgust, writing to Leeser:

". . . the folks here . . . are very willing to employ the best minister possible, but the truth is, they don't want to pay. They would like Mr. Touro to do that duty. It is quite honor sufficient that they have accepted his gift, and having secured that effectually, their obligations are ended. They have been playing a farce with me during the last fortnight . . . [Touro] is heartily tired of these continual drains on his purse, and I will no longer submit to be a pensioner on his bounty . . . Since my first engagement in Feby. 50, he has paid nearly two thirds of my salary. . . ."[21]

The situation had really not changed very much. The rich were disinterested—Asher Nathan, the rabbi's uncle, neither joined the congregation nor contributed to it—and the poor were unable to pay anything.

As a matter of fact, Shanarai-Chasset Congregation was faring much better. The 1843 appeal for funds to build a new synagogue had been a dismal failure. But in 1845 the congregation moved from St. Louis and Franklin streets to a building on Rampart street between Conti and St. Louis, and in 1850 brought Rabbi Gutheim from Cincinnati. Spurred on by the example of the Portuguese congregation, and, under the strong leadership of Alexander Hart's son Isaac, the members of Shanarai-Chasset determined to build a synagogue for themselves. It was more modest than the building which Touro had presented to the Dispersed of Judah, but it was the product of the effort of many people rather than the largesse of one man. One hundred members bought shares of $50 each, in addition to outright contributions which were made by others. A transformation had indeed taken place in Touro's nature: he gave the German congregation, as it was frequently called, $5,000, and loaned them an additional $6,528, for which he held notes at the time of his death. The new synagogue was erected at the same location on Rampart street on which the temporary quarters stood, at a total cost of $16,000, and was dedicated on March 5, 1851. Gutheim, who was to be identified with New Orleans Jewry's religious life for almost forty years, ultimately as the founding rabbi of the Reform Temple Sinai, left Shanarai-Chasset in 1853, and succeeded Nathan in the ministry at Dispersed of Judah. It was therefore he who officiated at the funeral of Judah Touro in January, 1854. One more word needs to be said about the members of the Portuguese congregation, however: no sooner had Touro died, than they sold the building and ground which Touro had presented to them, and moved to a new location, more convenient to the residences of the members. The land on Canal street was very valuable, and, together with the adjoining properties which Touro gave to the congregation in his will, brought $70,000. It would seem as though they were saying, however, that the synagogue renovated at such expense and trouble was not at all satisfactory, had been accepted only because it was a gift, and had not been a wise project after all. Sad commentary, perhaps, on the capacity of a man to help a community.[22]

Not only did both congregations now have their own synagogue buildings, but a third congregation was organized in the Lafayette suburb. An abortive effort was made in this direction in 1848, followed by the establishment of a benevolent society in 1849, and, finally, the founding of Congregation Shaarei Tefiloh (Gates of Prayer) in January, 1850. Lafayette was not too far from town, but the trip was uncomfortable and difficult. As New Orleans Jewry entered the sixth decade of the century, then, it had three centers of worship.[23]

It is not our intention to report on the details of Jewish life in New Orleans in the 1850's. That is another story, similar to the story of many other communities throughout America—the gradual integration into communal life of large numbers of recent immigrants from Germany, the struggle with problems of Jewish education and philanthropy, the creation of a host of Jewish organizations, lodges and charities, the gradual emergence of Reform tendencies, further losses through inter-marriage and assimilation, and, in New Orleans, the crises of secession, conquest and Reconstruction. That story is not a distinctive one; it is a duplication of the experiences of other communities in the South, in the North and in the Mid-West, and is best told in conjunction with an analysis of the gathering crisis in American Jewish life which finally culminated in the recognition of the truth of Leeser's contention that American Jewish communities would never be able to solve their problems in isolation, but had to band together to create a national union of congregations and a central Jewish theological seminary. These were finally established in the 1870's under the creative leadership of Rabbi Gutheim's friend, Rabbi Isaac Mayer Wise of Cincinnati.

But this early period of Jewish life in New Orleans which we have been tracing comes to an end only with Judah Touro's famous will. If Touro had died during the 1820's or 1830's, although he might have left large sums of money to charitable organizations, they would not have been Jewish ones. But he lived long enough for Leeser and Kursheedt to reach his heart. Whether it was the building of the Nefutzoth Yehudah synagogue which had a profound emotional and spiritual influence upon him, or whether his willingness to pay for the remodeling resulted from a repentant acknowledgement of his prior errors, is impossible to tell. But he had returned to his religion. He was now once more a Jew by more than birth. His regular attendance at Sabbath services demonstrated that. And, apparently, he had decided to leave part of his wealth to Jewish causes. When he fell ill, Touro brought Shepherd and Kursheedt to his bedside to discuss his ideas with them. Shepherd never wrote down what had happened in these talks, but Kursheedt did. He had argued mightily to persuade Touro to adopt Leeser's vision of a network of national American Jewish cultural institutions—a university, a rabbinical seminary, a publication society, a national synod of rabbis—but this was beyond Touro's power to comprehend. "Poor old man," wrote Kursheedt, "he had noble impulses, but his great misfortune was in his want of education. Some of his notions were good, and to the extent that I can, I will carry them out." Touro's emphasis was on charity for the needy, and help for struggling congregations and congregational schools, tokens of esteem for rabbis like Leeser and Nathan, the creation of the Touro hospital in New Orleans, and tangible help for the poverty-stricken Jews of Palestine. The larger vision of national American Jewish unity would have to wait. Kursheedt's emotion-laden explanation to Leeser is full of frustration:

". . . Oh my dear friend, if you knew how I had to work to get that Will made and how I strove to serve you, you would pity me. Alas, it was not altogether what I wanted, yet I am thankful to God that even if I injured myself I got the most of what I wanted for Israel—arguments, changes and counter-changes in the sums for Institutions, till my heart sickened. I appeared calm, but indeed was almost crazy, ever dreading that nothing would be achieved in the end. The list of Jewish Institutions I made up as well as I could. I had dreadful hard work to raise your Education Society from 10 to 20,000."[24]

Touro's bequests should not be underrated, however, because we now recognize how late he was in returning to the faith of his father, or because we understand how difficult it was for Kursheedt and Leeser to transmit to him the urgent awareness of the problems of American Jewish life. No one could force him to do what he did do. The decision was his alone. And it was a meaningful one. He recognized the need for the great gesture, a concrete expression of good will and optimism in broad, magnanimous terms. It is worth counting his benefactions. We do not know of any previous American will, written by Christian let alone by Jew, which ever before had spread such largesse among so many institutions. $75,000 went to various individuals and friends, including the executors, Parson Clapp, and Rabbis Leeser and Nathan; Shepherd was, of course, the residuary legatee. Gifts to orphans' homes and other Christian welfare agencies in New Orleans, and for the construction of a new almshouse, totalled $120,000. Philanthropic institutions in Boston, to which his brother Abraham had been devoted, received $20,000. In Newport, Rhode Island, his old home, $10,000 was given to the Old Stone Mill park, and $3,000 to the Redwood Library. The Jews of New Orleans received a total of $108,000, including property worth $48,000 to Dispersed of Judah, $40,000 in property (the Paulding estate) for a Jewish hospital (Touro Infirmary) in New Orleans, $5,000 for Shanarai-Chasset, and $15,000 for local benevolent societies including the utopian effort to send assistance to the dwindling Jewish community in China. An endowment of $10,000 was established for the Newport synagogue and cemetery. A total of $60,000 went towards the relief of the poor Jews of Palestine, $50,000 to be used at the discretion of the distinguished British Jewish leader, Sir Moses Montefiore. Congregations, religious schools, benevolent societies and Jewish hospitals in Boston, Hartford, New Haven, New York City, Philadelphia, Baltimore, Richmond, Charleston, Savannah, Mobile, Memphis, Louisville, Cincinnati, Cleveland, St. Louis, Buffalo and Albany, received a total of $143,000.[25]

Even generosity brings problems in its wake. Gershom Kursheedt and Sir Moses Montefiore had to make several trips to Palestine to attempt to carry out Touro's wishes, and

Montefiore complained that Touro's bequest cost him a great deal of money—but it was worth the trouble: instead of the hospital they originally intended to build, they constructed a number of homes in the first Jewish suburb outside the walls of the Old City of Jerusalem—a district called Mazkeret Moshe— Remembrance of Moses (Montefiore). The city government of New Orleans had a difficult time establishing the Touro Alms- houses, and they were no sooner constructed than they were taken over by the victorious Union Army. It was many years, too, before the Jews of Philadelphia finally used Touro's bequest to build an educational structure which was named for him. Some Jews complained that Shepherd had gotten too much out of his friendship for Touro, and Jewish organizations which were left out of the will were very upset. Kursheedt reported to Leeser just a month after Touro's death that the Jewish or- ganizational squabbles embarrassed him terribly:

> ". . . You cannot imagine the disgusting communications that come to Shepherd from some of our Societies, giving recitals of congregational difficulties, jealousies, etc. I have to blush fre- quently, and try to put the best face on it. . . ."[26]

Yet these were minor difficulties, at worst. The news of the terms of Touro's will was received with undisguised astonish- ment; tributes of the most laudatory character were published in New Orleans and throughout the country. The funeral services in New Orleans, despite the man's innate shyness, became a virtual public triumph; the *Bee* said that "it was one of the largest assemblages of citizens we have ever beheld . . . The funeral train was immense, almost every carriage in the city being filled." The final burial service, which was held in New- port, Rhode Island, early in June, was another occasion for public praise for Touro's magnanimity.[27]

Touro became in death what he had never been, never wanted to be, in life: a local and national hero; a leader of men; a dignitary; a man of inspiring presence; an exemplary Jewish philanthropist. His significance in American Jewish history, by reason of the remarkable manner in which he disposed of his wealth, is a major one. To dozens of Jewish congregations and institutions throughout the country, many of them newly created, practically all in financial straits, he gave both material and moral encouragement. To thousands of newly-arrived immigrants, hesitating on the threshold of a new life, he offered the example of a happy combination of self-respecting Judaism and avid Americanism, together with a high level of material success and generosity, which served to spur their own ambitions and hasten their acculturation to the new land. To the minds of many Americans he contributed a benevolent portrait of "the Jew" which contrasted forcefully with distorted folk-images tainted with prejudice. To Jews in Europe, from the exalted Sir Moses Montefiore to the lowliest villager in unhappy Poland, he gave a new impression of the American Jew which helped to counteract the concept of the rough, uncouth, materialistic, irreligious American-Jewish frontiersman. It was a supreme irony, and a strange twist of fate, that this simple man, so distant from Judaism throughout most of his life, should have brought such renown to the Jewish community of New Orleans which had been notable only for the extent of its accommodation to the environment, and for its delay in establishing the foundations of religious and communal continuity.[28]

NOTES

Abbreviations of Sources in Notes

(All newspapers cited in notes were published in New Orleans, unless otherwise indicated.)

AGI   Archivo General de Indias, Manuscript Collections in Seville and Cuba, divided into two main groups, Audiencia de Santo Domingo, and Papeles procedentes de la Isla de Cuba. Most of our citations are from photostats, microfilms or typescripts in the Library of Congress, Manuscript Division.

AJA   American Jewish Archives, Cincinnati

AJHQ   *American Jewish Historical Quarterly* (New York, 1961–   )

AJHS   Library of the American Jewish Historical Society, Waltham, Mass.

DAB   *Dictionary of American Biography* (New York, 1946)

JE   *Jewish Encyclopedia* (New York, 1901–1905)

JRBD   Joseph R. Rosenbloom, *A Biographical Dictionary of Early American Jews* (Lexington, Ky., 1960)

LC   Library of Congress

LG   *Louisiana Gazette* (New Orleans, 1802–26)

LHQ   *Louisiana Historical Quarterly* (New Orleans, 1917–   )

LSML   Louisiana State Museum Library, New Orleans: documents are from translations and summaries of originals in the Cabildo safe; death data from cemetery card files.

MSAJD   Malcolm H. Stern, *Americans of Jewish Descent* (Cincinnati, 1960)

NCC   Natchez Court of Chancery Manuscript Records, summarized in May Wilson McBee, *The Natchez Court Records, 1767–1805* (Natchez, 1953), but references are to Manuscript Transcripts of 1817–18.

NOCD   *New Orleans City Directories*, of varied titles, followed by year, as listed in Dorothea N. Spear, *Bibliography of American Directories through 1860* (Worcester, 1961), 222–29.

NOG   *New Orleans Genesis* (New Orleans, 1962–)

NONA   New Orleans Notarial Archives, Civil District Court, some numbered in series by notary's name, some identified only by year.

NOOR   New Orleans Office of the Registrar of Births, Marriages and Deaths.

NOPC   New Orleans Probate Court Records, Civil District Court.

OCC   *Occident and American Jewish Advocate* (Phila., 1843–69)

PAJHS   *Publications of the American Jewish Historical Society* (Baltimore, New York, 1893–1960)

REJ   *Revue des Etudes Juives* (Paris, 1880–)

SC   *Synopses of Cases in the U. S. District Court for the Eastern District of Louisiana, Cases #1 to 3000, 1806–1831* (WPA Mimeographed Volume) (Baton Rouge, 1941)

SLCBR   St. Louis Cathedral, New Orleans, Baptismal Registers, arabic numbers from 1771 on.

SLCCB   St. Louis Cathedral Confirmation Book, 1790–1840, published as *Confirmaciones* by Genealogical Research Society of New Orleans (New Orleans, 1967).

SLCFR   St. Louis Cathedral, New Orleans, Funeral Registers, unnumbered.

SLCMR   St. Louis Cathedral, New Orleans, Marriage Registers, arabic numbers from 1777 on.

SWFP   *Archives of the Spanish Government of West Florida* (WPA Mimeographed Volumes) (Baton Rouge, 1937–38), references are to the original volumes and pages as summarized in these transcriptions and translations.

WFP   British West Florida Provincial Papers, Public Record Office, London, Colonial documents, Section 5, from photostatic copies in the Library of Congress.

[1] Samuel Oppenheim, "The Early History of the Jews in New York, 1654–1664," *PAJHS* No. 18 (1909), 9–11.

[2] Ab. Cahen, "Les Juifs dans les Colonies Françaises au xviiie Siècle," *REJ*, IV (1882), 127–43, 236–48; V (1882), 68–92, 258–72; Nellis M. Crouse, *French Pioneers in the West Indies, 1624–1664* (New York, 1940), 179, 211, 265; I. S. Emmanuel, "New Light on Early American Jewry," *American Jewish Archives*, VII (1955), 22; I. S. Emmanuel, "Les Juifs de la Martinique," *REJ*, CXXIII (1964), 511; Lee M. Friedman, *Jewish Pioneers and Patriots* (Phila., 1943), 81–94.

[3] Friedman, *Jewish Pioneers*, 87; Cahen, "Les Juifs," IV, 128 ff; Arthur Hertzberg, *The French Enlightenment and the Jews* (New York, 1968), 22–25.

[4] Friedman, *Jewish Pioneers*, 88; Zosa Szajkowski, *Franco-Judaica* (New York, 1962), 1.

[5] Friedman, *Jewish Pioneers*, 90; Arthur Daniel Hart, *The Jew in Canada* (Toronto, 1926), 5–12; *JE*, VI, 63–64; Hertzberg, *French Enlightenment*, 88–92; B. G. Sack, *History of the Jews in Canada* (Montreal, 1926), 13–33; Z. Szajkowski, "The Jewish Status in Eighteenth-Century France and the 'Droit d'Aubaine,' " *Historia Judaica*, XIX (1957), 150, 154–55; Simon Wolf, *The American Jew as Patriot, Soldier and Citizen* (Phila., 1895), 476–82.

[6] Edwin Adams Davis, *Louisiana, A Narrative History* (Baton Rouge, 1961), 58.

[7] Anita L. Lebeson, in *Pilgrim People* (New York, 1950), 114–18, seems firmly convinced that Louis-Elias Stutheus, an agent for John Law's speculative Company of the Indies colonization scheme popularly known as "the Mississippi bubble," who came to Louisiana in connection with his official duties about 1720, was Jewish. It is difficult to discern from her footnotes whether or not she relies solely on J. Hanno Deiler's undocumented statement in *The Settlement of the German Coast of Louisiana and the Creoles of German Descent* (Phila., 1909), 21, where reference is made to Stutheus as "the Jewish business manager of Law." Professor Marcel Giraud, the leading authority on the early colonization of Louisiana, who has for many years studied the documents relating to Law's Company, has discovered no contemporary reference to Stutheus as a Jew. The name in the notarial records is spelled that way, rather than "Stultheus" as given by Mrs. Lebeson. Giraud bases his belief that Stutheus was not Jewish on the absence of any such positive identification and on the following facts: firstly, that Stutheus was, before joining Law's venture, a "commissaire de la marine," an unlikely post for a Jew; secondly, that one M. Pauger, referring to Stutheus' death in 1721, says that he died with "great sentiments of piety," a characteristic Christian comment of the time, hardly to be applied to a Jew. Father Charles O'Neill of Loyola University, New Orleans, has been in contact with Prof. Giraud about such matters as these in connection with his own research for his recent volume, *Church and State in French Colonial Louisiana*

(New Haven, 1966), and has been kind enough to share his correspondence with M. Giraud with me. Giraud refers to Stutheus in the third volume (1717–1720) of his *Histoire de la Louisiane Française* (Paris, 1966), 234, 241, 244. The Pauger letter (to M. de La Tour, April 14, 1721, Archives Nationales, 3 JJ 201 [5]) is not mentioned in this volume since it relates to 1721. The name Stutheus, which no Jew is known to have borne, may be of German, Dutch or Swiss origin; perhaps somewhere there is a reference to Stutheus as a Swiss which may have been misread by Deiler or someone else as "Juif." Father O'Neill has explained to me the error made by Pierre Margry, *Découvertes et Établissements des Français dans l'ouest et dans le sud de l'Amérique septentrionale, 1614–1754* (Paris, 1879–83), V, 576, in his published transcription of André Pénicaut's *Relation . . .* (Bibliothèque Nationale mss. Fr. 14613, p. 355). In the passage "In the beginning [of 1720] . . . there arrived seven ships . . . These ships had brought over more than four thousand persons, French as well as Germans and Swiss . . .," Margry, or his amanuensis, misread Pénicaut's handwritten "Suisses" with the old-style "ss" as "Juiffes." This is apparent when the Pénicaut manuscript is compared with the Margry transcription (B.N. mss. Fr. 9298, p. 358). See R. G. McWilliams, translator and editor of Pénicaut's narrative, published under the title *Fleur de Lys and Calumet* (Baton Rouge, 1953), 240, 257, for confirmation of this explanation. McWilliams, 241, transcribes "M. Lias" for Margry's reading of "Elias."

[8] Louisiana Historical Records Survey, *Inventory of the Church and Synagogue Records of Louisiana. Jewish Congregations and Organizations* (Baton Rouge, 1941), 1, and Samuel Proctor, "Jewish Life in New Orleans, 1718–1860," *LHQ*, XL (1957), 111, among others, contain these questionable references.

[9] Deiler, *The Settlement of the German Coast*, 84. Mrs. Lebeson (*Pilgrim People*, 116–17) is convinced that some of these people were Jews, but offers no evidence other than names which today are frequently regarded as Jewish. Many Central European Jews, however, did not even possess family names until much later into the eighteenth century.

[10] Father O'Neill had thought that "les nommés Isaak," who were working to develop a type of cotton gin in 1732–33, mentioned in a ministerial communication to Salmon, September 8, 1733, Archives Nationales, AC, B 59, f. 584–85, might be Jews simply on the basis of the name, but he recognizes the risk of such ascription without positive evidence of Jewish identification. In his own meticulous study relating to Catholics and non-Catholics in this early period, he has found no evidence of the presence of Jews in French Louisiana: *Church and State*, 269–70, 282.

[11] *Le Code Noir, ou Edit du Roi* (Paris, 1728), 2.

[12] *The History of Louisiana* (New Orleans, 1903), I, 362–63.

[13] Pope Gregory the Great (590–604) distinguished between slaves held temporarily by Jewish traders, and those permanently possessed by Jewish individuals, thereby encouraging Jewish merchants to take part in the slave trade. No definitive study of this subject has been published, but see Israel Abrahams, *Jewish Life in the Middle Ages* (second edition, revised by Cecil Roth) (London, 1932), 112–17; Salo W. Baron, *A Social and Religious History of the Jews* (Phila., 1957), III, 30–31,

219, 243–44, 252–53; IV, 9, 187–96; Jacob R. Marcus, *The Jew in the Medieval World* (Cincinnati, 1938), 5, 39.

Father O'Neill, *Church and State*, 269, regards the *Code Noir* ban on Jews as evidence of the concern of the French authorities for the loyalty of the colonial settlers; if they were all Catholics, they would have no political leaning towards a rival power, presumably Protestant. But there is no contemporary evidence that Jews constituted any kind of political force anywhere in the late seventeenth and early eighteenth centuries. If this was indeed in the minds of the French authorities, it is another indication of the utter unreasonableness of attitudes towards the Jews.

The *Code Noir* was officially reprinted in New Orleans as late as 1803 by order of Pierre Clément Laussat, who was the French Commissioner of Louisiana during the brief period between the announcement of the cession of the territory by Spain to France, and the occupation of the area by United States forces after the Louisiana Purchase. But a covering statement indicated that all provisions which were in contradiction to the U. S. Constitution were void. A copy of this rare pamphlet is in the Favrot Collection, at the Tulane University Library.

[14] Ms. Mémoires, Archives Nationales, Colonies, C13A, 4, p. 934, cited in O'Neill, *Church and State*, 265.

[15] Jacob Rader Marcus, *American Jewry. Documents. Eighteenth Century* (Cincinnati, 1959), 326–29.

[16] *LHQ*, XIX (1936), 1117; XX (1937), 222–23. Henriques was the grandson of Yeosua Henriques who was in Curaçao as early as 1654 and who died there in 1704. This Henriques family has been in longer continual residence in Curaçao than any other Jewish family. I. S. Emmanuel, *Precious Stones of the Jews of Curaçao* (New York, 1957), 203–204.

[17] This synopsis of a long and involved matter is based on the narrative and translations of relevant documents in A. P. Nasatir and Leo Shpall, "The Texel Affair," *AJHQ*, LIII (1963), 3–43. The *Annual Report, John Carter Brown Library, 1948–1949* (Providence, 1940), 14–20, gives some bibliographical data on the conflict. There is also an extensive description of the affair in Marc de Villers du Terrage, *Les Dernières Années de la Louisiane Française* (Paris, 1904), of which I have used Henri Delville de Sinclair's 1937–38 WPA mss. translation, in the Tulane University Library, hereafter cited as Terrage, *Last Years of French Louisiana*. The references to the *Texel* affair in this translation are pp. 158–70. The data on Dias Arias are in Emmanuel, *Precious Stones*, 295.

[18] Nasatir, "The Texel Affair," 27. This was a report to the Minister of Marine in Paris, dated March 25, 1759. Among the many other documents in the case, a letter of Pierre Henry Derneville, a military officer and one of Rochemore's associates, to Le Normand (Archives Nationales, Colonies, C13A, 41, p. 341) portrays the Jews as a serious economic threat: "The Jews who have established stores in this city for approximately the last eighteen months, are carrying off [monopolizing] all of the coined money, are negotiating bills of exchange at twenty per cent, are carrying off all the indigo and furs, with the result that if one of our vessels should come, I doubt that he could find anything to take back. . . ."

Derneville's reference would date Jewish settlement in New Orleans as early as the fall of 1757.

[19] State of Rhode Island Archives, Dept. of State, Providence, Public Notary Records, VI, 436, June 8, and November 23, 1757; Letters to the Governor of Rhode Island, VI, 15, May 11, June 22, 23, 1759; Algemeen Rijksarchief, The Hague, Old Curaçao Archives, No. 601, f. 375; LHQ, XXV (1942), 1178 (petition of Guillaume, September 27, 1763); XXVI (1943), 217–19 (answer of Monsanto, October 12, 1763); LSML: Doc. 63/109a (decision of the arbiters, November 19, 1763); Doc. 63/109 (petition of Monsanto, December 1, 1763); Doc. 63/109c (advice of Lafite, arbiter, undated and incomplete); Doc. 93/109c–2 (recommendations of Carresset, chief arbiter, December 2, 1763). No record of the case can be found in the incomplete Saint-Domingue records in the Archives Nationales in Paris.

[20] LHQ, XVIII (1935), 293, 301, 314.

[21] There is a mystery about Ester Levy which we have not been able to solve. The entry in the Gemeente Archief at The Hague, Recht. Arch. 75g, f. 2, which notes her civil marriage to David Monsanto on February 3, 1732, clearly states that she was born in the "Land van Munster." Yet the wills or death records of three children give the mother's name as Ester Barro, Bareo or Bareau, two stating that she was from the Barbados Islands: Gracia's will, Francisco Broutin, VII, 83, December 8, 1790, NONA; Manuel's first will, Francisco Broutin, XI, 56, March 8, 1792, NONA; Eleanora's death record, SLCFR, 1793–1803, p. 45. There are a number of alternative explanations: That Ester Levy Barrow had been born in Münster but lived in the Barbados before her marriage, but why is the Barrow name not given in any of the records at The Hague? That David married an Ester Barrow from the Barbados after Ester Levy Monsanto's death in 1747, and had by her a number of younger children, including Gracia and Eleanora, but Manuel was one of the oldest children, certainly born to Ester Levy Monsanto! That David married an Ester Barrow from the Barbados after the family moved to Curaçao, and she became so devoted a mother to the children of the first Ester that they regarded her as their mother. It may never be possible to resolve this contradiction which is largely of genealogical significance.

[22] The approximate date of Isaac's birth is recorded in the civil antenuptial agreement between Esther and David Monsanto, Gemeente Archief, The Hague: Notarial Archives, J. Sydhoff, no. 2053, act 17, January 28, 1732. The earliest reference to David Monsanto's connection with de Medina is in the latter's first will, November 20, 1715, also in the Sydhoff Notarial Archives. A thorough investigation of The Hague Gemeente Archief would undoubtedly reveal many transactions in which Monsanto represented de Medina and held his power of attorney. Two examples are given in J. H. Buzaglo, "Bijdragen tot de Geschiedenis der Portugeesche Israëlieten en Hunner Gemeenten te s'-Gravenhage van±1690 tot±1730," Die Haghe Jaarboek (The Hague, 1939), 98–99. In the first, Monsanto acted for de Medina in the sale of a property in Princessegracht to the directors and treasurers of the Honen Dal Congregation, March 12, 1725, for 1,100 florins; in the second, on February 14, 1729, he fulfilled a similar role in the sale of a property south of the synagogue for 4,200 florins. Data about de Medina is in Albert M.

Hyamson, *The Sephardim of England* (London, 1951), 54–55, and Cecil Roth, *A History of the Jews in England* (3rd ed.) (Oxford, 1964), 287–88. Dr. Oskar K. Rabinowicz of New Rochelle has permitted me to consult his unpublished monograph on de Medina and Marlborough. The final wills of de Medina and his wife are in the Sydhoff Notarial Archives, no. 2046, June 3, 1727. Monsanto was involved in the sale of de Medina's home for the large amount of 30,000 guilders to Rachel Teixeira Suasso in 1737–39 (Gemeente Archief, RA 519, November 12, 1737; Notarial Archives no. 2279, June 3, September 12, 1738). Some indication of de Medina's limited means or, at least, of the small amount of ready cash which he had at hand is revealed by the relatively small contribution which he made to the Honen Dal Congregation of The Hague, at the service on the eve of the dedication of its new synagogue building in 1726. Twenty-seven contributors gave a total of 4,225.5 florins. Eight of the contributors, Monsanto among them, gave 5 or 5.5 florins each. Eight others gave 500 florins each; de Medina was not one of them—his contribution was only 20 florins, four times as much as Monsanto's. But it is difficult to believe that he gave as much as he was able—perhaps he was just not interested (Buzaglo, "Bijdragen," 67).

[23] Most of these details are from reports by Dr. H. M. Mensonides, Director of the Municipal Archives of The Hague, September 22, October 5, November 4, 1966, and May 23, 1967, based on the manuscript archives of both the city and the synagogues. Grateful appreciation must be expressed to Dr. Mensonides for his extremely generous expenditure of time and effort. Some of the references to David Monsanto are as follows: civil records—Buurtboek 84, f. 70, 86; Rechterlijk Archief 556, November 2, 1739; 802, December 19, 1741; Tax List, O.A. 4763, 4764; synagogue records—Honen Dal Arch. 1, pp. 44–45; and entries for Cheshvan 11, 5503 (1742); Sivan 15, 5509 (1748–49); Teves 22, 5512 (1751/52); "Livro longo no. 4 de Promessas & Noticias do K. K. Honendal," entries for Nisan 5509 (1749) and Hanukah 5511 (1750). The antenuptial agreement referred to in the previous note states that Ester brought no dowry to David, but stipulated that if he predeceased her, she was to receive the substantial sum of 1,000 guilders from his estate. Even though he was not in The Hague at the time, David Monsanto was included in the 1743 list of members of the united congregation, Beth Jacob-Honen Dal. Interestingly enough, it indicates that just prior to that time he was associated with Beth Jacob, and was no longer a member of the Honen Dal Congregation in which he had been active in the 1720's and 1730's. Is this, perhaps, to be explained by his sense of embarrassment over the change in his financial status? (M. Henriquez Pimentel, *Geschiedkundige Aan Teekeningen, bettreffende de Portugesche Israelieten in Den Haag En Hunne Synagogen Aldaar* [s'-Gravenhage, 1876], 81).

[24] Unless more precise birth records can be discovered in Holland, we shall have to be content with the age variations offered in various legal documents. Manuel is called "about 50 years old" in his death record, July 10, 1796, SLCFR, 1793–1803, p. 32; but since he was the last of the Louisiana siblings to die, and none of the brothers or sisters remained to give his age, it is more likely that his own testimony that he was fifty years old in 1785 is correct: *LHQ*, XXVIII (1945), 617. Gracia's death record, January 3, 1791, SLCFR, 1784–93, p. 31, unfortunately does not give her age; in 1766 she was reported as being twenty-two years old:

LSML, Doc. 1957 (September 10, 1766), which also gives Angélica's age as twenty-one. But Angélica's tombstone and death record on a Girod St. Cemetery card in LSML list her as seventy-two years old at her death on October 21, 1821; the tombstone is in the possession of Dean Kenneth Trist Urquhart; the ms. eulogy of Angélica by General James Wilkinson, in Prof. Urquhart's collection of family memorabilia, says that she was born in June, 1749, in The Hague. Jacob's death record for June 5, 1789, SLCFR, 1784–93, p. 20, lists him as forty-three years of age, but he testified that he was thirty-seven years old in 1785; *LHQ*, XXVIII (1945), 617. Benjamin said that he was thirty-five years old in 1785, *LHQ*, XXVII (1944), 862, but the St. Louis Cemetery No. 1 card in LSML says that he was forty at the time of his death, September 30, 1794; the card also says that he was a native of Spain, undoubtedly an error . . . either Benjamin's widow made the mistake, or there was a deliberate effort to mislead. Eleanora's death record, SLCFR, 1793–1803, p. 45, says that she was about forty-five at her death on April 8, 1796. Angélica's marriage contract and wedding record indicate that she was born in Amsterdam (L. Mazange, Book I, 778–79, NONA; SLCMR, I, 114, September 9, 1781), but this mistaken information may have been supplied by her second husband, Dr. Robert Dow, unless her parents lived briefly in Amsterdam; this is the only Monsanto family record referring to Amsterdam as its city of residence, although David Monsanto is recorded in his civil marriage record as a native of that city. Sara's death is registered in O.I.T.B., Gemeente Archief, The Hague, for January, 1736; she is therefore not the same as the Sara Rodrigues Monsanto who died in Curaçao, December 20, 1754 (Emmanuel, *Precious Stones*, 508, no. 644). The births of two unnamed Monsanto children are recorded in Buurtboek 84, May, 1733, and May 25, 1734, Gemeente Archief. Ester's burial record is in O.I.T.B. 13, f. 1 g.

[25] Excerpt from *Livro de Termos, Rezolucoems do K. K. Honendal*, No. I, 73, entry for Teves 14, 5515 (1754/55), Gemeente Archief, The Hague.

[26] The reader is advised that Monsanto was a very common family name, but confusion is avoided to some degree by the realization that most Sephardic families had two names. Thus our Monsanto family was specifically the Rodrigues (or Rois/Roiz, a shortened form or abbreviation of Rodrigues) Monsanto clan; other Monsanto families in Holland and the Caribbean area were known by the names Abendana Monsanto, Gonzales Monsanto, Israel Monsanto, Mendes Monsanto, Molina Monsanto, Moreno Monsanto, and Nunes Monsanto. Strangely enough, a sister-in-law of David Dias Arias, Ester Yesurun, married an Isaac Monsanto, but he was of the Israel Monsanto family, and he died in Curaçao on September 12, 1758 (Emmanuel, *Precious Stones*, 295, 503). The decision to leave The Hague may have been motivated not only by failure and poverty; it is possible that the Monsanto family was attracted to Curaçao because David may have had a sister who lived there. Judith Roiz Monsanto, the wealthy widow of Raphael Alvares Correa, of Curaçao, may have been David's sister. David is not mentioned in her will (Old Curaçao Archives, Algemeen Rijksarchief, Vol. 862, dated March 15, 1747), but certain legal documents in the Old Curaçao Archives index to Vol. 836 seem to indicate a family relationship. Unfortunately the documents themselves have been lost, but the index notations, viz. no. 531, power of attorney

from Judith Roiz Monsanto to David Roiz Monsanto; no. 532, a transaction of her son, Manuel van Raphael Alvares Correa, with David; no. 533, a transaction of Abigael Alvares Correa, her daughter, with David, seem to indicate more than business relations. Some data about Judith Monsanto Correa are in H. M. Alvares Correa, *The Alvares Correa Families of Curaçao and Brazil* (The Hague, 1966), 23–24, but no reference is made to her parentage or family. Judith married Correa in Amsterdam on June 19, 1716, but unfortunately no information about her family is given in the civil record of the wedding (Amsterdam Gemeentelijke Archiefdienst, D. T. & B, no. 710, p. 291) other than that her parents were deceased. If she was indeed David's sister, perhaps she helped David and his sons to establish themselves in business in Curaçao after their transfer from The Hague. This would explain how they so swiftly became men of some success.

[27] David's name occurs in a list of inhabitants of Curaçao who petitioned the directors of the Netherlands West India Company, in 1757, in regard to the capture of Dutch ships by the British: Arch. Neth. West India Company, 421, f. 381. Certificates for Isaac and Jacob to act as brokers in 1758 are listed in the Old Curaçao Archives, 836, numbers 171 and 238. Documents authorizing David and Jacob to act as legal representatives of other persons are in the Old Curaçao Archives, 836, no. 498 (January 15, 1758) and no. 502 (January 16, 1758); 875, no. 310 (October 19, 1759); and 877, (June 6, 24, 1760). All of these records are in the Algemeen Rijksarchief, The Hague. If the Jacob Monsanto referred to in these documents is a member of our Rodrigues Monsanto family, then he must have been born a good deal earlier than 1746. On the other hand, since no middle name is given, he may have been a member of one of the other Monsanto families, and unrelated to ours. The tradition that David Rodrigues Monsanto was attorney-general of Curaçao has flourished for more than one hundred years; it appeared in print most recently in Edwin Adams Davis, *The Story of Louisiana* (Baton Rouge, 1960), IV, 141.

[28] The last record in the Old Curaçao Archives, Algemeen Rijksarchief, relating to this Monsanto family is OAC 889, No. 250 (August 12, 1763), Manuel's assignment of his power of attorney to his father. OAC 889, no. 187 (June 16, 1763), describes Manuel still as a merchant in Curaçao. A reference to Britto as a member of the business partnership of Britto and Monsanto (Isaac?) is in OAC 887, April 28, 1760. Our knowledge of the activities of Joseph and Judith is very skimpy, due largely to the relatively small number of manuscript records from Saint-Domingue which survived the ravages of revolution, and are preserved in the Outre-Mer Section of the Archives Nationales in Paris. We know only that Joseph was living in the Limonade district of Sainte Suzanne in 1783, when he purchased from Françoise Nicholas Dibonne for 3,960 livres two plots of ground, a main house, an outbuilding and a family of slaves (Michel Not. Arch., August 27, 1783, February 6, 1784). Judith and Moïse Julien are referred to as the parents of Abraham Julien who was married on November 30, 1788, in a ten-page marriage agreement (Pardevani Not. Arch.) in which the elder Julien is said to have been a native of Curaçao. It is natural to wonder if Moïse and Judith first met in New Orleans. A man named Julien, of the firm of Julien and Rodriquez, from the Caribbean area, was in New Orleans for an extended period of time before September 30,

1765. He was involved in business dealings with the Monsanto firm which resulted in litigation (LSML, Doc. 65–A–79). There may have been other Monsanto relatives in Saint-Domingue. One Daniel Monsanto had already settled on the island by 1765, and was still doing business in 1779–80, but since his middle name is not given, he may belong to another Monsanto family (Cahen, *Les Juifs*, IV, 245; Bordier jeune, Not. Arch., January 23, 1779, May 10, December 26, 1780).

[29] The documentation of Manuel's partnership with Fastio is in Old Curaçao Archives, Algemeen Rijksarchief, 889, No. 187 (June 16, 1763): the claim of Johan Jacob Faesch upon them for 1,777 pesos. The information about the departure of Ester Rodrigues Fastio, then thirty-one years old, from Bordeaux, is in the Archives Départementales de la Gironde, Bordeaux, Fonds de l'Amirauté de Guyenne, 6B.52, f. 93-verso, dated April 21, 1757. It lists Ester erroneously as the wife of Abraham Rodrigues, while giving her name correctly as Ester Rodrigues Fastio, Fastio must have gone on ahead, decided it was worth staying in Curaçao, and then sent for Ester and the children, to be accompanied by her brother and the servant. The recording officer at the port probably assumed that the man heading the family on such a trip was the husband. The names and ages of the children in this document are Rachel (10), Sara (8), Judica (6), and Rebeca (2). Only Rachel's and Rebeca's birth records—with the names of the parents given correctly—have been located in the Bordeaux Archives Municipales' Register of Portuguese Jewish Births: Rachel, born February 14, 1747, is Act 194; Rebeca. born June 27, 1755, is Act 438. Fastio's death record, March 14, 1804, is in SLCFR, 1803–1807, f. 5. The earliest documented reference to Fastio in Louisiana which we have been able to locate is in *LHQ*, XXIII (1945), 620–21, dated May 24, 1766, an account of the sums involved in ventures by Fastio and Isaac Monsanto to Campeche and Saint-Domingue. Unfortunately, the Pointe Coupee business and real estate transaction records for the period prior to 1771 are lost, so we have no way of ascertaining when Fastio actually moved there from New Orleans.

[30] Terrage, *Last Years of French Louisiana*, 222–23.

[31] LSML, Doc. 66A/29, May 9, 1766.

[32] References to dealings with Gradis are in *LHQ*, XXIV (1941), 829–31, and in LSML, Doc. 8671–P (73090–2) and Doc. 8671 (73088). These relate to the years 1763 and 1764.

[33] Some of these locations are noted in *LHQ*, XXVIII (1945), 579 ff, the inventory of Monsanto financial papers which was made in 1785. This is based on some lists in the Cabildo which are badly damaged and poorly repaired. It is difficult to make sense out of the lists, especially the financial data, but the names of locations are clear. Other, scattered references appear: Saint-Domingue: *LHQ*, XXIV (1941), 219 (1761–62); 1192–93 (1763); St. Eustatius: LSML, 65A/78, 65A/79, relating to the disposition of a crate of merchandise worth 600 livres sent on consignment in 1763—this transaction brought one Rodriguez, probably another Jew, to New Orleans and Mobile for a brief time, after which he returned to the island.

[34] The inventory in *LHQ*, XXVIII (1945), 579 ff; also XXV (1942), 571–72.

35 *LHQ*, XXVIII (1945), 579 ff; IX (1926), 330. One wonders if Monsanto, Britto or another member of the Monsanto firm could have been the "very worthy little French Jew" who took a letter from Kaskaskia, in the Illinois country, for George Morgan of Philadelphia, and promised to "send it by the First Vessel to New York or Philadelphia," to Morgan's partners, after he reached New Orleans. The letter was dated July 11, 1768. As we shall see, Monsanto was in the Illinois country the next year; he may well have been there in 1768 as well. Clarence W. Alvord and Clarence Edward Carter, *Trade and Politics 1767–1769* (Springfield, 1921), 349. One of Monsanto's correspondents was Pierre Laclede (c. 1724–1778), founder of St. Louis, who was in New Orleans in 1755–63 and probably knew Monsanto there. Dr. John Francis McDermott of St. Louis reports that the inventory of Laclede's possessions included "une liasse contenant sa correspondance avec isaac Monsanto," but the papers have not been preserved. Both men were extremely important traders, and it was natural for them to have had business contacts and dealings.

36 This voyage resulted in many accusations and counter-complaints. The third member of the partnership, Captain Raoult, owner of the *San Juan Bautista*, was charged by the Monsanto correspondent in Vera Cruz, Don Francisco Xavier de Acosta, with many irregularities, among them the following: refusing to pay his share (three-eighteenths) of the expenses involved in obtaining a license (through bribery) to dispose of the cargo; tampering with cases of goods which belonged to a passenger on the ship, Don Carlos Ricardo, the recent chargé d'affaires of the Spanish at Pensacola; and failing to keep an accurate record of the cargo. D'Abbadie's share of the expenses and profits (which were expected to be very small because of the cost of the bribe and the duty on the imports) was five-eighteenths. Monsanto's share was ten-eighteenths; he was obviously the major factor in the venture. Ricardo was eventually fined for spreading malicious accusations against the Captain, and the dispute between Raoult and Monsanto was submitted to arbitration, the result of which does not appear in the extant records. The case was the occasion, however, for the first Louisiana imprint of Jewish interest. Monsanto's legal brief against Raoult was printed by Denis Braud, the official printer of the colony, in a twenty-page pamphlet which bears the superscription: "Réponse/ Du Sieur Monsanto & Compagnie, Armateurs du/ Senault le St. Jean Baptiste, Demandeurs./ Au Mémoire du Sieur Raoult, Capitaine Commandant ci-devant/ ledit Navire, Deffendeur." The pamphlet is dated July 16, 1765, and is signed by Doucet, Monsanto's attorney. One of the two known copies is in the Library of the University of Texas; it is No. 4—the fourth earliest piece of Louisiana printing listed in Douglas O. McMurtrie, *Early Printing in New Orleans 1764–1810* (New Orleans, 1929), 20, 88. D'Abbadie apparently left the proceeds of the voyage on deposit with Monsanto. In 1783, the Governor's widow, Maria Magdalena Harrenger Dumesnil Rolland, was still trying to collect the money from the syndics who had charge of Monsanto's property (*LHQ*, XXI [1938], 330–32); the claim had been dragging on since 1771. The data about the voyage are in LSML, Doc. 65A, no date, letter from de Acosta, Vera Cruz; Doc. 65A/4, January 5, 1765, receipt by Francisco Madera Paragero for 3,000 pesos to be delivered to Monsanto, in connection with a cargo of wood loaded on the ship

for its return voyage; Doc. 65A/6, January 5, 1765, giving details of the bribe; Doc. 65A/5, letter of de Acosta, January 25, 1765, listing further complaints. The exoneration of Raoult is summarized in *Publications of the Louisiana Historical Society*, VIII (1914–15), 15. D'Abbadie referred to the venture briefly in his journal (Terrage, *Last Years of French Louisiana*, 333): "The sieur Monsanto, a merchant in this colony, having presented a request to me covering plans for an expedition to Vera Cruz to import from there some of the European merchandise now super-abundant in that colony, I have all the more readily given him my consent for the reason that a unique opportunity arose here that supplied a pretext for this expedition to a Spanish possession. Don Carlos Antonio Ricardo having been sent away from [Pensacola] by the British government, without being given time to await the arrival of a ship to transport him home, has just arrived here. . . ."

[37] As examples, canvas, cordage, sails, wine, handkerchiefs, for a cargo to Saint-Domingue, in association with Isaac Fastio: *LHQ*, XXVIII (1945), 620; guns, *LHQ*, XXIII (1940), 599; lumber, LSML, Doc. 68/42, March 28, 1768; indigo, sugar and lime, *LHQ*, XXVIII (1945), 616; bullocks, *LHQ*, XXVIII (1945), 590.

[38] LSML, Doc. 68/102, March 28, 1768; Doc. 68/102A, May 21; Doc. 68/128, June 4. Other slave transactions are reported in *LHQ*, XXVI (1943), 256; LSML, Doc. 68/41, March 28, 1768.

[39] *LHQ*, VII (1924), 84 ff; Régine Hubert-Robert, *L'Histoire Merveilleuse de La Louisiane Française* (New York, 1941), x.

[40] *LHQ*, XXVIII (1945), 618–19. The building measured fifty-eight feet by one hundred and twenty, was built of brick, and was appraised at 3,400 pesos in 1785, but brought only 2,100 at auction because it had been neglected for years.

[41] LSML, Doc. 1957, September 10, 1766; Doc. 66/A107, November 7, 1766; Doc. 66A/133, November 8, 1766; Doc. 1982, November 8, 1766. Baptiste Manuel Monsanto is referred to in Doc. 66, September 9, 1766, not relating to the Lomère case. Robles was probably Jewish, though we have been unable to identify him with any precision. Eleanora, Jacob, Manuel and Benjamin may have been in New Orleans in 1766, but were not called to testify in this case probably because they were not present during Lomère's attack on Robles.

[42] *LHQ*, IX (1926), 329 f. The document itself in the Cabildo safe is undated, but obviously stems from the period after 1769. It reports that the inheritance amounted to 835 pesos, which was sent to New Orleans in merchandise which Isaac sold for their account for 1,095 pesos, which in turn was left on deposit with him. As we have indicated, the fact that the inheritance came to them in cargo probably proves that David did not die in New Orleans.

[43] *LHQ*, VII (1924), 732–33, records a mortgage given by Monsanto to Nicholas Adam in 1766.

[44] N. M. Miller Surrey, *The Commerce of Louisiana during the French Régime, 1699–1763* (New York, 1961), 107.

[45] LSML, Doc. 359, May 17, 1767, September 28, 1773; *WFP*, Vol. 602, pp. 389, 398–406, contains the tangled record of this case.

[46] John Fitzpatrick Letter Book, Manuscript Division, New York Public Library, April 13, June 10, June 26, July 12, July 17, August 4, September 2, 1769. Monsanto may thus have been the first Jew known to us by name to have visited, traded or worked in the "Illinois Country" in this early period, even if he was not the "little French Jew" of 1768 referred to in note 35 above. Eastern Jews like Joseph Simon and Levy Andrew Levy of Lancaster, and David Franks and the Gratz brothers of Philadelphia, played an active role in trading operations and land speculation beyond the Alleghenies beginning in the 1760's. After the occupation of present day Illinois and Missouri by the British, these Pennsylvania Jews participated in various schemes for the exploitation of the commercial potential of the area, but so far as we know, none of them actually traveled beyond Pittsburgh. Their interests were represented by partners who penetrated to the upper Louisiana territory. Edwin Wolf 2nd and Maxwell Whiteman, *The History of the Jews of Philadelphia from Colonial Times to the Age of Jackson* (Phila., 1957), 65–75, 177–80, is the best available summary of data about these merchants. The first permanent Jewish resident in the Illinois-Missouri area appears to have been Isaac Levy who had settled in Cahokia by February, 1780, at the latest. Levy was a merchant trader whose knowledge of medicine seems to have earned him some repute as a physician. There are many references to Levy's activities during the period 1780–88, in the published Cahokia records: Clarence W. Alvord, *Collections of the Illinois State Historical Library, Vol. II, Virginia Series, Vol. I, Cahokia Records, 1788–1790* (Springfield, 1907). It is possible also that Jewish traders came down from Canada to do business in the Illinois territory; one manuscript which has survived in the New Orleans Cabildo safe (brought to my attention by Winston De Ville), Sp. Doc. 1842, Box 51, records the presence in Kaskaskia of one Simon Nathan some time during the period 1781–88. He may be identical with the man of the same name who was in Montreal in 1769 (*JRBD*, 133). John Hays, who settled in Cahokia in 1793, served as sheriff of St. Clair County for a long period of time (*JRBD*, 58). Ezekiel Block was in the Cape Girardeau District by 1803, and members of the Philipson family settled in St. Louis by 1807 (Donald I. Makovsky, *The Philipsons, The First Jewish Settlers in St. Louis, 1807–1858* [St. Louis, 1958]). The Jewish history of the Kaskaskia/ Cahokia/ Fort de Chartres/ St. Genevieve settlements requires further diligent investigation. No shred of evidence has been found to support the fantastic tale of Jews who were tortured and burned at the stake by the French in the Illinois country as published in the *Chicago Inter-Ocean*, October 1, 1899, and unworthily reprinted by Max J. Kohler, "Some Jewish Factors in the Settlement of the West," *PAJHS* No. 16 (1907), 33–35.

[47] Clarence W. Alvord and Clarence Edward Carter, *The Critical Period, 1763–1765* (Springfield, 1915), 423 ff. Alvord and Carter spell the name "Mansanto."

[48] Ms. French copy in the Gage Papers, Clements Library, University of Michigan, photostat in AJA, docketed on the reverse, "Copy of a letter from Lieut. Alexr. Maclellan 34th Regiment to Monsr. Monsanto Novr. 10 1766." Another sheet accompanying this document certifies that "I received this as a Copy of a Letter to Mr. Monsanto and as near as I can recollect, it corresponded exactly with that produced to me before by Mr. McLellan from which this was reported to me to have been Copied. Pensacola 29th March 1767." The signature is H. W. Bayles.

The docketed date is, of course, in error; the negotiations were in November of 1765. But the copy may have been made in 1766 in connection with an investigation of the expedition, or, more likely, during the court-martial of Major Robert Farmar on charges of misappropriation of funds and other fiscal offenses, of which more later.

[49] Contemporary translation (original French letter not present), Gage Papers, photostat in AJA.

[50] Peter J. Hamilton, *Colonial Mobile* (Boston, 1897), 189; Cecil Johnson, *British West Florida 1763–1783* (New Haven, 1943), 50 ff; LSML, Doc. P. 80914–24, extract of the session of the Superior Council of June 7, 1766; *WFP*, Vol. 625, pp. 235–57, and Vol. 632, pp. 102–108, which contain the text of Farmar's petition and the minutes of the Council of West Florida meetings on February 20, 26, 28, 1765.

[51] Hamilton, *Colonial Mobile*, 189. Governor Johnstone had already written to General Gage about this episode in a letter dated January 2, 1765, Mobile: "Monsieur D'Abbadie wrote to Major Farmar requesting the Loan of some Flower [sic] for his troops. The Major wrote back he could not spare any of His Majesty's Provisions, nevertheless the Stores were almost drained, and the Flower sent by one Pallachio, a Jew, to be sold at New Orleans. But D'Abbadie had the spirit rather to give sixteen Dollars, a Barrel, to Mr. Irving, than ten to Pallachio, tho' they offered it at that price." *WFP*, Vol. 574, p. 303. Unfortunately, it has not been possible to discover the court-martial records in order to ascertain what answer Farmar and de Palacios offered to this accusation.

[52] *WFP*, Vol. 601, pt. 1, p. 55; Items 124, 125 and 126, ms. Judah Hays Receipt Book, Virginia Historical Society. On June 1, 1764, Solomons had written Hays from Pensacola to give £30 to Samuel Israel, who was already in New York (item 120), and on the same day he ordered Hays to deliver £6 to his brother Haym (item 121). This marks Haym's first appearance in relation to British West Florida; this Haym Solomons is not to be confused with the Revolutionary War patriot of the same name, as was done by Harold Korn in his article "Receipt Book of Judah and Moses M. Hays, Commencing January 12, 1763, and Ending July 18, 1766," *PAJHS* No. 28 (1922), 213–29. During this same period, Alexander instructed Hays to turn over another £250 to Jonas Phillips "an Insolvent Debtor" (item 123).

[53] *WFP*, Vol. 625, p. 225; Vol. 632, p. 98; Clinton N. Howard, *The British Development of West Florida, 1763–1769* (Berkeley, 1947), 59, 66. Howard prints a chart showing the location of the lots. Another building lot, number 76, and garden lot number 71, were granted in 1767 to Samuel Judah, but this is the only reference to this person in the entire corpus of West Florida Papers, and it has not been possible definitely to identify him with any member of the various Jewish Judah families then in North America. Any one of several Jews bearing that name, of the correct age, might have been in Pensacola in 1767 (*WFP*, Vol. 602, pp. 308–309, 326; Howard, *The British Development of West Florida*, 72; *JRBD*, 81).

[54] *WFP*, Vol. 625, p. 29; Vol. 632, p. 134.

[55] *WFP*, Vol. 574, p. 428; Vol. 586, pp. 330–31, 625; Vol. 601, pt. 2, pp. 312–13; Vol. 632, pp. 136, 147. The grant of 500 acres, originally awarded on January 7,

1766, was confirmed on March 2, 1767; it included "an old Spanish plantation about three miles to the Eastward of Oyster Point" (*WFP*, Vol. 584, pt. 2, p. 429; Vol. 532, p. 193). *PAJHS* No. 27 (1920), 248; Fondo Floridas, Legajo 9, No. 27, f. 16–17, Archives of Cuba. According to Dr. Isaac Emmanuel, Isaac Mendes had been in Curaçao in 1760–61, when he disposed of a plantation, and when his daughter Ester died (the daughter's death is noted in *Precious Stones*, 518, no. 1154; other references to this man are in Dr. Emmanuel's manuscript history of the Jews of Curaçao). The same or another Isaac Mendes was involved in the Manuel Monsanto-Isaac Fastio venture of June, 1763, which marks their last appearance in the Curaçoan records (see note 29 above). It would not be a surprise if these references were to four different men bearing the same name, or if they were all to one man. Mendes is a common Sephardic name, and colonial Jews were remarkably mobile, seeking opportunities throughout the area. That one man should appear consecutively in Jamaica, Albany, Curaçao, New Orleans and Pensacola would not be unusual.

[56] *WFP*, Vol. 602, pp. 116–21, 218–22; Strachan and Co. Letter-book, National Library of Scotland, Edinburgh, 17b. Other more transient Jews probably came to British West Florida from time to time. One of these was Rodriguez, of the firm of Julien and Rodriguez, from one of the Caribbean islands, who was in Mobile in 1763 or 1765, after doing business with the Monsanto firm in New Orleans (LSML, Doc. 65-A-79). Members of the Gratz consortium did not go as far from Pennsylvania as the Gulf ports, but two of their agents, Cornelius Bradford and Cornelius Tucker, were in Mobile and New Orleans in 1766 (William V. Byars, *B. and M. Gratz, Merchants in Philadelphia, 1754–1798* [Jefferson City, Mo., 1916], 1766).

[57] *WFP*, Vol. 623, pp. 43–45.

[58] Ms. account and receipt, April 28, 1765, British PRO, Treasury I, Bundle 440, p. 110, copies in LC and AJA; *WFP*, Vol. 575, pp. 1–4; Vol. 583, pp. 33–43, reprinted in Dunbar Rowland, *Mississippi Provincial Archives, 1763–1766: English Dominion* (Nashville, 1911), I, p. 306.

[59] Hamilton, *Colonial Mobile*, 235–36; *WFP*, Vol. 602, pp. 55–56, November 28, 1765, filed in Pensacola, January 8, 1766; *WFP*, Vol. 615, pp. 226–70; *WFP*, Vol. 577, p. 78; *LHQ*, XXIII (1940), 55–68. For Montberault, who lived at "Lis Loy" when he was an official of the French government in Mobile, and served the British for a brief time as adviser on Indian affairs, see *The Memoire Justificatif of the Chevalier Montault de Monberaut . . .*, Translation and Introduction by Milo B. Howard, Jr., and Robert R. Rea (University, Ala., 1965).

[60] *LHQ*, X (1927), 148–51. The transcriber of the document misunderstood the names of the partners and thought that the name of the firm, Israel, Solomons, de Palacios, was the name of one person, hence "Israel Solomon de Palacios!"

[61] It has been impossible to identify him with any assurance, although he was probably the Samuel Israel who appears in the records of Shearith Israel Congregation of New York in 1770, and was active in its affairs in 1783–86: *PAJHS*, No. 21 (1913), 107, 142, 148–49, 159. A Samuel Israel also appears in Isaac Moses'

receipt book, in New York City, on September 1, 1786; copy in AJA. It was probably the same Samuel Israel of New York City who, in 1786, was identified as the brother of Joseph Israel Levy who was living in Calcutta, India, in 1772, whose mother Rosey Israel was still living "in Houndsdetch near algate London," and who had other brothers and sisters living in London. If so, this Samuel Israel appears to have returned to London during the late 1780's. Leo Hershkowitz, *Wills of Early New York Jews (1704–1799)* (New York, 1967), 161–64, 186–88.

[62] *WFP*, Vol. 580, pp. 171, 282; Vol. 595, pt. 3, pp. 784–815.

[63] *WFP*, Vol. 612, pp. 236–41; *WFP*, Vol. 615, pp. 477–79, 480–85; NCC, Book D, 539.

[64] Barnett A. Elzas, *The Jews of South Carolina* (Phila., 1905), 91, lists him as one of fifteen Jews among 300 Charlestonians who signed a petition addressed to General Lincoln. On August 4, 1785, he married the widow of Nathan Harriss of St. Eustatius, in Charleston; the press report identified him as a "factor and grocer . . . of the Portuguese nation:" Elzas, *Jewish Marriage Notices . . . of Charleston* (New York, 1917), x. His son by a previous marriage, Joseph de Palacios, Jr., was old enough to be listed in city records separately from his father: Elzas, *South Carolina*, 278. In 1786, the father participated as an important communal leader in the laying of the cornerstones of the wall around the new Jewish cemetery in Charleston: Elzas, *The Old Jewish Cemeteries* (Charleston, 1903), 103. Charles Reznikoff and Uriah Z. Engelman, *The Jews of Charleston* (Phila., 1950), 37, refers to the oath of allegiance.

[65] Elzas, *South Carolina*, 98. He is listed as a vendue master in the Charleston City Directory for 1801. The Mesne Conveyance Office of Charleston has the deed in Book M6, p. 190, of the sale by Solomons and a partner, on February 2, 1795, of a plantation in Christ Church Parish. Haym's will is in the Charleston County Probate Court, Will Book D, 164, copy in AJA. There is an Alexander Solomons who appears in the Charleston congregational records for 1802 (Elzas, *South Carolina*, 139), but it seems unlikely that he was our man, since he was not referred to in Haym's will of the previous year.

[66] Another Jew whose business visit to New Orleans was recorded was David Mendes France, probably a member of the well-known family which ultimately gave a Premier to the home country. Mendes France was in New Orleans in May, 1765, in a dual capacity, as captain of the vessel *Le Magnifique*, and as mortgagee of another ship, the *Saint Pierre*, which was also in port. He and the *Saint Pierre*'s captain, Pierre L'Eglis, appeared in court to establish the conditions of the loan—that it was for twenty-five percent of the value of the ship, and that losses or profits were to be shared proportionately by the two men. The division of profits and the repayment of the loan were to take place after the ship's return to Saint-Domingue. *LHQ*, XXIV (1941), 215–16.

[67] *LHQ*, XXIV (1941), 221–26.

[68] Doucet, Monsanto's attorney in 1765, was one of the rebels. He was sentenced to ten years in prison and confiscation of property but was freed within a year:

David K. Bjork, "Alexander O'Reilly and the Spanish Occupation of Louisiana, 1769–1770," *New Spain and the Anglo-American West* (*Historical Contributions Presented to Herbert Eugene Bolton*) (Lancaster, Pa., 1932), I, 172.

[69] John Fitzpatrick Letter Book, September 1, 7 (letters to Alexander McIntosh and Robert Barrows), 11, 20, 21, 1769 (letters to John Bradley and McIntosh). Fitzpatrick's reports help to clarify the daily tightening of the noose; the writer has been unable to discover any other sources which can cast light on the situation of the merchants who were affected by O'Reilly's orders. Indeed, neither Fitzpatrick's nor any other British merchant's name appears in any O'Reilly dispatches or reports which we have seen.

[70] This is the only time that the name Mets appears in reference to Monsanto and de Britto. The name is nowhere to be found in the records of the Monsanto commercial affairs which have been published in *LHQ* or which we have been able to examine in the safe at the Cabildo, or in any other records. Mets, or rather Metz, was the name of eighteenth century Ashkenazic Jews in France who obviously took their name from that of the city. The closest non-Jewish name which has been found in Louisiana records is Meitz (Susanne), which occurs in the SLCMR, 1731–33; *NOG*, September, 1966, p. 303. Mrs. H. L. Forsyth has been good enough to search the other marriage registers for a recurrence of the name, unsuccessfully. Another name which may be Metz, Mitz or Matz (Anne Barbe), is recorded in the marriage register of the "Little Red Church" at Destrehan, for 1739 (*NOG*, January, 1966, p. 52). It has occurred to the writer that the name could conceivably be a mistake for Mendes—perhaps the ubiquitous Isaac Mendes.

[71] Nothing specific is known about Britto even though he had been associated with the Monsanto family since early 1757, first in Curaçao, then, after 1763, in New Orleans. We have discovered no separate reference to him; every time his name is mentioned, he is connected with the Monsanto firm. Britto, or de Britto, was a fairly common Sephardic name in Great Britain, and in Curaçao and other Caribbean settlements, but it is a curious coincidence that one Moseh de Souza Britto was a member of Honen Dal Congregation in The Hague at the time of its merger with Beth Jacob (Pimentel, *Portugesche Israelieten*, 81). Perhaps Manuel de [Souza?] Britto joined the Monsanto family when they left The Hague. Equally peculiar is Manuel de Britto's total disappearance from view immediately following the expulsion. He did not go with the Monsanto family to Pensacola, or at least his name appears in none of the British West Florida Papers.

[72] Lawrence Kinnaird, *Spain in the Mississippi Valley 1765–1794* (Washington, 1949) (Annual Report of the American Historical Association, 1945), pt. 1, xxi–xxiii, 96–99, quoting AGI, Santo Domingo, legajo 80–1–7, October 17, 1769, No. 3, transcription in LC, p. 2. Kinnaird misspells the name "*N*onsanto." Among the other merchants who were expelled were the Durand brothers who had been involved with Monsanto in the order for eighty slaves in 1768.

[73] Kinnaird, *Spain in the Mississippi Valley*, pt. 1, p. 103.

[74] *WFP*, Vol. 587, pt. 1, pp. 13 f. Captain Philip Pittman, one of the instigators of the charges against Major Farmar, wrote in his 1770 memoir that ". . . other

orders were given out, by which all the English subjects, protestants, and Jews of every nation, were enjoined to depart from the province of Louisiana, and all commerce prohibited, except with old Spain and her islands. . . ." Frank Heywood Hodder, ed., *Pittman's Mississippi Settlements* (reprint of the 1770 edition) (Cleveland, 1906), 55.

75 AGI, Santo-Domingo, legajo 80-1-7, labeled October 17, 1769, No. 3, typescript in LC. These words are translated with only slightly different variations in Kinnaird, *Spain in the Mississippi Valley*, pt. 1, p. 103, and Bjork, "Alexander O'Reilly," 173.

76 AGI, Cuba, legajo 188, reel 2, LC, brought to our attention by Winston De Ville.

77 According to Fitzpatrick, some of these went back to France (Letter Book, May 31, 1770).

78 *LHQ*, IX (1926), 330; VII (1924), 732. Forstall had been associated with Monsanto in a business deal in 1768 and acted as his security: LSML, Doc. 68/41. It goes far beyond our purpose to attempt to evaluate the activities of all the merchants who were expelled, but this would be an important and revealing investigation.

79 *LHQ*, IX (1926), 329-35; XXVIII (1945), 579-91, 615-29.

80 Herbert Eugene Bolton, *Athanase de Mézières and the Louisiana-Texas Frontier, 1768-1780* (Cleveland, 1914), I, 151-52.

81 In anticipation of just such conditions as these, Whitehall had instructed Gov. Browne on July 17, 1769, that he should "avoid all Appearances whatever of inviting or encouraging [the] Migration [of French settlers who objected to Spanish rule]. But, as all His Majesty's Colonies have ever been open to Strangers of every Country, who have been desirous of settling therein, you are not to refuse reasonable Protection to such persons, as may voluntarily and without Invitation come from New Orleans to West Florida." *WFP*, Vol. 586, pp. 151-52. Obviously the British were hopeful that they would be able to add new settlers to their thinly populated Province through the harshness of O'Reilly's edicts.

82 *WFP*, Vol. 612, pp. 92-94. The deed was not recorded until August 19, 1770. This may, therefore, mean that the interest on the debt was back-dated, and that Isaac had not arrived in Pensacola quite as early as January. Monsanto still owed Waugh £90, 8½ pence of the debt in December, 1771; he had apparently sent a bill of exchange for that sum to London, but it was protested, and now he had to mortgage another slave, Fanchonet, to Waugh's agents, not only for the principal sum, but also for interest and damages.

83 *WFP*, Vol. 612, p. 48. George Urquhart and John Falconer were the witnesses.

84 AGI, Cuba, legajo 188-1, no. 48, quoted in Bolton, *Athanase de Mézières*, I, pp. 177-78.

85 Manuel did possibly buy some tobacco in Natchitoches the next year: on July 28, 1771, "253 twists of tobacco of Natchitoches, belonging to Jacob Moncento [sic]" were in dispute and were sold at auction in Pointe Coupee (Book 1771-72,

Doc. no. 437, Pointe Coupee Parish records, New Roads, La., brought to our attention by Winston De Ville).

[86] Fitzpatrick Letter Book, November 7, 1769; May 31, 1770.

[87] Fitzpatrick Letter Book, August 30, 1770; February 7, 1771; July 7 (a specific reference to Jacob), October 22, 1773; February 11, 1778; January 26, July 28, 1781. The final reference to the Monsanto brothers in Manchac in 1781 reflects the loss of commercial significance for the settlement. The Spanish had captured it from the British in September, 1779 as one phase of their participation in the Revolutionary War, a very convenient excuse. Manchac's major significance was as a center of illegal trade between the British and their French and Spanish neighbors.

[88] *WFP*, Vol. 612, pp. 206–207, 218–21, 258–61; Vol. 613, pp. 63–65, 147–48; Gage Mss., 237–39. Monsanto said that he was enclosing a letter for General Gage with this message, but that letter cannot be found.

[89] *LHQ*, XXVIII (1945), 586. Some of this information is from Prof. Kenneth Trist Urquhart, a direct descendant of Angélica and George Urquhart, Dean and Associate Professor of History at St. Mary's Dominican College in New Orleans. Prof. Urquhart has been extremely generous in sharing all of his knowledge of Urquhart family traditions, and the results of his own research into his family's background. The presumption is that the wedding was performed by the Anglican chaplain at Pensacola.

[90] Details of the marriage contract in *LHQ*, XVII (1934), 393. "J. Monsanto" is listed as a witness. This was probably Joseph, the brother who lived in Saint-Domingue, though it may also have been Jacob. Charles André's date and place of birth are given in Davis, *The Story of Louisiana*, IV, 141.

[91] *LHQ*, IX (1926), 329 gives a brief summary. These quotations are from a translation of the original document, in the Cabildo safe, made available by Mrs. Connie Griffith of the Tulane University Library.

[92] Fitzpatrick Letter Book, December 26, 1773.

[93] *WFP*, Vol. 613, pp. 392–93; Garic, Book for 1774, pp. 234, 238, NONA.

[94] The 1774 data are in *WFP*; the June 10, 1775, letter is in the Oliver Pollock Papers, LC, all provided by Prof. Urquhart.

[95] Pointe Coupee Parish, Office of the Clerk of Court, New Roads, La., Colonial Records, Book for 1778, pp. 918 ff, summarized by Winston De Ville.

[96] Perdomo, Book VIII, 408, 481, September 6, 15, 1786, NONA. Clara was probably the daughter of the Selomoh Motta whose wife Ribca Hana died on December 30, 1765 (Emmanuel, *Precious Stones*, 506); if so, she was a few years older than the New Orleans record indicates.

[97] Quiñones, Book V, 107 ff (the pages are misnumbered, but there are ten), February 15, 1787; Perdomo, Book IX, 118, February 21, 1787; Book XIV, 374, July 24, 1789, NONA.

98 SLCMR, 2, p. 52, February 27, 1787.

99 Roger Baudier, *The Catholic Church in Louisiana* (New Orleans, 1939), 210–12, 217–18.

100 Samuel S. Forman, *Narrative of a Journey down the Ohio and Mississippi in 1789–90*, With a Memoir and Illustrative Notes by Lyman C. Draper (Cincinnati, 1888), 56. Forman makes it abundantly clear that the Monsantos enjoyed the highest possible social position in Natchez: they, and a few other "families in town and country, formed our principal associates," together with "Governor Gayoso, [who] was very affable and pleasant. . . ."

101 *LHQ*, XXVII (1944), 86.

102 SLCFR, 1793–1803, p. 16. This death record contains the correct information that Benjamin was born in The Hague; the tombstone, on the other hand, as transcribed in LSML, reads "Don. Benj. Monsanto/ native of Spain, husband of Dona Clara Motau/ son of Don David Monsanto and Dona Ester Levis/ died Sept. 30, 1794 age 40." Don Francisco Gutiérrez de Arroyo, royal inspector in Natchez, wrote to Governor Gayoso: ". . . after nine days of difficulty on the river I arrived here day before yesterday in good health though unable to go out today because the short shoes have crippled my feet so much that I was unable to attend the funeral of Don. Benjamin Monsanto which took place this afternoon, and he died before I was able to see him since I arrived;" AGI, Cuba, legajo 47, brought to my attention by Dr. Jack Holmes.

103 Pedesclaux, Book XXII, 860, September 29, 1794, NONA.

104 NCC, E, 481–82, records the award of property which had belonged to Jacob Monsanto, to Scott as the husband of Clara, on March 30, 1804. Very little information is available about Scott. He was apparently new in the Natchez area when his brother Robert died, October 21, 1796, for Robert's will specifies a legacy for William so that he might become established in the town. A Rev. McLennan was a brother-in-law of Robert Scott; this probably indicates that the family were Protestants. NCC, Book C, 433–34. Scott's chief appearances in the Natchez legal records relate to his claims on behalf of his wife for lands which had been owned jointly by Benjamin and Jacob: NCC, Unrecorded Land Claims, 565–66. Scott had died before August 24, 1814, if he was the William Scott whose heirs owed taxes on 400 acres in Wilkinson County, Miss. (Natchez *Mississippi Republican*, January 18, 1815).

105 SLCFR, 1793–1803, p. 108. The child, whose name is not revealed in this record, was buried in New Orleans on April 6, 1802.

106 SLCFR, 1820–24, p. 61; LHML cemetery card for Clara's age, probably understated.

107 SLCBR, 3, p. 69b; the child was born on March 28, 1797, and named for her mother, Marie-Eulalie Tessier; the father was Pierre Roques, "a native of [Montauban] in the Province of Languedoc." SLCFR, 1793–1803, p. 45.

108 Francisco Broutin, Book VII, 83, NONA; SLCFR, 1784–93, p. 31.

[109] *LHQ*, XXVIII (1945), 617.

[110] St. Gabriel Church Baptismal Book, reference supplied through the kindness of Mrs. Elizabeth Becker Gianelloni.

[111] SLCFR, 1784–93, p. 20.

[112] Francisco Broutin, Book XI, 56, March 8, 1792; Ximenez, Book for 1795, p. 112, February 23, 1795, NONA.

[113] SLCFR, 1793–1803, p. 32.

[114] Leonard V. Huber and Guy F. Bernard, *To Glorious Immortality, The Rise and Fall of the Girod Street Cemetery* . . . (New Orleans, 1961), 36; *The Reminiscences of Bishop Chase* (New York, 1844), I, 73; reference to the prayer book is from Prof. Urquhart; B. Lafon, *Annuaire Louisianais* (New Orleans, 1808), 191.

[115] Will Book No. 4, pp. 15–17, NOPC.

[116] Huber and Bernard, *To Glorious Immortality*, 36; photograph on p. 20.

[117] The stone is in the possession of Dean Kenneth Trist Urquhart. The quotations from the eulogy are on pp. 3b, 4a and 4b of the mss., which Prof. Urquhart has loaned to the Mss. Division, Tulane University Library. One wonders if the General knew that Angélica's family was Jewish. He refers on p. 2a to Isaac's banishment as follows: "Mr. Isaac Monsanto was on a frivolous pretext banished from Louisiana and sought refuge in the then British Province of West Florida at Pensacola."

[118] SLCMR, 1, p. 114; the document does not contain any reference to a "public abjuration of their errors" as in the case of Benjamin's marriage record, and here the wedding joined together a Jewess and a Protestant! There was, of course, no way in which a Protestant could be married in New Orleans, other than in a Roman Catholic ceremony.

[119] St. Francis Church Register II, 221, Dept. of the Archives, Diocese of Baton Rouge, through the kindness of Mrs. Drouet W. Vidrine and Mrs. Elizabeth Becker Gianelloni; SLCMR, 2, p. 37, May 19, 1785. The marriage record gives the bride's name as Isavel, which is probably identical with the Elizabeth of the baptismal document. The baptismal certificate is the only colonial church record thus far discovered in which reference is made to a person as a Jew. Since Elizabeth's parents were not listed as being present at the baptismal service, as was customary, we may assume that they did not become converts. She died on February 27, 1796 (SLCFR, 1793–1803, p. 30); in this document her husband's name is given as "Jorge Roquembourg!"

[120] The earliest date is July 24, 1772; other dates are November 2, 1772; March 3, September 27, 1773; December 9, 1777. *WFP*, Vol. 610, pp. 125–27; Vol. 630, pp. 7b, 80, 140, 141b; Vol. 634, pt. 1, pp. 5, 68, 90, 148. Topham had probably come to West Florida shortly before the first application for a land grant.

[121] Fitzpatrick Letter Book, December 19, 1776; July 3, 1777; October 14, 1780.

[122] Pointe Coupee Parish, Office of the Clerk of Court, Colonial Records, Book 1778, p. 918.

[123] Judice Notarial Records, Donaldsonville, Ascension Parish Courthouse, Book A, 279-318, summarized by Prof. Urquhart.

[124] *NOG*, September, 1965, p. 362.

[125] Mazange, Book I, 408, June 9, 1780, NONA.

[126] Perdomo, Book IV, 412, September 22, 1784; Book V, 106, February 5, 1785, NONA.

[127] Francisco Broutin, Book VII, 83, December 8, 1790, NONA.

[128] *LHQ*, XVII (1934), 391-94. Benjamin Monsanto paid the expenses of the suit. The case was not finally decided until 1781. There are 55 pages of documentation relating to the suit, numbered 561-A, in the Cabildo safe.

[129] Mazange, Book IV, 784, August 8, 1781, NONA.

[130] Pedesclaux, Book XXIII, 457, May 28, 1795, NONA; SLCMR, 2, p. 101. Pierre Roques was a man of some substance and repute. In 1803 he signed the address of welcome to Laussat by citizens of New Orleans (reference to Archives Nationales, Colonies [Paris], C¹³ A⁵² f 200, from René J. LeGardeur, Jr.)

[131] *LHQ*, XX (1937), 364-65; *NOG*, June, 1962, p. 309; Davis, *The Story of Louisiana*, IV, 141; Dunbar Rowland, ed., *Official Letter Books of W. C. C. Claiborne, 1801-1816* (Jackson, Miss., 1917), VI, 252-53; 388-90 (Tessier's answer to Claiborne's for-the-record inquiry about the preparations for the defense of New Orleans prior to the British invasion). Davis, IV, 141, gives details of the civic activities of Eleanora's descendants in and around New Orleans.

[132] There are many references to Urquhart in the *WFP*. In regard to land grants and purchases, Vol. 591, under dates December 2, 1772, May 5, 1773; Vol. 603, No. 116; Vol. 607, pp. 10, 175 ff; Vol. 612, pp. 430-44; Vol. 613, pp. 315-17; Vol. 626, pp. 14b, 34-35; Vol. 630, pp. 9b, 78b, 87b; Vol. 632, pp. 159, 219, 235; Vol. 634, pt. 1, pp. 7, 43, 90, 98; see also Howard, *The British Development of West Florida*, 72, 90, 98; *NOG*, March, 1964, p. 178; June, 1965, pp. 268-69; September, 1965, p. 364. In connection with public service, *WFP*, Vol. 589, p. 115; Vol. 590, pp. 251-53; Vol. 591, p. 239; Vol. 634, pt. 1, p. 206; see also Mss. "Record of His Majesty's Sign Manuals or Book of Commissions," begun November 1767, copy in LC, 44. On business matters, *WFP*, Vol. 612, p. 594; Oliver Pollock Papers, LC, under dates February 25, April 3, May 5 and 17, 1775. The records of the Urquhart inventory are in the Judice Notarial Records, Ascension Parish Courthouse, Donaldsonville, which also contain many other references to George. Much of this material has been provided by Prof. Urquhart, with whom the writer has reviewed the Urquhart and Monsanto story. The quotation about his death is from a letter which George's mother wrote to Angélica, undated, in the Urquhart Papers, which also refers to the possibility of Angélica's going to Scotland.

[133] *LHQ*, XIV (1931), 132; see also XXII (1939), 891; Garic book for 1779, p. 603, December 16, 1779, NONA.

[134] Mazange, Book III, 377-80; Book IV, 778-79, September 22, 1781, NONA; SLCMR, 1, p. 114.

282

[135] Details of Dow's medical career are in John Duffy, *The Rudolph Matas History of Medicine in Louisiana* (Baton Rouge, 1958), I, 143 ff, 163, 169, 181, 270 (the quotation from Gayarré), 306 (Claiborne's tribute), 312 and 491. The Claiborne offer is in *Official Letters*, II, 374, dated October 10, 1804; it is also noted in Clarence Edwin Carter, *The Territorial Papers of the United States*, Vol. IX, *The Territory of Orleans, 1803–1812* (Washington, 1940), 277, 346, where Dow is mentioned as "highly respected." At the same time the Urquhart brothers were considered for the post of Federal Marshall (308). Carter, 987, 1014, refers to Dow's service on the boards of the Charity Hospital and University, both in New Orleans. Duffy reports that Dow was a founder of the College of Orleans, and president of the first New Orleans medical society, 1822. Dow testified in regard to his activities, "I arrived in this country from the West Indies in September 1776. I settled in the practice in New Orleans in 1778, and was shortly after appointed by General Galvez, physician to the hospital. I continued in this station til the year 1785, when I left the country, and returned in 1786, since which time I have resided here as a practitioner. I have also during the said period, been consulted by the Spanish government, as to the causes and means of arresting certain diseases which have appeared in their hospitals. . . ." Deposition by Dow, August 23, 1810, printed in *Memoirs of My Own Times By General James Wilkinson* (Phila., 1816), II, Appendix CIX, unnumbered page.

[136] Wilkinson, *Memoirs*, II, 109; eulogy ms., 4b; René J. Le Gardeur, Jr., *The First New Orleans Theatre, 1792–1803* (New Orleans, 1963), 18; *NOG*, March 1964, p. 117.

[137] Angélica's will is in Will Book No. IV, 15–17; NOPC. The quoted letter from Dow to the boys is dated New Orleans, June 17, 1821, a copy of which is in the Urquhart Papers, Tulane University—written at a time when Angélica was ill, it discusses the division of property on which Dow and his wife had agreed, together with the estimate of their net worth, and submits these decisions to her sons. In 1789 Dow had invested in Natchez real estate, probably at Benjamin's suggestion; the property was sold shortly before Benjamin died: NCC, Book B, 539; Book C, 146–47. Some slave transactions during the earlier period of their married life are in the following notarial records: Francisco Broutin, Book VII, 101, December 20, 1791; Book XV, 225, 296, July 4, September 24, 1792; Book XXVI, 234, February 26, 1794; Book XXX, 63, March 14, 1794; Book XLVI, 197, September 4, 1797; Francisco and Narciso Broutin, 33, February 6, 1799; Pedesclaux, Book II, 179, February 14, 1788; Book IX, 240, March 23, 1790; Book XXXVI, 107, March 1, 1800, NONA. Other business matters are treated in Pedesclaux, Book III, 446, April 4, 1788; Book XIV, 365, June 16, 1792; Book XVII, 419, May 24, 1793; Book XXIX, 92, 136, February 15, March 22, 1797; Book XXX, 478, August 24, 1797; Francisco Broutin, Book XXX, 63, 262, March 14, October 2, 1794; Book XL, 318, December 31, 1796, NONA. In some of these transactions, Dow acted as attorney or executor for others, indicating the trust which was placed in him by his friends. Quiñones, Book I, 96, September 1, 1779, NONA, is an example of many cases in which he appeared as a physician at the request of the court. AGI, Cuba, in Havana, includes a document, dated December 9, 1786, in which Dow requests a grant of 40 arpents of land for Angélica, to replace an

Urquhart piece of land on which some Acadians had been settled. A copy of this document was obtained from Cuba by a friend whom I am unable to name because of the present political situation. The citation about Dow's trip to England in the first sentence of the paragraph is from this document.

138 Fitzpatrick Letter Book, May 23, 1785. On May 31, Dow gave Angélica his power of attorney; Perdomo, Book VI, 374, NONA.

139 The slaves were bought and sold on July 7 and 23, 1800 (Pedesclaux, Book XXXVII, 443, 463, NONA). The quotation from the Rush commonplace book is in George W. Corner, *The Autobiography of Benjamin Rush* (Princeton, 1948), 252–53. The July 8, 1802, letter is in the Urquhart family papers at Tulane. Madame Miró was the widow of Esteban Miró, Governor of Louisiana, 1782–1791. Baron Joseph Xavier Pontalba (1754–1834) had made a fortune in New Orleans real estate before retiring to Paris in 1797; the Pontalba family estate was Château Mont l'Evêque (Leonard V. Huber and Samuel Wilson, Jr., *Baroness Pontalba's Buildings* [New Orleans, 1964], 22–23). Dow's reference to the New Orleans climate is in Duffy, *History of Medicine in Louisiana*, I, 143, 270. Narciso Broutin, Book I, 157, June 22, 1799, NONA, contains a copy of Dow's power of attorney to his brother. Some fine tributes to the character of Angelica's son Thomas Urquhart appear in Carter, *Territorial Papers*, IX, 97, 869–70. In the latter, dated March 4, 1810, Governor Claiborne says that Urquhart "is a well informed Merchant, in High Credit, & enjoying an independent fortune;—He is President of the Louisiana Bank, & of the New-Orleans Insurance Company; he is also a Member of the House of Representatives of the Legislature.—Mr Urquhart supports a most amiable Character in private life, & discharges with great fidelity the public Trusts reposed in him. . . ." Angélica had good reason to be grateful for the accomplishments of both sons; some of the credit must be accounted to her and to Dr. Dow.

140 Manuel's will is in Carlos Ximenez, Book IX, 112, February 23, 1795, NONA; Gracia's, Francisco Broutin, Book VII, 83, December 8, 1790, NONA; Benjamin's, Pedesclaux, Book XXII, 860, September 29, 1794, NONA. There is some confusion in the wills over the names, but it is clear from the antenuptial agreement in the Pardevani Not. Arch., November 30, 1788, Outre-Mer-Section, Archives Nationales, Paris, that Judith was married to Moïse Julien or Julian and that their son, Abraham, was about to marry Rachel Lopes Dias, "niece de Salomon Madoura, fille de feu sieur Abraham Lopes Dias et de demoiselle Lia Madoure, veuve en secondes noces de Josué Depinis." Gracia and Manuel both speak of Rachel in their wills as though she were Judith's daughter rather than daughter-in-law. Rachel's father, Abraham de Jacob Lopes Dias, who had been an active member of the Jewish community of Curaçao, serving as building inspector in 1764–65 and chairman of the synagogue school in 1751, died at sea in 1775. He had been married to Rachel's mother (his third wife), Lea de Moses de Isaac Levy Maduro, on September 18, 1768 (Emmanuel, *Precious Stones*, 502 ff, in which the Lopes Dias family genealogy may be traced).

141 Fitzpatrick Letter Book, May 31, August 30, 1770; February 7, 1771; July 7, October 6, 22, 1773; February 7, 1778; January 26, July 28, 1781. In *The Favrot*

Papers, 1769–1781 (New Orleans, 1941), III, 6, a deed for the sale of a slave by Manuel to Don Pedro Favrot, dated February 19, 1782, is given in full; Manuel is called "vecino de Puesto de Manchac," indicating that the Monsanto firm's headquarters were still in that captured post. This is, however, the last such reference.

142 *WFP*, Vol. 634, pt. 1, p. 4, Council meeting held on July 24, 1772.

143 For these developments, see Jack D. L. Holmes, "Some Economic Problems of Spanish Governors of Louisiana," *Hispanic American Historical Review*, XLII (1962), 521–43, and Holmes, *Gayoso, The Life of a Spanish Governor in the Mississippi Valley, 1789–1799* (Baton Rouge, 1965), 77–84. Some of the official Spanish communications, promising that American settlers coming to the Spanish dominions from Kentucky and northern Mississippi "will not be molested in religious matters, although no other public worship will be permitted to be publicly exercised than that of the Roman Catholic Church," dating from 1789, are in D. C. and Roberta Corbitt, "Papers from the Spanish Archives . . . 1783–1800," *East Tennessee Historical Society's Publications*, No. 20 (1948), 104; No. 21 (1949), 89–90.

144 AGI, Santo Domingo, legajo 2582 (LC photostats, 86–7–19, 289–304), reviewed for me by Dr. Jack D. L. Holmes.

145 *WFP*, Vol. 634, pt. 1, pp. 236–37, Council meeting of March 4, 1775.

146 *WFP*, Vol. 634, pt. 2, p. 383, Council meeting of September 5, 1776. The deed was signed by Governor Peter Chester on December 29, 1777 (*WFP*, Vol. 608, p. 362).

147 Account for September 27 and October 3, 1776, submitted on February 10, 1777, Oliver Pollock Papers, LC; *Favrot Papers*, II, 104; *WFP*, Vol. 612, p. 375, dated October 11, 1773; George Urquhart inventory, Judice Notarial Records.

148 Fastio finally recovered only 846 pesos, 4 reales from the much larger sums which Isaac Monsanto owed him from their joint ventures in 1766, documented in *LHQ*, XXVIII (1945), 620–21, 629; IX (1926), 333, 335. On September 5, 1780, Benjamin and Fastio were listed among Pierre Methode's creditors: *LHQ*, XIV (1931), 631–33. On February 23, 1781, they appealed to the Commandante of Pointe Coupee for help in collecting a debt from Pierre Le Doux (Pointe Coupee Parish Archives, New Roads, La., Office of the Clerk of Court, provided by Winston De Ville). The dissolution of partnership document is in the same records, under date of January 3, 1788, also provided by Mr. De Ville. Isaac Fastio died a pauper in 1804. His death record reported that he was "aged 78, a resident of this colony about 50 years, worth at one time a considerable amount, but lately reduced to privation . . . a native of Bordeaux . . ." (SLCFR, 1803–1807, 5, March 14, 1804). In 1794, Fastio was the third largest debtor to the Monsanto firm, owing $664.

149 *LHQ*, XXIII (1940), 332–34.

150 Rodriguez, Book V, 720, August 30, 1785; Perdomo Book IX, 40, January 24, 1787; Book X, 454, September 4, 1787; Book XVI, 492, September 24, 1790 (when the thirty-one slaves were paid for), NONA. In addition to the statistics cited above, thirteen slaves were bought and sold within the family.

151 I have been unable personally to search all of the Pointe Coupee records, but Winston De Ville and Sidney Villeré, who have worked in them extensively, have shared their notes with me. Detailed information about Benjamin's plantation to which the Fastio-Benjamin Monsanto partnership termination refers is not available to me. On February 19, 1787, Benjamin purchased 2 arpents of land, including a house and other buildings, from Simon Croiset for $1,300; this reference is from Mr. Villeré. The record of the 1784 purchase and 1785 sale is in NONA: Rodriguez Book IIa, 306, April 26, 1784; Book IV, 225, March 11, 1786. The first Natchez purchase is in NCC, Book A., 242, February 19, 1785.

152 *LHQ*, XXVII (1944), 861–915.

153 The precise date of the move to Natchez is not known, but it was probably about the time of the termination of the partnership with Fastio. During 1787 and 1788 Jacob, too, was buying land in Natchez, possibly for use by Benjamin, because some of it adjoined Benjamin's plantation: May 13, 1787 (NCC, Book A, 371); June 18, 1787 (NCC, Book A, 382); March 15, 1788 (NCC, Book E, 476); December 16, 1788 (NCC, Book B, 192).

154 NCC, Book E, 168, June 19, 1790; Book B, 504, June 1, 1791; Book C, 77–79, September 21, 1793. Jacob may possibly have moved to Natchez prior to Benjamin's arrival. He was busy selling slaves there in 1787–88, and in some of the deeds (for instance, NCC, Book B, 173, 174, 181, October 29, 31, November 12, 1788) refers to himself as "I, Jacob Monsanto, of this District, merchant. . . ." In 1786 Jacob was the court interpreter at the trial of another resident on the charge of treason (NCC, Book F, 92–95, August 4, 1786). In 1788 Jacob was appointed to the job of taking inventory and giving an appraisal for the estate of Christopher Thompson (NCC, Book D, 40, 44, November 13, December 6, 1788). Unfortunately Jacob's will cannot be discovered; therefore we cannot report on his holdings in the Natchez area. But his death record calls him a resident of the New Orleans parish of St. Louis Church. It is possible, however, that Jacob and not Benjamin was the first of the brothers to establish residence in Natchez.

155 David probably met his future bride while visiting his Uncle Benjamin. The two men witnessed Williams' will and were present at the reading: NCC, Book C, 177–78, April 7, 1792. David and Mary were married on November 17, 1803, when she was sixteen years old. David had already known her for at least eleven and a half years.

156 The description of the Natchez property and the inventory of its contents are in the estate papers, NCC, Book C, 315–31, beginning October 10, 1794; this file also contains the correspondence relating to the financial troubles of the firm.

157 NCC, Book C, 408.

158 NCC, Book F, 186–87. The decree is dated March 15, 1794, but no date appears on the creditors' petition.

159 NCC, Book C, 323–26.

160 NCC, Book C, 326–31.

[161] Pedesclaux, Book XXII, 860, September 29, 1794, NONA.

[162] NCC, Book D, 137, December 10, 1794; Book C, 408, June 17, 1792, July 22, 1796; Book B, 244, February 12, 1789, May 10, 1800; Unrecorded Land Claims, Nos. 1629, 1630; *Transcriptions of County Archives of Mississippi. Adams County. Vol. II: Minutes of the County Court, 1802–1804* (Jackson, 1942), cases numbered 5, 60, 140.

[163] Ximenez, Book IX, 112, February 23, 1795, NONA.

[164] Rosa's emancipation is in Francisco Broutin, Book XV, 181, May 29, 1792, NONA. The emancipation of Maimi is in Rodriguez, Book I, 729–30, August 4, 1783, NONA. Sophia's purchases of slaves and property are referred to in Ximenez, Book IX, 92, February 9, 1795; Narciso Broutin, Book I, 202, August 9, 1799; Pedesclaux, Book XXXVII, 637, October 27, 1800, NONA. *New Orleans in 1805. A Directory and a Census* (Heartman's Historical Series No. 48) (New Orleans, 1936), 49, lists Maimi as living at 64 Bienville and Sophie at 61 Bienville. Maymi William Monsanto's will and inventory are in NOPC, under date of April 8, 1817. Sophia, or Sophie, Monsanto outlived Angélica. The last record of her activity which has been traced is her purchase from Jacob Hart of five slaves in a transaction recorded in the Record Conveyance Office (Civil District Court) Book II, p. 36, on October 22, 1827.

[165] One of Angélica's sons spent the summer in Philadelphia in 1829 and he and his wife became friendly with Rebecca Gratz. We do not know which son this was, but cannot resist wondering whether Rebecca knew that Angélica Dow had been a Jewess. David Philipson (ed.), *Letters of Rebecca Gratz* (Phila., 1929), 101.

[166] The writer has been unable to discover who was originally responsible for the identification of these two men as Jews. The earliest, chronologically, thus far, is Rabbi Max Heller, *Jubilee Souvenir of Temple Sinai, 1872–1922* (New Orleans, 1922), 2, who has been followed by Leo Shpall, *The Jews in Louisiana* (New Orleans, 1936), 7; Lebeson, *Pilgrim People*, 114; and Samuel Proctor, "Jewish Life in New Orleans, 1718–1860," *LHQ*, XL (1957), 110–32. Perhaps Rabbi Heller, reading Gararré, *The History of Louisiana*, IV, 347–49, presumed that men bearing these names simply had to be of Jewish background.

[167] Data about Solis and Mendez in the production of sugar are in Henry Rightor, ed., *Standard History of New Orleans* (Chicago, 1900), 649–51; Alcée Fortier, *A History of Louisiana* (New York, 1904), II, 158; V. Allen Moody, "Slavery in Louisiana Sugar Plantations," *LHQ*, VII (1924), 198. Details of the Solis family's lineage are in *NOG*, June, 1962, p. 277; Almonester y Roxas, Book II, 155, July 29, 1771, NONA; SLCFR, 1793–1803, p. 54. H. L. Forsyth, who traces his family back to the Solis family, has gone over its genealogy with me in helpful detail.

[168] See Cecil Roth, *A History of the Marranos* (Phila., 1932), 271, for the general background of "new" Christians in America. *Limpieza* certificates were printed in Mexico as early as 1580 and as late as 1810. Proceedings in New Orleans in regard to *limpieza* certification are described in *LHQ*, XI (1928), 331–32; XVIII (1935), 200 ff; XIX (1936), 542 ff; *NOG*, January, 1965, p. 75; March, 1965, p. 127. See also the application of Lieut. Col. Nicholas Fabre Dauncy for a certificate for his

son Carlos so that the latter might join the "Spanish company of royal guard corps, which was organized for the benefit of the American nobility," in 1793, in *Dispatches of the Spanish Governors of Louisiana* (W.P.A. Survey) (Baton Rouge, 1939), IV, 149–63.

169 *LHQ*, XXIV (1941), 842–43.

170 *LHQ*, IX (1926), 333; XXVIII (1945), 615; Rightor, *Standard History of New Orleans*, 649–51. SLCCB, 70, records the confirmation of two of his children, and two slaves, in New Galvez, on February 12, 1797.

171 *Letter Books of W.C.C. Claiborne*, I, 372–73; II, 350–51, dated July 5, 1806, which contains another description of the case; IV, 147, November 28, 1807, the appointment of Mendez as Justice of the Peace for St. Bernard Parish; VI, 185, October 6, 1812, Mendez' resignation from that office. Under the regime of Governor Bernardo de Galvez, 1777–1784, large-scale immigration to Louisiana was encouraged. Among those who responded to the propaganda campaign and the practical inducements were large numbers of Canary Islanders. In 1779 alone, 499 Islanders came to the colony. Davis, *Louisiana, A Narrative History*, 110, 120, 130–31; Elizabeth Becker Gianelloni, *Love, Honor and Betrayal: The Notarial Acts of Estevan de Quiñones 1778–1784* (Baton Rouge, 1964), vi; Kinnaird, *Spain in the Mississippi Valley*, pt. 2, xxiii. Paradoxically, many of these Canariotes carried typical Sephardic "New" Christian and Marrano names; the records abound with family names like De Leon, Mendes, Rodriguez, Lopez, and the like: *NOG*, June, 1964, pp. 215 ff. Perhaps some of these people had been made to feel inferior because of their ancestry, back in the islands.

172 Francis Newton Thorpe, *The Federal and State Constitutions* (Washington, 1909), III, 1360, 1365, 1369, 1373–74.

173 Archives Départementales de la Gironde, Bordeaux, 3L–182 (October 27, 1795–March 22, 1796); 3L–184, Section 1 (March 22–May 22, 1796); references supplied by René J. LeGardeur. See also Z. Szajkowski, "Jewish Emigration from Bordeaux during the Eighteenth and Nineteenth Centuries," *Jewish Social Studies*, XVIII (1956), 121–22.

174 Archives Départementales de la Gironde, Bordeaux, 3L–184, Section 3 (July 12–September 21, 1796), through the courtesy of Mr. LeGardeur; see also Szajkowski, "Jewish Emigration from Bordeaux," 121. The name Manuel Diaz occurs in New Orleans and Natchez from 1789, but no evidence connects him with our Lopes Dias family (NCC, Book B, 265 ff; *NOG*, September, 1962, p. 37); four children of Jose and Maria Dias were confirmed in Ascension Parish on May 25, 1796 (SLCCB, 34).

[1] *Delta*, quoted in Leon Huhner, *The Life of Judah Touro* (Phila., 1946), 108.

[2] Dun and Bradstreet manuscript record books, Louisiana, Vol. 9, p. 273, entries for June, 1847 et seq., Baker Library, Harvard University.

[3] Dun and Bradstreet, Vol. 9, p. 31, entry for Alexander Levy & Co.

[4] Letters of Gershom Kursheedt to Rabbi Isaac Leeser of Philadelphia, December 18, 1848, May 2, 1849, May 3, 1853, in Leeser Collection, Dropsie College Library.

[5] *New York Herald*, June 18, 1855, cited in *PAJHS*, No. 27 (1920), 420–21.

[6] Jacob R. Marcus, *Early American Jewry* (Phila., 1951), I, 154–55; Isaac Touro mss. petitions, March 13, 1780, December 12, 1782, and list, dated September 30, 1782, naming refugees from Newport in New York City, Carleton Papers, William and Mary College, copies in AJA; Jacob A. P. M. Andrade, *A Record of the Jews in Jamaica* (Kingston, 1941), 51. Huhner, *Judah Touro*, 20, and Morris A. Gutstein, *Aaron Lopez and Judah Touro* (New York, 1939), 71 f, both seem reluctant to admit that the elder Touro was a Tory.

[7] Kursheedt to Leeser, January 25, 1854, Leeser Collection.

[8] Huhner, *Judah Touro*, 151, n. 19, gives a host of sources for the romantic episode, none earlier than the time of Touro's death. An undated clipping in the Virginia Historical Society reports that Rebecca was the object of Touro's affections; Leeser in *OCC*, X (1854), 589, indicates that he heard the story (probably from Kursheedt) on one of his visits to New Orleans, and he too thought the young lady was Rebecca. The letter from Catherine Hays Myers to Touro, dated January 4, 1854, is in the Virginia Historical Society, copy in AJA. Rebecca was almost six years older than Judah; Catherine was a year younger.

[9] *LG*, February 19, 1805.

[10] *LG*, March 12, 1805.

[11] Letter and account, December 7, 1809, Storer Collection, Massachusetts Historical Society.

[12] Ms. letter, Rhode Island Historical Society.

[13] Ms. letter, New York Public Library, reproduced in Huhner, *Judah Touro*, 29.

[14] Huhner, *Judah Touro*, 33–58, and the appropriate notes, offers some detailed data on Touro's business activities, but exaggerates their importance. The Thwing firm of Boston was Touro's agent from 1846 until his death. None of Touro's letters to them were preserved, but their letter books contain large numbers of reports to him. At the time of his death, he had $105,000 on deposit with them, which was invested in bonds, bank stocks, mortgages, notes and property in Maine. Early Touro advertisements are in *LG*, September 16, 30, November 15, 1806; March 3, 1807; November 11, 1808. *LG* references to Touro cargoes during 1820 are in the

issues of January 10, 25, February 2, 11, March 4, April 21, May 2, 6, 11, 16, 30, June 3, 10, 11, August 28, September 1, October 5, November 10, 22, December 1, 6, 15. Touro's purchase of the interest in the *Highlander* is in John Lynd, Book XII, August 4, 1815, NONA. *Ship Registers and Enrollments of New Orleans, La.* (WPA Survey of Federal Archives), Vol. I: 1804–1820 (Baton Rouge, 1941), contains the data on Touro's participation in the ownership of various vessels. Among his partners were Laurent Millaudon, R. D. and James H. Shepherd, and John A. Merle. Touro and R. D. Shepherd were co-owners of ships built and named for them. Altogether, he was associated with the ownership of twelve vessels over the years, but no more than a few at any one time.

15 New Orleans *Bee*, May 3, 1828; August 3, 1837.

16 *New Orleans in 1805. A Directory and A Census* (Heartman's Historical Series No. 48) (New Orleans, 1936), 70.

17 The inventory of the Touro estate is Act No. 3 in Thomas Layton, Book III, January 30, 1854, NONA, extending for forty-nine pages.

18 *OCC*, XI (1854), 590. Parson Theodore Clapp also testified to Touro's extremely modest manner of living, in the eulogy which he preached after Touro's death (*Asmonean* [New York], February 17, 1854).

19 *American State Papers. Documents in Relation to the Public Lands* (Washington, 1834), II, 269; Robert Lynd, Book XV, 972, December 10, 1818, NONA; Huhner, *Judah Touro*, 48–56; the contents of the relevant Thwing papers in the Massachusetts Historical Society.

20 It is worth noting that in August, 1803, when a report was drawn up for Governor Claiborne's guidance, listing the names of the principal persons in New Orleans, Creoles, foreigners and American citizens, Touro's name was not included, although his friend Shepherd's was: Carter, *Territorial Papers*, IX, 10–11.

21 Carter, *Territorial Papers*, IX, 290, 337.

22 *Natchez Gazette*, February 4, 1807.

23 *LG*, March 27, 1807.

24 *Orleans Gazette*, April 20, 1807; *LG*, April 27, 1807.

25 *LG*, February 5, 1812; *Moniteur*, February 8, 1812.

26 *LG*, January 3, 7, 1812; January 5, 1813; *Moniteur*, January 7, 1812. The results of the elections of 1814 and 1815 were not published. By 1816, Touro was no longer listed as a director. In 1819 he was recommended, together with others, for the board of the State Bank of Louisiana, but was not among those who were elected: *LG*, February 6, 9, 1819.

27 *Jackson and New Orleans. An Authentic Narrative of the Memorable Achievements of the American Army, Under Andrew Jackson, before New Orleans, in the Winter of 1814, '15* (New York, 1856), 267–72. Marion J. B. Pierson, *Louisiana Soldiers in the War of 1812* (Baton Rouge, 1963), 108, 117, lists Touro as a private in Dejan's First Regiment, and Shepherd as a private in Captain Ogden's Company of Dragoons. Documentation about the service of civilians in the battle is very scarce. Much of

what is known is derived from memoirs and reminiscences, rather than from official military records. There is no indication that Touro had previously been a member of the militia or that he had been trained for any military duties. To picture him as anything other than a civilian volunteer, doing whatever he could in the military emergency, is an unwarranted assumption.

[28] Touro's will is printed in full in Huhner, *Judah Touro*, 129–39, and in Morris U. Schappes, *A Documentary History of the Jews in the United States, 1654–1875* (New York, 1950), 333–41. The estimate of one-half million dollars is based on the assessed value of the estate in the manuscript inventory; Schappes (657) quotes a newspaper report which rates Shepherd's share at the higher figure.

[29] Some information about Shepherd has been supplied by Senator Saltonstall and the family genealogist, Louise Emerson Carlile of Chestnut Hill, Mass. During his period away from New Orleans, Shepherd maintained residences in Massachusetts and Virginia; his business affairs in New Orleans were apparently handled by James. Some material about the litigation over James's estate is in printed briefs by attorneys for Rezin's nieces and nephews against Rezin's daughter, dating from 1867, which I found in an old bookstore. I have been unable to locate a complete description of the issues and outcome of the case anywhere. The major importance of the case, for us, is James Shepherd's heavy indebtedness to Touro, and Touro's involvement as a witness on Rezin's behalf. In one of the briefs, which we have labeled "A", page 53, an attorney for the opposing side accuses Shepherd of sinister motives in "causing all his books and those of Judah Touro, one of the executors of J. H. S. [James H. Shepherd] of whom he had been the executor, to be burned." In another brief, labeled "C", page 32, Rezin Shepherd said in a letter of April, 1844, "I believe [I] would have given up all as lost, including my own ruin, had it not been for my inestimable friend Judah Touro, who came to my aid with all his force and power." The suggestion transmitted by Schappes, *Documentary History*, 657, and in his review of the Huhner book in *Jewish Life*, April, 1947, pp. 21–24, that Touro was reminded by a newspaper editorial which appeared a short time before his death, of Shepherd's devotion to him at the time of the Battle of New Orleans and that this was his motivation for his making Shepherd his residuary legatee, seems to be very far-fetched. The closeness between the two men over the long years demonstrates Touro's awareness of his indebtedness to his friend. New Orleans Directories list Shepherd as living in Touro's home in the 1840's and 1850's. The papers which refer to Shepherd's acting on Touro's behalf in the settlement of Abraham Touro's estate are in the Suffolk County Court records, Boston, transcriptions by Samuel Broches in AJA.

[30] Schappes, *Jewish Life*, April, 1947; *Jewish Messenger*, XXVI, October 1, 1869, p. 4. Parson Clapp said that Touro was invalided for twelve months after the battle, and that he always walked with a slight limp thereafter (*Asmonean*, February 17, 1854).

[31] *Autobiographical Sketches and Recollections during a Thirty-Five Year's Residence in New Orleans* (Boston, 1857), 102.

[32] Clapp, *Autobiographical Sketches*, 102, says explicitly that Touro "had just signed a document resigning his legal title to the entire estate of an only sister, recently

deceased. It was worth, if I remember aright, about eighty thousand dollars. He refused to take the smallest fraction of it, and requested his friends at the north to distribute it for charitable purposes. . . ." If the document ever existed, it is not now in the Suffolk County Court House in Boston with the other papers relating to Rebecca's estate. Rebecca's money had been her share of brother Abraham's residuary estate, which was divided equally between her and Judah. Judah's representatives were still selling Rebecca's property in 1840, after Rezin had returned to New Orleans.

33 Huhner, *Judah Touro*, 68, writes as though the building had actually been erected and served an important purpose. Roger P. McCutcheon, "Libraries in New Orleans, 1771–1833," *LHQ*, XX (1937), 152–58, offers a more factual report. Other data on the library are in *LG*, January 23, March 27, May 10, 22, 1824. As late as 1832, books belonging to the library were still kept in the church, according to *NOCD*, 1832.

34 *Bee*, October 13, November 15, 1830; June 25, 1831; November 6, 1832; May 7, June 24, 1838. The earliest public campaign for funds was in 1810, when subscriptions were solicited for the College of Louisiana. Touro was not among the donors. *Courier*, December 10, 1810, January 4, 1811.

35 Huhner, *Judah Touro*, 78–79, 162, gives the sources for the contributions to the Bunker Hill Monument and the Redwood Library; in the latter case, Touro's letter to the Library (November 27, 1843, in the Archives of the Redwood Library) acknowledges that Shepherd had already talked to Touro about the need for repairs to the portico of the Library's headquarters and to the sidewalk . . . it therefore seems probable that Shepherd had suggested to the Library that Touro be honored by election as a member, as an inducement for him to make the contribution. The amount of money paid for the Paulding estate is reported in the Touro estate inventory, January 30, 1854.

36 *Picayune*, January 4, 1852; *Delta*, January 6, 1852.

37 Huhner, *Judah Touro*, 69.

38 *New Orleans in 1805*, p. 70.

39 *LG*, December 23, 1808.

40 *LG*, September 8, 1812.

41 *LG*, August 25, 1823.

42 Schappes, *Jewish Life*, April, 1947, pp. 21–24, is quite correct in stating that there is no evidence that Touro was opposed to slavery, but he goes too far in blaming Touro for a pro-slavery sermon which Parson Clapp delivered, and, in general, for being himself used (after his death!) as support for the pro-slavery argument. It makes just as much sense to give Touro credit for the fact that the Touro Infirmary was open to slaves, following his death (*Spectrum* [New York], IX [1961], 113 ff, which reports that twenty-six of thirty-eight patients listed in the admission book of the Infirmary for August–September, 1856, were slaves).

43 The information about Ellen Wilson is in the Touro estate inventory. John Touro is listed in *NOCD*, 1855, 1856; he was also one of a number of New Orleans residents

who made claims on the Federal government during the Civil War (*Collected Works of Abraham Lincoln* [New Brunswick, 1953], VII, 492). That Judah and John Touro were not strangers, however, is indicated by a page in the Thwing papers, photostat in Broches Collection, AJA, which reveals that John Touro as "Ship Broker" took care of the agency for the ship *Judah Touro* when it was in New Orleans in December, 1856–January, 1857. It is difficult to believe that the names are coincidental, but John's name appears nowhere in Judah's will or estate papers. The report that Judah Touro freed Shepherd's slaves is in Alexander Walker's essay on Touro in Freeman Hunt, *Lives of American Merchants* (New York, 1858) II, 466.

[44] Robert C. Reinders, "The Free Negro in the New Orleans Economy, 1850–1860," *Louisiana History*, VI (1965), 279–80; reports in Dun and Bradstreet mss. records, through Professor James P. Baughman.

[45] Hunt, *Lives of American Merchants*, II, 448.

[46] It is unrealistic to suppose, as does Huhner (*Judah Touro*, 59), that any businessman like Touro could have avoided litigation. We have already cited a number of suits in which he was involved; another is listed in François-Xavier Martin, *Louisiana Term Reports*, I (New Orleans, 1824), 425–27. But it is true that he did his best to avoid them. In a letter of November 21, 1826, to Titus Welles of Boston (Washburn Collection, Mass. Historical Society), in reference to his brother's estate, Touro said, "I hate any *law Suit or Altercation* and wish to avoid them if possible. . . ."

[1] Davis, *Louisiana, A Narrative History*, 158.

[2] Our attention will be confined largely to the areas which were part of the economic market of New Orleans, although even those Jews who originally settled in Baton Rouge, which still belonged to Spain until 1810, ultimately moved to New Orleans. One interesting personage who lived a good deal farther away, near the settlement on the Arkansas River, was Louis Levy, who by 1803 had a farm of 750 arpents on the river about forty leagues above the village. On July 7, 1808, Maurice Fortnay testified, in connection with Levy's claim to the land, that "the premises were cultivated and Inhabited about 5 years ago, a dwelling house was then built, had a wife and one child" (*American State Papers*, II, 431; III, 317; ms. record of the same claim, from the Office of the Secretary of State of Missouri, Jefferson City). The claim was rejected in 1808 and 1811, but was reconsidered and granted on February 2, 1816, Levy still apparently being there at the time. Levy may have been in New Orleans at one time or another, but his closest trip on record was to Baton Rouge in August, 1808, when he bought an undershirt and two pairs of pantaloons at auction (*SWFP*, XIII, 154–56).

[3] Carter, *Territorial Papers*, IX, 289; 337 (another petition which Spitzer signed on November 22, 1804). Data on the father are in Jacob Rader Marcus, *Early American Jewry* (Phila., 1953), II, 151–52; Samuel Oppenheim, "The Jews and Masonry in the United States before 1810," *PAJHS*, XIX (1910), 42–43; JRBD, 166; Wolf and Whiteman, *Jews of Philadelphia*, 413. The Kursheedt family's genealogy is in *MSAJD*, 106.

[4] *LG*, June 21, 1805; April 11, May 20, September 9, 23, 26, 1806; May 8, 1807; *SC*, numbers 12, 25, 67, 68; *Le Télégraphe*, August 30, 1806; *New Orleans in 1805*, p. 45; *SWFP*, XI, 245–46; Henry Brown, Book for 1804–1806, June 2, 1806, NONA; *Courier*, February 8, 1830; *Bee*, June 8, 1832.

[5] At least two and possibly three other men in New Orleans bore the same name. One was Philadelphia-born Jacob Hart who served in Capt. Burt's Company of Florida Volunteers and who died May 26, 1836 (*Bee*, May 26, 1836). He may be identical with the Jacob Hart of New Jersey, who was listed as a deserter from the U. S. Army in 1816 (*LG*, September 16, 1816). A second or third Jacob Hart bore the middle name Moses; he was German-born, had been in Louisiana since 1806, and was a well-known police official (*Bee*, April 20, 22, 27, May 11, 1835). There is no evidence that any of these men were Jewish, or that any of them were engaged in commerce. To R.E.S. goes the credit for discovering our Jacob Hart. According to his obituary in *Crescent*, December 21, 1849, he had been "for the last 46 years a resident of this city"—but this would take us back to 1803, an error of a year. His tombstone card in LSML reports his date of birth as March 28, 1781; *MSAJD*, 71, gives it correctly as March 29, but reports his death in 1836 instead of 1849. The mss. Record of Interments in the Nefutzoth Yehudah Cemetery, Touro Synagogue Archives, copies in AJA, lists Jacob Hart as a non-member burial.

[6] David de Sola Pool, *Portraits Etched in Stone* (New York, 1952), 76, 78, 80, 102, 104, 358, 411–13; *PAJHS*, No. 21 (1913), 163–64, 167, 169; No. 27 (1920), 51, 54–55, 57–58, 66, 69–70, 83, 86, 253.

[7] John Lynd, Book I, October 27, 1805, NONA.

[8] The first of a large number of Hart's advertisements appeared in *LG* on April 29, 1806. *Ship Registers and Enrollments*, I, 107–108, reports his ownership of the schooner.

[9] Hart's business life is reflected, in miniature, in his dealings with the Hendricks firm of New York City. On May 12, 1809, he received a consignment of 25 boxes of spermaceti candles from Hendricks, on board the ship *Luminary*. Not finding an immediate purchaser at a fair price, Hart had to store them for a year; Hendricks then suggested that they be sold at auction, where they brought $379.29. Hart's charges and commission amounted to a modest $27.32. He sent the remittance to the Hendricks firm in the form of a bill of exchange on his father in New York City. This kind of transaction has to be multiplied a thousand fold in order to visualize the activity of a businessman like Hart at that time. Hendricks Letter Book, entries for May 12, 1809; May 9, June 25, 1810; letter, Hart to Hendricks, July 11, 1809 (Hendricks Collection, New-York Historical Society).

[10] *LG*, July 8, November 22, 1808; *SWFP*, Vol. 18, pp. 294–95. On November 3, 1809, de Armas had mortgaged a tract of land in Baton Rouge to Hart as security for a loan of 1,590 pesos. There is no indication that the two transactions were related. *SWFP*, Vol. 15, pp. 224–25.

[11] "Liste par ordre alphabétique, Des Négocians, Marchands, &c, &c, résidans a la Nlle—Orléans," *Annuaire Louisiananais Pour L'Année 1809 Par B. Lafon* (New Orleans, 1808), 209.

[12] *LG*, March 27, May 8, June 2, 1807; February 12, August 9, 1808; *Courier*, June 3, 1808; ms. petition, citizens of New Orleans to Jefferson, January 25, 1808, New-York Historical Society, copy in AJA.

[13] *LG*, January 6, February 20, 1807.

[14] Stanley Faye, "Louis De Clouet's Memorial to the Spanish Government, December 7, 1814," *LHQ*, XXII (1939), 802 ff; Faye, "Privateersmen of the Gulf and their Prizes," *LHQ*, XXII (1939), 1024; *SC*, No. 411; *Official Letter Books of W. C. C. Claiborne*, V, 7–13; *LG*, July 14, 1809; April 14, 1810; September 3, 1810. Dunbar Rowland, the editor of the Claiborne letters, misread Hart's signature on the letter of November 16, 1809, and transcribed it as "Jacob y Cart." The original correspondence, brought to my attention by René J. LeGardeur, Jr., is in the National Archives, Department of State, Territorial Papers, Orleans, Year 1809, ff. 304, 310, 387, 389, 391–92. Our transcription of the Hart letter differs in some minor details from that printed by Rowland, beyond his misreading of Hart's signature.

[15] Stanley Clisby Arthur, *Jean Laffite, Gentleman Rover* (New Orleans, 1952), 222–23; Jane Lucas de Grummond, *The Baratarians and the Battle of New Orleans* (Baton Rouge, 1961), 4–5.

16 *The Journal of Jean Laffite* (New York, 1958), 9–11, 29, 33. There is also, on an unnumbered page, the reproduction of a handwritten note from a page in the supposed family Bible, which says that "I owe all my ingenuity to the great intuition of my Jewish-Spanish grandmother, who was a witness at the time of the Inquisition." The journal does not refer to Laffite's first marriage to "Christina Levine, of Jewish descent, a native of St. Croix ... [who] died on shipboard in the Gulf of Mexico ... in 1804" (Arthur, *Jean Laffite*, 224). Although there were Jews in the West Indies, Jamaica for instance, who bore the name Levien, not all Leviens or Levines were Jews; the first husband of Alexander Hamilton's mother, John Michael Levine, seems not to have been Jewish (*DAB*, VIII, 171; Harold Larson, "Alexander Hamilton: The Fact and Fiction of His Early Years," *William and Mary Quarterly*, Third Series, IX [1956], 139–51, esp. 142). References to members of the Jamaica Levien family are in Jamaica *Royal Gazette*, June 16, 1781, and *Kingston Journal*, March 10, 1787 supplement.

17 *Journal of Laffite*, 147.

18 Pool, *Portraits*, 384–92; Marcus, *Early American Jewry*, II, 132 ff.

19 *MSAJD*, 71; John Lynd, Book XVI (1819), 500, NONA: *LG*, November 22, 1819.

20 *LG*, January 30, April 4, 1823.

21 *LG*, July 3, 1822. Nathan Hart is listed in *Ship Registers and Enrollments*, I, 105, as owner of the *Marsouin* in 1819.

22 The newspaper advertisements of 1820–21 indicate that the import-export business had continued at least that long: *LG*, October 5, 31, November 25, 1820; September 21, October 30, 1821. His scale of living is demonstrated by the special tax which he paid in 1818–19 on a horse and carriage (Tax List, Miscellaneous New Orleans Manuscripts, New-York Historical Society).

23 *LG*, April 8, 1831; July 24, 1832; *Ship Registers and Enrollments*, III, 13.

24 *Ship Registers and Enrollments*, II, 60–61, 116; III, 13; Edward Barnett, Book I (1838), acts 148, 201, 252; Book X (1840), act 41; and many others in succeeding years, NONA. During June of 1827, for instance, Hart bought and sold four slaves: Record Conveyance Office (Civil District Court) Book I, pp. 128, 216–17, 219–20, 321–22; in October of the same year, as we have seen, he sold five slaves to Sophie Monsanto.

25 Carlisle Pollock, Book VI (1820), 520, NONA.

26 *LG*, May 17, November 1, 1826; *Courier*, January 13, 1830; *Bee*, July 31, 1830; November 20, 1839.

27 Information is unavailable as to the exact year of the Marks family's arrival in New Orleans. Their second grandchild, Katherine, was born there in 1845 (*MSAJD*, 133).

28 The date of Barnett's birth is established by his tombstone in St. Louis Cemetery No. 1; his death record, NOOR, No. 483, September 27, 1865, says that he was a native of France. Rabbi Max Heller, who knew Maurice Barnett, Jr., reports in his *Jubilee Souvenir of Temple Sinai*, 129, that the elder Barnett was a Napoleonic

soldier. Heller knew that Barnett was Jewish; family records have been destroyed, but Prof. Samuel Burwell Barnett Carleton of the University of Texas, Austin, reports the family tradition that the elder Barnett was a Dutch Jew, who had served in Napoleon's army. The marriage record is in the Marriage Register, 1793–1821, p. 57, St. Joseph's Cathedral, Baton Rouge, in the Dept. of History and Archives, Diocese of Baton Rouge. Maurice's father's name as given in that record, Flamphor, is startling; it may have been a French equivalent of the Hebrew "Meir" (giver of light); if so, perhaps Maurice was a French adaptation, too, and our Maurice may be identical with the "Myer Barnett, Senior," otherwise unknown, who is listed in the *Constitution and Bye-Laws of the Israelite Congregation, of Shanarai-Chasset* (New Orleans, 1828). The identification of Maurice as the Dutch-born son of Lazarus Barnett is suggested by the SLCBR, 9, p. 19, record of the baptism on July 25, 1818, of Marie Eliza Barnette, daughter of Edouard, "a native of Philadelphia," with "Dame Marie Trahan, wife of Mr. Maurice Barnette . . . aunt of the baptized" as godmother. Another baptismal record, that of Maurice's son Edward, SLCBR, 8, p. 51b, May 25, 1816, refers to Maurice as a native of Philadelphia, and gives his parents' names as "Luis Bernet and Susana Mayer." "Luis" is closer to "Lazarus" than "Flamphor," but the mother's name is the same in all family records in Louisiana churches. Lazarus Barnett's Philadelphia story is given in Wolf and Whiteman, *Jews of Philadelphia*, 171; *Independent Gazetteer* (Phila.), June 4, September 13, November 15, 1783; *Pennsylvania Packett*, December 1, 1784; February 22, 1785; Mikveh Israel correspondence files, October 26, 1783, copy in AJA. Lazarus' bankruptcy in London is reported in *The London Chronicle*, February 2, 1785, p. 114; *Morning Chronicle* (London), February 2, 1785; *The London Gazette*, February 1, 1785, p. 118; April 16, 1785, p. 118. References to Barnett in *SWFP* are in Vol. 11, pp. 15, 91, 221; Vol. 12, p. 299. Marie Trahan's year of birth is given on her tombstone in St. Louis Cemetery No. 1 as 1789; she died January 17, 1850. But her death record, NOOR, No. 153, January 19, 1850, and SLCFR 1848–1853, p. 213 (no. 605), say that she was sixty-two years old. Many members of the Trahan family had come to Louisiana as exiles from Acadia, but there is no evidence that her father Juan (Jean) was one of them. Marie's mother's family name, Le Jeune, was a common French Catholic name in Louisiana, but, as we shall see, it was also the name of a few Jewish families.

[29] *SWFP*, Vol. 14, pp. 289–91.

[30] *SWFP*, Vol. 17, p. 73: Ganucheau & Co. of New Orleans sued Barnett in 1810 for payment of a debt going back to 1808. Other debts are referred to in *SWFP*, Vol. 16, p. 304 (1809); Vol. 17, p. 100 (1810).

[31] *SWFP*, Vol. 11, p. 182–A, ff.

[32] *SWFP*, Vol. 12, p. 78 (1807); Vol. 13, pp. 76, 171 (1808); Vol. 18, p. 123 (1810).

[33] *SWFP*, Vol. 14, pp. 285–93.

[34] *SWFP*, Vol. 13, p. 251 ff. The Negroes were, apparently, not slaves, since they were armed.

[35] *SWFP*, Vol. 16, p. 182 (1809); Vol. 19, pp. 110, 112, 131, 373, 432, 465–68 (1811).

[36] Maurice, Jr.'s recollections are in *Picayune*, December 6, 1898 (an obituary quoting from an interview which he gave the previous year), from which are taken other reminiscences in the following paragraphs. Helene Barnett Audler, Maurice Barnett, Sr.'s daughter, is said in her succession record to have been born in New Orleans in 1810 (case 33,096, NOPC); her stone in St. Louis Cemetery No. 1 reports her birthdate as July 3, 1810, but gives no place of birth; her death date was July 18, 1869. An Isaac Moses appears in a solitary record for June 27, 1808, as a witness to a Baton Rouge business transaction of no great significance (*SWFP*, Vol. 14, p. 284); there were many Jews at the time who bore that name, none of whom can be definitely located in Louisiana; it was probably not the distinguished New York City merchant who would hardly have been traveling on the frontier at the age of sixty-seven.

[37] In 1814 he was suing the estates of a number of former customers in Baton Rouge for the payment of old bills: Probate Records 206 and 207, Baton Rouge Court House. He continued to own land in the Baton Rouge area, which was occupied and cultivated from 1811 on; in 1843 he was given final patent on a quarter section of land: Book O, f. 69, Baton Rouge Court House. Practically the only records of the Barnett family's presence in New Orleans during this period which we have discovered are the baptismal registry entries for Maurice's and Edward's children. Maurice's son Edward's baptismal certificate, dated May 25, 1816 (he was born on February 20), SLCBR, 8, p. 51b, refers to his parents as residents of the city. Maurice and Marie were involved in the baptismal ceremonies for his brother Edward's children, Heleonore, SLCBR, 8, p. 26, December 19, 1815; Marie Eliza, SLCBR, 9, p. 19, July 25, 1818; Theodore, SLCBR, 9, p. 139b, August 16, 1820; Edemond, SLCBR, 11, p. 294, February 9, 1827 (this is the only record which gives the grandfather Barnett's name as "Lazare.") *NOCD*, 1822, lists Edward Barnett as a trader at 55 Bourbon street. Perhaps Maurice worked with his brother.

[38] *Bee*, June 1, 1838. *Picayune*, June 15, 1904, has an obituary of William Boswell Barnett, and calls him the "last of a long line of notaries." SLCBR, 8, p. 51b (Edward, born February 20, 1816); 9, p. 19 (Alphonse, born August 22, 1823). Edward and Alphonse were buried the same day, November 12, 1850, according to St. Louis Cathedral Sexton Record Book, entries 919 and 920.

[39] *Bee*, December 15, 1830; March 10, 1831.

[40] Characteristic slave advertisements in *Bee*, October 20, November 12, December 11, 17, 1835; March 5, 26, 1836.

[41] The Dun and Bradstreet record book, La., Vol. 9, p. 119, does not speak well of Maurice, Sr. Entries from April 9, 1852, through April 25, 1854, refer to the father's dishonesty and roguery, and accuse various members of the family of having transferred funds to each other, at various times, before going bankrupt for amounts as high as $150,000. As Maurice, Jr., and Lewis or Louis take over the business, with the father still continuing as "crier," however, there is a change in tone: "He never stood well & during his administration complaints were genl. Since the yng men hv. had the mangt. things hv. gone on better. Parties here who wd. hv. ref. to do with the old man are not afraid to entrust them with limited amts . . .

But the char. of thr. fath, (& they being Jews) weakens confide." Before long the references to roguery, suspicion and dishonesty cease; by June 24, 1858, the sons are reported to be "prudent men . . . doing a safe snug bus." Just six years previously, the investigator said that "all the famy are rogues." One cannot escape the feeling that the early reports were severely biased. All of the Barnett men could not have been corrupt, one pocketing the profits in such amounts as $40,000 before another declared himself a bankrupt, and then suddenly reformed to such an extent that they were believed to be "Hard workg. indus. men, dg a mod bus, have a gd Cr & stand well." It seems apparent that the father had made some enemies during his active commercial life. The Hope Mutual Insurance Company would hardly have taken Louis on as Secretary in 1859, if his reputation had been as black as earlier reports had described it. One note of interest is that all of the family are described by the Dun and Bradstreet investigator as Jews, even though the sons had been reared as Catholics.

[42] *Picayune*, September 26, 1865; December 6, 1898.

[43] St. John the Baptist Church, Edgard, Marriage Register I, 139. Marie Emeronthe and Pierre Brou's wedding is in the same volume, 86, dated June 2, 1799. Samuel Edmond's birth is in that church's Baptismal Register, III, 114 (June 21, 1807). In the old St. Charles Parish records of Antoine D. St. Amand, Commandant of the area in 1800–1803, now in the Department of Archives, Louisiana State University, the following documents have been preserved: a family meeting of the Brou-Becnel clan, held on May 12, 1802, at which it was decided that Ambroise Brou, Emeronthe's brother-in-law, would serve as guardian of Pierre and Emeronthe's sons, Florestan (about two and a half years old) and Valsin (about ten months old); a receipt for a loan of money which Emeronthe signed as young Pierre's widow. In regard to the approximate time of Samuel Hermann's emigration from Germany, a German periodical, making reference to a trip which Hermann made to Europe in 1835, said that he had gone to America thirty-one years previously—which might locate him in Louisiana as early as 1804 (Rudolf Glanz, "Source Materials on the History of Jewish Immigration to the United States, 1800–1880," *YIVO Annual* VI [1951], 149). The LSML cemetery card for Samuel's tombstone in St. Louis Cemetery No. 2 gives his age as seventy-five years at the time of his death on June 3, 1853; his death record in NOOR, and *Picayune*, June 4, 1853, give his age as seventy-six. He was born, then, in 1777 or 1778, and was twenty-eight or twenty-nine at the time of his marriage.

[44] The Becnel and Brou genealogies have been studied by many persons. Among the correspondents who have been most helpful to me in tracing this background are J. M. Webre of Rosedale, La., Msgr. Daniel J. Becnel, Pastor of the St. Aloysius Church of Baton Rouge, Mrs. G. A. Becnel of Lake Charles, Mrs. E. A. Broders of Baton Rouge, and members of the de Tarnowsky family. The Hermann slave transactions are in the "General Repertoire" conveyance records in the St. John the Baptist Parish Courthouse in Edgard, November 21, 1809 and March 26, 1811; later Hermann activities in the area are documented for January 24, 1818, and July 31, 1824, but he was then living in New Orleans. Louis Florian's birth and baptism are in the St. John the Baptist Church Baptismal Register III, 126; perhaps Samuel had just received news of the death of his father, and felt prompted

by Jewish tradition to preserve his father's name in this new son. Samuel Hermann's name appears in the printed census list, *Federal Census of 1810, Territory of Orleans, Excluding the Parish of Orleans* (Baton Rouge, 1961), but this publication does not give the complete data included in the manuscript originals.

[45] John Lynd, Book X, 94, 187; Book XI, 164, NONA. On May 27, 1814, Hermann resold the slaves to Weinbrenner; this may have been only a money-lending transaction so that Weinbrenner could repay his debt to Rochelle and Shiff, save his plantation, and then pay off Hermann with the proceeds of the year's crops. Like other merchant-bankers, Hermann's participation in the slave system throughout the years was extensive. In 1825, for instance, he sold sixteen slaves to various farmers in St. Charles Parish: Reg. 5, pp. 32–51, St. Charles Parish Courthouse, Hahnville, La.

[46] LSML cemetery cards, from St. Louis Cemetery No. 1; SLCBR, 8, p. 104; Carlisle Pollock, Book I, 626 f (1818); *LG*, August 5, 1823.

[47] In reference to the Shiff interests, letter, Shiff to Senator Josiah S. Johnston, signed by Hermann & Co., May 10, 1830, in the Johnston Collection, Historical Society of Pennsylvania, and *Argus*, April 14, 1828, where Shiff announced to the public that his business activities would be conducted during his absence by the Hermann firm. *Argus*, November 20, 1828, first refers to the firm as Samuel Hermann and Son. Carl Kohn, in his Letter Book, in the possession of Maunsel White Hickey, New Orleans, speaks of Lucien as a partner in the Hagan firm, on July 7, 1833, and of his income on September 23, 1833. The enlargement of the firm of Samuel Hermann, Sr., is in *Bee*, November 18, 1833; the inception of Thomas Barrett & Co. is reported in *Bee*, August 1, 1834; *Bee*, June 11 and November 17, 1834, report the importation of specie; the closing of the firm of Byrne, Hermann & Co. and the formation of Hermann, Briggs & Co. are reported in *Bee*, July 2, 1836.

[48] Carl Kohn Letter Book.

[49] The Hermann home is described in Samuel Wilson, Jr., *A Guide to Architecture of New Orleans* (New Orleans, 1960), 31; Stanley Clisby Arthur, *Old New Orleans* (New Orleans, 1959), 131. Mr. Wilson, the leading historian of New Orleans architecture, has kindly given me blueprints of the home, which include his own renovations, and a copy of another article on the building, "Grima House on St. Louis One of Best Early Examples," *States*, May 16, 1953. Samuel Hermann's contracts for the construction of this home are in William Christy, Book VII, February 16, March 16, 1831, NONA. Virginie's great-grandson, Mr. James Reiss, was the first to show the home to me. It is sad that the building is known as the Grima House, in honor of the family which purchased it from the Hermann family, and that the plaque in front of the home erroneously refers to Samuel Hermann as a physician. Carl Kohn writes of his troubles with Virginie in his Letter Book, June 12, 1833. Virginie's wedding is in SLCMR, 6, p. 65; Samuel, Jr.'s on February 16, 1835, in the same location, 72; Florian's in SLCMR, 5, act 43.

[50] *Bee*, November 15, 1830; November 6, 1832; February 15, 1833; July 15, September 19, 1834; May 30, 1836; January 27, 1837; June 24, 1838; March 4, 1839; March 5, 1840; *Courier*, October 13, 1830.

300

[51] *Bee*, February 29, April 28, 1832; April 30, September 8, 1834; February 4, 16, April 4, 29, June 27, 1835; January 6, February 3, 8, 19, April 26, May 4, 1836; January 6, 1837; March 4, April 1, 1839.

[52] *Das Fuellhorn* (1835), 378, quoted in Glanz, "Source Materials," 149.

[53] Stephen A. Caldwell, *A Banking History of Louisiana* (Baton Rouge, 1935), 59–66; Albert A. Fossier, *New Orleans, The Glamour Period, 1800–1840* (New Orleans, 1957), 68–74; Ralph W. Hidy, *The House of Baring in American Trade and Finance, 1763–1861* (Cambridge, 1949), 186; *Bee*, November 16, 1836; April 21, 1837; March 13, 1838; June 28, December 13, 1839; June 1, 1840.

[54] Emeronthe's death is in *Picayune*, March 12, 1851; Samuel's, June 4, 1853. Both are in SLCFR 1848–1853, pp. 360 (no. 842), 622 (1623). The two are buried in St. Louis Cemetery No. 2. Lucien's commission as a notary ran from 1839 to 1850: *NOCD*, 1856; *Bee*, October 19, December 3, 1839. Dr. Landreaux's death on September 13, 1853, at the age of forty-four, is from his LSML card for St. Louis Cemetery No. 1. References to him occur in *LHQ*, XXVI (1943), 59, 77. Lucien was an active Mason for many years; he was a leader in the effort to compromise the struggle between the lodges which favored the use of the English language and those which favored French (James B. Scot, *Outline of the Rise and Progress of Free Masonry in Louisiana* [New Orleans, 1923], 77). A letter from the Grand Secretary of La., D. Peter Laguens, Jr., August 18, 1967, reports that Lucien was Grand Senior Warden, 1843–1844, and Deputy Grand Master, 1846–1848, before achieving the highest office. The approximate date of his removal from New Orleans is derived from the fact that Lucien demitted from his lodge, Perfect Union, No. 1, on March 19, 1854 (communication from the Grand Lodge of Louisiana, F. & A. M., New Orleans, March 19, 1965). Lucien and young Samuel appear first in the San Francisco directories in 1854 as merchants, in 1856 as notaries. Lucien disappears from view after 1856; Samuel continues to be listed in the directories through 1878, but the date of his death cannot be found. Samuel Hermann, Jr.'s daughter Alice married Henry Palmer—their daughter May (Marie) Eugenie Palmer married Chauncey Depew in 1907; Samuel's daughter Louise married Hall McAllister (brother of the famous socialite Ward McAllister)—their daughter Edith married Francis G. Newlands in 1888. (Extensive genealogical data on the Hermann family, of little interest here, are in the writer's files.) The inventory of Emeronthe's effects was discovered after this was already in type. It is not in the records of the probate court, but in John Claiborne, Book III, acts 234 (June 19, 1851), and 328–31 (November 13, 1851), NONA. She lived with Virginie and her husband at the time (and so, presumably, did Samuel). The worth of Emeronthe's possessions amounted to only $1,953.65, including five slaves. No inventory of Samuel's possessions appears in Claiborne's books or those of any other notary consulted. If his wife had only $168 in bedding and furniture, $178 in jewelry and $137.65 in cash, he may have had even less.

[55] Lucien Wolf, *Essays in Jewish History* (London, 1934), 55–59 ("The Romance of a Bohemian Village," reprinted from the *Jewish Chronicle* [London], April 19, 1895). Details supplied by Wolf, recalled from conversations with his father, are corrected by data in the State Jewish Museum and State Central Archive of

Prague, reported to the writer on June 24 and October 31, 1963. Wolf says that Samuel's mother was a widow when he ran away; but the Prague records indicate that Samuel's father, Nathan Kohn, died on January 18, 1831. Wolf says that there were three sons and one daughter; Prague reports that there were seven sons, but has no records of daughters (perhaps they were not considered important enough to register). The names of the sons in the Prague records are Löwy; Simon (born 1781); Samuel (born 1783); Seligman (born 1786); Joachim (born 1800); Hermann (born 1806); and Joseph (born 1808). Wolf implies that the Kohn family had lived in Hareth for a long time, but the Prague records state that in 1778 Nathan lived in Petersburg/Petrohad—about forty miles from Hareth/ Hŏrany—when he married Kiwy/Eva Löbl (October 27, 1778). Nathan's parents' names were Simon and Bela—hence his Jewish name was Nathan ben (son of) Simon, or Nathan Schimml; some time later the family took the name Kohn, probably because they were Cohanim, preserving the tradition that they were descended from ancestors who had been priests in the ancient temple in Jerusalem. In view of the Nazi destruction of so much of the documentation of Jewish life in Central Europe, it is almost miraculous that even these few shreds of facts should have been preserved in Czechoslovakia.

[56] *LG*, July 4, 1806. The name Kohn was an unusual spelling for Cohen or Cohn in this period in America. One therefore wonders how there could possibly be two men of that name in early American Louisiana. Carter, *Territorial Papers*, IX, 593, notes that, in 1805, one "Jno Kohn" withdrew from the Company of Orleans Fusileers. Could "Jno" be a misreading of an entry for "Saml" in a manuscript?

[57] The Rapides Parish sales are recorded in Lynd, Book XIII (1816), 198–99 (April 16, 1816, referring to a transaction on November 23, 1808) and 562 (November 11, 1816, relating to land purchased on April 18, 1809), NONA. *Courier*, May 10, 1813, lists Kohn as owing taxes of $5.80 on property in Rapides Parish—perhaps these two parcels—and refers to him as a non-resident. The 1810 mortgage is in Fitch and Ross, Book for 1809–10, p. 113, December 17, 1810, NONA; the mortgage was renewed on April 15, 1811, and was finally paid in full on June 2, 1818 (Carlisle Pollock, Book V, 192, NONA). The building contract is in Quiñones, Book XII, 9, August 17, 1810, NONA. Kohn's endorsement of the notes is in *LG*, January 21, 1812.

[58] *LG*, December 16, 1823; September 17, 1824; *NOG*, June, 1962, p. 299; *Courier*, July 17, December 8, 1829; February 10, 1830; *Bee*, March 14, 1828; May 6, 1831; November 6, 1832; June 10, 1835; May 18, August 17, 20, October 7, 1836; August 11, 1839; February 24, 1840; L. T. Caire, Book XIX, act 297, March 22, 1832; Book XXII, act 785, August 1, 1832; L. Hermann, Book I, acts 189, 203, September 22, November 3, 1840, NONA.

[59] If Joachim was the Kohn who was a partner in the commission firm of Kohn and Coit, he was already in New Orleans in 1819 (*LG*, July 23, August 23, December 6, 1819); this may, however, have been one Matthew Kohn, of whom we know nothing else, who was in town in 1820–21 (*LG*, May 17, 1820; January 14, 1821; Carlisle Pollock, Book VI, 488–89, NONA). The earliest reference to Joachim by name is December 6, 1820, when he is listed as a passenger on the schooner

Daedalus from Bremen, arriving in the port of New Orleans that day (Milton P. Rieder, Jr., and Norma Gaudet Rieder, *New Orleans Ship Lists, I: 1820–1821* [Metairie, La., 1966], 49, which lists Joachim as eighteen years old, a merchant, from Germany). The same source, p. 26, records Samuel Kohn's arrival in New Orleans from Havana, on May 2, 1820, possibly returning via Cuba from a trip to Europe during which he decided to bring Joachim to the United States. *NOCD*, 1823, lists Samuel and Joachim together as merchants at 116 St. Ann street. In 1824 Joachim entered into a partnership with John L. Bernard (*Courier*, October 23, 1824, where he is called Joachim Kohn, Jr., probably to distinguish him from the elder Kohn who must have been well-known in the business community). The Kohn-Bordier partnership first appears in *LG*, November 24, 1826.

60 *Bee*, April 24, 1833; April 2, 1834; February 3, April 8, 1835 (when the complaint was voiced that Joachim and three other directors bought up all of the available stock of the Marine Fire Insurance Company, although other prospective purchasers were at the designated place earlier than they); April 11, July 1, 1835; January 1, February 3, May 4, 1836; January 6, 1837; January 3, 1838; January 8, 1840; Fossier, *New Orleans*, 41; *NOCD*, 1838, pp. 346, 351; *Historical Epitome of the State of Louisiana* (New Orleans, 1840), 346.

61 *Bee*, June 25, 1834; *Advertiser*, June 26, 1834; SLCMR, 5, p. 367. Uncle Samuel did not return to New Orleans for the wedding, but Joachim's former partner, J. L. Bernard, served as a witness. Little is known about Marie, since she died in such a brief time. One newspaper reports that she was a member of a committee which planned a fair as a benefit for the orphan girls who were in the care of the Sisters of Charity (*Bee*, June 29, 1839).

62 Baptismal certificates for Samuel and Joseph are in SLCBR, 15, pp. 488–89. Some notes on the Kohn family were given to me by the late George A. Kohn of New Orleans. There is an article on Joseph Gustave Kohn's life and collections in *Louisiana Conservation Review*, August 1931, pp. 26–27. The Dun and Bradstreet record books, La., Vol. 10, p. 555, report the success of the Heine brothers and indicates that most of their capital was invested in real estate and stocks.

63 Marie Alice is referred to in *Enciclopedia Universal Ilustrada* (Barcelona), Vol. 36, pp. 13–15; *Jewish Exponent* (Phila.), March 30, 1917. *The Book of the Israelites of Louisiana* (New Orleans, n.d.), 52, refers to contributions made by Michel to the Children's Home. Wolf, *Essays*, 58, mixed up the Heine brothers, and thought it was Amélie and Armand's daughter who married Prince Albert; he also presumed that the wedding of Marie Alice's parents took place in a New Orleans synagogue. I have heard the story verbally that Marie Miltenberger or her parents insisted that Michel adopt Catholicism, but the marriage record in SLCMR, 10, p. 593, indicates that Michel was still a Jew, and there is no subsequent reference to him as a convert in the Cathedral's Baptismal Registers. *NOG*, September, 1967, p. 332, gives some details of the Miltenberger genealogy. Marie was born in 1832, the daughter of Alphonse Miltenberger and Céleste Dorfeuille.

64 Samuel Kohn estate papers in the NOPC, Succession No. 163,144. Record Conveyance Office (Civil District Court) Book II, pp. 300–301, January 11, 1828, located after this was set in type, identifies Delphine as a free Negress.

65 *Archives Israélites* (Paris), CVI (1895), 124–25; Wolf, *Essays*, 55, 58; *JE*, III, 226–28; XII, 326.

66 *Price-Current*, January 10, 24, 1835; *Bee*, January 1, December 16, 1835; January 26, 1837; January 17, March 6, 1839; January 15, 1840; Lucien Hermann, Book V, act 251, *et seq.*, November 2, 1842, NONA: *NOG*, March, 1962, p. 169; *Delta*, June 28, 1850; Carl Kohn will and succession papers, NOPC, No. 46,980; *Picayune*, August 28, 1895; Carl Kohn Letter Book, May 15, October 27, 1833. The de La Ronde line has been well investigated; the first Pierre Denis, born in Tours October 8, 1631, died in Quebec May 6, 1708. But we are not certain of the names of Carl's parents; if he was the son of Samuel's brother Levi, who married Rachel Feldstein on January 26, 1802, according to the family records in the Prague archives, his Hebrew name was Abraham. If the religious record of his marriage to Clara could be located, it might reveal his parents' names, but Protestant archives in the United States are rarely preserved with the same care and concern as Catholic records.

67 Carl Kohn Letter Book, November 16, 1833; Wolf, *Essays*, 57.

68 John Lynd, Book III, 111–13, NONA; *LG*, May 6, 1808; September 11, 12, 1810.

69 Rochelle's will is dated July 1, 1824; his succession papers in NOPC include notarized statements from the Registrar of German Jews of Hamburg, Heyman Sander May, certifying the marriage of Ruben's parents, the date of Ruben's birth, the dates of his brothers' and sisters' births, and the death of their father on May 31, 1824, at the age of seventy-six. The brothers were Jacob Levin Rothschild, born March 13, 1776; Moses (Maritz), born April 16, 1782; and Berend (Bernhard), born August 4, 1784. The sisters were Golda, the wife of Lazarus Esaias Cohen, born December 14, 1777, and Rachel, born February 3, 1798.

70 John Lynd, Book III, 111–13, NONA.

71 *JE*, XI, 96 ff; Alexander Dietz, *Stammbuch der Frankfurter Juden Geschichtliche Mitteilungen über die Frankfurter jüdischen Familien von 1349–1849* (Frankfurt, 1907), 257–59, 381; Cyrus Adler, *Jacob H. Schiff, His Life and Letters* (New York, 1928), 2–3. The genealogical charts in *JE* and Dietz should be used with caution; they have been corrected extensively through the diligent research of Dr. Fritz Ettlinger, whose data in the Stadtarchiv of Frankfurt I have been permitted to use. Our Hart Moses was also the uncle of Moritz Schiff (1823–1891), the distinguished physician and physiologist.

72 During 1818–19, *LG* reported the names of the merchants to whom ship cargoes were consigned. Rochelle and Shiff received twice as many as Judah Touro. From 1820 on, large shipments of cotton were delivered to them from the river steamboats. They were part owners of two of these vessels, the *Mississippi* and the *Independence* (*Ship Registers and Enrollments*, I, 93; II, 80). In 1818 they purchased the ship *Hamburg Packet* from R. D. Shepherd for $2,250 (Carlisle Pollock, Book I, April 13, 1818, NONA). The inventory of Rochelle's estate lists him as the owner of 150 shares in the Louisiana State Bank, and of a smaller number of shares of stock in other enterprises. Their election to the bank board is in *LG*, February 6, 1821; February 12, 1822; February 17, 1824; February 9, 1825; February 7, 1826.

Courier, April 11, 1826, reports that Shiff purchased seven shares in the Louisiana Insurance Company; Rochelle had already subscribed to nine—these were purchased by his estate, represented by Montgomery. A fire in their three large tobacco warehouses is described in *LG*, November 12, 1823. In view of the fact that Rochelle's brothers were merchants in Hamburg, it is probable that they were Rochelle and Shiff's purchasing agents for such large shipments of dry goods as are reported in *LG*, December 5, 1823; they may also have placed orders with Rochelle and Shiff for tobacco, for which the New Orleans partners advertised "liberal advances on Tobacco to be shipped to Hamburg" (*LG*, April 15, 1824).

73 The public notice of the termination of the partnership is in *LG*, July 16, 1824; Rochelle's announcement that Shiff has his power of attorney is in the same issue; the report of his death is in *LG*, October 1, 1824.

74 The Martineau-Johnston suit is reported in Martin, *Louisiana Term Reports*, n.s., I, 497–510, and in the Johnston Collection, letters of October 8, 1823; June 13, 1825; September 25, November 22, 1827; April 4, August 5, September 8, 1828; May 10, December 12, 1830. Maritz' suits are in *SC*, 263, 295. The property in the Faubourg St. Mary was all that Rochelle had retained from a huge tract of land which he and Shiff, together with W. and J. Montgomery, sold at auction on January 29, 1823; it had consisted of twenty-six lots of various sizes on some of which homes and warehouses had been erected. This sale was challenged by the redoubtable John Gravier, because the land was part of his famous claim to possession of the New Orleans Batture (*LG*, January 11, 27, 1823).

75 The wedding is recorded in SLCMR, 3, p. 134, and *NOG*, June, 1967, p. 211; Basilique's parents' wedding on April 12, 1787, is in SLCMR, 3, p. 52, and *NOG*, June, 1962, p. 281. Chesse was 2nd Lieutenant of the Third Regiment of Louisiana Militia in 1808 (Carter, *Territorial Papers*, IX, 826). The earliest-dated Shiff card in LSML is a St. Louis Cemetery No. 1 card for Mary Louise Shiff, who died on October 25, 1811, at the age of 22 months; if the card is not in error, then Shiff had an earlier wife, or he and Basilique lived together as man and wife after a civil ceremony or none at all before their Catholic wedding. SLCFR, 1803–15, p. 277, records the burial of another child, Clara, on October 2, 1814. Two other children who did not survive childhood were Louise Marguerite, born December 25, 1815 (SLCBR, 8, p. 76), and Richard, who was buried at the age of 18 months on July 5, 1822 (SLCFR, 1820–24, p. 60). The children who survived their father, as listed in his succession papers, were Eugène, Théodore, Gustave and Henry (none of their dates of birth is known); Marie (who became the wife of A. H. Despaigne of Santiago, Cuba); Cora (who married George Gaultier of Paris); Arthur (born in 1823); and Edward (born in 1817, baptized December 21, 1824, the same day as Marie, who was born February 25, 1819)—data from SLCBR, 10, p. 148, acts 690, 691. Hart's travels are documented in letters in the Johnston Collection, and in *Argus*, April 14, 1828; *Bee*, March 7, 1836. The plantation is mentioned in Pierre A. Degelos, *Statement of Sugar Made in Louisiana in 1828 and 1829* (New Orleans, 1829); *Argus*, July 24, 1828. Edward's activities in his father's name are in Lucien Hermann, Book IV, act 63, March 14, 1842, Book VIII, acts 194–226, and Book X, acts 61–77, 136, 163, 172–74, 227 (1844–45), NONA, where so much of Samuel Kohn's and Hart Shiff's property was sold.

[76] Shiff's death is reported in the *New York Herald*, February 28, 1851; his New York City residence was at No. 5 Depau Row, Bleeker Street. The Hart Shiff inventory is in NOPC, succession No. 4841; it must be read together with the papers relating to Edward's estate (numbers 17346, 26067, 28600, in NOPC), in order to gain an understanding of the family's complex affairs, investments and relationships.

[77] Browning writes of the Shiff case in *The Diary of Orville Browning* (Springfield, Ill., 1925) I, 689–91, under date of October 27, 1864.

[78] Henry Shiff's service record in the National Archives, Washington, is incomplete. He enlisted in July, 1861, and gave his place of birth as France. His pay vouchers cover the period from October, 1861, to March, 1862. Emilie Shiff's experience is detailed in the Provost Marshal Records of New Orleans, Special Orders No. 24, June 5, 1863, in the National Archives, and in *Times*, February 8, 14, 21, 25, 1865.

[79] *Courier*, March 7, July 13, 15, August 8, 1808; *LG*, January 21, 1812; *SWFP*, XIX, 366.

[80] LSML, Girod Street Cemetery card; *Courier*, November 13, 1822, recording the brother's death on November 9.

[81] *LG*, January 16, 1823; *Bee*, March 8, 1838; May 18, 1839.

[82] His death record, NOOR, No. 248 for the year 1852, gives his name as Salomon Salomon De Jonge, although this hardly seems possible; the first and middle names never appear in full in advertisements or other records. The succession record, NOPC, is numbered 5507. M. M. Cohen, whom we will meet later, was the attorney for Nichols. Two different years are given for his birth in the succession papers, 1774 and 1780, but the death record and tombstone both give his age as seventy-two, which would date his birth in 1780. There is no evidence that De Jonge was related to the Abraham H. de Jung or De Jonge who was in Philadelphia in 1824, was in New Orleans in 1827, when he joined Congregation Shanarai-Chasset, and then went bankrupt in 1834 and 1837 (Wolf and Whiteman, *Jews of Philadelphia*, 356; *Bee*, June 21, November 7, 1834; February 16, April 2, 1835; July 6, 1836; April 28, 1837), or to a later Abraham De Jung or De Young who was one of the founders of Gates of Prayer Congregation in New Orleans (*Centennial Volume, Congregation Gates of Prayer* [New Orleans, 1950], 2).

[83] *SWFP*, Vol. XVII, 142–79, 230–31. Data on the bankruptcy also appear in John Lynd, Book VII, July 23, 1810, NONA; *LG*, May 26, June 29, 1810; June 1, 1811; *Courier*, June 3, 1811.

[84] The Nathan genealogy is in *MSAJD*, 163; an incomplete Hart line is given in *MSAJD*, 74A. Asher is located in Charleston in Elzas, *South Carolina*, 138. An obituary of Alexander (*Bee*, February 17, 1839) reports that he was in his sixty-second year, and was a native of Portsmouth; but a family note-book, in AJA, gives the town of his birth as Portsea, which *MSAJD* follows. The note-book gives no name for either wife, and no date or place of birth for Isaac. The *Bee* obituary signed by "M" calls Hart "Rev." and reports that he was for "many years a resident of the city of New York," but makes no reference to his congregational affiliation. The obituary pays high tribute to his piety and charitableness. Hart's

service is noted in Israel Goldstein, *A Century of Judaism in New York: B'nai Jeshurun, 1825-1925* (New York, 1930), 84, and Hyman B. Grinstein, *The Rise of the Jewish Community of New York, 1654-1860* (Phila., 1945), 485. Rabbi William Berkowitz has transcribed for me the Hebrew and English texts of the marriage record in the congregation's archives. Betsy Kokernot's arrival in New Orleans from Amsterdam on January 14, 1820, is listed in *Letter from the Secretary of State, with a Transcript of the List of Passengers who Arrived in the United States from the 1st October, 1819, to the 30th September, 1820* (Washington, 1821), 37, and Rieder, *New Orleans Ship Lists, I,* 5. The announcement of the firm of Alexander and Isaac Hart, together with the new Mrs. Hart's appeal to her old customers to support her under her new name, is in *Bee,* December 22, 1836.

85 The wedding record is in St. Joseph's Church Marriage Register, 1793–1821, in the Dept. of Archives of the Baton Rouge Diocese. Asher's mother's name is given as Elizabeta. Dalton had remarried after Ana or Hana Burke's death; his wife in 1807 was Caty Yair. The records of the Dalton estate are in *SWFP,* Vol. XII, 290–311. SLCCB, 30, notes Marguerite's confirmation on May 8, 1796.

86 *SWFP,* Vol. XIX, 485–86; Marguerite's succession record, NOPC. Her death record, NOOR, reports that she was born in Charleston.

87 *SWFP,* Vol. XIX, 187, 262, 366 (Antonio Gras' sale of property to Marguerite, witnessed by S. S. De Jonge), 424, 431, 508, 524, 525, 533, 539. Marguerite's choice of Gras as her guardian is in Vol. XII, 297 f, February 17, 1807. If the transcription of the name "Antonio Ros" in *NOG,* January, 1967, p. 85, is an error for Antonio Gras, Marguerite's choice is explained by the fact that Antonio's son Jayme married Marguerite's sister Ana Dalton on November 3, 1792.

88 *LG,* January 21, 1812. One other note is of interest, "executed by Joseph Lange in my favour, endorsed by Fergus Duplantier, for $105." This Joseph Lange had sold a lot on St. Louis street in New Orleans to Nathan for $500 on August 16, 1811 (*SWFP,* Vol. XIX, 431). Joseph may have been a member of a family of refugees from Saint-Domingue who arrived from Cuba during the summer of 1809. The Lange family may have been converts to Catholicism in Saint-Domingue or in Cuba; they did follow Catholic patterns in New Orleans when they did not need to. But perhaps they had lived in a Catholic environment for so long a time that they simply assumed the guise of nominal Catholics. The father, Joseph Lange Vidal, "a native of Bordeaux in France, sixty-six years of age, married to Isabel Rodriguez, residents of Saint-Domingue," was buried, without charge because of his financial condition, from St. Louis Church on July 15, 1809. His daughter, Marie Rose, was married to James Smith on January 1, 1816; Marie Aline to Jean Baptiste Latour on September 10, 1817; Marthe Claire to William Thompson on May 13, 1820; and Marie Rose, after Smith's death, to François Delaup on February 7, 1826 (SLCFR, 1803–15, p. 59; SLCMR, 3, pp. 166, 199, 240; 4, p. 78). The French records concerning the restitution of the property of refugees from Saint-Domingue (*Etat Détaillé des Liquidations* [Paris, 1828–34], VI, 526–27), list this Lange family under their Hebrew names, but with the correct identification of the names of the New Orleans husbands: Esther for Marie Rose Delaup; Rebecca for Marthe Claire Thompson; Judaïque-Rachel for Marie Aline Latour; Mardochée

for the father Joseph. Two sons are listed in the French record, Abraham and Joseph. It is this son, Joseph, who may have had the business transactions with A. M. Nathan. The value of the family's coffee and cotton plantation in the Parish of Jérémie in Saint-Domingue, was 168,700 francs. René J. Le Gardeur, Jr., who is the authority on the refugees from Saint-Domingue who came to the United States, has very generously shared this information with me. The identification of the Joseph Lange who is mentioned in the A. M. Nathan records with this family from Saint-Domingue is strengthened by the absence of any other Joseph Lange in Louisiana records of this period, although the Lange name is not an unusual one.

[89] Nathan and Williams are described as partners in John Lynd, Book XI, 106 f, March 16, 1814, NONA; *LG*, September 29, 1814; April 17, November 11, 1817. Nathan advertises a house and lots for sale (*LG*, December 30, 1817); solicits customers (*LG*, March 18, 1820); offers Louisiana Bank stock for sale (*LG*, February 12, 1822) after his association with Hermann; offers a reward for the return of his slave Sally (*LG*, February 26, March 29, 1822); sells lottery tickets for a property (*LG*, August 2, 1822); receives cases of merchandise (*LG*, March 24, May 15, 1823); deals in cotton (*LG*, March 11, 1825); subscribes to shares of stock in the Orleans Draining Co. (*Bee*, June 29, 1835); clears a ship (*Bee*, November 30, 1835); advertises bills of exchange on Paris and London (*Bee*, June 29, 1836); advertises for a runaway slave (*Bee*, March 19, 1839). His bankruptcy is attested by the listing of a note for $1,805 (labeled "insolvent debtor") in the Shiff succession papers. His activity in Baton Rouge as late as 1822 is documented in the *Baton Rouge Gazette*, October 1, 8, 15, 1822.

[90] *MSAJD*, 68, 163, contains the Nathan-Harris genealogical data. The Hyam Harris succession papers are in the NOPC. Jacob and Henry Harris are not mentioned in the estate papers; they may have remained in Charleston. Hyam's death is reported in *Courier*, June 2, 1828; the sale of his effects is in *Bee*, July 20, 1828, and *Argus*, July 29, 1828. The Harris-Goodman marriage certificate is in the possession of the Southern Jewish Historical Society, the gift of their granddaughter, Adele Clark of Richmond, brought to my attention by Saul Viener of Richmond. Moses Harris—Asher Nathan dealings are referred to in *Mobile Commercial Register*, February 4, 1837; August 4, 1841; October 26, 1842.

[91] Dun and Bradstreet record books, La., Vol. 11, p. 6; *NOCD*, 1855, p. 275; *Second Annual Report. New Orleans, Jackson and Great Northern Rail Road Company* (New Orleans, 1854), 11–14; Marguerite's succession papers, NOPC; Asher's will, No. 21124, but not the inventory of his estate, NOPC. Adolph Mazureau, Book for 1859, act 23, NONA, records the adoption on March 28, 1859. Achille Lion, Jules's son, is in L. Hermann, Book IX, act 232, October 15, 1844, NONA. Conveyance Books 75, June 30, 1857, and 82, November 12, 1860, New Orleans Civil District Court, record sales of slaves by Asher, but these transactions were personal rather than business. There were Jews named Lion in the New Orleans area in the late 1850's. Both H. Lion of New Orleans and L. Lion of Donaldsonville made contributions to the Association for the Relief of Jewish Widows and Orphans (Association board minutes, 79, 136, AJA). *NOCD*, 1855, lists Jules Lion (f.m.c.) at 304 St. Claude; A. Lion of Lion and Pinsard, French goods, at 66 Royal; A. L. Lion, clerk, at 22 St. Louis; and Herman Lion, of Lion Brothers, at 30 Camp street.

⁹² St. Joseph's Church Marriage Register, 1793–1821, p. 179, Dept. of Archives, Diocese of Baton Rouge; Rosina's will, dated January 24, 1876, in her succession papers, No. 3850, NOPC; *The Israelites of Louisiana*, 27–28 (the source of the quotation); Wolf and Whiteman, *Jews of Philadelphia*, 353, 491; Carter, *Territorial Papers*, IX, 970–72 (one Abraham Phillips is also listed as a signer of this document, but he cannot be identified as a relative of our Alexander). The actual date of Phillips' move to New Orleans may be recorded in *Courier*, March 2, 1812, where his name appears on a list of those for whom letters are being held at the New Orleans Post Office. Very possibly he was just then on his way from Baton Rouge to New Orleans.

⁹³ Phillips' business activities can be traced in *LG*, May 30, June 27, November 6, 11, 20, 26, December 7, 1818; September 23, 1822; January 11, 1823; *Bee*, January 7, 1839; *The Israelites of Louisiana*, 27–28, Carlisle Pollock, Book XI, 210–12, February 28, 1823, NONA. His Masonic interests are noted in *LG*, August 16, 1826, and Scot, *Free Masonry in Louisiana*, 37–38, 45 (he was Grand Treasurer in 1832). His political activities are described in *Argus*, March 22, July 4, 1828; *Bee*, June 26, 1832; April 21, July 2, September 19, 1836; and *Administrations of the Mayors of New Orleans* (W.P.A. publication) (New Orleans, 1940), 34, 42. Documents referring to his two homes are in Carlisle Pollock, Book XIV, 226 f, June 9, 1824, NONA; F. de Armas, Book III, act 191, March 22, 1825, NONA.

⁹⁴ John Lynd, Book XI, 434 f, October 29, 1814, NONA; *LG*, January 3, 1818; *Bee*, May 2, 1835; Barnett, Book VII, acts 746 ff, April 19, 1839 (in which Isaac sold fifteen lots of land for $5,910, purchased a few years previously from Samuel Hermann), and act 824, July 31, 1839 (Rosina's marriage agreement, certifying to her dowry of $1,000 in cash, and a slave worth $1,000), NONA. The tombstone attesting to Rosina's piety is illustrated in Huber and Bernard, *To Glorious Immortality*, 41. An obituary noting Isaac's death on February 27, 1851, was published in the *New Orleans Christian Advocate*, a Methodist paper (reprinted in *Genealogical Register* [Baton Rouge], VI [1959], 28).

⁹⁵ Asher's succession papers in NOPC, and a notarized document in Barnett, Book VI, act 294, March 13, 1839, NONA, confirm the brothers' relationship. The estate papers refer to the brothers' parents as Victor Abraam Phillips and Alla Matemem; Alexander's wedding certificate gives them as Pedro Phillips and Elizabeth Matheman. Such variations occur frequently in family documents of the time. Johanna, Asher's wife, was the daughter of Michel Debott and Elizabeth Vander Abadies, according to her husband's succession record; whether she was Jewish cannot be ascertained. An obituary of Asher in *Picayune*, March 5, 1839, gives virtually no facts about him. Johanna's arrival in New Orleans is documented in *Letter from The Secretary of State*, 83, and Rieder, *New Orleans Ship Lists*, I, 2.

⁹⁶ The names of the children are given in *The Israelites of Louisiana*, 27–28, and in Rosina's succession papers. Young Rosina's marriage to Haber is in the Nefutzoth Yehudah Marriage Book, January 31, 1846, AJA. Unfortunately, Alexander's own will, death record and succession papers have not been located.

⁹⁷ This is a summary, with revisions, of the writer's monograph, "Benjamin Levy: New Orleans Printer and Publisher," *Papers of the Bibliographical Society of America*, LIV (1960), 241–64.

[98] George L. McKay, *A Register of Artists, Engravers, Booksellers, Bookbinders, Printers and Publishers in New York City, 1633–1820* (New York, 1942), 43, 56; *Spectator* (New York), September 5, 1810. Olmstead (1779–1823) had also been a bookbinder, was later a bookseller and publisher. Genealogical data and details about Simeon compiled from *PAJHS*, No. 4 (1896), 213; No. 27 (1920), 51–52, 85, 95, 192, 347; No. 33 (1934), 203; Pool, *Portraits*, 400–401; *MSAJD*, 116.

[99] Carlisle Pollock, Book for 1824, act 13, copy of letters of Isaac Riley, dated December 19, 20, 1814, NONA; *NOCD*, 1838 (which lists Mary as residing at 13 Jackson street); Levy's will, No. 16,298, NOPC, filed January 17, 1860, seven days after his death.

[100] Benjamin Levy's wedding is in SLCMR, 3, p. 205; the baptisms are in SLCBR, 9, pp. 80, 132. Some data about Emilie's family are to be found in Jay Higginbotham, *Family Biographies* (Mobile, 1967), 22–23. Isabel's wedding (SLCMR, 7, p. 327) is reported in *Commercial Bulletin*, May 22, 1840. The marriage caused international comment, on the mistaken ground that Isabel had been reared as a Jewess. Dr. M. Wiener, writing in the *Allgemeine Zeitung des Judenthums* (Berlin), VI (1842), 294, about his trip to the United States, said, "During my stay in New Orleans I witnessed an example of tolerance on the part of the Catholic clergy which would appear incredible to any European. The daughter of the Jewish bookseller Benjamin Levy in that city married an attorney of the Protestant faith. After the bridal couple had been married in a civil wedding, the husband and wife . . . went to the Catholic church, to have their marriage consecrated there by a Catholic priest. Think of it! a Jewish bride, a Protestant bridegroom, and a Catholic priest administering the sacrament of marriage to them!" Ainsworth had been born in Providence, R. I., in 1809, was a graduate of Brown University, was a notary at the time of his marriage and, in 1846, was a Commissioner for Texas (*Picayune*, October 6, 1846; Providence *Directory*, 1828). He was in Montgomery, Ala., in 1832, apparently before coming to New Orleans (*Mobile Commercial Register*, July 13, 1832).

[101] Roger Philip McCutcheon, "Books and Booksellers in New Orleans, 1730–1830," *LHQ*, XX (1937) 610–13; *LG*, May 6, 1811; July 21, 1812; August 30, October 6, 1814; October 26, 1815; *SC*, No. 752; Orleans Parish Court Minute Book, June 1814–September 1815, Civil District Court, New Orleans; *Spectator* (New York), September 12, 1823; *Price-Current*, October 11, 1823.

[102] See *Argus*, May 19, 1826, for a typical array of books; *Price-Current*, November 15, 1829, for a variety of stationery items, and October 24, 1829, for the list of types of printing which he offered to do. Levy's 1842–43 bankruptcy files, in the National Archives, divide his stock into "School, Medical and Miscellaneous Books," and "Law Books." Theater tickets are offered in *LG*, April 24, 1822, and lottery tickets in June 25, 1818 *et seq*.

[103] Levy's first advertisement of the Darby volume is in *LG*, February 18, 1817. Olmstead may have printed the *Counting-House Calendars* which Levy advertised for sale in *LG*, December 18, 1818; December 28, 1819; February 24, 1821. *LG*, November 22, 1821, announced the opening of his print shop; November 30, 1821, advertised one of the Martin volumes. The bibliography of Levy's imprints

is in Korn, "Benjamin Levy," and in Korn, "Additional Benjamin and Alexander Levy Imprints, *PBSA*, LXII (1968), 245–52. Prieur is listed as Mayor in the *NOCD*, 1832, 1834 and 1838; Arthur, *Old New Orleans*, 53; *Biographies of Mayors of New Orleans* (W.P.A. mimeographed volume) (New Orleans, 1939), 26–29. Kate Wallach, "The Publication of Legal Treatises in America from 1800 to 1830," *Law Library Journal*, XLV (1952), 136–48, refers to Levy's legal publishing.

104 New printings of Livingston's *Penal Code* were published both in Paris and New York City in 1873; the American republication was undertaken by the National Prison Association of the United States, and the introduction was written by Salmon P. Chase, Chief Justice of the Supreme Court. One of the most notable discussions of Livingston's work is Elon H. Moore, "The Livingston Code," *Journal of the American Institute of Criminal Law and Criminology*, XIX (1928), 344–66.

105 *Price-Current*, March 21, 1835; *Documents Relative to the Banks of New Orleans* (New Orleans, 1837), 61, 67, 176; Levy bankruptcy files, unnumbered papers.

106 All of this detail is from the Levy bankruptcy files. *Price-Current*, March 23, 30, December 21, 1839, report Levy's withdrawal from activity in the paper's publication, although, probably because his name was so important to its success, and possibly out of respect, Alexander and Cook continued to print on the mast-head the words "Printed at the Office of Benjamin Levy," until the issue of December 26, 1842.

107 Alexander Levy & Co. imprints, as well as those of F. Cook and A. Levy, are listed in Korn, "Benjamin Levy." The prostitutes' license is reproduced in Herbert Asbury, *The French Quarter. An Informal History of the New Orleans Underworld* (New York, 1949), 261. Dun and Bradstreet, La., Vol. 9, p. 128, reports Alexander's business reputation ("gd. for Jews") and failure.

108 Details of the death-dates are from *Commercial Bulletin*, May 6, 1851; *Delta*, July 23, 1852; *Crescent*, August 16, 1860; certified copies of death certificates from NOOR. Information about Mary Levy is from her great-grandniece, Irma Peixotto Sellars of Beverly Hills, California.

109 Levy bankruptcy file; will no. 16298, and inventory of his estate, dated July 18, 1860, NOPC. Alexander declared at the inventory that five shares of stock in the Louisiana State Bank in Benjamin's name belonged to the grandchildren "of whom he was the tutor." If he was still alive, Richard was freed by the Civil War. Benjamin was buried in the Protestant Girod Street Cemetery. Alexander did not long outlive his father; he died on February 7, 1866, at the age of forty-eight, at the home of his niece, Aline Mary Ainsworth, then Mrs. Frederick Jordy (*Picayune*, February 8, 1866).

110 *Bee*, September 24, 1839; *LG*, May 1, 1812.

111 The roster, in the Department of Archives, Louisiana State University, is reproduced in de Grummond, *The Baratarians*, 163–70.

112 Stanley Clisby Arthur, *The Story of the Battle of New Orleans* (New Orleans 1915), 249 f; *Picayune*, September 9, 1865.

113 *Genealogical Register*, VI (1959), 28.

114 Pierson, *Louisiana Soldiers*, 34, 59, 94, 102, 108.

115 We have not attempted to investigate the participation in the battle of Jews from other areas. One such report which has come to our attention concerns Isaac Henry of Savannah and Washington, D. C., who is supposed to have fought in the forces under Jackson (ms. letter of John Samuel, Philadelphia, January 29, 1898, to Judge Mayer Sulzberger, in AJHS Library).

116 Fossier, *New Orleans*, 200; *Bee*, April 2, 15, May 7, 28, June 20, July 2, August 4, 6, September 29, October 30, November 17, 1829; January 5, February 25, March 11, April 21, May 11, 24, October 2, 1830; April 8, 1833; August 29, 1836.

117 *Bee*, August 29, 1836; John Lynd, Book XV, 1002–1003, December 27, 1818; Carlisle Pollock, Book II, 163, 175, from October 25, 1818, NONA; *NOCD*, 1822.

118 SLCBR, 15, 77, May 9, 1836; SLCFR, 1833–36, p. 362. Simon's father's name is given as Mortier, but the mother's name is not reported in either record, strengthening the view that Cohen may even have been unconscious when the rites of baptism and extreme unction were administered. It is significant that the baptismal record also notes his death date, as though it had been recognized all along that the two events were related. The funeral record says that Cohen was about fifty; the obituary says fifty-five.

[1] Alan Conway, "New Orleans as a Port of Immigration, 1820–1860," *Louisiana Studies* I (1962), No. 3, pp. 1–4; the statistics are from a letter report, August 12, 1966, from the Chief of the Bureau of the Census, U. S. Dept. of Commerce.

[2] Ira Rosenswaike, "The Jewish Population of the United States as Estimated From the Census of 1820," *AJHQ*, LIII (1963), 141, 177. Rosenswaike's "Heerman" is, of course, our Samuel Hermann, not to be confused with other men named Heerman. Rosenswaike overlooked Samuel Jacobs, on Bourbon street, one male under 45, one female under 26, 20 slaves. Nowhere in the returns, as Rosenswaike realizes, is there a mention of the name of Manis Jacobs. Nor are the following listed anywhere in the returns: Rochelle, Barnett, Samuel Kohn, Asher Phillips, Isaac Phillips, De Jonge. If the census information on which other Jewish population estimates are based, omit as many Jews as the New Orleans returns, our present estimates need to be drastically revised upward.

[3] Letter to one of his sisters, May 6, 1815, Mordecai Papers, Southern Historical Collection, University of North Carolina. Sam wrote of the host of ships and craft along the river, the narrow streets "filled with dust or mud," and the curious fact that the ladies did not go shopping: "The Shop Keepers send their goods out for sale." Sam did not try to meet any local Jews. He was interested in the fashionable set, and felt that his ignorance of French prevented his having a good time.

[4] *LG*, January 15, 1823.

[5] Wolf and Whiteman, *Jews of Philadelphia*, 319–20; John S. Kendall, *The Golden Age of the New Orleans Theater* (Baton Rouge, 1952), 9–13; *LG*, March 2, 8, 13, 23, 27, 30, 1819; January 19, March 3, 9, 11, 16, 1820; April 14, 16, 18, 25, 28, 1823. Other performances of Noah's plays are in *LG*, January 8, February 10, 1824; February 18, May 15, 1826; and Kendall, *passim. She Would be a Soldier* was performed twenty-seven times between 1823 and 1842, and Noah's melodrama *The Wandering Boys* was on the boards twenty-five times from 1823 through 1838 (Nellie Smithers, "A History of the English Theatre at New Orleans, 1806–1842," *LHQ*, XXVII [1945], 85–276, 361–572).

[6] *LG*, September 7, October 21, 1825; February 10, 1826; *Argus*, December 19, 1828. Other apparent transients in New Orleans were the following immigrants, of whose subsequent presence in New Orleans there is no indication: arrived on the Brig *Johanna Catherine* from Amsterdam, January 14, 1820: Aaron Levy Dehann, 36, with wife and three children; Isaac Levy Dehann, 30, with wife and two children; Samuel Levy Dehann (no age given)—all three listing themselves as merchants from Germany; and arrived on Brig *Jupiter* from Bremen, July 10, 1820, Michael Levy, 27, a watchmaker from Bavaria (Rieder, *New Orleans Ship Lists, I*, 6, 17).

7 Will Book III, 94–95, NOPC. He died on July 6, 1818. Henry G. Schmidt, his partner, was designated as his executor. We do not know if Schmidt, who was a good friend of the Kohn family, and, later, a partner of Daniel Warburg, was Jewish.

8 Will Book III, 93, NOPC.

9 *LG*, December 23, 1820 (when his luggage is listed in the steamboat's cargo list); January 2 (the first advertisement in his name, but dated December 29, 1820), January 6, May 12, 1821; October 23, 1822 (his name appears in a list of estates with out-of-town heirs, giving the date of death). Heller, *Temple Sinai*, 2; Shpall, *Jews of Louisiana*, 8; and Proctor, "Jewish Life," 118, all assume that Salomon had come to New Orleans at a much earlier time. See Wolf and Whiteman, *Jews of Philadelphia*, 468, 495, for his prior activities in that city. Ezekiel had been cashier of the Lexington branch of the Bank of the United States beginning in 1816 (Lewis N. Dembitz, "Jewish Beginnings in Kentucky," *PAJHS*, No. 1 [1893], 99; AJHS has some 1819 correspondence between him and Langdon Cheves, president of the Bank).

10 *LG*, November 25, 1820; LSML cemetery card. Rev. Bernard Susser of Plymouth, England, the acknowledged student of the Jewish history of the area, has searched the British records in an effort to discover a precise identification of our Baruh, but, he says, "There was probably an army of [Jonas] cousins called Baruch!" Baruh's oldest brother may have been the Joseph Jonas who arrived in New Orleans from Havana on May 29, 1823 (Rieder, *New Orleans Ship Lists, II* [New Orleans, 1968], 80).

11 *LG*, September 17, 1822.

12 *LG*, November 24, 1819; January 17, March 14, July 21, August 1, 1820.

13 *LG*, December 13, 18, 1819; January 10, March 2, 20, May 6, 1820; *Courier*, November 3, 1826; *Argus*, March 15, September 30, November 21, 1828; Conveyance Book I, 72, May 14, 1827; XII, 227, 554, September 2, 1832, March 28, 1833, Civil District Court, New Orleans. The wedding is in *Bee*, May 7, 1832. Fossier, *New Orleans*, 188, for Joans' forgery and disappearance. A "Levi Jacobs" was in Charleston in 1818 (Elzas, *South Carolina*, 135); this may have been our man just before he came to New Orleans.

14 *MSAJD*, 95; *LG*, August 15, 1823; *Bee*, April 6, July 6, June 25, July 30, 1829; September 30, 1830; June 27, 1832; January 17, 1835; April 10, June 13, 1839; January 8, 1840.

15 Sam had difficulty in having his name printed properly. His first advertisement about his wife, Rosia or Rosette Abas or Abasse, gives his name correctly, but the retraction in *LG*, September 24, 1824 is over the name Jacob Solomon; even the census taker got his name wrong in the manuscript returns for 1820 and gave him the name Jacob Samuel. The legal notices concerning his separation give the correct name (*LG*, December 22, 27, 1824; January 4, 1825). Sam's financial difficulties are in *Bee*, September 15, November 21, 1834; May 26, 1835; January 22, 1839.

16 SLCBR, 10, p. 7b.

[17] SLCMR, 4, p. 39; SLCBR, 10, p. 77, December 4, 1823.

[18] References to the two Souza men are in *Courier*, September 30, 1826; *Argus*, March 21, 1828; *Bee*, April 3, 21, May 19, 1828; May 7, 1832; April 22, May 8, June 4, 8, 14, 1834. The terms "Junior" and "Senior" were not reserved for father and son; they were applied also to brothers and even cousins who lived at the same address or were in business together. We have already noted that Joachim Kohn was referred to as "Junior." A copy of the civil marriage certificate of the wedding, at which Souza was a witness, of Edouard Ursin Pasdeloup and Léa Chimène, May 31, 1846, is in AJA; Andre Doriocourt, Book IX, act 249, NONA, contains a rental agreement, dated Nov. 10, 1853, in which Souza took part. The data about Souza's subsequent career are in the Dun and Bradstreet record books. Baiz obtained a passport to go to New Orleans on August 9, 1827, and returned on May 20, 1829 (Szajkowski, "Jewish Emigration from Bordeaux," 119, 122). He is certainly not identical with the Abraham Baiz noted in *MSAJD*, 161, as being in St. Thomas in 1816, but could have been related to that family.

[19] Audler is in Elzas, *South Carolina*, 133, which also gives Myer's earliest appearance in Charleston as 1817. Dr. Audler had been in the Charleston area by 1814; his remedy is advertised in *Spectator* (New York), May 11, 1819. Sol was in New Orleans early enough to be elected secretary of the congregation in 1827. Helene Barnett Audler (July 3, 1810–July 18, 1869) is buried with her father and mother in St. Louis Cemetery No. 1; there is no record of Sol's death or burial. His financial troubles are in *Bee*, June 9, 1830, Myer's in March 8, 1832. The record of the Levy-Audler quarrel is in *Bee*, May 31, June 1, 2, 1836. For Lewis A. Levy see Korn, *Eventful Years and Experiences* (Cincinnati, 1954), 3, 23.

[20] The Gomez genealogy is in *MSAJD*, 63. The New Orleans newspapers contain no record of the duel, but this was at the end of a cholera epidemic, and one more death was not that newsworthy. Pool, *Portraits*, 432–33, presents material on Matthias' family and his father's concern with his education. *Bee*, November 16, 1833, notes the disposition of his property. Wolf and Whiteman, *Jews of Philadelphia*, 320, report that the stagecrafter Mathias Lopez "was killed in a duel in New Orleans in 1833," but I have discovered no confirmation of this; perhaps the authors confused Lopez with Gomez. Carl Kohn's identification of Gomez as an "American" is worthy of note—not particularly because he did not know or care that Gomez was a Jew, but because he was contrasting him with the French Creole socialites, with whom he himself was identified, and of whom Bosqui was perhaps one.

[21] A clipping, probably from a Baltimore newspaper, dated New Orleans, November 29, 1836, in AJA. Dyer later became a distinguished citizen of Texas.

[22] Memorandum dictated by E. M. Bodenheimer, on the stationery of J. Fair Hardin of Shreveport, in AJA.

[23] David told his story in great detail in his reminiscences of "Early Days in Texas," published in *Gonzales Weekly Inquirer*, June 22, 1878, and following issues, reprinted in the Seventieth Anniversary issue of the paper, July 19, 1923, obtained for me by Irving S. Forgotson of Gonzales. David mentions only his father for the early

New Orleans years. The immigration records of 1820, to which we have already referred, report Betsy as coming to New Orleans from Germany, not from Holland. It may be that Betsy and Louis had already come to America, and that she then returned to Europe on a buying trip for their store. The only reference we have been able to discover to Levi Kokernot is the sale of a slave on December 18, 1823, in Carlisle Pollock, Book XII, 360, NONA.

24 Louis' first appearance in the records is on May 26, 1821, when he appeared before the mayor to complain that one J. B. Falter had threatened to kill him; Solomon Ferth, another dry goods merchant recently come to town, appeared as a witness of the altercation (Miscellaneous New Orleans Mss, New-York Historical Society). Betsy's buildings along the rail road are referred to in L. T. Caire, Book XIX, act 263, March 15, 1832, NONA; *Bee*, January 12, 1832; April 23, 1833; April 19, 1834; January 1, 1835. Betsy's financial troubles, in which David was involved, are in *Bee*, April 18, May 30, July 21, 1832. Betsy's advertisements dealing with runaway slaves and slaves with money, *Bee*, May 6, August 5, 1833; July 12, October 13, 1834; January 30, October 24, 1835. *Bee*, July 21, 1831, reports that "an order subscribed by Widow Kokernott & Son, date not recollected, promising to pay the cabin passage of Mrs. Beugel, and her two children, from Amsterdam to this place," has been lost; Betsy's maiden name is given as Van Der Beugel or Vander Beugel in a number of documents. David Van Ostern's death certificate, signed by his brother Joseph, March 22, 1859, says he was a native of New Orleans, and that he was thirty years old at his death on March 15. The first mention of the father, Levi, was in 1828 when his stock of flannels, blankets, shoes, ready made clothing, and cottons was sold at sheriff's auction (*Argus*, June 2, 1828). Louis' partnership with Ben is in *Bee*, December 21, 1836. Ben was active in the affairs of the Washington Fire Co., No. 4, and was a member of the association of fire company representatives (*Bee*, October 3, 1837; February 17, March 1, 1838). The divorce is in *Bee*, July 3, 1839. The two children of Nancy and Louis were buried in the oldest Jewish cemetery, as were the mother (death-date unrecorded) and Louis (died at sixty-four on February 22, 1864); the children were George W. and Miriam (cemetery cards at LSML). The family's business and fiscal difficulties are reported in *Bee*, June 21, August 8, 1839; February 3, March 9, 1840; E. Barnett, Book V, act 195, 1839; Book XII, act 408, 1840, NONA. The Van Osterns are in *Transcription of Baptismal, Marriage and Death Records of Christ Church Episcopal Cathedral* (New Orleans, n.d.), 95.

25 Daniels testified, in the probate hearing for S. S. De Jonge's succession, NOPC, that he himself had come to New Orleans in 1822. His own succession papers, No. 18791, NOPC, reveal that he was born in Prussia, and was eighty-six years old when he died. His death certificate identifies him as a widower. In the census of 1830, a young man, twenty-thirty years old, is listed in his household, but we know nothing more of this person—it may have been a son or other relative, or a clerk; Daniels owned eight slaves in 1830. Further reference to Daniels is made in *LG*, January 7, 1826; *Bee*, June 16, September 30, 1828; June 25, 1829; November 15, 1830 (where he contributes $10 to the fund for the victims of the French July Revolution); September 19, 1834; May 4, 1835; February 3, October 18, 1836; May 8, 1838 (an offer to purchase $25,000 in Mississippi banknotes at one percent

discount); May 18, June 8, 1840 (bankruptcy order). Goodman's death certificate, signed by his son George on November 13, 1858, NOPC, reports his father's age and nativity. Daniel Goodman's active organizational career is in *Courier*, December 26, 1826; *NOCD*, 1834, 254–55; *Bee*, April 25, September 28, 1837. Mrs. Adele Clark of Richmond has given the Southern Jewish Historical Society the handsomely printed memorial resolution which was adopted by his Masonic Lodge on November 22, 1858.

[26] Soher-Andrews data are in *MSAJD*, 195; the dates of birth and death of Soher are not known. Herbert T. Ezekiel and Gaston Lichtenstein, *The History of the Jews of Richmond from 1769 to 1917* (Richmond, 1917), 87, reports that Soher was in Richmond in 1817. The Soher-De Jonge partnership was dissolved in early 1823 (*LG*, January 16, 1823). Some of Soher and Daniels' purchases were very large—10,000 pounds of peltries, for instance (*LG*, April 4, 1826). The steamboat ownership information is in *Ship Registers and Enrollments*, II, 28, 122, 140. They lost one of their steamboats at a sheriff's sale in 1830 (*Bee*, April 28, 1830). *Mercantile Advertiser*, August 3, 1830, reports Abraham Harris' withdrawal from the firm. A slave was sold for Soher in 1836, after he had left town (E. Barnett, Book I, index, NONA). The saga of Miriam's brothers' dramatic rise to and fall from economic power deserves an independent study. Some data about them are found in Lewis E. Atherton, *The Southern Country Store, 1800–1860* (Baton Rouge, 1949), 25–26, 84, 120, 124, 160–61. Their advertisements in New Orleans begin in the *Bee*, May 28, 1835. They sent out a special edition of the *Price-Current Letter Sheet* to their own customers; one example, dated October 7, 1843, is in the Mississippi Dept. of Archives and History, Jackson. Solomon Andrews settled in Mobile in 1835, but was caught in the panic of 1837, and closed down the operation (*Mobile Commercial Register*, May 2, 1837), but *Bee*, June 28, 1839, reports that Zalegman would continue to represent the firm in New Orleans, with Joseph in New York City, while Eliezer Lewis would move from Huntsville to Mobile. Eliezer Lewis and Salomon both died on April 22, 1848, in a suicide pact, the former in Mobile and the latter in New Orleans. The number of Haym Salomon's children and grandchildren who came South is little short of astonishing, but it demonstrates the economic attraction of a booming frontier during this period.

[27] *MSAJD*, 33, notes the Davies-Cromelien relationship. *LG*, November 11, 1823, lists M. Cromelien, J. M. and D. Davies as traveling together. R. Cromelien was married on September 15, 1824, to Amelia Judah, in New York City (*LG*, October 22, 1824), and Mr. and Mrs. R. Davies and a Mr. Cromelien returned to New Orleans from New York on December 2, 1824 (*LG*). Cromelien, Davies, had to sell two slaves and some merchandise to settle a suit with the Bank of Louisiana in 1826 (*LG*, June 13, 1826), but they did not then go out of business, nor were they bankrupted.

[28] See the writer's "Note on the Jewish Ancestry of Louis Moreau Gottschalk, American Pianist and Composer," *American Jewish Archives*, XV (1963), 117–19. After that article was written, my friend and congregant, Jeanne Behrend, while preparing a new edition of the younger Gottschalk's *Notes of a Pianist* (New York, 1963), received more precise evidence from the genealogist R. J. D'Arcy Hart of

317

London: the Gottschalk family appears in the records of the Great Synagogue of London, but not all of the children are listed in the birth records because entries for the period December 25, 1794–September 12, 1801, are missing. There is no question about the identification of the family: Edward's marriage certificate (SLCMR, 4, p. 120, act 548, May 26, 1828) gives his parents' names as Mr. Lazare Gottschalk and Mrs. Harris; the Great Synagogue birth book lists a child Flora, born January 19, 1792, whose parents were Jane (Shinah) Harris and Lezer, the son of Gottschalk Levi from Nancy. Two other children listed are Judah, born in August, 1796, and Moses (Morris), born August 13, 1802—listed in the circumcision book. In 1796, the family lived on Charlotte Street in Blackfriars, and in 1802 on Prescot Street in Goodmans Fields. This additional information should put to rest any doubts about Edward's birth into the London Jewish community. Edward's advertisement of the theft of his imitation jewelry wares is in *LG*, June 12, 1823. Since he is not listed in the *NOCD*, 1822, it is a safe guess that he arrived in New Orleans in the fall of 1822 or the winter of 1822–23. Edward's death certificate, No. 350, dated November 4, 1853, NOOR, says that he was fifty-eight years old at the time of his death on October 23, 1853; but he testified at the probate hearing of his brother Joseph Victor that he was forty-four at the time (1837), which would carry his birth back to 1793. Gottschalk signed one of Shiff's letters in the Johnston Collection, June 13, 1825.

[29] Jeanne Behrend's sober introduction to the younger Gottschalk's autobiographical memoir is the best source for his life and musical achievements. The imaginative biographical reconstruction by Vernon Loggins, *Where the Word Ends* (Baton Rouge, 1958), needs to be used with caution.

[30] The announcement of the admission of James into the firm is in *Courier*, April 1, 1829. James first appears in *LG*, December 27, 1825, as receiving a shipment of cordials and wine bitters from Philadelphia. The death of the third brother, listed only by his initial "G.," is in *LG*, August 25, 1824. This was not the brother George who appears in newspaper advertisements during the 1830's. James's business dealings in land and dry goods, in his own name, are documented in *Bee*, July 8, 1835; November 1, 1836; June 25, 1839. In 1835 he was involved in a public dispute over the ownership of land in Pass Christian, Miss., with the famous attorney Edward Livingston.

[31] The bankruptcy and sales of property are in *Courier*, June 5, 1830; *Bee*, March 2, 20, 25, 1833; August 1, 20, September 12, November 5, 1834; January 1, May 2, 1835; May 19, 1837. The birthdates are given in Loggins, *Where the Word Ends*; they had a total of eight children.

[32] Loggins, *Where the Word Ends*, 139 ff, describes the father's financial position in the 1850's. *Bee*, November 11, 1834; September 8, 1835; August 29, 1836, gives examples of Edward's business activities before the 1837 panic. A careful examination of the Notarial Archives would undoubtedly provide much data on Edward Gottschalk's financial vicissitudes.

[33] Doctor Gottschalk's death certificate, signed by Edward, on July 12, 1837, NOPC, reports that Joseph had come to New Orleans from Pyritz in Pomerania. It seems likely, therefore, that Joseph had attended medical school in Germany.

318

Marianne's first husband, David Lucas, had died in 1820. Brothers Edward, James and George Gottschalk attended the family meeting required by law to discuss custody of Joseph's children. The doctor's announcement of his arrival is in *Bee*, November 19, 1836; the news of his death is in *Bee*, July 11, 1837. In a lengthy report of yellow fever deaths in *Bee*, September 9, 1837, Joseph is listed as having been buried in the Protestant cemetery. Joseph died intestate; his succession papers are in NOPC.

[34] *LG*, February 1, 1823.

[35] Hanns G. Reissner, " 'Ganstown, U.S.A.'—A German Jewish Dream," *American Jewish Archives*, XIV (1962), 22, 26.

[36] *Argus*, May 10, 1828; *Bee*, May 10, 1833; Carl Kohn Letter Book, June 12, 1833.

[37] The father first advertised his skills in *Argus*, January 22, 1828; he had practiced as a dentist in Charleston as early as 1802 (*MSAJD*, 54). The earliest appearance of the brothers is in *Advertiser*, June 11, 1825. William is listed in *LG*, July 1, 1826, as a captain in the Militia; Henry is described as an aide-de-camp of the 1st Militia Brigade in *NOCD*, 1838, p. 253. Jacob's political activities are reported in *Bee*, April 4, October 19, 1835; March 30, April 4, 26, 1836; April 3, 1839. William's bankruptcy is in *Bee*, March 2, 1838; the conversion of Jacob's hotel is in *Bee*, November 5, 1839. Jacob built the hotel in 1834 for $13,300 (William Christy, Book XVII, 86, January 27, 1834, NONA). Evelina Gleaves Cohen, *Family Facts and Fairy Tales* (Wynnewood, Pa., 1953), 92–94, offers some interesting details of the family's background.

[38] *Courier*, March 17, 1829; March 31, 1830; *Bee*, March 20, 1828; May 29, September 19, 1829; January 1, February 3, October 2, 1830; May 18, November 1, 1832; February 12, November 18, December 11, 1833; February 18, June 30, 1834; September 23, 1835; March 20, 1837; Fossier, *New Orleans*, 200; Manis Jacobs estate inventory, October 2–3, 1829, NOPC. In the 1830 census Lasalle was listed as being between forty and fifty years old; he owned four female slaves; a free Negro family lived in the same building.

[39] Lavergne, Book III, acts 411–12, March 25, 26, 1820, NONA: *Courier*, September 13, 1830; *Bee*, May 12, 1835; March 24, 1837; March 13, 1838; April 20, 1839. Szajkowski, "Jewish Emigration from Bordeaux," 122–23, lists a number of Sacerdote departures from Bordeaux: "Izaac Sacerdotte, to join his father in New Orleans," September 18, 1827—this was probably Simon's son; "Esther Erera, her husband and Isaac Sacerdotte" to Ile de France, 1820—but see the entry which reports that "Salomon Sacerdote and the widow Ester Erera Sacerdote" went to Madrid—perhaps this was Salomon and his mother, and the prior entry is really an error for "her husband, Isaac Sacerdote." The differences in spelling are, of course, meaningless. Another Szajkowski entry is for the passport of Louis Delvaille, to New Orleans on March 12, 1827—probably another brother of Sipora's. A merchant named M. Delvaille came to New Orleans from France by way of St. Thomas on February 25, 1820; he too may have been a relative (Rieder, *New Orleans Ship Lists*, I, 17). It has not been possible to establish a relationship between these Sacerdote brothers and another man with the same last name,

Joseph Cohen Sacerdote, who was in Charleston in 1819 (Elzas, *South Carolina*, 139), in Mobile in 1830, running a store on Spring Hill Road (*Mobile Commercial Register*, July 1, 1830), and then turned up in Montgomery, in charge of the Alabama Exchange, offering liquor and refreshments, including "COFFEE, hot and strong, every morning" (*Alabama Journal*, September 10, 1831; January 28, 1832). Joseph Sacerdote was probably the first Jewish resident of Montgomery. In 1835 he was auctioning off property which he owned in East Wetumpka, Ala. (*Mobile Commercial Register*, November 14, 1835).

[40] Salomon's age at his death, fifty-three, is obtained from the data on his passport for a trip to Europe, 1828, in the writer's collection of Jewish Americana. Salomon was in New Orleans early enough to pay taxes on a horse and buggy in 1818–19 (mss. tax list, Miscellaneous New Orleans Collection, New-York Historical Society). Frascati advertisements are in *LG*, March 26, July 20, 26, 27, 31, 1821. NOCD, 1822, lists Salomon at Frascati, with a dwelling at 104 Royal. The bankruptcy is in *LG*, January 16, 31, 1822; June 13, 1826. It is possible that the bankruptcy applied to a business at 67 Chartres, also listed in *NOCD*, 1822, and not to Frascati, with which he still seems to have been associated in 1823 (*LG*, July 8, 1823). His legal problems connected with the gambling license are in Martin, *Louisiana Term Reports*, n.s., IV, 26–28. He was already on St. Philip street in 1826 (*LG*, May 6, 1826). Jonau's connection with the Ball Room and with Salomon is in *Bee*, August 27, November 10, 1834; April 1, 1835. Sacerdote died intestate; the inventory of his estate is in NOPC. Fossier, *New Orleans*, 359, 363, 460, 469, gives some realistic background about the Ball Room, "the scene of many scandalous and disgraceful brawls, fights and even murders," to counteract some of G. W. Cable's attractive, but fictional accounts.

[41] *Stamm- und Nachfahrentafeln der Familie Warburg Hamburg-Altona* (Hamburg, 1937), charts 2, 21, 22. A distant cousin of Daniel's, Frederick Warburg, came to Florida in 1821, briefly, to work for Moses Levy (Senator David Levy Yulee's father), but he did not remain in the United States very long (*PAJHS*, No. 25 [1917], 2 ff, 132–34); Frederick was already in Liverpool on January 2, 1822 (letter to his brother Martin, Historical Society of Pennsylvania).

[42] *LG*, June 19, 1821, is Warburg's first newspaper appearance. *Bee*, October 30, 1827, reports his return to New Orleans from a trip to New York. *Bee*, July 2, 21, August 23, September 6, October 18, November 21, 28, December 5, 21, 1831; February 2, 13, 1832, mark various stages in the organization of the Levee Steam Cotton Press, in which Warburg took a leading role. *Bee*, December 4, 1834, refers to buildings of which Warburg and the Architects Company were co-owners. Among many documents referring to real estate purchases and sales, and the construction of buildings, are L. T. Caire, Book IV, 239, August 13, 1828 (sale of a lot for $4,500); 326, October 10, 1828 (sale of a lot for $2,000); Wm. Christy, Book VI, 36–37, April 17, 1829 (purchase of land for $11,500); Caire, Book XII, act 678, August 5, 1830 (construction of three large buildings on Camp street); act 704, August 21, 1830 (construction of a building on Common street), NONA. The Caire notarial books record many other real estate operations during the 1830's. *Bee*, February 11, 1840, reports the auction of Warburg's interest in a plantation in St. Bernard Parish.

[43] *Bee*, April 4, 1835 (his candidacy for office); August 14, 1835 (quoting the St. Francisville paper); July 9, 14, August 7, 1836 (the "Lion and Serpent" communications). The two pamphlets are unrecorded in any bibliographies; the Library of Congress seems to have the only extant copies, the first of which is autographed by Warburg—they were accessioned in 1860.

[44] The Warburg family in Hamburg knew of the existence of Eugène and Daniel; they are listed in the family's genealogical charts in the *Stamm- und Nachfahrentafeln der Familie Warburg*. Eugène's birth year is given as 1826, young Daniel's as 1836, the latter's date of death as September 16, 1911, but the names of the other children and their mother are not included in the family tree. The elder Daniel's year of death is listed as 1860. We have been unable to discover any information about his death in the New Orleans press or in the notarial records. The elder Daniel was apparently so poor in 1853 that slaves held in his wife's name had to be sold for the benefit of the children. Eugène appeared at these transactions, and received $252.36 as his share of the proceeds. It may be that Eugène insisted that his mother's property be sold and divided before his departure for Europe. On the other hand, there is a St. Louis Cemetery No. 1 card in LSML for a Marie Rose Warburg, alias Blondeau, native of Santiago, Cuba, daughter of Venus Warburg, alias Blondeau, colored, died November 1, 1837, at the age of thirty-three. The date cannot be verified, but it seems to be too early, in view of the sale of Marie Rose's slaves in 1853 (A. Doriocourt, Book 9, acts 2–4, January 5, 1853, NONA). The elder Daniel's emancipation of Eugène is in Caire, Book V, 499 ff, March 27, 1830, NONA; the mother's purchase of a slave is in W. Y. Lewis, Book XXII, 327, February 10, 1837, NONA. The elder Daniel still owned a piece of real estate in the Washington suburb in 1856 which he sold for $600 (Conveyance Book LXX, 314–15, September 12, 1856, Civil District Court, New Orleans). Some data on Daniel and Eugène are in R.-L. Desdunes, *Nos Hommes et Notre Histoire* (Montreal, 1911), 95–98; James A. Porter, *Modern Negro Art* (New York, 1943), 46–47; Cedric Dover, *American Negro Art* (New York, 1960), 26. The Frick Art Reference Library has been helpful in assembling information about the sons. Desdunes reports that Eugène did some statuary for the St. Louis Cathedral, and that some of Daniel's cemetery monuments were impressive, but no precise evidence has identified any of these works.

[45] *MSAJD*, 68, for the Harby genealogy; Sam was born March 23, 1813, in Charleston. *NOCD*, 1838, lists his office at the *Bee*. Harby's earliest literary contribution which we have been able to discover was in the July 18, 1835, issue of the *Louisiana Recorder*, an early New Orleans literary periodical (*Bee*, July 20, 1835). His first marriage is in *Picayune*, March 25, 1842; Frances' death is in the LSML cemetery card file, November 9, 1850. The marriage to Sarah is in *NOG*, I (1962), 163—November 22, 1851. His death is in *Delta*, June 13, 1862. His succession papers, in NOPC, value his interest in the *Bee* at $15,000. His other possessions were worth almost $21,000.

[46] We know nothing about George's prior activities. He may have taught school in Charleston under his brother, or in Louisville, where he met Mary Lucas. On the other hand, he may already have begun dabbling in stagecraft: when Mary

died of cholera on October 12, 1834, while on a visit there, George was notified through a letter from Samuel Drake, the pioneer actor-impresario of the Kentucky area (*DAB*, V, 432), whom Harby could not have met in Charleston. James Rees, the theatrical writer, of whom more later, was at the family meeting in New Orleans, after Mary's death, when Sam (the first mention of his presence in the city) was chosen to serve as guardian for Margaret Porter, Mary's half-sister, NOPC. The information on George's Academy is in *Bee*, September 26, 1834, and *Picayune*, April 2, 1839; other notes on his educational activities are in *Bee*, January 11, 22, 1834; February 14, 1835; September 23, 1836. The fire is described in *Bee*, January 13, 1840. The second annual report of Harby's public school is in the *NOCD*, 1842, pp. 164–65. Some information about the development of New Orleans' public school system is in Robert C. Reinders, *End of an Era, New Orleans, 1850–1860* (New Orleans, 1964), 131 ff. The *NOCD*, 1855 and 1856, list George as a teacher.

[47] Information about Mary is in her succession papers, NOPC. Her estate was worth only $901, including a fifty-year-old slave. *Bee*, December 18, 1835, carried the report of the second marriage, which is also recorded in SLCMR, 6, p. 152.

[48] Neither *Tutoona* nor any other play by George Harby was ever published; there is, however, a photostatic copy of the manuscript of *Tutoona, or The Indian Girl*, as it is titled, probably in Harby's hand, in the AJA. With the manuscript are some clipped reviews, including that from an unidentified newspaper, from which our quotation is taken; these clippings do not include the critical one in the *Advertiser*, April 23, 1835. Rees's comments are in his *Dramatic Mirror and Literary Companion* (Phila.), II (1842), 51, and are reprinted in some of his other books and essays on the American theater. The presentations of *Tutoona* are listed in Smithers, "A History of the English Theatre at New Orleans." *Bee*, April 9, 1835, reports the benefit; *Bee*, May 10, 1835, describes the cornerstone ceremony.

[49] James Rees, *The Dramatic Authors of America* (Phila., 1845), 30, 88–89; *Dramatic Mirror*, I, August 14, 1841; *Picayune*, March 18, 20, 22, 23, 1838; Smithers, "A History of the English Theatre at New Orleans," 227; William G. Carson, *The Theater on the Frontier, The Early Years of the St. Louis Stage* (Chicago, 1932), 268, 271 (the report that in 1839 Harby went to St. Louis with the Sol Smith company for the performance of *Nick*, and even took part in the play as an actor). George's death is reported in *Bee*, June 28, 1862; his wife survived him by thirty years, dying at the age of seventy-two in 1892 (*Item*, February 19, 1892).

[50] Jacob Florance to Lavinia Florance Minis, February 10, 1861, Minis Papers, AJA.

[51] SLCMR, 5, act 286. The precise date of the wedding has hitherto not been published; no one, apparently, sought the information from the authorities of the Cathedral. It is difficult to explain Hermann's presence at the wedding for any reason other than that he was Benjamin's former employer and subsequent friend. A Jewish patron of great wealth who had also intermarried with a Roman Catholic might be a meaningful personage at this impecunious young Jew's wedding to a socially prominent young Catholic woman. It is, on the other hand, possible, but less likely, that Hermann was present on the invitation of the St. Martin family;

Natalie's father, Auguste, had been secretary of the New Orleans Insurance Company since 1824 (*LG*, August 13, 14, 1824)—and the Hermann family owned enough stock in the company for Samuel, Jr., to be elected to its board in 1834.

52 R. D. Meade, *Judah P. Benjamin, Confederate Statesman* (New York, 1943).

53 The Hyams genealogy is in *MSAJD*, 87. *JE*, VI, 512, reports his admission to the bar. *MSAJD* gives December 30, 1832, as the date of Eliza's wedding, but a compilation of family data by Elzas, ms. copy in AJA, reports the date given here. Elzas lists a number of weddings which the father conducted for relatives and friends. Marks, not to be confused with one James B. Marks (probably non-Jewish) who was in New Orleans during the same period, began his activities as a notary about 1836 (*Bee*, March 9, 1836); his estate is no. 4620 in NOPC.

54 *Bee*, January 17, 1834; August 17, 1835; *NOCD*, 1838; William W. Howe, "Reminiscences of the Bar of 1865," *Louisiana Bar Association Proceedings* (New Orleans, 1899), 94–95; *Picayune*, June 25, 26, 1875; *Times*, June 26, 1875; data in AJA from Judith Hyams Douglas, Baton Rouge.

55 Elzas, *South Carolina*, 134, 142, 168, 189, 205, 207; *Bee*, December 12, 1836; March 16, November 29, December 8, 1837; May 11, 1838; February 5, March 20, July 4, November 8, 1839; May 8, 1840; J. S. Whitaker, *Sketches of Life and Character in Louisiana, The Portraits Selected Principally from the Bench and Bar* (New Orleans, 1847), 34–37; Robert Gibbes Barnwell, *The New-Orleans Book* (New Orleans, 1851), 340–44—an essay by Cohen on "Gratitude;" *To the Members of the Permanent Committee on the New Orleans, Algiers, Attakapas and Opelousas Railroad* (New Orleans, 1851), signed by Cohen as Chairman; *Proceedings of the Convention and Central Executive Committee of the South-Western Industrial Fair* (New Orleans, 1852), 3–4, 23–24, 31; *Picayune*, February 24, 1887; *Proceedings at the Annual Meeting, of the New-Orleans Commercial Library Society, with an Address by M. M. Cohen, Esq.* (New Orleans, 1837); O. Z. Tyler, Jr.'s introduction to the 1964 reprint of Cohen's *Notices* in the Quadricentennial Edition of the Florida Facsimile and Reprint Series, published by the University of Florida Press.

1 *The Israelites of Louisiana*, 24, reports the tradition of services in 1750.

2 *Asmonean* (New York), August 2, 1850.

3 Appeal of Bene Israel Congregation, Cincinnati, to "The Elders of the Jewish Congregation at Charleston," July 3, 1825, photostat in AJA, printed in *PAJHS*, No. 10 (1902), 98–99.

4 J. S. Solis-Cohen, Jr., "Jacob S. Solis: Traveling Advocate of Judaism," *AJHQ*, LII (1963), 310–19; *MSAJD*, 196–97; Wolf and Whiteman, *Jews of Philadelphia*, 356, 452, 456, 495; *PAJHS* No. 27 (1920), 84, 120, 321, 327–28.

5 The resolutions are printed in *Courier*, February 10, 1830, and are included in the letter which Solomons sent to Charity Solis (AJHS Library). On March 13, 1828, Solis had purchased some real estate for $200 and promptly mortgaged it to Manis Jacobs, according to a memorandum of 1867, when Solis' children were attempting to clear up their father's estate (papers in the possession of J. S. Solis-Cohen, Jr., of Philadelphia); *Bee*, March 31, 1828, reports his receipt of some merchandise from New York City. A letter from Manis Jacobs to Solis, June 4, 1828 (AJHS Library)—printed in full later in this narrative—and a resolution of the Cincinnati congregation, August 7, 1829 (also AJHS Library), report on Solis' movements during 1828 and 1829. Solis' copy of Moses Lopez, *Lunar Calendar* (Newport, 1806) (copy in AJA), lists the birthdate of "Phebe Elizabeth" and implies that he was there at the time.

6 We have discovered no reference to Plotz earlier than this. His obituary in *Picayune*, June 15, 1881, reports that he was a native of Amsterdam, eighty-seven years old at the time of his death; the Mrs. J. Plotz who died at the age of twenty-nine on May 12, 1833, may have been his wife (*Argus*, May 15, 1833). He was in business with one or another of the men named Barnett in 1829–30 (*SC*, No. 2718; *Bee*, August 28, 1832). He and his wife were between twenty and thirty years old in the 1830 census, with a male child under five and a female slave. The N. M. Plotz who signed the 1847 constitution of the congregation (Touro Synagogue Archives) may have been this son.

7 Abraham Green is listed in the *NOCD*, 1822, as operating a clothing store at 79 Tchoupitoulas, above Poydras. In 1826 he sued a debtor, and some rigging from a brig was sold to satisfy the judgment in his favor (*LG*, July 21, 1826). In the 1830 census he is listed as thirty-forty years old, his wife between twenty-thirty, two sons five-ten and ten-fifteen and two daughters of similar age. One of the earliest known congregational records lists the birth of his son Salus, March 15, 1833, circumcised on April 30 by someone whose Hebrew name was Joseph ben Wolf (ms. digest of the congregation's history by Rabbi Emil Leipziger in AJA). An "A. Green" was a member of the Dispersed of Judah Congregation from

June 4, 1847, its date of incorporation, until his death some time before 1860 (*Constitution and By-Laws of the Hebrew Congregation of the "Dispersed of Judah"* [New Orleans, 1860]).

[8] Not a resident of New Orleans, but of Louisville, according to a letter of Manis Jacobs to Jacob S. Solis, June 4, 1828 (AJHS Library).

[9] This may have been the Bernard Lejeune who was active in the Bene Israel Congregation of Cincinnati and died there about 1833 (*MSAJD*, 157). Another Lejeune family came to New Orleans from Rotterdam, but David M. Levy of Philadelphia, who provided this information, does not know the date of their migration. The Bernard Lejeune of New Orleans was sued by creditors in 1832; property he had owned since 1828 was sold at auction (*Bee*, April 23, 1832; May 15, 1833).

[10] This may have been the Levy S. Levy, born in Charleston in 1806, who died in Vicksburg on July 30, 1833 (*MSAJD*, 1). The succession papers of his wife Mary, 1834, are in NOPC; she had a fifteen-month-old child named Sarah. J. L. Florance acted as curator of Mary's estate. The file indicates that the couple had been married in New Orleans. Another L. S. Levy is in the 1830 census: fifty-sixty years old, four male children between five and thirty, three female children between infancy and fifteen, with two female slaves and one free woman of color. Either or neither of these men may be the one who was a member of the congregation.

[11] *MSAJD*, 122, describes this man as coming to the United States from France with Lafayette in 1777, married to Rachel Salomon in Charleston, first child Alexander, born December 10, 1810. He must be identical with the New Orleans David Lewis whose wife's name was also Rachel Salomon, and who died on May 18, 1839 in New Orleans, succession records in the NOPC. *MSAJD* says that he was born in Strasburg about 1761; the succession records report him as a "native of Wurzburg, on the River Maine, Bavaria," and "about sixty-six years old" in 1839. His home was at 180 Tchoupitoulas street. He had done business with Daniel Goodman, Hart and Labatt, and Solomon Ferth; Isaac Phillips acted as curator of the estate. There is no mention of any children in these probate records.

[12] This may have been another brother of Jacob, Benjamin and Nathan Hart, born 1783; but this was an exceedingly common name at the time.

[13] Perhaps this was the M. J. Myers listed in the *NOCD*, 1822, with a dry goods store at 25 St. Louis street.

[14] When Manis Jacobs wrote to Solis on August 26, 1829, he reported that Prince had recently died.

[15] This man is unknown other than in the 1830 census, where he is listed as twenty-thirty years old, no one else in the household.

[16] Ferth was in New Orleans by 1821, when he testified as a witness to a complaint by Louis Kokernot. *NOCD*, 1822, listed him as a tailor at 77 Tchoupitoulas street. His age is forty-fifty in the 1830 census, with a wife forty-fifty, and a son under five.

[17] *JRBD*, 34; *MSAJD*, 47. Born in New York City in 1794, married Frances Polock August 30, 1821, died in New Orleans September 1, 1829. He had been in

Charleston in 1818 (Elzas, *South Carolina*, 134). On October 2, 1828, in New Orleans, he was sued by a creditor, and a small quantity of hats, shawls and other dry goods was sold to satisfy the debt (*Bee*, October 2, 1828). See Pool, *Portraits*, 276–77, for his father.

[18] This is probably Morton Phillips Levy, brother of Commodore Uriah P. Levy, husband of Rebecca Phillips, father of six children, one of whom, Mitchell, was born in New Orleans July 1, 1836 (*MSAJD*, 114). Newspaper references to his business affairs as follows: in 1832 he received a shipment of apples, butter, rope and other merchandise from Charleston; in 1834 and 1839 he entered suits against debtors (*Bee*, October 18, 1832; March 27, 1834; August 17, 1839). He was a member of the Dispersed of Judah Congregation from December 12, 1847, to his death before 1860 (*Constitution . . . "Dispersed of Judah"*).

[19] This may be the Solomon Emanuel Hunt in *MSAJD*, 86, who was born in Amsterdam in 1792, and died on May 7, 1846; he was married on May 15, 1827, to Rachel Peixotto. Another Solomon Hunt is a more likely candidate—his wife, Esther Millam Hunt, was in New Orleans by 1827, and appears in the notarial records in the 1830's (*Bee*, November 24, 1827; Edward Barnett, Book I [1836], acts 129–30; Book V [1839], acts 42 and 195, NONA); she was a widow by 1836 at the latest. This Mrs. Solomon Hunt was somehow related to the Kokernot family, and, like them, came from Amsterdam. She was buried in the Dispersed of Judah cemetery after her death in Biloxi on July 15, 1848 (Ms. Interment Book, AJA).

[20] Manis Jacobs' letter of August 26, 1829, to Solis reported that Leopold Jones, formerly of New York City, had died recently.

[21] An Andre Kerkhan is listed in the 1830 census, thirty-forty years old, with a young man twenty-thirty, a young woman fifteen-twenty, and a female slave. *Letter from the Secretary of State*, 37, lists one A. Solomon Kirkham, waxmaker, twenty years old, migrating from Germany to New Orleans in 1820; but Rieder, *New Orleans Ship Lists, I*, 5, reads the same name as A. Solomon Kirkhaus. Alexandrine and Catherine Kirkham are in the list of oldest burials in the Shanarai-Chasset cemetery in the congregational archives, with no dates assigned to any of the names included.

[22] This is probably the man who went bankrupt in 1840 (*Bee*, March 9, 1840), the brother of Israel Solomons, listed below, and the father of Aaron Solomons, the secretary pro-tem who signed the condolence letter to Mrs. Solis. Aaron was born in Charleston in 1791, died in New Orleans March 15, 1851. Another brother of Joseph and Israel, Chapman, died in New Orleans on June 28, 1849 (*MSAJD*, 200).

[23] Block probably never lived in New Orleans, but was an early settler in Washington, Arkansas. He was a member of a large family of Bohemian Jews who were in the United States by about 1810. *MSAJD*, 19, lists some fragmentary, tentative data about the family. Many members of the Block family married members of the Cincinnati-Quincy-New Orleans Jonas family.

[24] Died in New Orleans July 23, 1828; more about him later.

326

25 This may be the Daniel De Pass who was born in Bordeaux, married Ann Watson Smith in Richmond, one of whose children was born in New Orleans in 1845 (*MSAJD*, 42). *Bee*, June 26, 1834; April 16, 1838, refer to business matters of the New Orleans De Pass.

26 We presume that this was Levi Jacobs, and that the L. Jacobs, Jr., listed below, was his son. L. Jacobs is listed with a son thirty-forty years old, in the 1830 census.

27 *MSAJD*, 136, reports a Morange family in the United States at this time. B. Morange & Son were in the dry goods business in New Orleans in 1827 (*Bee*, October 30, December 20, 1827); B. Morange's Medicated Oil remedy for the cure of various diseases is in *Courier*, May 18, 1826. Benjamin Morange had been a founder of Bnai Jeshurun in New York City in 1825 (Pool, *Old Faith*, 437).

28 Workum apparently did not live in New Orleans, but in Kentucky. He may have had business dealings with merchants in New Orleans, or may have been persuaded by Solis to make a contribution. Jacobs sent Solis a copy of the *Constitution* (letter, June 4, 1828).

29 This is probably Lewis Solomons, listed as a watchmaker in 1822 *NOCD*, and who sued David Kokernot, owed taxes, and went bankrupt, during the period 1832–34 (*Bee*, April 16, 1832; November 5, 1833; May 16, September 22, 1834).

30 This may be the man listed in *MSAJD*, 42, 223, as born in Savannah on July 12, 1786, married to Hannah Hart in Charleston in 1813. But De Pass was a common Jewish name in America and the West Indies during this period. In 1839 a Joseph De Pass was in the auction business in New Orleans (*Bee*, October 17, 1839).

31 From what we know of the brothers, this was probably Simon, rather than Salomon.

32 Samuel De Pass advertised ships for Mexico in 1835–39 (*Bee*, April 17, 1835; April 2, 1839). Both he and Joseph De Pass were incorporators of Dispersed of Judah Congregation in 1847.

33 In *NOCD*, 1822, M. Joseph is listed as a trader at 54 Orleans. He was apparently not in New Orleans in 1828 when Jacobs sent copies of the *Constitution* to Solis for delivery to him and others in Kentucky and elsewhere. He may be the Moses Joseph who married Abigail Audler in Charleston, May 24, 1818 (Elzas, *Marriage Notices*, 11); Audler is such an unusual name that it is presumed that she was a sister of Sol and the other Audler men. This would link M. Joseph to New Orleans in several ways.

34 It would be encouraging to believe that this was one of the family of refugees from Saint-Domingue, but we have no certain evidence of this.

35 This is another fairly common name. He was probably not the physician Isaac Montgomery Lyons who was with the Texian Army and died at A. C. Labatt's home in New Orleans on January 14, 1837, at the age of twenty-six (Will Book V, 426–28, NOPC), but he could conceivably have been the father (1774–1843): *MSAJD*, 130.

36 This may be the Israel Solomons, a native of Amsterdam, who was in Georgetown, S. C., by 1800, and the brother of Joseph and Chapman (*MSAJD*, 200).

37 This man had already left New Orleans for New York City by the time that Jacobs wrote to Solis in June, 1828. In *Argus*, January 19, 1828, he advertised lace goods, ladies' clothing, jewelry and perfume, for sale at his shop at 111 Royal street "all of which will be sold by wholesale or retail, at very reduced prices, as the subscriber contemplates leaving the city in a short time for New York."

38 These were civic officials, merchants, bankers, attorneys and notaries who must have had close business relationships with Jews who were active in the formation of the congregation.

39 Jacobs' succession papers, in NOPC, dated September 28, 1839, say that he was about fifty-seven years old at the time of his death. *Bee*, September 24, 27, 1839, report variously that he had been in New Orleans for twenty-eight and thirty years. *LG*, May 1, September 5, 1812, reports the theft, and the dissolution of the partnership. Jacobs' suit against Cholros on January 22, 1814, is in the Miscellaneous New Orleans Collection, New-York Historical Society. The slave purchases are in Nicholas Broutin, Book for 1817, pp. 194–95; Carlisle Pollock, VIII, 376, April 14, 1822; IX, 677, June 24, 1822, NONA.

40 Bernard Hart died in Havana, Cuba, while on a business trip; his succession papers in NOPC report that he was twenty-nine years old, a native of Beaufort, South Carolina, the son of Simon Moses Hart and Rachel Levy. He and Irma had one son, Arthur. Manis' own succession papers refer to Irma as his daughter, not Angélique's. Data about Angélique is from René J. Le Gardeur, Jr., *The First New Orleans Theatre, 1792–1803* (New Orleans, 1963), 23–26, and correspondence with Mr. Le Gardeur. The time of the wedding of Manis and Angélique is estimated from the fact that in the January 2, 1826, marriage agreement between her son and Marie Chevalier of Saint-Domingue, the mother still bore the last name Verneuille, while on July 12, 1826, Angélique and Manis signed an agreement whereby he was to take charge of her financial affairs (Chr. de Armas, Book XIII, acts 4 and 200, NONA); this probably indicates that they waited to get married until her son had settled down. Angélique's cemetery card at LSML says that she was sixty-nine at her death on August 4, 1851, a native of Paris. Angélique's compensation for her Uncle Fontaine's losses in Saint-Domingue amounted to 19,350 francs (*Etat Détaillé des Liquidations*, IV, 60; VI, 28).

41 *NOG*, September, 1962, p. 3; *LG*, November 1, 1823; *Bee*, April 27, June 26, July 14, 19, 1832; February 19, 1834; April 30, 1835; March 19, 30, 1838; July 16, August 10, December 16, 1839; succession records of Manis Jacobs and Bernard Hart, NOPC.

42 *Bee*, September 27, 1839; his family certainly thought of him as the "Rabbi"— his son-in-law, Bernard Hart, said in the death certification, in the succession papers, that Manis had been "late a merchant and Rabbi of the Israelite congregation . . . of this city."

43 *Allgemeine Zeitung*, VI (1842), 295.

44 Heller, *Temple Sinai*, 4; it has been impossible to locate these descendants.

45 Schappes, *Documentary History*, 179–81, prints the wording of the charter as it appeared, with many errors, in the legislative journal.

[46] The *Ketubah* is in the possession of the Southern Jewish Historical Society, a gift of Mrs. Adele Clark, Daniel and Amelia's granddaughter. Heller, *Temple Sinai*, 2, errs when he says that Adolphus Sterne's wedding to Rosine Ruff on June 2, 1828, was a Jewish ceremony.

[47] The sale of property by Jacobs to the congregation is in Conveyance Book III, 522, Civil District Court, and Carlisle Pollock, Book for 1828, 347–48, NONA. The act of incorporation is in *Argus*, April 10, 1828; the exchange of letters (in French) is in *Bee*, April 26, 1828; the notice to sign and pay up is in *Courier*, April 15, 1828; the first of dozens of advertisements notifying the congregants of the deadline is in *Bee*, June 12, 1828—the last appearance is August 12, 1828.

[48] Jacobs left a space here for the insertion of the number of *Constitution* pamphlets which he was sending, but he forgot to fill it in after listing all the people who were to receive copies.

[49] The officers of the congregation were so proud of the *Constitution* and of the useful calendar which it included that they advertised copies for public sale at one dollar each (*Bee*, July 1, 1828). But it had obviously been published early enough for Jacobs to send copies to Solis with this letter.

[50] Lurie may have been the Jacob Lurie whose Torah scroll was loaned to New Orleans by Shearith Israel Congregation in 1833 (Pool, *Old Faith*, 434). There was a Jacob Luria in New Orleans in 1835–36, however, who went bankrupt, spoke at an anti-abolitionist meeting, and opened a law office at 3 Bourbon street (*Bee*, April 23, August 12, December 18, 1835; April 30, 1836).

[51] There is an indication here of the date of Solis' departure from New Orleans. Jacobs does not tell Solis the name of the deceased, Hyam Harris, who died on June first (*MSAJD*, 68); the implication is that Solis left after the death, but before the burial of Harris actually took place, or else Solis would have given his answer to the question about interment—on which subject there are many divergent opinions. Harris' is reported to be the first death in the congregation after the purchase of the cemetery (Isaac Markens, *The Hebrews in America* [New York, 1888], 89, which however gives the wrong date). The request for letters from Natchez and subsequent stops would lead one to believe that this letter was sent to Solis in Natchez.

[52] This would suggest that Solis was soliciting contributions for the New Orleans congregation from Jews in these towns. Certainly the reverse was true—on August 7, 1829, the Cincinnati people passed a resolution which expressed appreciation to Solis for "his liberal donation and his useful exertions in getting subscriptions from our Israelite brethren in New Orleans in aiding us to erect a place of worship" (letter from Bene Israel to Solis, in AJHS Library).

[53] This letter is in the AJHS Library; it was previously published in Shpall, *Jews of Louisiana*, 19–20. Our reading differs from Shpall's in a number of places. "Mr. Marks" must have been A. J. Marks and, as we shall see, it was just like him to complain about the length of the service.

[54] Stern's bankruptcy is in *LG*, June 23, 1824; June 24, 1826. Isaac was Stern's son by Jeanette, according to the succession papers, NOPC. Adolphus was Stern's

son by a first wife, whose name is not known. How Isaac was related to the Van Ostern family is not indicated, nor is there any suggestion of how Jeanette Hunt Stern may have been related to Solomon Hunt. But in view of the dealings Mrs. Kokernot had with Mrs. Hunt, it is possible that all of these people constituted one vast clan through natural and marriage relationships. Emanuel had not been successful. He owed Edward Gottschalk $900; his furniture and stock of dry goods had to be auctioned off so that the debt could be settled. Gottschalk was curator of the estate. Stern had paid $100 per month rent. Two slaves who belonged to the Sterns were also sold at auction; one was eighty years old! (*Argus*, July 29, August 13, 15, 26, 1828).

[55] Adolphus Sterne deserves a full-scale study, but his significance for New Orleans is a minor one. His diary for 1840–44, 1851, is in the *Southwestern Historical Quarterly* XXX (1926) –XXXVIII (1934). The introductory sketch (XXX, 139) reports that he was born in Cologne, April 15, 1801, the son of a Jew and a Lutheran. This is difficult to believe. His diary indicates that he had a knowledge of Jewish ritual and some rudimentary ability to write Hebrew or Yiddish—on October 6, 1840 (XXXI, 65) he wrote "to night is *erev Yom Kippur* [in Hebrew]"; on July 15, 1841 (XXXII, 165, 179) he reported that a neighbor with whom he was very friendly, Michael De Young ("a German Jew of the *old reverend class*") had sent him "A Book . . . containing the Service of *Yom Kippur* in the portuguese *minik* [minhag—rite]"; on October 1, 1843 (XXXVI, 221) he wrote "to day is *Yom Kippur* Mr. Flateau [a Jewish partner of De Young] is doing Penance, nonsense, to keep up a Religion only one day in the year." Sterne relished the fact that T. M. Flateau (who would ever know him to be a Jew with that name?) was going to be co-publisher of the *San Augustin Literary Intelligencer*—"a Methodist Paper—(oh! dear)—& to be under the management of a *Son of Abraham*" (XXXVII, 43—entry for December 22, 1843). All of this speaks too clearly of Adolphus' rearing as a Jew, which would have been unlikely in Europe, if his mother had really been a Christian; it is hard to believe that an intermarriage would have been conducted anywhere in Germany without the father's conversion, and Emanuel had obviously remained a Jew. Perhaps some descendant confused Adolphus' mother with his wife, Eva Catherine Rosine Ruff, whom he married in Natchitoches on June 2, 1828. Catherine had come to Louisiana from Germany with her father, mother, sister and two brothers on February 22, 1820, when they landed at New Orleans from the brig *Eugene* (Rieder, *New Orleans Ship Lists*, I, 13); she was then ten years old. Other relevant material in Adolphus' diary includes: the report that Isaac, orphaned in 1828, was keeping a store and "a Billiard Table and Bar Room— (no good place for him)" in Natchitoches in 1842 (XXXV, 321); information that Adolphus also had a sister named Nancy, unmentioned in the succession papers, who kept in touch with Isaac; she was married to a man named Stevens or Steevens (XXXI, 82–83); a note that Michael De Young's mother-in-law was a Mrs. Morange—it is natural to wonder if she was a member of the Morange family of New Orleans (XXXV, 153); a reference to a stepbrother of Adolphus, in New Orleans, named Bernard Cohen (XXXVII, 49, 59, 137). Rabbi Newton J. Friedman of Beaumont, Texas, who has worked with the Sterne materials, is convinced that Adolphus was not reared as a Christian, or converted to Christianity, despite

330

the many references to Catholic and Protestant ideas and faith in his diary; I am inclined to believe that, while Adolphus was in no way an observant Jew, if he was anything at all, he was one of those secularized Jews who make Masonry their religion. It is impossible to explain how Adolphus could have had a stepbrother named Bernard Cohen unless the first Mrs. Emanuel Stern was divorced and married a Mr. Cohen, or the second Mrs. Emanuel Stern had had a first husband named Cohen—but there is no confirmation of either of these possibilities in the Stern succession papers.

[56] "Doct A Costa" was Dr. Isaac Da Costa who did not practice medicine in New Orleans, but had a little store at 32 Canal street. He died in 1830. The inventory listed his stock as worth only $653.96, according to the succession papers, NOPC, June 7, 1830. Da Costa's widow, Jane, moved to Mobile in 1832 and opened a "fancy" store there, with Dr. Da Costa's sister Sarah's husband, Ralph Canter, as her partner: *Mobile Register*, May 6, 1832; *MSAJD*, 22, 222.

[57] Letter in AJHS Library.

[58] Pool, *Old Faith*, 434. No answer from Hendricks has been found. The deed of sale of the lot of ground by the city of New Orleans to the congregation is in Felix de Armas, Book for 1829, No. 903, August 25, 1829, NONA, brought to my attention by Samuel Wilson, Jr.

[1] Letter, November 1, 1807, quoted in *Parke-Bernet Auction Sale Catalogue*, October 17, 1961, lot 109. *Courier*, May 3, 1811, includes "Gratz and Co." in a list of recipients of letters to be called for at the New Orleans post office. Either Joseph or Ben Gratz might then have been in New Orleans on business. In later years Ben had extensive business relations with New Orleans firms, shipping the bagging that he manufactured in Lexington, Kentucky, down the Ohio and Mississippi rivers. See *Letters of Rebecca Gratz*, 93, 96–97, for reference to a visit to New Orleans by Ben Gratz' wife.

[2] Carl Kohn Letter Book, September 23, 1833. "Salaud" is the equivalent of "dirty dog."

[3] Carl Kohn Letter Book, November 16, 1833.

[4] Reissner, " 'Ganstown,' " 26.

[5] *PAJHS* No. 21 (1913), 169; No. 27 (1921), 91, 315; Wolf and Whiteman, *Jews of Philadelphia*, 362, 496 (there is an error in the statement that A. M. Nathan was buried in Mikveh Israel cemetery in 1841); Goldstein, *A Century of Judaism*, 383; Simon Cohen, *Shaaray Tefila* (New York, 1945), 6, 14, 62–64; Rochelle's burial in Philadelphia as a non-member of Mikveh Israel brought an unexpected $250 to the congregational treasury (report by Maxwell Whiteman based on an examination of the Mikveh Israel records); the description of Hermann's contribution, May 26, 1836, from Dr. Andernacht of the State Archive of Frankfurt am Main.

[6] For an earlier treatment of Touro's relationship to Judaism, see Korn, "A Reappraisal of Judah Touro," *Jewish Quarterly Review*, XLV (1955), 568–81. Pool, *Old Faith*, 49, reports that both Touro and Jacob Hart were asked for donations to Shearith Israel, but neither responded. David Philipson, "The Cincinnati Community in 1825," *PAJHS*, No. 10 (1902), 99, records the request to Touro from Bene Israel. Much later, in 1848, the Savannah congregation asked for Touro's help in paying a *hazan's* salary, but he refused the request (Mickveh Israel Congregation minute book, August 21, 1848, AJA, quoted by Floyd Herman in a term paper, "Jewish Life in Savannah, 1790–1880," AJA).

[7] *OCC*, XI (March, 1854), 591.

[8] *Christ Church History* (New Orleans, 1947), 11, where the date is given as 1819; but it was more likely to have been 1816, when sixty-one pews were sold for a total of $13,000. Hodding Carter and Betty Werlein Carter, *So Great a Good* (Sewanee, 1955), 7–8, 20, 411, give details of Shepherd's interest in and service to the church, but do not print the list of purchasers of pews.

[9] Clapp, *Autobiographical Sketches*, 94, 101–103.

10 *OCC*, XI (March, 1854), 590; *Niles' Weekly Register* (Baltimore), December 27, 1823.

11 Carter, *So Great a Good*, 72, 76; *Christ Church History*, 11.

12 Leonard V. Huber and Samuel Wilson, Jr., *The Basilica on Jackson Square* (New Orleans, 1965), 31–34; Touro inventory.

13 Clapp, *Autobiographical Sketches*, 101–102; Reinders, *End of an Era*, 119–20.

14 Clapp, *Autobiographical Sketches*, 97 (italics his).

15 *OCC*, XI, 590.

16 Parson Clapp said in his laudatory sermon after Touro's death that "He knew well that many of the recipients of his bounty hated the Hebrews, and would, if possible, sweep them into annihilation. He consulted not their ill-desert, meanness, prejudice and sin, but only how they might be best raised from debasement and destitution." "Hated the Hebrews," and "sweep them into annihilation," are strong words indeed. Were these Clapp's conclusions or Touro's? (*Asmonean* [New York], February 17, 1854).

17 Peter Guilday, *The Life and Times of John Carroll* (New York, 1922), 711.

18 *Bee*, September 5, 1834; Parker also said, "The Protestants can hardly be said to be in a much better state." See also Rabbi Isaac Leeser's comment in *OCC*, VIII (1850), 116: "The Christian population itself was but little given to religious observances, and formerly a degree of freedom in living was indulged in but little promotive of the growth of piety."

19 Joseph Lyons, quoted in Jacob Rader Marcus, *Memoirs of American Jews, 1775–1865* (Phila., 1956), I, 260–61.

20 *LG*, June 26, 1824. Samuel Hermann and A. M. Nathan had their office on Chartres street; Rochelle and Shiff were on St. Louis. Clay was a tobacco inspector who ran for alderman of the first ward and lost. The sale of his home, property, four slaves and some stock was held in January, 1825 (*LG*, April 6, 24, May 3, 21, June 3, December 7, 1824).

21 *LG*, May 26, 1826. News of Noah's colony in *LG*, February 25, 1820, and *Courier*, March 29, 1820. Several attempts to mimic the accent of German Jews appeared in *LG*, November 30, 1822; September 8, 1823.

22 *Bee*, December 3, 21, 1835. Edward Gottschalk was secretary of this society, which met at 113 Chartres street; it was open from 4 to 10 p.m. every day and all day Sunday. Cohen added to his income by serving as a "Transcriber, Translator and Book-keeper."

23 Kendall, *The Golden Age of the New Orleans Theater*, 323.

24 Quoted in Marcus, *Memoirs of American Jews*, III, 104. After the Civil War, Hyams' law partner, Benjamin Franklin Jonas, became, successively, city attorney of New Orleans, a member of the state legislature, Senator from Louisiana (1879–

1885), and collector of the port of New Orleans (*Picayune*, December 22, 1911). For a brief biography of Moïse, who was in Woodville, Mississippi, in 1836, and in New Orleans by 1840, and who served as a member of the Louisiana legislature for about fifteen years, see Harold Moïse, *The Moïse Family of South Carolina* (Columbia, S. C., 1961), 48–50.

[25] *Charter and Rules of the Boston Club, of New Orleans* (New Orleans, 1879), 18–20; *Picayune*, August 28, 1895; Stuart O. Landry, *History of the Boston Club* (New Orleans, 1938), 220–49; Augusto P. Miceli, *The Pickwick Club of New Orleans* (New Orleans, 1964), 24, 87, 95, 207–208, 220. The social exclusion of Jews in contemporary New Orleans was the subject of a journalistic essay by Calvin Trillin in *The New Yorker*, March 9, 1968, 138–44. Landry, 165 f, identifies Louis J. Salomon as the first Mardi Gras Rex, in 1872. He was the son of Jacob Hart's nephew, Ezekiel Salomon, and a great-grandson of Haym Salomon of the Revolutionary War. He was buried in the Shearith Israel Cemetery of New York City, May 6, 1925 (New York City Health Dept., Certificate No. 2388, dated April 26, 1941), courtesy of his grandniece, Muriel Schaeffer Carter, via Rabbi Malcolm Stern.

[26] Marcus, "Light on Early Connecticut Jewry," *American Jewish Archives*, I (1949), No. 2, esp. 27, 37. Malcolm Stern, "The Function of Genealogy in American Jewish History," *Essays in American Jewish History* (Cincinnati, 1958), 85, ventures some conclusions about the rate of intermarriage on the basis of available data, but Stern's list of families is far from complete, and he would be the first to admit that those Jews whom he did not trace were the most likely to have disappeared from the Jewish community through intermarriage. It is hoped that a name-by-name and family-by-family search, such as we have pursued for New Orleans, may be undertaken for other frontier cities and areas; an accumulation of such studies may help to answer our question about the extent of assimilation and disappearance during the first generation of the settlement of Jews as individuals.

[27] Cohen's succession papers, NOPC; after the inventory was taken, the property was sold at auction (*LG*, October 9, 21, 1826).

[28] *The Dedication of the Home for Jewish Widows and Orphans of New Orleans, January 9, 1856 . . . together with the Oration of B. F. Jonas, Esq . . .* (New Orleans, 1856), 18; Association for the Relief of Jewish Widows and Orphans, minute book of the board of directors, AJA, 7 ff. R. D. Shepherd gave a contribution of $250, in May, 1855. Armand and Michel Heine and Joachim Kohn were elected honorary members on March 29, 1857; Carl was elected on May 19, 1857; after the Heine brothers moved to Paris they were elected life members. Armand had been a member of the Dispersed of Judah Congregation (*Constitution*, 1860). When a new "Home" was erected in 1886, a plaque listed the names of major contributors, including Michel Heine (*Israelites of Louisiana*, 52). A brief sketch of Adolph Meyer, called "General," is given in *Israelites of Louisiana*, 117. Both Victor and Adolph Meyer figure in Carl's estate papers, succession no. 46,980, NOPC. Stanley Clisby Arthur, *Old Families of Louisiana* (New Orleans, 1931), 398, lists the White genealogy, but skips the generation between Carl and Clara Kohn and Evelyn and Victor Meyer's children. The obituary tribute to Edouard Kohn in *Archives Israélites*, V (1895), 124–25, gives some data about his philanthropic activity; the files of the

Alliance on Edouard are fairly slim—from 1881 to 1895 he lived at 49 Rue Blanche, Paris; some of his correspondence with the Alliance office was written from Meggenhorn, Switzerland, while he was visiting his cousin Marie Amélie Heine; Edouard regularly made large financial contributions to the Alliance. André Chouraqui, *Cent Ans d'Histoire l'Alliance Israélite Universelle et la Renaissance Juive Contemporaine (1860–1960)* (Paris, 1965), 420, 428, reports that Edouard was first elected to the central committee of the Alliance in 1876, and served as treasurer from 1885 until his death in 1895. Adolph Meyer, incidentally, married Benjamin F. Jonas' daughter Rosalie.

[29] Korn, "Judah P. Benjamin as a Jew," *PAJHS*, No. 38 (1949), 153–71, reprinted in Korn, *Eventful Years and Experiences* (Cincinnati, 1954), 79–97. For several of Benjamin's early Jewish clients, see the succession papers of Levy S. Levy, 1834, NOPC, and *Bee*, May 31, 1834 (J. L. Florance was curator of the estate); *Bee*, April 1, 1835, the bankruptcy of H. M. Hart and L. Solomon.

[1] Little is known of this synagogue building, other than references to it in various newspaper notices about annual meetings. It is located on Zimpel's 1834 map of New Orleans and is keyed in the list of churches.

[2] Shearith Israel Trustees' Minute Book, June 18, 1833, pp. 428–29, microfilm in AJA. Some excerpts from this letter are in Pool, *Old Faith*, 434. The Minute Book also refers to a letter from Luria asking that the Torah be sent to New Orleans.

[3] *Bee*, September 21, 1837. There seems to be no clear record of Dr. Bensadon's arrival in New Orleans. Elzas, *South Carolina*, 206, reports that he graduated in 1838; but the following year he was practicing in Mobile as a former New Orleans physician (*Mobile Commercial Register*, October 25, December 27, 1839). The father had served as Mikveh Israel's *hazan* in Philadelphia in 1817, 1819 and 1822 (Wolf-Whiteman, *Jews of Philadelphia*, pp. 251, 363).

[4] The Reas weddings are in *Bee*, May 5, 1835, where Moses is referred to as "the Revd. Moses S. Reas, of the Israelitish Congregation." One wonders if he could be the B. Rees who was so enterprising as to advertise his Comb and Variety Store, 44 Canal street, New Orleans, in the *Mobile Commercial Register*, November 26, 1828. Wedding ceremonies conducted by Jacobs are announced in *Bee*, March 16, 1837; January 31, 1838; February 9, 1839. Some Jewish couples were married first by a parish judge, then by a Jewish officiant: *Bee*, April 3, 1839 (Jacob L. Levy and Sarah Edwitha Marks), November 16, 1839 (David Aaron and Sarah Jacobs).

[5] *Bee*, October 28, November 7, 1834; October 11, 1836; *NOCD*, 1838; *Bee*, October 8, 1839.

[6] Sarah Cohn will, filed September 23, 1833; Marius Cohen succession papers, 1836; David Lewis succession papers, 1839—all in NOPC; *Bee*, August 29, 1837. The procedure whereby the congregation acted as a sort of "family" for strangers in the community, or for members without relatives, was embodied in a by-law adopted in 1841, which authorized the officers to apply to the courts for appointment as administrators of the estate, and to conduct the inventory in accordance with legal procedures (1841 ms. By-Laws, Touro Synagogue archives).

[7] 1841 ms. By-Laws; Heller, *Temple Sinai*, 8.

[8] *Bee*, July 19, 1832, the text of Crémieux' letter of April 4, 1832, in response to the resolutions which had been passed on August 10, 1831 (the Abbé died on May 28, 1831); this letter was still in the possession of descendants of Manis Jacobs in 1922 when Rabbi Heller wrote his *Temple Sinai*, 4. The synagogue lectures are advertised in *Bee*, October 16, 18, 1834.

[9] Marriage Contract books of the congregation, beginning in 1839, the oldest surviving congregational records, in the Touro Synagogue archives, copies in AJA. The oldest certificate with his signature is that of Jacob L. Levy and Sarah E. Marks, March 30, 1839—not in the congregational books—given to AJA by

336

their grandson, Charles B. Levy; this was a wedding previously conducted by a judge, reported in *Bee*, April 3, 1839. The grave registers in the Touro Synagogue archives, dating from fairly recent times, but listing some of the oldest interments, do not report the name of the officiating rabbi.

[10] Carson, *Theater on the Frontier*, 127, 130; William Bryan Gates, "The Theater in Natchez," *The Journal of Mississippi History*, III (1941), 87; Kendall, *Golden Age of the New Orleans Theater*, 78, 86, 162, 167, 229–30; N. M. Ludlow, *Dramatic Life As I Found It* (St. Louis, 1880), 269–70 (our quotation), 303–304, 380–81, 389, 423, 561, 660; Sol Smith, *Theatrical Management in the West and South for Thirty Years* (New York, 1868), 201–202; Smithers, "History of the English Theater," 133, 170, 187, 192, 235, 251, 266, 274. The Missouri Historical Society, St. Louis, has playbills for Sol Smith's Natchez season of 1830, with Marks appearing in twenty-four performances, sometimes in two different roles the same evening. Marks as fireman is in *Bee*, July 16, 1834; May 17, 1836; September 2, 28, October 16, 1837; March 18, 1840. Other Jews who were active in the fire companies at this time were A. H. Harris, A. C. Labatt and B. Van Ostern.

[11] *Bee*, August 22, 28, September 4, 10, October 11, 1839; February 18, May 22, 1840; *Picayune*, February 5, 1842.

[12] *Allgemeine Zeitung*, VI (1842), 295; *Bee*, July 10, 11, 1835—one James Lawler advertised a $100 reward for another actor named Marks accused of stealing $350 in cash, and jewelry worth more than $200, describing this man as "a London Jew by birth and bad address for one of the sect," but stating that this was not Roley, who had a good family reputation. The New Orleans Public Library's manuscript list of plays and casts takes Marks through 1849; his last appearance was on October 31, 1849, touted as a benefit for him. The Harvard University Library's theater collection has dozens of playbills which include his name during the period 1843–47. The Sol Smith collection at the Missouri Historical Society includes a letter from Marks to Smith and Ludlow, June 9, 1847, New Orleans, offering his services for the fall season at the St. Charles Theater; in the same collection is a list of expenses for a season in Mobile, year not noted—with Marks listed at $12 (per week?). Marks's name does not appear in the incomplete list of early interments in the Shanarai-Chasset cemetery which is in the Touro Synagogue archives, nor in the Dispersed of Judah cemetery register in AJA. He is not in the cemetery card file at LSML, but his daughter Miriam is in that file, as having died on January 6, 1838, buried in the Shanarai-Chasset cemetery. The 1840 census lists Marks with a male child under five years of age, four males between twenty and thirty, one female child between five and ten, one between fifteen and twenty, two females between twenty and thirty, and eleven slaves. His daughter Bell Virginia married Henry William Canney on July 11, 1860, in Christ Church (*NOG*, June, 1963, p. 229); an Albert Stonewall Canney was buried in the Hebrew Rest Cemetery, April 6, 1904, born January 1, 1863 (LSML cemetery card)—he was probably Virginia's son. Eliza Marks, Roley's wife, died on September 8, 1880, while on vacation in Knoxville in the company of her granddaughter Minnie V. Canney. The Knoxville Jews assisted in making arrangements for the shipment of the body, and Eliza's son, Harry H. Marks, came to Knoxville to accompany his

mother's remains back to New Orleans. Eliza had been born in New Berne, N. C., in July, 1812 (Knoxville *Daily Chronicle*, September 9, 11, 1880; LSML cemetery card).

[13] A brief sketch of Leeser is in Korn, *American Jewry and the Civil War* (Phila., 1951), 6; further information is given in Maxwell Whiteman, "Isaac Leeser and the Jews of Philadelphia," *PAJHS*, XLVIII (1959), 213–14. Some discussion of the problem of rabbinical leadership in this period is in Korn, *Eventful Years and Experiences*, 35–36, 39–40. Korn, "Isaac Leeser: Centennial Reflections," *American Jewish Archives*, XIX (1967), No. 2, pp. 127–41, is an effort to evaluate Leeser's significance.

[14] The two most informative sketches of Kursheedt's life are obituaries in the *Jewish Chronicle* (London), May 15, 1863, and *Jewish Record* (New York), June 5, 1863. There are many references to the father in Ezekiel and Lichtenstein, *Jews of Richmond;* in Pool, *Old Faith* and *Portraits;* and in *PAJHS*. The first mention of Gershom in New Orleans concerns meetings of the Whig Party, in *Bee*, May 14, 27, June 24, 1840. Gershom's activity in the Howard Association is reported in the *Record* obituary, and in *Commercial Times*, January 1, 1849. Leeser's tribute to the father, and his recollection of their meeting, friendship and scholarly contact, are in *OCC*, X (1852), 162–67.

[15] *OCC*, I (1843), 216, 352–53, 516; II (1844), 512; III (1845), 416; mss. by-laws, Shanarai-Chasset, 1841, copy in AJA; *Israelites of Louisiana*, 41; *Constitution of "Dispersed of Judah"* (New Orleans, 1860), 18. *OCC*, VIII (1850), 198, reports that a Society Bikkur Cholim (Visiting of the Sick) had been organized in 1845—this, presumably, was different from the Benevolent Society, which was for charity rather than personal service.

[16] *DeBow's Review*, V (1848), 240.

[17] Kursheedt to Leeser, December 18, 5608 (1847), Leeser Collection, Dropsie College.

[18] Kursheedt to Leeser, March 20, 5608 (1848).

[19] Kursheedt to Leeser, January 1, May 2, 5609 (1849).

[20] *OCC*, VIII (1850), 109–19; XI (1854), 590–91; Isaac Hart to Leeser, September 9, 1851, Leeser Collection; *Delta*, January 6, 1852.

[21] Nathan to Leeser, January 9, 1853, Leeser Collection.

[22] *OCC*, VIII (1850), 8, 262–63, 317, 432; IX (1851), 57–59; Cenas, Book 47, f. 17, July 5, 1850, NONA; Huhner, *Judah Touro*, 89–92; Heller, *Temple Sinai*, 5–7, 48 ff.

[23] *Centennial Volume, Gates of Prayer* (New Orleans, 1950); *Israelites of Louisiana*, 42.

[24] Kursheedt to Leeser, February 19, 5614 (1854).

[25] The most accurate printed version of Touro's will is in Schappes, *Documentary History*, 333–41, 656–62, which also contains information on the background of the various beneficiary institutions.

[26] Kursheedt to Leeser, February 19, 5614 (1854); David de Sola Pool, "Some Relations of Gershom Kursheedt and Sir Moses Montefiore," *PAJHS*, No. 37 (1947), 214–20; Huhner, *Judah Touro*, 105, 123 ff; Michael Avi-Jonah (ed.), *Jerusalem* (New York, 1960), 162. One M. Solomons wrote a mocking letter to Leeser, from New York, February 8, 1854, commenting sarcastically about Shepherd's inheritance. It is worth noting that Shepherd gave large sums of money from his own portion of the Touro estate to the city of New Orleans, amounting to about a quarter of a million dollars (*Asmonean* [New York], February 10, 1854; *Daily Crescent*, January 21, 1859).

[27] Details of these services are in Huhner, *Judah Touro*, 102–17. The quotation is from *Bee*, January 21, 1854.

[28] In the weekly issues of the *Asmonean* (New York), beginning with January 24, 1854, and continuing for months, the reader senses the tremendous excitement which was generated by Touro's will in the non-Jewish as well as the Jewish press. Memorial resolutions were passed by congregations and institutions throughout the country, and printed in the *Asmonean*. News about Touro's benefactions was printed in Jewish papers in London, Paris, Berlin, and Italy. Touro's bounty to the Jews of Palestine was publicized again after Sir Moses finally had the houses built outside of Jerusalem. Touro's name appeared frequently in the European Jewish press throughout the decades as an example of noble generosity.

Acknowledgements

The author gratefully acknowledges the assistance of the following librarians, scholars and friends: Mr. David Cohen, Secretary of the Touro Synagogue; Mr. Boyd Cruise; Mr. Solomon S. Goldman; Mrs. Connie G. Griffith, Director, Manuscripts Division, Tulane University; Miss Louise Hubert Guyol; Mr. Isaac S. Heller; Mr. Maunsel White Hickey; Mr. Leonard V. Huber, Louisiana Landmarks Society; Mrs. E. LeBourgeois, Superintendent, St. Louis Cemeteries; Miss Marjorie Le Doux; Mr. René J. Le Gardeur, Jr.; Reverend Vincent Liberto, O.M.I., St. Mary's Church; Mr. Albert Louis Lieutaud; Mr. Charles R. Maduell, Jr.; Mr. Donald Meyer; Mrs. Josephine Moise; Miss Dolores Morgadanes; Mrs. Mary Oalmann, Librarian, State of Louisiana Military Department, Jackson Barracks; Reverend Charles E. O'Neill, S.J., Loyola University; Dr. Robert C. Reinders, Tulane University; Mr. James Reiss; Miss Margaret Ruckert, Head, Louisiana Department, New Orleans Public Library; Mr. Ray Samuel; Mr. A. L. Schlesinger; Reverend Nicholas S. Tanaskovic, O.M.I., St. Louis Cathedral; Dean Kenneth Trist Urquhart, St. Mary's Dominican College; Mr. Sidney L. Villeré; Mrs. Marie L. Weiss; Mrs. Dorothy Whittemore, Reference Librarian, Howard-Tilton Library at Tulane University; Mr. Samuel Wilson, Jr.; all of New Orleans, Louisiana. Also, Dr. H. Andernacht, Director, Stadt Archiv, Frankfurt Am Main, Germany; Monsignor Daniel J. Becnel, St. Aloysius RC Church, Baton Rouge, Louisiana; Mrs. G. A. Becnel, Lake Charles, Louisiana; Dr. Virgil Bedsole, Director, Department of Archives and Manuscripts, Louisiana State University, Baton Rouge, Louisiana; Miss Jeanne Behrend, Philadelphia, Pennsylvania; Rabbi William Berkowitz, Congregation B'nai Jeshurun, New York, New York; Mrs. Eleanor C. Bishop, Baker Library, Harvard University, Cambridge, Massachusetts; Mrs. Carl Black, Jackson, Mississippi; Miss Katherine F. Bridges, Librarian, Northwestern State College of Louisiana, Natchitoches, Louisiana; Mrs. E. A. Broders, Baton Rouge, Louisiana; Mr. F. H. Brunner, New York, New York; Mrs. S. R. Campbell, Vacherie, Louisiana; Miss Charlotte Capers, Director, Department of Archives and History, State of Mississippi, Jackson, Mississippi; Professor Samuel Burwell Barnett Carleton, University

340

of Texas, Austin, Texas; Miss Louise Emerson Carlisle, Chestnut Hill, Massachusetts; Mr. Clarkson Collins, III, Librarian, Rhode Island Historical Society, Providence, Rhode Island; Miss Pollyanna Creekmore, Chief, McClung Historical Collection, Knoxville Public Library, Knoxville, Tennessee; Miss Essae M. Culver, State Librarian, Baton Rouge, Louisiana; Mr. Alan d'Anglade, Archives Départementales de La Gironde, Bordeaux, France; Mr. J. Clarence Davies, New York, New York; George de Tarnowsky, M.D., Wilmette, Illinois; Mr. Jacques de Tarnowsky, Baton Rouge, Louisiana; Mr. Pierre A. de Tarnowsky, Chicago, Illinois; Messrs. Charles and Lindley Eberstadt, New York, New York; Dr. Isaac S. Emmanuel, Cincinnati, Ohio; Mr. Irving S. Forgotson, Gonzales, Texas; Miss Esther Frank, Montgomery, Alabama; Rabbi Newton J. Friedman, Beaumont, Texas; Dr. L. Fuks, University Library, Amsterdam, Netherlands; Mrs. Elizabeth B. (Mrs. S. J.) Gianelloni, Jr., Archivist, Diocese of Baton Rouge, Baton Rouge, Louisiana; Mr. Samuel Giberga, Miami, Florida; Miss Sarah Grossman, American Jewish Archives, Cincinnati, Ohio; Miss Lenore Harrington, Librarian, Missouri Historical Society, St. Louis, Missouri; Mrs. Henry W. Howell, Jr., Librarian, Frick Art Reference Library, New York, New York; Dr. Nathan M. Kaganoff, Librarian, American Jewish Historical Society, Waltham, Massachusetts; Rabbi Arthur B. Lebowitz, Temple B'nai Israel, Natchez, Mississippi; Mr. and Mrs. Harold Leisure, Natchez, Mississippi; Miss Evangeline Lynch, Librarian, Louisiana Room, Louisiana State University Library, Baton Rouge, Louisiana; Dr. John Francis McDermott, St. Louis, Missouri; Mlle. Marie-Antoinette Menier, Le Conservateur, Archives Nationales, Section Outre-mer, Paris; Dr. H. M. Mensonides, Director, Gemeente Archief, The Hague, Netherlands; Rabbi Isidore S. Meyer, Editor, American Jewish Historical Society, New York, New York; Mr. Stanley Morris, Philadelphia, Pennsylvania; Mr. James E. Moss, State Historical Society of Missouri, Kansas City, Missouri; Mr. Louis Raphael Nardini, Natchitoches, Louisiana; Professor A. P. Nasatir, San Diego State College, San Diego, California; Mr. D. Nuhlicek, State Archives, Prague, Czechoslovakia; Dr. James W. Patton, Director, Southern Historical Collection, University of North Carolina Library, Chapel Hill, North Carolina; Dr. David De Sola Pool, Rabbi, New York, New York; Dr. James A. Porter, Head, Department of Art, Howard University, Washington, D. C.; Dr. Oskar K. Rabinowicz, Scarsdale,

New York; Dr. H. G. Reissner, Flushing, New York; Mr. M. P. H. Roessingh, Keeper, First Section, Algemeen Rijksarchief, The Hague, Netherlands; Rabbi Kenneth D. Roseman, Hebrew Union College, Cincinnati, Ohio; Senator Leverett Saltonstall, Boston, Massachusetts; Mr. George A. Schwegmann, Jr., Chief, Union Catalogue Division, Library of Congress, Washington, D. C.; Mrs. Irma Peixotto Sellars, Beverly Hills, California; Dr. Clifford K. Shipton, American Antiquarian Society, Worcester, Massachusetts; Miss Mildred Steinbach, Assistant Librarian, Frick Art Reference Library, New York, New York; Rabbi Malcolm H. Stern, New York, New York; Mr. Zosa Szajkowski, New York, New York; Mr. W. Wichard Timmers, Leyden, Netherlands; Miss Anne Urquhart, New York, New York; Mr. Vilém, Director, State Jewish Museum, Prague, Czechoslovakia; Mrs. George H. Warren, Newport, Rhode Island; Mrs. Ruth Warren, Mobile Public Library, Mobile, Alabama; Mr. J. M. Webre, Rosedale, Louisiana; Miss Jeanette Weiss, American Jewish Archives, Cincinnati, Ohio; Mr. Maxwell Whiteman, Philadelphia, Pennsylvania; and Miss Helen D. Willard, Curator, Theatre Collection, Harvard College Library, Cambridge, Massachusetts.

INDEX

Index

345

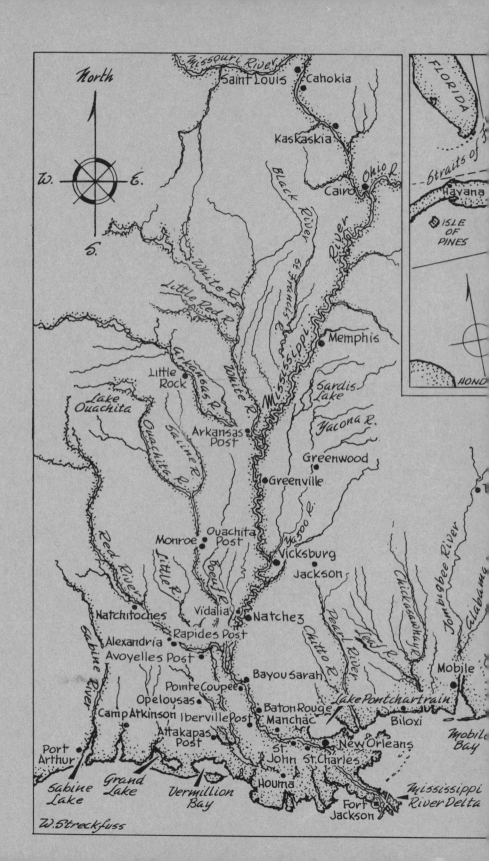